Charles Corm

The Levant and Near East:
A Multidisciplinary Book Series
Series Editor: Franck Salameh

The Levant and Near East series publishes works reflecting the region's hybridity and offers new perspectives on an area in permanent transformation. This series studies the Near East from a broad, diverse, inclusive, and cross-multi-disciplinary purview, with the aim of bringing into focus its larger conceptual, geographic, social, linguistic, and cultural settings. In line with its commitment to this "ecumenical" approach, *The Levant and Near East* series is designed to present clearly, accurately, comprehensively, and objectively research in a variety of Near Eastern studies sub-fields and disciplines—examining narratives, histories, cultures, ideas, and intellectual traditions often overlooked in traditional scholarship, with the purpose of appealing to both experts and general audiences. The series' objective is, therefore, to deal with the Levant and the Mediterranean from the perspective of Middle Eastern studies, cultural and intellectual history, political science, religion, philology, anthropology, linguistics, literature, security studies, women studies, and other disciplines of the humanities and social science, with the aim of advancing an inclusive, deep understanding of the Near East, and casting a broad look at the region beyond soothing familiar settings and prevalent dominant models.

Titles in the Series

Charles Corm: An Intellectual Biography of a Twentieth-Century Lebanese "Young Phoenician," Franck Salameh

Charles Corm

An Intellectual Biography of a Twentieth-Century Lebanese "Young Phoenician"

Franck Salameh

LEXINGTON BOOKS
Lanham • Boulder • New York • London

Published by Lexington Books
An imprint of The Rowman & Littlefield Publishing Group, Inc.
4501 Forbes Boulevard, Suite 200, Lanham, Maryland 20706
www.rowman.com

Unit A, Whitacre Mews, 26-34 Stannary Street, London SE11 4AB

Copyright © 2015 by Lexington Books

Cover image: Charles Corm at the age of 17, during his first visit to New York (ca. 1912). This is the adolescent Charles Corm who convinced Henry Ford that he was the "right man" to be the exclusive agent of Ford Motor products in the Levant. Charles Corm's Archives and Private Papers, Beirut, Lebanon.

All rights reserved. No part of this book may be reproduced in any form or by any electronic or mechanical means, including information storage and retrieval systems, without written permission from the publisher, except by a reviewer who may quote passages in a review.

British Library Cataloguing in Publication Information Available

Library of Congress Cataloging-in-Publication Data

The hardback edition of this book was previously catalogued by the Library of Congress as follows:

Salameh, Franck, 1962-
Charles Corm : an intellectual biography of a twentieth-century Lebanese "young Phoenician" / Franck Salameh.
pages cm.
Includes bibliographical references and index.
1. Corm, Charles, 1894-1963. 2. Authors, Lebanese--20th century--Biography. 3. Authors, French--20th century--Biography. 4. Intellectuals--Lebanon--Biography. 5. Philanthropists--Lebanon--Biography. 6. Businesspeople--Lebanon--Biography. I. Title.
PQ3979.C6Z86 2015
848'.91209--dc23
[B]
                        2015012037

ISBN 978-0-7391-8400-4 (cloth)
ISBN 978-1-4985-1768-3 (pbk)
ISBN 978-0-7391-8401-1 (electronic)

To my wife, Pascale;
To my children,
Zoé, Chloé, and Tristan:
May the Lebanon of Charles Corm's yearnings one day become their reality.

Quand reverrai-je hélas, de mon petit village Fumer la cheminée et en quelle saison Reverrai-je le clos de ma pauvre maison Qui m'est une province et beaucoup d'avantage?

Joachim DuBellay (1522–1560)

Contents

Acknowledgments		xi
Prologue		1
1	A Brief Introduction to a Monumental Life-Story	27
2	Poet, Humanist	65
3	Entrepreneur, Patriot	153
4	Child and Disciple of Humanism: Conclusions	233
References		245
Index		251
About the Author		257

Acknowledgments

Rare are the biographers who remain unchanged after having, for years, poured over the smallest detail of their subject's life. For the time it takes to complete a biography, writers may catch themselves often masquerading as their subject matter, savoring their tastes, feeling their feelings, suffering their setbacks, enduring their fears, celebrating their victories, and basking in their triumphs. Indeed, it may be said that a biographer can do his subject a great injustice by attempting to paint an impartial picture of him, instead of, say, donning his skin, humanizing him, rendering him alive, reading his ideas aloud and broadcasting his ideals, so as to inject life into what may otherwise yield a drab, lifeless narrative. A biography is after all an account of a person's life, and a "lifeless" biography can hardly be deemed a fitting "life story."

Not unlike novelists, biographers are perforce obsessed, consumed, often possessed by their main characters. This compulsion may be all the more acute when the subject of the biography in question, even in death, still has relevance in the collective memory of a country, in its politics, in its cultural and intellectual life. Yet between a hagiography, that is to say a partisan uncritical study of a "patron saint" who can do no wrong, and a sensationalist exposé corralled by *partis pris*, where a character may be subjected to an author's slander and bombast, there lie a biography *tout court*. It is in this latter category that this intellectual biography of Charles Corm must be placed; a life's account that is not necessarily disinterested, but one that is not captious either: a life story in which the subject, his works, his diaries, his personal archives, the accounts of family members and friends, as well as relevant public records, are all laid bare and subjected to the biographer's close scrutiny. And therein lies the risk that Charles Corm (1894–1963) might have taken by according me the task of writing this intellectual biography; a particular rendition of a life story shedding a peculiar shade of light on a man's thought, imparting a distinct reading of his life's work, and bringing a different kind of sensitivity into the intensity, the subtlety, and the singularity that was Corm during his lifetime, and thereafter.

I cannot begin this missive of gratitude to those who have helped me bring this biography to life without noting that this book was researched and written in times of great personal and professional challenges. Its contents and subject matter incarnated in the person of Charles Corm—a Lebanese national poet and disciple of humanism, a man of taste, erudition, youthful energy, and optimism—were at once cathartic, therapeutic, and healing in more ways than I can mention. So, in a sense, this biography, at once intellectual history, life-story, and an act of discovery, was also a work with a personal impetus and personal ramifications: a labor of love as much as a quest for knowledge, and a work that owes much to Charles Corm himself.

Yet, as I sit down to draw up this act of recognition to all of those others who have helped me along the way, I am racked with a feeling that this biography may not do Charles Corm justice. The monument that were this man's personal story and his life's labors seem impossible to cram into a 300-page narrative that will, after all, remain cursory. But I have done my very best in the limited space to which I am constrained, and I do sincerely hope that this furtive foray into Charles Corm's life will open the door to those who may come after me to further parse this truly fascinating life, and draw more from the vernal headspring that was Lebanon's "child poet."

I cannot tell how the years 2012–2014 might have ended for me professionally and personally had Charles Corm not occupied my labors, preoccupied my yearnings, and aroused my curiosity, pushing me forth, goading me on to delve deeper into his mysticism and humanism—spurring me to write when I wanted *not*. What I can tell, however, is that there is a host of friends, mentors, colleagues, and family members who are owed a great tribute and a greater debt of gratitude for keeping me grounded and sane and safe these past few years, dropping a kind word, lending a warm smile, casting a gentle gaze, and sending my way a friendly nudge keeping me focused in the direction of Charles Corm, and firm on the path to completing this manuscript. I would be remiss not mentioning them here.

Of the many owed thanks, I should like to begin by speaking my profound gratitude to those who stood by me and brought light into (sometimes) dark places these past few years, and others who discussed, read, and commented on segments (and at times the entirety) of this work's incarnations, at various stages of its development. Knowingly or not, those friends and colleagues helped me retain my sanity, and shepherded my work from its early inchoate form, as jumbles of ideas and notes and fragmentary translations, to a motley of conference papers, and into its present book form. Those owed my thanks include Walid Phares, Avigdor Levy, Michael Welch, Sylvia Kedourie, Helen Kedourie, Carole Corm, Virginie Corm, Joumana Corm, David Corm, Hiram Corm, Charles Corm Jr., Grace Salameh, Joseph Kiwan, Hanin Ghaddar, Eli Khoury, Roger Makhlouf, Bruce Maddy-Weitzman, Norman Stillman, Itamar Rabinovich, William Harris, Maxim Shrayer, Michael Connolly, Margaret Thomas, Sarah Beckjord, Ourida Mostefai, Atef Ghobrial, Cynthia Simmons, Uzi Rabi, Kathleen Bailey, Joshua Landis, Sabah Ghulamali, Jo-Ann Deso, Tom Deso, Michael Kerr, Shelley Deane, Habib Malik, Marius Deeb, Nadim Shehadi, Brian Hill, Nicolette Amstutz, Brighid Klick, Alex Guittard, Jeff Skowera, George Somi, Luke Hagberg, John Myhill, Randy Geller, Gershon D. Lewental, Mordechai Nisan, Roderick Williams, Youssef Bassil, David Silverstein, and Suzanne Kurtz Sloan. I am also intellectually indebted to Asher Kaufman, whose own pioneering work on Lebanon and the "Young Phoenicians" intellectualized and brought into the mainstream a topic that many still considered an outlier just a decade ago. Robert Rabil's friendship and his generous commentaries and encouragements were refreshing and reassuring, going a long way toward keeping me grounded and focused and deliberate and thorough. The advice, insights, and mere presence of all of those aforementioned colleagues, friends, and mentors, *and* the comments of the anonymous peer-reviewer for whom I am infinitely grateful, all have refined my thinking, brought discipline to my writing, gave order to my life, and greatly improved this manuscript. The errors that may still remain are the result of my own failings.

Several colleagues at various institutions and foundations also deserve special recognition for the support and encouragement that they lent. At my home institution, Boston College, I am immensely indebted to my colleagues in the Department of Slavic and Eastern Languages and Literatures who for many long years protected my time and dispensed me from many departmental obligations in order to facilitate my research and writing. My faculty mentor Maxim Shrayer is owed a special debt of gratitude not only for his friendship and advice and guidance, but also for his ongoing interest in the development of my scholarship. My Department Chair Michael Connolly was a wise advisor and a generous friend who never wavered offering leadership, comfort, and motivation. Likewise Cynthia Simmons, Margaret Thomas, Atef Ghobrial, Lydia Chiang, Mariela Dakova, Thomas Epstein, and Fang Lu were beyond thoughtful and graceful, always ready with a kind gesture, a sympathetic ear, and much needed advice and backing. Additionally, Atef Ghobrial, despite his demanding obligations, graciously read various drafts of several of my English renditions of Corm's French texts, and offered a wide range of helpful commentaries and suggestions.

The Boston College Dean's and Provost's offices were crucial emotional and pecuniary resources. I am particularly indebted to the Dean of the College of Arts and Sciences Gregory Kalscheur SJ, to the University Provost and Dean of Faculties David Quigley, and to the Vice Provost for Research

Bill Nuñez for allocating generous subventions and other grants thanks to which I was able to secure some of the hard to get copyrights, and without which my travels to Beirut, Paris, and New York over the past few years would have proved more challenging. Other help and subventions have also come from Boston College, namely from a 2012 university Teaching Advising and Mentoring Grant which contributed to developing different themes in this book. Also at Boston College, head librarian Jane Morris, Anne Kenny and Duane Farabaugh of the College Libraries Interlibrary loans, and Nina Bogdanovsky, my subject specialist and the Managing Editor of *The Levantine Review*, deserve special recognition. It is thanks to the assistance of my BC Libraries colleagues that I was able to track down elusive copyrights, and identify and work with crucial New York Public Library newspaper archives without having to leave the comforts of Boston College.

I am also grateful to the New York Public Library's Manuscripts and Archives Division (Astor, Lenox, and Tilden Foundations,) and namely Weatherly Stephen, Susan Malsbury, and Tal Nadan, who helped me identify a sizeable archive relevant to Lebanon's participation in the 1939 New York World's Fair, and for allowing me to cite materials from the New York World's Fair 1939–1940 records crucial to this biography. New York Public Library Archives Reading Room staff Lea Jordan and John Cordovez, who took particular interest in my work and put up with my tight schedule with much charm, courtesy, and grace, deserve special recognition.

The Association for the Study of the Middle East and Africa is owed gratitude and recognition for travel and research grants that helped me fund important portions of this book project. In Beirut, deserving my infinite thanks and indebtedness are the ever devoted and enthusiastic David and Hiram Corm of the *Éditions de la Revue Phénicienne*, who spared neither resource nor asset or time, putting at my disposal a wealth of archives, family anecdotes and heirlooms, advice, personal backings, and relevant contacts and acquaintances as I excavated their family archives and parsed their father's diaries, personal effects, and unpublished papers. I should stress that without David and Hiram Corm's friendship and assistance, without their opening many doors for me in Beirut, without Carole Corm's close reading and meticulous commentary on early versions of this text, and without the exceedingly charming and generous assistance of the *Éditions de la Revue Phénicienne* and the Charles Corm Archives' staff, in particular Grace Salameh and Joseph Kiwan, many aspects of this project would have never materialized. It is not always easy to have an intrusive outsider poke around and write about one's parent, and do so often in dry academic fashion— although it was not always easy to write about Charles Corm without getting sucked into the lyricism of his world. But David, Hiram, and Carole Corm were incredibly graceful and generous and accommodating friends, and proved a crucial resource, from the day I took on this project some four years ago, through the drudgeries of editing and proofreading, and into this final finished form.

At Rowman and Littlefield, a number of wise, skilled, and proactive editors made this book project what it is today. Sabah Ghulamali took a personal interest in my work, in Charles Corm, and in this book project in particular while still Assistant Editor for Politics and Area Studies at Lexington Books, and while the book was still in its early gestation. I am grateful to Sabah for having shepherded this project from its inception, and for passing it on to the able hands of Brian Hill, and later to the exceptionally thoughtful and patient Nicolette Amstutz. Without Nicolette's perspicacity, diligence, and insights, this book would not be what it is today.

My wife, who brings balance to my life and Cartesian order to my tempestuous Mediterranean temperament, lent exquisite Gallic discernment and composure to many of my oversights and inconsistencies during this project. In addition to embellishing my defects and hiding my vulnerabilities, she was, as ever, the perfect partner-in-crime. During my work in France, and at the New York Public Library Archives, Pascale was my ideal accomplice and double; only she was more deliberate, methodical, efficient, and discerning a researcher than I can ever be. Without her, without the discipline that she brought to my research, without the simplicity and literary charm that she compelled in my writing, and without the clarity that she brought to French texts that I was working with, many more failings would have still tarnished this text. I am grateful for the love, the friendship, the harmony, and the discipline that Pascale brings to the turbulence of my work and life. Five years ago, as I concluded the Acknowledgments for my first book, *Language, Memory, and Identity in the Middle East: The Case for Lebanon*, I spoke of my three beautiful children and the maturity, patience, and poise—betraying their young age—with which they always answered my absences from home (*even* when at home,) and dealt with my taxing work habits and my many neuroses. Missed recitals, forgotten school plays, ignored teachers' conferences, nixed vacations, and cancelled family outings and movie nights—"because dad is working"—were always met with compassionate bright smiles, precocious resignation, and a happy house sparkling with laughter and noise. Today Zoé, Chloé, and Tristan are a little older and, alas, a lot quieter, making me wistful for those fleeting delicious moments of happiness when their "children's voices" punctuated my life and intruded on my work. Memories of events and places from our past, wrote Marcel Proust in *À la Recherche du Temps Perdu*, "are but regrets over lost moments in our lives; and the homes, the houses, the roads, and the avenues of times past are, sadly, ephemeral and elusive, like the years of our lives." I cannot bring back Proust's "times past." But I can hold on to their happy memory in my own life. It is in this spirit that I wish to dedicate this book to Zoé, Chloé, and Tristan; to the children that they were, to the children that they are, and to the children that they will always be. May they evermore bring their happy disorder to our house, and may they always sprinkle sparkles of their beautiful noises and bright smiles onto our lives!

F. S.
January 1, 2015
Andover, Massachusetts

NOTE ON TRANSLATION AND TRANSLITERATION

Spellings of non-Western place-names and proper nouns were employed in conformance with common usage in Lebanon and in keeping with Lebanese localisms as well as dialectal and phonological peculiarities. This was done even in places where others might have adhered to standards of the International Journal of Middle East Studies (IJMES). For instance, the author uses Saïd Akl and not Sa'id 'Aql; Ashrafiyyé and not Ashrafiyah—because those are the norms in Lebanon. Unless otherwise indicated, all translations from French, Arabic, and dialectal Lebanese originals are the author's own.

Prologue

After many long years of doubt and hesitation, I finally made my way to Beirut. For far too long I had entertained the prospects of writing a biography of Charles Corm. But the Corm Archives had for the past fifty years been an anonymous jumble bolted shut in a Beirut sanctum, and for more than thirty years—and for a variety of personal reasons and security concerns—Beirut had been off limits to me. I have had plenty trepidation about "going back" to Lebanon. But Charles Corm and I go a long way. His literary works have haunted my boyhood and my school days in Lebanon, and as an adult, educated and socialized in the United States of the early 1980s, his lure had tugged at my academic and research trajectories for a number of years. English translations of considerable fragments of Charles Corm's poetry and prose were the mainstay of my first book, *Language, Memory, and Identity in the Middle East: The Case for Lebanon* (Lexington, 2010). Through the decade invested in that book project, writing a biography of Charles Corm still weighed heavily. And so, finally, on the evening of Tuesday July 10, 2012, in an "ivory tower" abutting the Jesuit Université Saint-Joseph and Beirut's National Museum, in the heart of Ashrafiyyé's Quartier Nazareth, I came at last to meet Charles Corm (1894–1963), face to face.

Being in the Corm family compound, in the home of one of Lebanon's iconic national figures of the early twentieth century, was like moving in the midst of an aged gallery of memories and cultural artifacts. The home itself was replete with musty heirlooms and echoes of times past, redolent with fragrances and ghosts of Charles Corm, his craft, the bustle of his learned salons, the frenzied animation of his creative endeavors, and the energy and enterprise of his business and commercial ventures. Meeting Charles Corm's descendants, the curators and "keepers" of this monument to Lebanon's national memory—and making most recently the acquaintance of his son Hiram on this very day in July—was like being in the presence of Charles Corm himself; the father, the family patriarch, the child-poet, the entrepreneur, and the chief architect of Lebanese nationalism of the early twentieth century.

At first glance the physical resemblance between Charles Corm and his children was striking. Likewise, their mannerisms, language, inflections, and above all their general energy and warmth bespoke a familiar familial flair. Yet Hiram's likeness to his father was uncanny on a plane quite distinct from that of Charles's other offspring—namely his eldest son, David, whom I had known for a number of years now, his daughter Virginie, whom I had also met during the summer of 2012 in Beirut, and Virginie's younger sister Madeleine, known to me only through photographs.

Peering into Hiram Corm's prying—almost mischievous—eyes was like touching the very soul of Charles Corm. The likeness was as otherworldly as it was real; one soothing, enchanting, and disconcerting at the same time. Hiram's gaze radiated a familiar sparkle, at once inquisitive, impish, and gentle, gleaming in the same luster of yellowed sixty-year-old photographs of Charles Corm's own piercing look. In one's eyes are revealed all the mysteries of one's being leading to the gates to one's very soul, often mused Charles Corm in his literary compositions.[1] Even in his early teens, in vernal essays some might judge too clumsy to be deemed serious literature, Corm had already been overtaken by the "power of the eye." At seventeen, in a letter sent to his mother from aboard the RMS *Olympic* that was ferrying him to New York, a clearly melancholy Charles Corm, longing for home, wrote,

> To my beloved mother: to you I send these kisses, bubbling with affection. Unforgettably etched in my heart, I carry with me a most exquisite image of you, the finest and most delicate of medals hanging from my neck. With me I also carry your smile, a light and subtle fragrance, pervading and embalming the depths of my being. Oh, and your eyes! They are alive within me; they are my sweet and comforting night-light, discrete and devoted, burning softly in the sanctum of the shrine that you have raised in love to our family. Yours, with all of my soul, Charles Corm, 1912.[2]

Reflecting "the sweetness of a smile," "the splendors of daytime," "the secrets of nightfall," and "cascades of starlight," all of life's zest, deliriums, and woes rested in the eyes, according to Corm.[3] And now, whether a Providential coincidence or a heaven-sent assent to Corm's poetic supplications, his progeny came to fully incarnate the ardor and enchantment that he saw and held dear in the human eye—most remarkably perhaps, bestowing upon his children his own sprightly, burning, prurient gaze.

In his eulogy of Charles Corm, Lebanese poet Youssef Ghsoub (1893–1972), a high-school friend of the author's, described his sharp bewitching eyes as "garrulous tireless sparkles that cannot be overcome once they begin talking; so you submit to their magic, you take heed, and you listen, enraptured. [. . .] Even in illness, his captivating eyes lit up his ashen face, energized his visitors, and filled his sick-man's bedroom with a healthy glow."[4]

Like his ubiquitous eyes, long after he'd been gone, Charles Corm's very presence remains, and is undeniable in his children, in the lives they lead, and in the memories that they have kept of him, faithfully kindling his life's work, preserving his legacy, and, as it were, holding down the fort, the citadel of a nation, that he had erected almost singlehandedly, brick by brick. Any father would be envious of the special relationship and the evident affection in which these offspring—now in their sixties and seventies—held, and still hold, their father. Something magical takes place when these child-like adults begin speaking of their long-departed parent. Even now, some fifty years after his death, none of them (particularly not Virginie, in whose arms he had literally breathed his last) can recall that evening on September 19, 1963, without welling up with emotion.

She had come home late on that fateful night, racing up the stairs to her father's bedroom for a kiss goodnight. She was his little *Asfoora*, his beloved "Birdie girl" as he nicknamed her, and he wouldn't sleep a wink, no matter how tired or unwell he had been, without that cherished nighttime kiss.[5] That evening the ailing Charles Corm had an unusual radiance to him as *Asfoora* recalled. He wasn't sleepy, he wasn't tired, he wanted to talk. He wasn't even in bed. Rather, he had been pacing in his room, rummaging through his books and notes, reading, writing as he walked, itching for a conversation. So he asked Virginie to stay a bit longer, keep him company, and he proceeded to discuss with her the plot and historicity of the movie she had just returned from watching, Elizabeth Taylor's *Cleopatra*. To the bitter end the ever-curious indefatigable humanist and man of culture, an intellect of widely varied interests, Charles Corm was animated, almost ebullient, consumed by that evening's conversation, elated by his daughter's presence, as if possessed of a fresh, newfound energy and a new craving for life—even in the throes of illness, and even as he'd been teetering on the edge of his final days. Yet, as he paced back and forth, spirited, garrulous, absorbed by the ongoing conversation, things unexpectedly fell silent—as if air, light, sound, space, and time itself had all abruptly got sucked out of the room. By the time Virginie took stock of what had just happened, an eerie blast of stillness was already settling in, and she watched her father slowly toppling over. She leapt in his direction, almost diving to catch him. But movement had become inert, as if cast in slow-motion, and her frantic dash to break her father's fall felt like an eternity. She caught him in time. But it might have been too late. Something popped in her ears as she held him. She felt the wind get knocked out of his and her own breast. She recalled that "popping sound" from mere seconds earlier. She wondered what it might have been. She watched the slow ticking of a wristwatch gradually come to a standstill. And there she stood, alone, dazed, as if in a void, her limp father laying in her tiny arms, tears streaming down her face, her small frame grieved, bruised, crushed by the enormity of that mournful moment. Yet she remained standing, riveted, erect, unbowed, like a tiny wounded (five-foot, one-hundred-pound) warrior carrying a fallen comrade. That pop, she now speculated, must have been the sound of Charles Corm's wristwatch shattering against the bedroom floor as she ran to cushion his fall. But it might as well have been the sound of time coming to a halt; the sound of the void being created as her father let go of his last gulp of air—what she described as "something vast departing; a light being snuffed out; a universe shrinking and shriveling to nothingness."[6] The Corms still wonder to this day what extraordinary strength possessed tiny teenaged Virginie that evening, enabling her to lift her father's lifeless body off the ground and carry him the length of the eight-hundred-square-foot bedroom to lay him on his bed. She remained at his bedside, massaging his chest, hoping to bring him back to life. But he was gone; peacefully, albeit not willingly and not in silence. He died doing what he loved, engrossed in conversation, debating, ever-ready to voice an opinion, defend an idea, or express admiration for peoples and things.[7]

Days later, as David and Hiram Corm flew back home from Germany, where they had been attending university, and as preparations were being made for the modest burial service that Charles Corm had requested in his will, another "will and testament," in the form of a sonnet, was found among papers strewn about on his bedside table. It should be noted that during his lifetime Charles Corm had written a variety of sonnets titled *Le Testament*, all of them published posthumously, most recently in a 2004 multi-volume collection covering a good portion of his previously unpublished papers and manuscripts along with works already available in print. What is notable about the poems titled *Le Testament*—and others under different headings but treating the same topic—is that they were all similar in spirit, all sparkling with joy, all bespeaking Corm's gratitude for having lived his life, all exuding hope, and all calling upon his children to be joyful and happy and grateful for being alive, in spite of the trials and adversities that they may encounter along the way.

To wit, in "Le Testament" published in *The Little Sentimental Cosmogony* collection, Corm urged his children to promise him never to grieve, regardless of their hardships, and instead to always take the high road, always "choose the highest peak, and always scale it with eagerness and energy and fortitude"; and once there, in the hill country, he pressed them to exult in the peace of mind and euphoria of nature's highest shrines, "where thanks to the open air of the higher altitudes, / one beholds and sees strewn at one's feet, all injuries thwarted, all evils tamed."[8] Likewise, another "Le Testament" poem, published in *The Rose and the Cypress*, was an entreaty for Corm's children to not grieve or memorialize him when he passes on, and to not even plant a single seedling at his gravesite;

> not a weeping willow, not even a flower, / so that neither the blackbird, nor the mournful pigeon, / may disturb the peace of my final resting place. / And so as to prevent / the terrible twilight from taking pleasure cloaking my proud remains, in cowardly pallor, / I ask that I be lain quietly, under the gaze of tearless eyes, / in the deepest of dust, mingling with the elements of creation. [9]

In a similar vein, a poem titled "Bye Bye," written in almost puerile baby-talk, addressed Corm's children as follows:

> You see, my beloved children, I really did my best,
> To bring you happiness, more than I gave myself,
> And despite my ailing health, and despite my old age,
> With you I always tried, to remain ageless, to always keep the faith.
> But since I must soon bid you my last farewell,
> Please know that I have tried to remain always upright,
> Steeped in honesty. And having, like the gods,
> Lived for the sake love, I shall die without fright!
> So please do not grieve, do not cry over me,
> But instead thank the Lord, for having pardoned me.
> It is now your turn, to do your very best,
> To push a little further, and lift a little higher,
> The passionate fervor of building the future,
> Of praising, serving Life, and kindling its Light! [10]

Like all the preceding, the final "Le Testament" of September 19, 1963, though it did have a peculiar kind of finality to it, read with the same emotion and plaintiveness and the same reluctance to depart the world of loved ones and family and friends. But it also ended on a similar note of hope and contentment and gratitude; an "ode to joy" as it were; a mark of Charles Corm's inveterate youth and youthfulness, and his incorrigible idealism and optimism and grace, even in times of gloom and profound pain and sorrow. And so read the "final" *Testament*:

> I am leaving you against my will, without fear, yet hardly without pain,
> Farewell my wife! Farewell my children! Farewell my friends!
> Please don't cry. Long has my heart made battle and long has it hurt,
> And so, in the end, this peace and quiet are mine, as they are well deserved!...
> Please don't fuss with eulogies, obituaries, or funerary rites;
> No flowers, no incense or candles, no vigils and no wakes;
> After all the battles that I have waged, let only the stillness of night
> Watch over the silence of my grave.
> So my beloved, please, no ceremonies, not the least;
> Except that, when without me, you shall for the first time come home again,
> Gather around, one more time, in memory of me,
> And listen to Beethoven's Ninth Symphony.

May God bless you forever, and may He
Everyday, cradle you and keep you in His grace![11]

David Corm recalls walking home from the grave on that day, with his mother and siblings in tow, all bereaved, taciturn, somber, beat. And when he suggested they all gathered in his father's reading room, in that mournful day's final act of remembrance, to fulfill the last of Charles Corm's wishes, his widow, Samia, protested. The mere thought itself—let alone the act of listening to a composition culminating in an "Ode to Joy"—was anathema to her. "It was his wish," insisted David. She still demurred. In her mind, listening to music—to an "Ode to Joy" no less—on a day such as this, was utterly out of the question; an aberration that defied all reason and defiled all precepts of propriety and decency. How could she be made to listen to music when all she felt like doing was weep for a beloved that she had just lain in the grave? How could her departed husband leave them—*her*—with such an onerous clause? But the children stood firm, overruling her, and she deferred.

As they all filed into the reading room, sitting down quietly, surrendering to the initial crackling sounds of vinyl spinning on the turntable, something "magical" began to take place. Even the stormy mood of the Ninth Symphony's first movement had a soothing calming quality to it, perhaps a reminder of the "passion" and "power" in Charles Corm's own life seeping back from beyond. But by the time the symphony's famous choir finale began creeping up, a sort of "healing" and "recovery" started to settle in, a catharsis perhaps communicated by Charles Corm himself, from the yonder, announcing the night was over, telling his loved ones, in words borrowed from his poetic lexicon, the story of how pain goes away, how personal tragedy is always overcome, by rising above sorrow, by choosing "the highest peak," by scaling it "with eagerness and energy and fortitude," by exulting in the peace of mind and euphoria of nature's highest shrines, "where one beholds and sees strewn at one's feet, all injuries thwarted, all evils tamed."[12] Even in death, it seems, Charles Corm was able to bring a curious ray of brightness and comfort and joy into the lives of those who knew him.

And so I knew, from the moment that I set foot in the Charles Corm Archives, that the history of the man that I set out to write was about to become a personal one indeed; a vicariously written posthumous autobiography, recorded through me, evidently, but dictated by a living gallery of recollections, a living shrine to Charles Corm, and a rich inventory of untapped manuscripts and private papers pining to get parsed.

My subject was to *be* Charles Corm, modern Lebanon's national poet. It was also to be the cultural and intellectual history of Corm's Lebanon through his published literary work, his unpublished manuscripts, his unexplored monographs, sketches (and scribbles on Lucky Strikes cigarette wrappings), his public addresses, and his private, corporate, and commercial correspondence between 1919 and 1963.[13] But what I suddenly had before me was much more than a rich private archive of untouched primary sources; it was much more than manuscripts and collections of cultural and intellectual testimonials that had once been Charles Corm's life and his craft's vessel and carriage. My playground was now a veritable living memory of Charles Corm, and a breathing pulsating palpable likeness of his very being, his demeanor, his mindset, and his temperament. Charles Corm died in 1963, but one can still find him hot-shot, exuberant, a spirited cultural-dynamo engrossed in his craft, engaged and engaging, coming alive in the persons of David and Hiram Corm, and haunting the home he prematurely (and grudgingly) departed. The *Fondation Charles Corm* cultural center, an archival trust which Corm's children are currently preparing to house these private collections, ultimately aiming to turn them into the holdings of a research institute and academic foundation, underpin the essence of this biography.

CHILD-POET AND BUSINESS TYCOON

The eight-story building currently housing the Charles Corm Archives had been the family home since the late 1930s. In 1928, it had begun serving as the corporate headquarters of Charles Corm's *Société Générale Industrielle & Commerciale*; the Middle East's exclusive Ford Motor Company subsidiary, and at the time the world's largest franchise of Ford car dealerships, auto part warehouses, and agricultural machinery shops and distribution centers. Indeed the famed *Maison Blanche de Beyrouth* (as the building was known colloquially) eventually became the corporate nerve center of one of the Levant's most successful business ventures of the 1920s and 1930s.

At its height, Corm's *Société Générale* could boast dozens of Ford showrooms, and a number of Firestone, John Deere, and McCormick International Harvester branches, assembly shops, dealerships and distribution centers stretching from Turkey to Transjordan and Mandatory Palestine, and from Damascus to Baghdad and Teheran. Some of the dealerships were strewn about in forlorn underdeveloped outposts as far afield as Aleppo, Alexandretta, Amman, and Antioch; others were closer to the nearer metropolises of Beirut, Haifa, Jaffa, Jerusalem, Tripoli, and Damascus. In all, Corm's enterprises employed upwards of a thousand Turks, Lebanese, Syrians, Iraqis, Transjordanians, Iranians, and Palestinians (Jews, Christians, Bahaïs, and Muslims alike), became the livelihood of thousands of families, and contributed to developing the infrastructure and networks of roads, railways, and bridges in countries that hadn't even come into being yet.

It may be argued that Corm's commercial ventures, and indeed his charisma and personal magnetism had served as a prelude to the budding of neighborly contacts, and ultimately the establishment of diplomatic relations, among emerging Middle Eastern states. In his memoirs, early twentieth-century Iranian (Bahaï) industrialist Habib Sabet related an anecdote attesting to Beirut's station as a Levantine financial and cultural hub in the early decades of the twentieth century, and spoke of the role that Charles Corm himself had played in those heady days—attributing Sabet's own entry into the business world, and eventually his industrial fortune, to Charles Corm. It should be noted that for peoples emerging from centuries of Ottoman stagnation and a devastating World War, the measure of modernity and sophistication was assessed by the availability and access to Western technologies, Western luxury goods, and more importantly Western ideas and knowhow. Given its position as a major port-city astride Mediterranean Europe and a torpid Middle East coming out of its slumbers, Beirut was well placed to relay the faintest "life-ripples of the Mediterranean, of Europe, and of the universe [. . .] to the [Middle Eastern] realms of sands and mosques and sun. Such [was] an element of 'Eternal Truth,'" wrote Lebanese statesman Kamal Jumblat in 1946.[14]

Channeling this, Beirut's energy and savoir vivre, and its cultural and commercial dynamo that was Charles Corm, Sabet also spoke fondly of our young poet's own worldliness, commercial savvy, and personal charm. Sabet knew, from his first encounters with Corm and the Beirut of his times, that his own fortunes were about to change. His "first break" as it were was in that Beirut of the mid-1920s—a major commercial entrepôt that arguably launched his business career and prepared him for the international industrial tycoon that he would later become. It all began with Sabet's purchase of a car from Corm's *Société Générale*, driving it south to make a pilgrimage to the Bahaï shrine in Haifa, then heading back East to Teheran, reselling the vehicle for twice its purchase price, and repeating the exercise a number of times. The rest, as the saying goes, was history.

Subsequent to this modest experimentation with interstate automotive trade, Sabet would end up launching his own import-export ventures between Beirut and Teheran, starting a passenger transport service for pilgrims traveling to Persia and Mesopotamia, and eventually becoming one of pre-Revolutionary Iran's chief industrial magnates. What follows is Sabet's own description of his first encounters with Lebanon and Charles Corm of the 1920s:

> [Beirut] was a big and active port, which opened a gate between the Arab countries and Europe and was the center for the sale of a variety of imported cars. [. . .] My first voyage to Beirut [. . .] that beautiful and historical city that lies on the slope of Mount Lebanon and on the coast of the Mediterranean Sea, was very pleasant and generated an unprecedented joy and excitement in me. I had heard a little bit about the history of this port city, which had been a major commercial and cultural centre during the heyday of the Phoenician, Roman, Islamic, and finally Ottoman civilizations, and about how in the present centu-

ry its civic and cultural development had reached the highest levels both in its Islamic and Arab, and its Western and Christian aspects. But hearing things never equals seeing them. When I saw this display of Lebanese civilization, everything I had known and heard was confirmed. I enjoyed looking at the city's bazaars and shops, which were full of European goods, of chairs, furniture, elegant fabrics, graceful clothes, and dishes made of crystal and china. For hours I wandered around the streets and shops, and lost myself looking at the goods. Of course I bought a few souvenirs, including a pair of black patent-leather shoes for my sister, which everybody fell in love with in Iran, for until then nobody had seen shining black leather shoes in our country. All my relatives and acquaintances asked me to bring them these types of new shoes when I went on my next trip. After a few days, [. . .] I looked for a car. Almost all European and American car manufacturers had representatives in this illustrious city, and as one of my acquaintances put it, Beirut was the Paris of the Middle East.[15]

For all intents and purposes, like Beirut itself and the glittering new world that it laid bare before Sabet's bewildered eyes, cars were still a novelty in those days, and Sabet himself knew very little about them. Although he did not know how to drive, he ended up purchasing a Ford vehicle; a Tin Lizzie that was sold to him on its own merits no doubt, but not without the enticing shopping experience afforded by Corm's customer-friendly facilities and his own delicate and engaging personal touch. "Corm was a dignified, well-mannered man," wrote Sabet; "a poet and a scholar who had left behind a number of books and poems. He was very well dressed and always wore pastel-coloured silk shirts and elegant suits."[16] Shrewd merchants, talented engineers, skilled ship builders, intrepid mariners, elegant intermediaries, and inspired artisans and poets are some of the qualities attributed to the Phoenicians by admirers and adversaries alike.[17] Sabet evidently noted those qualities in Charles Corm. And from his narrative in the preceding—as well as from what shall follow throughout this biography—Charles Corm seems to have incarnated those Phoenician archetypes, and carried proudly the mantle of those Canaanites of classical antiquity, whom he deemed ancestors, guiding lights, and mentors.

Charles Corm had the subtlety and the elegance of a poet, even in the way in which he conducted his commercial transactions and managed his business emporium. This is evident in his fastidious record-keeping, his lyrical internal memos, and the literary quality of his corporate dispatches, which often read more like poetry than plain business audits and inventory reports. To wit, in some of his early correspondence with the Ford corporate office in London, Charles Corm described to his British correspondent how, "in spite of the country's economic austerity," his *Société Générale* remained undaunted and determined in its commercial and social endeavors. He further noted that "thanks to our capable and effective organization, our robust social and financial means, and especially thanks to our steadfast energy [. . .] we have succeeded in maintaining more than satisfactory Sales figures for the year; [. . . Sales figures] of which we are duly and legitimately proud."[18]

In this same letter Corm would go on to describe his marketing method; how he'd sold Ford vehicles to the most unlikely of customers—to the French High Commissioner no less, a representative of the French government, and French "colonial authorities," who should ordinarily be seen driving in iconically French automobiles, like Citroëns and Renaults, not American Ford products—and how this marketing device had boosted the sales of Ford Motors among those officials and common citizens who wanted to emulate the French High Commissioner.[19] It should be noted that among the automotive subsidiaries represented in Beirut of 1921, Renault, Studebaker, Opel, Fiat, Lancia, Dodge, and Austin figured prominently and put up a stiff competition to Corm's enterprises.[20] Yet Corm's firm was the only dealership providing "non-traditional" finance options and payment plans to those wishing to purchase an automobile and who did not issue from the region's affluent classes to whom such an expense would not have been an onerous financial burden. "Despite hard economic times," wrote Corm in his correspondence with the Ford corporate office in Europe,

> despite penury and the lack of money, despite the political turmoil, and despite many other challenges that seem to threaten our country on a daily basis, [. . .] we have resolved to employ novel marketing means; selling cars on credit and providing potential customers with incentives and long-term re-payment plans so as to afford them the opportunity of truly appreciating the merits of owning a Ford automobile, rather than any of the other makes.[21]

Corm would go on to disclose how since June 20, 1921, the date at which the first shipment of Ford automobiles was unloaded at the Beirut harbor, until September 5, 1921, his company had assembled and sold a total of ninety vehicles, ordered some sixty more, and paid the Ford company a thirteen-thousand-dollar advance toward the purchase of spare parts.[22] More importantly, at a time when automobiles were still more of a curiosity than a necessity, and when they most probably still shared cluttered dirt roads with mules and horse-drawn coach and carriages, increased sales at the scale described by Corm would have been a phenomenal accomplishment. Furthermore, increased reliance on automobiles would have entailed a rapid expansion of Ford's business territories, and led to the paving of new roads and the construction of bridges to relay the headquarters to new branches and new Corm business subsidiaries. This also contributed to the building of new homes and lodging facilities to accommodate new employees, and the launching of new small businesses (grocery stores, pharmacies, restaurants, and the like) to cater to an ever-growing population and an expanding labor force.

CHARLES CORM'S *MAISON BLANCHE DE BEYROUTH*

The nerve center of this enterprise had been the *Maison Blanche de Beyrouth*. This structure, housing the Charles Corm *Société Générale* Headquarters, the Beirut "White House" as it was commonly known in its heyday, was designed by Charles Corm himself. Unlike Beirut's traditional sandstone and red-roof, Ottoman-era buildings, Corm's White House was made of steel and cement. It is no wonder that it withstood the 1956 Chehim Earthquake—a 6.0 tremor along the Dead Sea Transform fault system that caused much damage and heavy casualties throughout Mount-Lebanon and Beirut.[23] The building likewise defied Lebanon's devastating 1975 civil war, which wreaked havoc on the city's traditional structures and flattened the most robust of its constructions.

Charles Corm's son David vividly recalls the Chehim Earthquake, and how, as the tremors began convulsing the city of Beirut, his father calmly steered the family out of the building and into the safety of its surrounding gardens. A few moments later, from some distance, they all watched in consternation their eight-story home sway like a giant metronome, from left to right, to left to right, to finally settle into stillness—seemingly intact. Not a single window was broken, proudly recalls David Corm. An architect by formation, David speaks today—not without a hint of glee in his voice—of the visionary architect and master-builder that was his father. Though not a trained engineer himself, Charles Corm had evidently the instincts, the skill, and the discernment of one. Down to the minutest details, his *Maison Blanche* blueprints—and the final product itself—reflected Corm's professional savvy and scientific perspicacity as much as they did his subtle instincts, his exquisite taste, and his lyrical sensitivity.

Like art, architecture was to him the "other" human endeavor, which wrapped Man in an elegantly engineered edifice; an enchanting man-made space that offered at once physical sanctuary, peace of mind, and aesthetic charm. It is no wonder that in 1921, when French symbolist author Paul Valéry gave Corm a copy of his new book *Eupalinos*, he'd inscribed it with the following encomium: "To my friend Charles Corm who, naturally, knew Eupalinos better than anyone else."

Valéry's inspiration had been the historic Eupalinos; an ancient Greek hydraulic engineer whose feats are well documented in the *Histories* of Herodotus. The literary Eupalinos on the other hand, the one extoled in Valéry's work, was a romanticized version of the real historical figure; the incarnation of an amalgamation of philosophy, art, science, and music. To have deemed his friend Charles Corm someone "who, naturally, knew Eupalinos better than anyone else," Valéry must have grasped the very essence of Charles Corm and his craft; he must have been intimately acquainted with all his faculties in all their varied facets: Charles Corm the artist, the humanitarian, the patron of the arts, the man of letters, the merchant, and the amateur architect, engineer-apprentice, and master-builder.

Staged in fifth-century BC Greece, Valéry's *Eupalinos* was an afterlife dialogue between Phaedra and Socrates; a lengthy interchange during which Phaedra calls up remembrances of the famous architect Eupalinos, a resourceful, scrupulous, and talented builder of temples who, not unlike an inspired poet communing with the word, could make a stone quiver and sing to the emotions and the soul of its future worshiper, visitor, and onlooker.[24] Eupalinos was a man who stood for and *by* his precepts, claimed Valéry's Phaedra; "he neglected nothing" in his craft, and left nothing to chance; he brought thought, scrutiny, detail, and attention to all the visible and hidden points of his constructions; with his creations, he was fastidious to a fault, treating them with diligence and concern "as if they'd been parts of his own body";[25]

> He turned the stone into a matchless musical instrument, readied it for the light of day, diffused it in clear, open, incandescent forms, appealing to the eye, but possessing almost musical properties discernable even in the spaces where mortals roam the afterlife [. . .]—"It is my aim that my temples stir the emotions of Men in the same manner in which Men are moved at the sight of their beloved," [Eupalinos] was often heard whispering to himself.[26]

The bulk of the *Eupalinos* dialogue is one outlining the regrets of Socrates, the philosopher, who'd allegedly wished he'd become an architect, but had evidently missed his calling and resigned himself to remaining an orator and a teacher. For, as Eupalinos makes Socrates realize, it is "alas in actions [. . .] not words, that one finds the most immediate sense of the Divine's presence."[27] Conversely, though an exquisite poet and literary enchanter in his own right, Charles Corm was above all a man of action to whom "production" was as important as "conception." This was the essence of the doctrine of Valéry's *Eupalinos*; a doctrine of creation, dynamism, and movement, which later in the dialogue meanders and relays itself to the doctrine of Tridon the Phoenician, another fifth-century BC master-builder and shipmaker, whom Valéry *also* likens to his twentieth-century Lebanese friend and latter-day Phoenician, Charles Corm.

One must have known Charles Corm—as, obviously, had Valéry—to have written about Tridon and the Phoenicians with such sympathetic language remarkably evocative of Charles Corm himself, his life, his thought, and most importantly his achievements. For, so were creation, dynamism, and movement Charles Corm's own creed and his life's calling.

"And so, you have come to know Eupalinos?" asked Socrates at one point in the dialogue.

"I am naturally curious about merchants and tradesmen," answered Phaedra:

I avidly seek out those men whose thoughts and actions question and answer one another with alacrity and clarity. My Piraen wiseman was a Phoenician of striking diversity. His beginnings were those of a slave in Sicily. From a slave he mysteriously morphed into a boat-master, and from a sailor he grew into a master-caulker. Over time, having grown weary of the docks, he let go of old vessels to throw himself in the embrace of new ones, soon willing himself a master ship-builder. His wife kept a tavern at a stone's throw from his shipyard. I have yet to see a man of more varied means, of more skilled artifice, of more exquisite art and workmanship; a man more curious about that which does not concern him and more competent at that which does. [. . .] He conceived all of his business enterprises strictly in terms of relationships between practice and method. Even vice and virtue were for him pursuits with their own time and place, and with refinements all their own, which he practiced as he and the circumstances deemed fitting. I have a suspicion that he'd saved many a man at sea, and perhaps even murdered a few along the way, most likely due to hazards of the brothel or heat of the marketplace. Yet this whole, he executed with delicious acumen and exquisite skill.[28]

This was, indeed, a most charming (and accurate) description of Charles Corm—in the person of a Piraen Phoenician—as it flowed from Paul Valéry's reed. And though one would be hard pressed imagining him a murderer of men, Charles Corm was certainly a lover of mankind, a man of many talents, an enterprising businessman, a skilled architect, an inspired poet, and a humanist at heart, always adroit in adventure, always eager for a new challenge, always wedding thought to movement, and theory to action. Seeing the charm and elegance emanating from his craft, "one feels oneself becoming an architect" wrote Valéry of Eupalinos—with Charles Corm evidently in the background.[29]

Ahead of his time, like the historical Eupalinos whom he "naturally, knew [. . .] better than anyone else," and acutely aware of Beirut's "fluid" marine soil and its high levels of water retention (after all, what descendant of Phoenician mariners wouldn't make room for water?), Charles Corm conceived of his "skyscraper" as one built with strip footings and floating foundations to accommodate the tectonic plate and subsoil streams upon which Beirut and the Levantine littoral as a whole sat.[30]

But as expected, Charles Corm's contemporaries mistook his modernist and avant-gardist instincts for eccentricity and deviation from accepted norms. Let alone was he building an eight-story structure in the middle of nowhere—that part of Beirut was still an uninhabited hillside of terraced olive groves in the mid-1920s[31]—he was also using cement, aluminum, and steel-beams in blatant contravention of his times' traditional stone and mortar building practices. Furthermore, in this second decade of the twentieth century, Corm was also flirting with a streamline Art Deco architectural style then still in its infancy, a trend even Europe and the Americas had not begun appreciating until the 1930s. The eclecticism of Art Deco was described by

F. Scott Fitzgerald as a tendency developed by "all the nervous energy stored up and unexpended in the War."[32] This pent up energy clearly found release in Charles Corm's enterprises, whether literary, commercial, artistic, or architectural. Among the "eccentric" attributes of Corm's building—which ultimately came to embody his entire creative, mercantile, national, and charitable work—one can mention its geometric curves, its ziggurat shapes, its chevron-like motifs, and the floodlights that illuminated both the structure itself, and by night the Beirut "skyline" that it dominated. In this, Charles Corm had accomplished modernity and innovation wedded to ancient Phoenician—and other local Semitic—motifs and techniques.

Marrying simplicity, symmetry, beauty, and functionality, Corm willed his building into a crossroads and a meeting place of peoples and ideas, reflecting the hybrid resurrected Lebanese nation that he was yearning for. The building's twenty-foot cathedral ceilings—reminiscent of airplane hangars more than the car-business headquarters that Corm was originally constructing—featured light fixtures echoing Ford's Model-T headlights. The railings of the building's marble staircases were modified Ford steel bumpers, and its moldings and ceiling and door frames were reminiscent of *streamline moderne* industrial tubes, most probably inspired by mufflers and car undercarriages, suggesting mobility, speed, and efficiency. The building's ornamental style, both inside and out, seemed suitable for a nascent nation reeling from wars and famines—in tune with the aspirations, dynamism, mobility, and energy of its youthful representatives, incarnated most notably in the person and vision of Charles Corm and his circle of colleagues and friends.

Still, the eclecticism and futuristic aura of the *Maison Blanche* notwithstanding, and despite the reproof that it earned locally at the time of its construction, its progressive unorthodox structural design was above all functional, and was most probably the main feature that might have contributed to it surviving catastrophic earthquakes, devastating wars, and a company of upheavals that had stricken and shaken Lebanon (and Beirut particularly) since 1928.

The other inspiration behind the *Maison Blanche* might have been the archetypal New York City skyscrapers of the 1920s. Charles Corm had, after all, called New York City home for a few years prior to the Great War, and he came to imbue that city's bustle and energy and distinctive architectural flair during those times. The *Maison Blanche*'s eight floors were completed in 1928—the date at which Corm's Ford Motor Company's Corporate Headquarters moved from *Les Halles de Beyrouth*'s fruit and vegetable downtown market to the city's eastern suburb Nazareth Quarter. Despite the ire it had initially caused, the *Maison Blanche* eventually became one of Beirut's most recognizable landmarks and cultural emblems—not unlike New York City's own Empire State Building. It dominated the sparsely inhabited Nazareth hills of Ashrafiyyé, remaining Lebanon's—and indeed the whole of the Levant's—sole "skyscraper" until 1968. Today, nestled between the Lycée Franco-Libanais, the Beirut National Museum, and Université Saint-Joseph's sprawling campus, it is drowned in drapes of cement buildings, in a city of ever-sprouting gardens of glass and steel skyscrapers.[33]

The *Maison Blanche* was ravaged by multiple fires and suffered devastating damage through different phases of the Lebanese wars of 1975–1990. It has also gone through multiple renovations and rehabilitations—rising from the ashes as it were—preserving its emblematic character and its will to remain a beacon of culture and hope in a city gripped by conflict. It should be noted that although the Empire State Building—which was completed in 1931, three years after the *Maison Blanche*—derives its name from New York State's nickname, Corm's building owes its sobriquet to its distinctive white color. Otherwise, it bears no kinship, in either style or size, to the American White House. Nevertheless, Charles Corm's infatuation with American culture, energy, and entrepreneurship made it that he wore the label, *Maison Blanche*, with the insinuation to the White House, with much pride and satisfaction.

HUMANITARIAN AND MAN OF TASTE, AHEAD OF THE TIMES

Today, a library of some 40,000 volumes lie in boxes in the basement and on the second floor of the building—the original "Corm Library"—where Charles Corm had held his *Amitiés Libanaises* cultural salons throughout the 1930s, 1940s, 1950s, and early 1960s. One might guess how this intellectual society would before long become a trendy and much coveted weekly gathering, to which flocked a number of eminent local and international political and intellectual figures, among them Pierre Benoît, Paul Valéry, Eliahu Epstein, Charles Plisnier, Paul Morand,[34] and F. Scott Fitzgerald—but also a number of Lebanese literati, politicos, and aspiring authors who, hard as they might have tried, seldom escaped the binding spell of their host's charm and infectious energy.[35] Many a twentieth-century Lebanese patriot and cultural icon, from Michel Chiha to Saïd Akl, and from Amin Rihani to Fouad Ephrem Boustany, imbued the "national glow" emanating from the thicket of Charles Corm's *Amitiés Libanaises*.

There is even evidence suggesting that Israeli scholars (or at least members of the pre-state *Yishuv* in British Mandatory Palestine) might have also partaken of the cultural and intellectual activities issuing from Charles Corm's salons.[36] Among those, one could count the Hebrew poet Haim Nahman Bialik, author Rachel Ben-Zvi, and Semitist Nahum Sloucshz. Of course this was at a period in time where the (spiteful) borders of an emerging Middle Eastern state-system had not yet been finalized, and when the brewing animosities between Muslims and Jews had not yet reached their pinnacle. Regardless, Charles would always remain outside of the petty disputes of competing nationalisms in the region, and as mentioned earlier, his business emporium, cultural exchanges, and friendly collaborations reached across borders and bypassed ethnic, religious, and political barriers. And so, Corm's *Amitiés Libanaises*, bringing together Muslims, Christians, Jews, and others, was a natural order of things, and a reflection of Charles Corm's own humanism and his ecumenical temperament—in life, in literature, in politics, in personal relationships, and in commercial endeavors.

In a series of letters exchanged between Charles Corm and Eliahu Epstein between 1935 and 1938, there figure a number of invitations by Corm, extended to Jewish archaeologist Nahum Sloucshz, diplomat Victor Jacobson, and sculptor (and Marc Chagall friend) Chana Orloff, to present their work at the *Amitiés Libanaise* and a number of other Beirut venues. Naturally, Corm was particularly interested in Slouschz's work on the Phoenicians, and in Orloff's personal ties to a number of French and European artists whom he admired a great deal and occasionally hosted in his salons.[37] During a 1933 talk at the *Amitiés Libanaises*, Victor (later Avigdor) Jacobson, who had business interests in Beirut and quite possibly with Corm himself, spoke of the Biblical relationship tying together King Solomon and the Phoenician King of Tyre, Hiram, the builder of the Temple of Jerusalem. This talk, naturally, drew enthusiastic applause form the Lebanese audience, a reception which was indeed a reflection of the affection that many Lebanese in Charles Corm's circles exhibited toward both the Jews of classical antiquity and their descendants in modern times. Indeed, Charles Corm himself, a few years later, would name his two newborn sons David and Hiram—the former after Corm's own father (Daoud) *and* King David, and the latter a namesake of King Hiram of Phoenicia, Solomon's friend and the "architect" of the Temple of Jerusalem. This may be deemed a familial nod to the millennial kinship that, in Charles Corm's telling, tied all the peoples of the Levant in the same ancient bond.

Remarkably, Lebanese author and avid Arab nationalist Amin Rihani, who was a close friend of Charles Corm's and a fixture at his salons (Rihani was also the godfather of Corm's son Hiram), became friendly with Eliahu Epstein, in spite of their presumably antagonistic political views on the future of British Mandatory Palestine. This, again, is in attestation of the spirit of openness, receptivity, and ecumenism radiating from the cultural encounters that Corm put together—and indeed a reflection of his own temperament and worldview.

Yearning for those interrupted weekly gatherings, Lebanese author Rushdy Maalouf (1914–1980), father of Francophone novelist and member of the *Académie Française* Amine Maalouf (b. 1949), noted in his elegy of Charles

Corm that although the meetings of the *Amitiés Libanaises* had become sparse in Charles Corm's final days, the legacy that he left behind, "like the Cedars of Lebanon, never ceased to lavish glory and grandeur to the altar of Humanism that is his Lebanon."[38] Charles Corm was "our first teacher" claimed Maalouf; he was Lebanon's "national school," its "national museum," its "national torch and beacon," and its "national fountainhead and spring eternal."[39] Charles Corm, stressed Maalouf,

> was the first one to show us *how* to love Lebanon; *how* to chant and rhapsodize Lebanon, *how* to vaunt and defend Lebanon, and how to become masterbuilders of this Lebanon of his yearnings; Humanists, Cosmopolitans, Ecumenical friends and allies to mankind, yet steadfast in our love and affection for our homeland.[40]

Maalouf noted that it was not unusual for artists, intellectuals, and cultural and political figures visiting Lebanon for the first time to have Charles Corm and his *Maison Blanche* on their itinerary of peoples and places to see: "they visited Lebanon seeking Charles Corm the same way some of us may visit France to see Da Vinci's *Mona Lisa*, or the way we may visit Athens to see the Acropolis."[41] This is the veneration that many, Lebanese and foreigners alike, held for Charles Corm, and it is still this mystique of Charles Corm's that haunts the walls and halls of his now-muted *Maison Blanche de Beyrouth.*

Yet one can still make out the murmurs of this once-bustling intellectual beehive. What remains of the halls of the *Amitiés Libanaises*, its walls, and its library's giant, solid wood bookshelves and era furniture are a powerful reminder of "the eternal presence of Charles Corm, the compassion of Charles Corm, and the apostles that he left behind; even when he is no longer physically with us."[42]

There are other salient physical traces that this dainty man managed to leave behind: relics of Charles Corm's personal charm, his exquisite taste, his subtle spirit, and his powerful mind. Battered Marcel Breuer, Ludwig Mies van der Rohe, and Lilly Reich furniture and "office chairs" line the now-barren walls of his library. When Corm initially acquired those items during the early 1930s, he was mocked by his Lebanese contemporaries for furnishing his home and reading rooms with tubular metal and animal-skin chairs; "who in their right mind would sit on metal tubes?" they sneered. Like his architectural predilections, Corm's taste in furniture was deemed strange and absurd by the elegant standards of his generation. Of course, van der Rohe and Lilly Reich furniture today, with their minimalist framework and sleek structural order—"skin and bones," or "less is more," as they are often called in architectural circles—have come to define "popular classics" in home and office furnishings throughout the world, and are considered masterpieces of modern design today.[43]

Initially developed for the German Pavilion at the 1929 International Exhibition in Barcelona, the van der Rohe and Lilly Reich designs immediately caught Charles Corm's eye and his predilection for the distinct, the delicate, and the dignified—even though their reception at the time was mixed. He set out to purchase as many of these items as he could, despite the banter and sarcasm of those who insisted "normal people" sat on "normal" wooden furniture—not metal pipes. Yet, in mint condition, Lilly Reich and van der Rohe furniture like the ones strewn about Corm's library today can fetch upwards of $100,000 a piece. As mentioned earlier, Corm, of course, had not acquired any of his possessions strictly with an eye for profit—only with the cultured man's passion for the exceptional, and the artist's feel for the timeless. But it doesn't hurt that he was also gifted with a flair for the timeless and a predilection for the invaluable.

Many of the *Maison Blanche*'s inestimable documents and some ten thousand volumes of its prized library holdings were consumed by fire, or otherwise succumbed to squatters and looters' abuses in the war years. I remember a high school French professor, who was a talented violinist—and incidentally a fan of Charles Corm's work—lamenting the possibility of his treasured Stradivarius, at one time stored in a bank safety vault on the infamous "Green Line," one of Beirut's war frontlines, ending up as fuel for warring militias seeking warmth during the winter of 1979. Needless to say, my French professor never recovered his violin. Likewise, David and Hiram Corm alluded to the fact that many of the damaged papers and books in their father's library—which stood at a stone's throw from that "Green Line"—did in fact end up as fire fuel (and perhaps even as "toilet paper") for various warring militia groups that had at different times expropriated and squatted on the property between 1975 and 1989.

Built in 1928, the *Maison Blanche* grounds once extended to where the Beirut National Museum now stands, on the Damascus Road. A major thoroughfare during Ottoman times connecting cosmopolitan Beirut to the sleepy rural interior and the *Vilayet* (State) of Damascus, the Damascus Road had been a major commercial artery for coaches and grain traders traveling from the Eastern Ottoman provinces to the Mediterranean port-cities; a land-bridge, as it were, between Europe and the East. It was therefore natural for a major business emporium to be headquartered on that thoroughfare. And Charles Corm had indeed made a conscious "business" decision to build on that "central location," desolate as it might have been prior: He viewed the Damascus Road not only as a "crossroads" of sorts, but indeed as a "lighthouse" pulling merchants and weary travelers, coming down from Damascus, into the city of Beirut.

As *Société Générale*'s corporate headquarters once, Ford Motor vehicles, Firestone products, John Deere equipment, and McCormick International Harvester machinery would ordinarily pass through the Beirut Harbor, before continuing on for assembly and distribution at the *Maison Blanche*. Twelve hangar-like bays flanking the main structure—spaces which today serve as parking garages, storage depots, and office space for the Corm brothers and the *Éditions de la Revue Phéniciene* Press—were the workshops, car assembly stalls, and showrooms that were the foundation of Corm's business emporium. The *Société Générale* ordinarily received Ford vehicles in disassembled parts and pieces, shipped in wooden crates—the equivalents of today's metal shipping containers. All the assembly and different stages of operation and maintenance took place in Beirut, with Charles Corm himself—who incidentally never learned how to drive—taking part hands-on in the building and assembly process.

It should be noted that following the Armenian Genocide of 1915, and the subsequent expulsions of Armenians from Cilicia and Deir ez-Zor through the early 1920s, many survivors and victims (of what is often referred to as the "Armenian Genocide" today) took refuge in Lebanon; more specifically in the Bourg Hammoud and Karantina districts, very near to the Beirut Harbor. Bourg Hammoud would eventually become a separate municipality within Beirut and a major urban, industrial, and commercial center in the country. One might argue that Ford Motor Company and Charles Corm's *Société Générale* played a major role in the rehabilitation and integration of Armenian refugees in Lebanon, facilitating their transition from destitute outcasts and forlorn victims of "ethnic cleansing" into industrious, valuable, and much admired Lebanese citizens. And while the Bourg Hammoud that had received them in the early 1920s had been no more than a distressed shanty town, it quickly evolved into a major urban center, its first dwellings—and eventually its businesses and storefronts—initially constructed out of the wooden crates in which Charles Corm received shipments of his Ford Motor products.

Having served as the president of the Post-War Beirut Relief Committee—charged with bringing assistance to needy families reeling from the famines and devastation that had plagued Lebanon during the Great War—Charles Corm developed the resourcefulness, the wherewithal, and the drive to build a town from scratch—so to speak—and develop infrastructures, roads, bridges, economies, and above all, breed hope, confidence, and faith in the future. This would serve him well in years to come. It was an experience that brought him face to face with the devastation wrought by the Great War—the famines, the disease, the death, and the wonton deforestation that it left in its wake—but it was also an experience that gave him determination and hope, and honed his "building" skills.

One cannot overstate—and the Charles Corm Archives confirm—the fact that the Great War (and later World War II) had a profound impact on Charles Corm and his worldviews. They taught him the value of tolerance and humanism, they put him in touch with the absurdity of violence and the futility of resentful nationalism, and they made him realize that only a spacious, humanist, hybrid, universalist "patriotism," bereft of all manners of orthodoxy and chauvinism—religious, linguistic, and national alike—could offer a panacea to the Levant's violent inter-identity quarrels, and give Lebanon respite from its endemic ethnic dissentions.

As this work will show, Charles Corm's lifelong literary, intellectual, commercial, and humanitarian work was intended as an act of defiance and confrontation directed at orthodoxy—*all* orthodoxy, whether in art, architecture, politics, history, or literature. But his work was also a summons to the inherently pacifist impulses of the peoples of the Levant, and namely Lebanon's much disputed and debated Phoenician forefathers.

In a spate of angry words disputing the claim of some Lebanese to Phoenician descent (namely those who may still valorize Charles Corm's work in our time), leading Arabophone commentator and journalist Hazem Saghieh reminisced in the summer of 2014 at how, as a proud young Arab nationalist during the 1960s, he and his radical colleagues took great pleasure mocking Lebanese nationalists who paraded Phoenician rather than Arab ancestry. The intent of Saghieh's article, titled "ISIS and the Hazards of Our Abysmal Histories," was clearly not a disputation of the Phoenician past—he had himself long since abandoned the rhetoric and reductionism of Arab nationalism. Instead, Saghieh's essay was an indictment of Arab intellectuals and lapsed Arab nationalists of his persuasion in the face of the abomination that was now the Islamic State of Iraq and Syria, and the Caliphate that it spawned in June 2014—in his view an accursed progeny of Arab nationalism. Yet in his caustic charge against ISIS and Islamic fundamentalism, Saghieh took also a swipe at both Arab nationalists and their failures, *and* at those Middle Eastern advocates of minority nationalisms who harked back to pre-Arab Phoenician, Pharaonic, or Mesopotamian progenitors. "This kind of discourse" valorizing pre-Arab progenitors, he wrote, "in our Arabist-Leftist circles" of the 1960s,

> was deemed an exemplar of absurdity and stupidity, laden with depravity and bad intentions. The depravity of this Phoenicianism, in our view, stemmed from the challenge that it posed to our assumed Arabism, whose language we spoke and to whose history we ardently subscribed, both as individuals and as a collective. The absurdity of this overblown Phoenicianism on the other hand, dwelt in that, to our sense, its effects were dead, its relics were meager, and its inscriptions and artifacts remained negligible, even as they were overly and unduly memorialized in our official history textbooks.[44]

To this "indignity," the response from Lebanon's "Phoenicianist" camp came swiftly and firmly, spilling from the pen of Eli Khoury the very next day, on the very same pages of the Lebanese online journal *NOW*, where Saghieh's article first appeared. In a lampoon of Saghieh's own title, now rendered "ISIS and the Hazards of Our Not So Abysmal Histories," Khoury wrote the following:

> It was with immense pleasure and a big smile on my face that I read the recent NOW editorial of my friend Hazem Saghieh [. . .] and I was in agreement with him as far as the essay's intent, although I had to disagree with some of his opinions. You see, and this is by pure coincidence, I happen to be one of those absurd, depraved [Phoenicianist] dunces that Hazem Saghieh spoke of in his piece. Therefore, I have a brief comment to make and two objections to voice in this regard. Concerning the "other's" alleged affront to Arabism, it is perhaps worth remembering that the onus here is not on the Phoenician, Pharaonic, Mesopotamian, or even Kurdish and Berber civilizations, as my esteemed colleague suggests; they, after all, are not the ones who trespassed on the Arabs. It is in fact the Arabs themselves, and Arabism in particular, that affronted and abused all those who were not Arab. No need to remind anyone here of the ethics and (less than becoming) conduct of Arabists in the heyday of Arab nationalism. Indeed, Arabism was to a large extent the ISIS of its day. Arabism and its hollow strident acoustics was the only acceptable benchmark of selfhood in those times; if one dared disclaim his imputed Arabness, he was deemed a traitor (instead of, say, an Infidel today), and his reward would have been the gallows (instead of, say, meeting the sword today). At a minimum, those who contravened the sacrosanct Arabist narrative in those days were dismissed as "idiots" worthy of being ridiculed and abused. And so, the difference between the Arabists and ISIS today is in that ISIS may not have yet acquired Arabism's sense of humor, which in time, might have entitled ISIS to call others "idiots" [instead of outright killing them.][45]

Khoury's response concluded by assuring Saghieh that

> the legacy and history of the Phoenicians need not be defended, nor exaggerated, nor even bragged about. The Phoenicians' legacy and history speak for themselves. One need only quickly leaf through the scholarship that the West has been producing on the Phoenicians in recent times to realize how profound an imprint they have left on our world. [. . .] The Phoenicians took little from the Continents and took much from the Seas; they never colonized, they never brutalized, they never subjugated like others might have done. And perhaps that might have been their main failing.[46]

The preceding in many ways condenses Charles Corm's own view of Lebanese society and the legacy of the Phoenicians that he hallowed and rhapsodized. It is also in line with, as Khoury noted, what "others" have written and continue to write about the Phoenicians—perhaps most aptly expressed by French poet Jean-Louis Vaudoyer, more than hundred years ago, observing how

> the Phoenicians commanded and dominated all the known and unknown oceans. [. . .] They established their fabulous trading posts along the world's finest shores. [. . .] They came, they left, they came back again. But they never ever colonized, they never brutalized, and they never subjugated. They simply conquered by way of cultural seduction. They were sailors, teachers, traders, prophets, and poets. [. . .] They were pacifist, versatile, adaptable, and elegant. They were Sidonian Phoenicians. The fountainhead of their fortune had always been beyond the seas, always at the other edge of the world.[47]

This humanism of the Phoenicians all but populated the literary production of Charles Corm. "If I dare remind my countrymen of our Phoenician forefathers" began one of the poems of his celebrated *La Montagne Inspirée* (The Hallowed Mountain),

> It is because back in their Times, long before we had become mere Muslims and Christians, / we were a single nation at the forefront of History, united in the same glorious past. [. . .] / Today, having grown into what we've become, / [. . .] we owe it to ourselves, to love one another, / in the same way we did, when we were still splendid humanist pagans.[48]

It is hoped that the present biography will offer Anglophone readers and students of the Middle East a glimpse into the fascinating and supremely humane universe of Charles Corm, and help shed some light on his innocuous and compassionate brand of nationalism. A biographer, wrote François Bédarida, is neither prosecutor nor defense lawyer; instead, he is a referee and a thoughtful commentator.[49] No doubt, Charles Corm in this biography will now and then come to be defended and critiqued; but defended and critiqued he will be only in as far as he will be evaluated, on the basis of his work, his private papers, and the context of his times. Based on the wealth of papers that Charles Corm has left behind, this intellectual biography of the man, the patriot, the poet, cannot be but a first offering; a glimpse into the life of a towering cultural figure of modern Lebanon. Other historians and biographers will hopefully follow and parse other aspects of Charles Corm's work and life. And so, this biography shall remain a brief and hurried survey—perhaps even too hurried and antsy, like Charles Corm himself. But it shall be a survey that incarnates Corm's entire corpus; a capstone as it were, that is also a gateway to the enchanting universe of Lebanon's immortal child-poet.

Some poets come to define and enshrine the spirit of their nations. In that sense, France had its Hugo, Greece its Homer, Spain its Cervantes, England its Shakespeare, and Italy its Dante. For Lebanon, Charles Corm was (and remains) Hugo, Homer, Cervantes, and Dante, all at once, and so much more; he is also arguably Lebanon's George Washington, Henry Ford, King Solomon, Chaucer, and Hiram-Aviv all at once.

NOTES

1. See for instance *Les Miracles de la Madone aux Sept Douleurs* (Beirut: Éditions de la Revue Phénicienne, 2010), 83–85, and *Contes Érotiques; Variations sur le Mode Sentimental, 1912* (Beirut: Éditions de la Revue Phénicienne, 2011), 14.
2. Charles Corm Archives, postcard from the Atlantic Ocean, Royal Mail Steamer *Olympic*, July 20, 2012. It should be noted that this vessel was a transatlantic liner, the "flagship" and namesake of the "White Star Line" triumvirate of "Olympic-class liners," which included the *Titanic* and *Britannic*. On this trip, Charles Corm would go on to set up shop on Broadway Avenue, where he would eventually learn English, and later meet Henry Ford and Fiorello La Guardia, laying the groundwork to his very successful future business ventures, and eventually a triumphal return to New York City in 1939–1940 to represent Lebanon in the New York World's Fair of Flushing Meadows–Corona Park.
3. Charles Corm, *Les Miracles de la Madone aux Sept Douleurs* (Beirut: Éditions de la Revue Phénicienne, 2010), 85.
4. Youssef Ghsoub, *Shaarl Qorm; Sawt Lubnaan al-Madwiyy* [Charles Corm; The Resounding Voice of Lebanon] (Beirut: Charles Corm Archives, ND), manuscript, 1. See also *Al-Hikma* (Beirut: The Hikma Institute, Volume 11, Number 9, December 1963), 451.
5. *Asfoora* was also the subject of one of Charles Corm's short stories, the "Palm Sunday Story," featured in the *Miracles of Our Lady of the Seven Sorrows* (Beirut: Editions de la Revue Phénicienne, 1948.) Based on Virginie's own struggles with a childhood illness that almost took her life, the "Palm Sunday Story" relates little *Asfoora*'s and her parents' trials, until she is miraculously healed by the Lady of the Seven Sorrows.
6. Conversation with Virginie Corm, July 2012.
7. Ghsoub, "Charles Corm; The Resounding Voice," 451.
8. Charles Corm, "Le Testament," *Petite Cosmogonie Sentimentale* (Beirut: Éditions de la Revue Phénicienne, 2004), 376.
9. Charles Corm, "Le Testament," *Sonnets Adolescents, La Rose et le Cyprès* (Beirut: Éditions de la Revue Phénicienne, 2004), 212.
10. Charles Corm, "Bye Bye," *Petite Cosmogonie Sentimentale*, 375.
11. See image of original manuscript in Corm's longhand: *Je m'en vais malgré moi, sans peur, mais non sans peine, / Adieu ma femme! Adieu mes enfants, mes amis! / N'en pleurez pas. Depuis que mon coeur se démène, / La paix et le repos me sont enfin permis!... / Je ne veux point de faire-part, de funérailles; / Pas de fleurs ni d'encens, de cierge ou de flambeau; / Mais que seul le silence, après tant de batailles / Qu'il m'a fallu subir, veille sur mon tombeau. / Donc mes chers, pas la moindre ceremonie; / Mais quand vous rentrerez sans moi sous votre toit,*

Veuillez vous recueillir en souvenir de moi, / Pour écouter de Beethoven la Symphonie Numero Neuf. Dieu vous bénisse! Et chaque jour / Qu'Il vous embrasse et qu'Il vous garde en son Amour!
12. Charles Corm, "Le Testament," *Petite Cosmogonie Sentimentale*, 376.
13. After the collapse of the Ottoman Empire, and as Lebanon achieved its autonomy under the auspices of the French Mandate, Charles Corm, the young poet and militant on behalf of his country's independence, took a respite from "political activism" and threw himself into the business fray, at one point becoming the Middle East's exclusive agent for Ford Motor products. His business was booming throughout the 1920s and 1930s, and his Ford car dealerships and showrooms were sprawling throughout the Levant. Though he never neglected his social, cultural, and literary activities, he still managed to maintain a close oversight over his many business interests—visiting all his dealerships, in multiple countries, at least once a month. This task would have been burdensome even in our own times of information superhighways,

where air travel, computer networking, instant messaging, and interstate parkways are necessities often taken for granted. Charles Corm on the other hand was limited to technologies—cars and often dirt roadways—that were still in their infancy. The less than one hundred miles that separate, say, Beirut and Haifa, would take today's traveler less than an hour—whether by car, train, or airplane. In the 1920s and 1930s, this same route meant a five- to six-hour red-eye in a Ford Model-T—then one of the most efficient "high-speed" modes of transportation on the roads of the Levant. Although the exclusive agent and distributor of the Model-T, and one who often got his hands dirty, so to speak, assembling the vehicles and seeing to their maintenance and repair, Charles Corm never drove. And so, with his chauffeur at the wheel, he would make these regular overnight "business" trips to Haifa, Jerusalem, Antioch, and Lattakieh in the backseat of one of his Tin Lizzies. Before succumbing to sleep, during long, often dusty, bumpy rides, Corm would chain-smoke Lucky Strikes and turn the empty cigarette wrappers into writing paper where he would record his thoughts, sketch out a poem, or draw up the outlines of a new play or short story. These Lucky Strike wrappers constitute a considerable portion of Charles Corm's archive; boxes upon boxes of documents and manuscripts and folders, mingling helter-skelter with old neatly smoothed cigarette wrappers, filled with Charles Corm's longhand, still fragrant with the tobacco aroma wafting out of the 1930s.

14. Kamal Jumblat, "La Mediterranée, Berceau de Culture Spirituelle," *Les Années Cénacle* (Beirut: Dar al-Nahar, 1997), 99.

15. H. E. Chehabi and Hassan I. Mneimneh, "Five Centuries of Lebanese-Iranian Encounters," in H. E. Chehabi's *Distant Relations: Iran and Lebanon in the Last 500 Years* (London and New York; Centre for Lebanese Studies, I. B. Tauris Publishers, 2006), 23–4.

16. Chehabi, *Distant Relations*, 24.

17. Gerhard Herm, *The Phoenicians; The Purple Empire of the Ancient World* (New York: William Morrow and Company, 1975), 52.

18. Charles Corm, "Letter to FORD MOTOR CO., Caxton House, London, S.W.1" (Beirut: Charles Corm Archives, September 5, 1921), 1.

19. Corm, "Letter to FORD MOTOR CO.," 6.

20. Corm, "Letter to FORD MOTOR CO.," 3.

21. Corm, "Letter to FORD MOTOR CO.," 6.

22. Corm, "Letter to FORD MOTOR CO.," 6. According to the Consumer Price Index, $13,000 in 1921 would be the equivalent of $160,000 in 2013.

23. According to Boston College seismologist John Ebel, "There were actually two earthquakes that are known as the Chehim or Chouf earthquakes. The name Litani is also associated with the second earthquake. Both took place on March 16, 1956. The first earthquake occurred at 10:32 GMT and has been assigned magnitude 6.0. The second earthquake occurred some ten minutes later at 10:43 GMT and has been assigned magnitude 5.8." J. P. Rothe's *La Seismicité du globe, 1953–1965* notes the following: ". . . 136 killed, 6000 houses needing repair, 50 villages too badly destroyed to be restored to their former state. The epicenter was situated in the mountainous zone of Chouf, which runs from the anticlinal slope of Mount Lebanon to the Mediterranean [. . .] Machghara [. . .] was badly damaged; [. . .] among other places affected (intensity VIII-IX) were Jezzine, Machmouche, Chehim. There were two successive shocks at an interval of 10 minutes; most of the inhabitants fled after the first shock, whereas the collapse of houses occurred after the second." John Ebel notes a number of factors that may control damage during an earthquake. "First and foremost is the type of construction. Sandstone walls with heavy tile roofs are probably not very strong in the lateral shaking of an earthquake, and so they might be prone to damage even in moderately strong shaking. If a steel and cement building is constructed with proper earthquake-resistant design, it could withstand a pretty strong shake without taking any appreciable damage. Another factor that controls earthquake damage is the local soil conditions. Soft soils (unconsolidated river bottom sediments, landfill, sands, etc. . .) can amplify local earthquake ground shaking compared to the shaking experienced on hard rock. Furthermore, if such soils are water saturated, they can lose their strength and become like a rather viscous liquid. If this happens, building foundations can be affected and the buildings themselves can take damage." Dr. Ebel argues, based on images of the *Maison Blanche* that he consulted, that "such buildings are prone to be built in locations where there are firmer soils or rock for their foundations. Even in the strongest earthquakes, some

buildings take less damage than others. Some buildings seem to ride through even the strongest earthquakes with relatively little damage. Designing and constructing buildings is both a science and an art." Finally, notes Dr. Ebel, "it must be remembered that distance to the earthquake epicenter is an important parameter along with the magnitude of the earthquake. For example, one might experience more damage from a magnitude 6.0 earthquake centered only 3 kms away than from a magnitude 7.0 earthquake that is centered 50kms away. The earthquakes at Christchurch, New Zealand in 2010 were classic examples of these, as seismic waves decay in strength as they propagate away from an epicenter." It should be noted that the distance between Chehim and Beirut is about 40 kilometers.

24. Paul Valéry, *Eupalinos ou l'Architecte, Précédé de l'Âme et la Danse* [Eupalinos or The Architect, Preceded by the Soul and the Dance] (Paris: Éditions de la Nouvelle Revue Française, 1921), 59.

25. Valéry, 58–59.

26. Valéry, 59.

27. Valéry, 59–60.

28. Valéry, 60.

29. Valéry, 60.

30. It should be mentioned that the etymology of "Beirut" has its origins in the Canaanite-Phoenician word "Birot," plural of "Bir," which means "water-wells." This toponym, as evidenced by the majority of Lebanon's Canaanite and Aramaic place-names, was evidently a reflection of local topology and geology. Incidentally, the term "Bir" and its plural "Birot" are still used in modern spoken Lebanese to connote exactly the original Phoenician meaning; "water-wells."

31. French poet and traveler, and longtime resident of Beirut and Mount-Lebanon during the nineteenth century, Lamartine, described this quaint port-city as a picturesque harbor surrounded by hills, covered with the richest of vegetations; trees of mulberry, carob, figs, pomegranates, and hosts of others foreign to our French climes. See Alphonse de Lamartine's *Voyage en Orient 1832–1833* (Paris: Librairie de Charles Gosselin, 1843.)

32. Ghislaine Wood, *Essential Art Deco* (London: Bulfinch, 2001), 21.

33. It should be noted that the expanding campus of Université Saint Joseph owes its recent growth (and increasing space) in no small part to the Corm family. In early 2004, Virginie and Madeleine Corm sold—and given the times' market values one might even say "bequeathed"—to the Jesuits more than two acres of land that had been part of the Corm residence gardens. It is into these newly acquired lots that the university is currently expanding.

34. In addition to being a member of the *Académie Mediteranneène* and, like Charles Corm, a lover of the Mediterranean, Paul Morand was Coco Chanel's biographer.

35. Eliahu Epstein (later Eliahu Eilat) was a Jewish (later Israeli) diplomat, journalist, and Orientalist scholar, who studied and resided in Beirut during the 1920s and 1930s. He became a good friend of Corm's and maintained active correspondence with him after the establishment of the State of Israel in 1948—and the souring of relations between countries beholden to the Arabist narrative, Lebanon included, and the nascent Jewish State.

36. Charles Corm Archives; see for instance letters between Corm and Eliahu Epstein, dated January 25, 1938; February 22, 1938; March 3, 1938; April 26, 1938, etc.

37. Charles Corm Archives; Letters from Eliahu Epstein dated May 6, 1935, and January 25, 1938. In the 1938 letter, Epstein informs Corm that Nahum Slousch was currently "out of Jerusalem but is expected back next week. On his arrival I shall discuss with him the matter in a more definite fashion and will let you have details."

38. Rushdy Maalouf, "Yabisat Arza" [A Cedar Has Dried Up], *Al-Hikma* (Beirut: The Hikma Institute, Volume 11, Number 9, December 1963), 463.

39. Rushdy Maalouf, 463.

40. Rushdy Maalouf, 463. Emphasis in original.

41. Rushdy Maalouf, 463.

42. Rushdy Maalouf, 463.

43. It should be noted that the *Maison Blanche de Beyrouth* was met with the same kinds of negative reactions from the artistic, architectural, and literary elites of Beirut at the time. Not that Corm's structure should be compared to the Eiffel Tower, nor that like the Eiffel Tower

being today's most salient and charming symbol of the city of Paris, so should the *Maison de Beyrouth* be deemed a symbol of Beirut. Yet, it is interesting to note that avant-gardist non-traditional ideas are often met with violent opposition by the guardians of orthodoxy. The Eiffel Tower was almost torn down after the 1889 *Exposition Universelle* World's Fair for which it was initially built. A collection of renowned and respected French artists referred to it as a "grotesque monstrosity" at that time, and protested with much indignation the bad taste in which it was conceived, viewing it as an affront to French art, French history, and French elegance and good taste. Gustave Eiffel on the other hand was convinced of its beauty and ultimately its endurance, prompting him to predict that he would live to become jealous of his own creation one day. He is alleged to have said "je vais être jaloux de cette tour; elle est plus célèbre que moi" (I will one day become jealous of this tower; it is more famous than I).

44. See Hazem Saghieh, "ISIS and the Hazards of Our Abysmal Histories," *NOW*, Beirut, August 5, 2014, http://mme.cm/PM2U00.

45. Eli Khoury, "ISIS and the Hazards of Our Not So Abysmal Histories," *NOW*, Beirut, August 6, 2014, http://mme.cm/U22U00.

46. Khoury, "ISIS and the Hazards."

47. See Michel Chiha's *Visage et Présence du Liban* (Beirut: Cénacle Libanais, 1964), 168.

48. Charles Corm, *La Montagne Inspirée* (Beirut: Éditions de La Revue Phénicienne, 1987), 53.

49. François Bédarida, *Churchill* (Paris: Fayard, 1999), 21–25.

Chapter One

A Brief Introduction to a Monumental Life-Story

This study reflects on an aspect of modern Middle Eastern life that, although having shaped an important facet of the region's cultural and intellectual landscape since the early twentieth century, is often overlooked in the history of ideas of the late Ottoman period. In many respects, this biography is an intellectual history of the modern Middle East; the Levant in general terms, Lebanon in particular. Most importantly, the present work is an inquiry into Lebanese intellectual, cultural, and political life as incarnated in the ideas and as illustrated by the times, works, and activities of Charles Corm (1894–1963), the guiding spirit behind modern Lebanese nationalism and a leading figure in the "Young Phoenicians" movement of the first half of the twentieth century. As such, Charles Corm was a devoted Lebanese patriot, and an outspoken advocate on behalf of identity narratives that are often dismissed in the prevalent Arab nationalist paradigms that have come to define the canon of Middle East history and scholarship of the past century. But Charles Corm was much more than a man of letters upholding a patriotic mission.[1]

As poet and entrepreneur, socialite and orator, philanthropist and patron of the arts, and as a leading businessman, Charles Corm commanded immense influence on modern Lebanese political and social life, popular culture, and intellectual production during the interwar period and beyond. In many respects, Charles Corm had also been "the conscience" of Lebanese society at a crucial juncture in its modern history as the autonomous *Sanjak/ Mutasarrifiyya* (or Province) of Mount-Lebanon and the *Vilayet* (State) of Beirut of the late nineteenth century were navigating their way out of Ottoman domination and into a French Mandatory period (ca. 1918), before culminating with the independence of the Republic of Lebanon in 1943.

Yet, what attention Charles Corm has received from scholars has traditionally been limited to his role as a leading figure in the "Young Phoenicians" movement, which, in itself, is neither faulty nor deficient. However, relegating Corm's contributions to a single deed, an intellectual current that is often denigrated—in spite of its legitimacy in the eyes of large segments of Lebanese society—does not do him (or his times) justice, provides an inadequate context to the history of ideas in the modern Middle East, and consequently leaves us with an incomplete, skewed, and ideologically tainted image of a region that is anything but the monochromatic uniform monolith that it is often made out to be in traditional literature.[2]

Indeed, in this second decade of the twenty-first century, the Arab-Muslim Middle East that the majority of area specialists have come to take as a given—as the exclusive preserve of cohesive, uniform, and harmonious Arabs and Muslims alone—seems to be coming undone, revealing in its folds *another* Middle East; one populated by Arabs and Muslims to be sure, perhaps even a majority of Arabs and Muslims, but a universe that can ill-afford continuing to neglect an important indigenous non-Arab and non-Muslim element in its midst. Indeed, just as the autarky of a seemingly uniform and immutable "Ottoman universe" had unraveled in the second decade of the twentieth century, so is the dominance of the Ottomans' successor "Arab Order" as monolith being called into question a mere hundred years later, in this second decade of the twenty-first century. In January 1918, President Woodrow Wilson had proclaimed "self-determination" and "autonomy" as inalienable human principles under which all "non-Turkish nationalities" then subject to Turkish rule be granted safety, security, and opportunity of autonomous development.[3] Wilson's "non-Turkish nationalities" referred to those Middle Easterners (and Europeans), subjects of the Ottoman Empire, who were not Turks, and who protested being referred to as such and folded into a then resurgent "Ottomanism" and an irredentist pan-Turkism. It is worth recalling that, from a Western perspective, the Middle East had (wrongly) been synonymous with Turkey back in those days—to the same extent that it may be identified (also wrongly) with the "Arab world" today. Likewise the term "Turk" prior to the emergence of twentieth-century nationalism in the Middle East was often used interchangeably with "Muslim"—to the same extent that the terms "Arab" and "Muslim" are often conflated in our times. This anarchic taxonomy proved disastrous in the early twentieth century—just as the nomenclature deeming the "Middle East" an "Arab world" may yet prove catastrophic for our times. President Wilson's advisor in 1918, Colonel Edward Mandell House, cautioned about the risks of such over-simplifications. He warned that the early twentieth-century British map of the Middle East, giving primacy principally to Arab interests—to the neglect of others—would render the region "a breeding place for future wars."[4] Issuing from the administration of a then unseasoned young America, often belittled for its shallow "sense of history," Colonel House's admonition was prescient, betraying subtlety of spirit, political foresight, and a grasp of history to which even the courtly Europeans of his day were no match. With the volatility and woes of today's "Arab Middle East" as backdrop, Colonel House's forewarnings of a century ago may yet convey a different kind of poignancy and pertinence.

ON TAXONOMY, AND THE MAKING AND UN-MAKING OF THE MODERN MIDDLE EAST

The studies and predictions that have emerged in the aftermath of the misnamed and ill-defined "Arab Spring" since early 2011 were manifold and varied. Yet, they often lacked in depth of analysis and grasp of the history and "cultural ecology" of the Middle East. They were therefore selective and static in their approach, largely predicated on "Arab" taxonomy as essence and seed of everything Middle East, and predicting widespread democratization—sometimes Islamization—when other possibilities and other parameters of identity remained unexplored.

After all, the current map of the Middle East, plotting states with "national" names boasting "national" anthems, unfurling "national" flags, and trotting out "national" armies, is a reflection *not* of a law of nature *nor* of time-honored Middle Eastern precedents and traditions. Rather, this model is the product of European fancy, European history, European toponymy, and European romantic conceptions of the Middle East as a preserve, exclusively or predominantly, of "Arabs" and "Muslims." Yet the Middle East by its very nature, and in dutiful observance of its millennial history, is hardly the fixed, homogenous "Arab-Muslim world" often depicted in the yearnings of Arab nationalists and their European advocates. Likewise the Arabs' conquests and colonization of a non-Arab Middle East beginning in the seventh century—which, no doubt might have colored Christian Europe's, and by osmosis the West's, perceptions of the region as a uniform "Arab world"—never wholly Arabized or Islamized the new colonial chattels. Indeed,

> Some peoples of the [Middle East] resisted the forces of Arabicization, Islamicization, or both: even among those who underwent both these processes, this was not always accompanied by a total abandonment of their earlier culture. Thus, there are still pockets across the Arab world using languages other than Arabic and practicing religions other than Islam, and there are still [Middle Eastern] groups convinced that their ancestors belonged to a people different from [the Arab and Muslim peoples.][5]

In truth, there had never been a united "Arab world" or a cohesive "Arab nation" antecedent to the modern twentieth-century Middle Eastern state-system that the British willed into being after the collapse of the Ottoman Empire. Even T. E. Lawrence, the celebrated Lawrence of Arabia, one of our time's most committed advocates of Arabism, scoffed at the notion of an "Arab nation" and a putative cohesive "Arab people" as such, calling them a "manufactured" nation.[6] "Arab unity," upon which the current Middle Eastern state-system was constructed, was described as an illusion by Lawrence; a fairytale akin to "English-speaking unity [. . .]; a madman's notion—for [the twentieth] century and the next."[7] Lawrence even conceded the Arabic language itself—the supposed cement of Arabness—to have gained primacy in the Middle East *only* recently, and *only* by sheer "accident and time," maintaining its ostensible dominance to "not mean that Syria—any more than Egypt—[was] an Arabian country," and further noting that on the Mediterranean "sea coast there [was] little, if any, Arabic feeling or tradition."[8]

As pertains to the role that the Arabic language itself might have played in coloring prevalent conceptions of the Middle East, linguists are in agreement as to the puzzle that is Arabic, and the ambivalence that users of the Arabic language feel when speaking about, or naming, their spoken idioms. And whereas this "ambivalence" may be incomprehensible to English-speaking audiences who are unanimous as to what constitutes "good spoken English"—that is to say, English that adheres closely to the "written language"—users of Arabic don't have an equivalent to "good spoken Arabic," and mean only one thing when uttering the phrase "Arabic language."[9] To them Arabic is strictly speaking the "Classical" or "Koranic" idiom brought forth by Islam, and its more recent nineteenth-century descendant—Modern Standard Arabic. Simply put, Arabic is *not* any of the Middle East's modern spoken languages—which Arabs themselves often dismiss as "vernaculars," or "colloquials," or simply "vulgar accents."[10] Yet many of those so-called "accents" can indeed be deemed languages in their own right, differing from each other, and from Arabic *tout court*, as French may be different from English, and as both French and English may differ from Latin.[11] Even in the early decades of the twentieth century, when an inchoate Arab nationalism was beginning to unfurl its irredentist banner on the entire Middle Eastern mosaic, noted Egyptian writer Tawfiq Awan was cautioning that,

> Egypt has an Egyptian language; Lebanon has a Lebanese language; the Hijaz has a Hijazi language; and so forth—and all of these languages are by no means Arabic languages. Each of our countries has a language, which is its own possession; so, why do we not write [our native language] as we converse in it? For, the language in which the people speak is the language in which they also write.[12]

But, as remarked Bernard Lewis, were this reality to come to pass, and were "the Egyptians, the Syrians, the Iraqis, and the rest" to heed Awan's advice in 1929 and "develop their vernaculars into national languages, as the

Spaniards, the Italians, and the rest had done in Europe, then all hope of a greater Arab unity would be lost."[13] Yet the engine of history seems to be heading in that direction. And so, rather than being an aberration, the upsurge in a discourse fashionable in the second decade of the twenty-first century about the impending collapse of the Sykes-Picot political order in the Middle East to reflect the diversity of its mosaics, may be looked upon as an honest, ideologically neutral reading of the region's past—that is to say a past defined by hybridity and multiplicity of identities, languages, and cultural accretions.

Moreover, it is worth noting that in this early twenty-first century's fragmenting Syria and Iraq—to name only those two—there had never been a uniquely Syrian or Iraqi territorial identity as such—perhaps less so a cohesive unitary Syrian or Iraqi political will to live in a single unitary state. In fact, what became the Kingdom of Iraq under British Mandate in 1920 had previously constituted three distinct Ottoman administrative units—that is to say three *Vilayets* or "states" in today's parlance, each as discrete and divergent from the other as, say, a Prague, a Vienna, or a Budapest would have been disparate in an Austro-Hungarian Empire. To wit, the Ottoman Vilayet of Mosul in the north, today the capital of Iraq's Nineveh Governorate, which was declared the seat of a new "Caliphate" by a nascent Islamic State during the summer of 2014, had, historically speaking, consisted of a majority mix population of Kurds, Turkmens, Assyrians, Armenians, and others, often with more kinships—as well as historical, cultural, linguistic, and geographic ties—to Aleppans in present-day Syria, and even Anatolian Turks and Iranians in the north, than to populations further south in what became Iraq proper. Likewise, the Vilayet of Baghdad, with even the etymology of its name recalling Persian rather than Arab origins, shares equally in the heritage of ancient Akkadians, Babylonians, as well as Persians and Arabs, and until the middle of the twentieth century still boasted a majority Jewish population, remnant of the sixth-century BC Babylonian Exile. The same hybridity and multiplicity of identities and cultural accretions apply to the southern Iraqi province of Basra; another district with a storied past, corralling Sumerians and Elamites in ancient times, Aramaeans, Arabs, and Persians in more recent history. Today, with its majority Shi'ite population, the province of Basra is deemed—perhaps inaccurately, but not unfairly or without reason—to be more Persian than it may be Arab.

In 2003, former Iraqi dissident author Kanan Makiya wrote that the new Iraqi state that he yearned for ought to become demilitarized, federal, and non-Arab for it to remain relevant, viable, and whole.[14] Makiya's object had been to recognize and valorize the sizeable non-Arab elements of modern Iraqi society; sacrificing as it were the dominance of "Arabness" (or the Arab identity upheld by the "many" in an Iraqi state that was once a bastion of Arab nationalism and a model of Arab identity), in order to valorize the identities and the narratives of the non-Arab "few." But Makiya's candor angered many relics of Arab nationalism, who, defying history, geography, and hope, still aspired to a united uniform "pan-Arab State," spurning the region's non-Arab element, and still spouting the musty slogans of an "Arab World" extant only in parched nationalist yearnings.

Revealing this stubborn attachment to an idea that, for all intents and purposes, seems to have outlived its usefulness, an observer attending a 1994 Arab nationalist convention in Beirut of all places—arguably the least Arab of Arab capitals—poignantly condensed the bankruptcy of an ideology that had smudged the mosaic of identities that is the Middle East. "From where I sat," wrote this observer,

> the [Arab nationalist] conferees appeared to represent an extinct tribe using strange words—indeed a language incomprehensible in our time. Most of them had grey hair and stooping backs. Some needed canes to help them walk. Some had hearing aids and shaking hands that made it difficult for them to write, and others had difficulty getting the words out. Astonishingly, none of this stopped them, [even though they were] blowing in a broken bagpipe.[15]

This is an indictment of a certain political and intellectual rigidity that has for far too long colored common perceptions of the Middle East, and, for the sake of ideological conformity, occulted its congenital diversity. In 1999, long before the fitful rise and fall of the 2011 "Arab Spring," former Arab-nationalist author and public intellectual Hazem Saghieh published a scathing critique of what he considered outmoded Arab dogmas and delusions. His book, *The Swansong of Arabism*, was a work of painful introspection in which he called for casting aside the jingles of "Arab Unity" and discarding the assumptions of "Arab identity." Saghieh urged his former comrades-in-arms to bid farewell to the corpse of the Arab nation.[16] "Arabism is dead," he wrote, and Arab nationalists would do well bringing a healthy dose of realism to their world's changing realities: "They need relinquish their phantasmagoric delusions about 'the Arab world' [. . . and let go of their] damning and outmoded rhetoric of unity and uniformity [. . . in favor of] liberal concepts such associational and consociational identities."[17]

But Arab nationalism was not the bane of Iraq alone. The above Mesopotamian ethno-religious conundrum has a parallel that is equally puzzling in neighboring Syria. In fact, just as historically speaking there had never been a distinct political or cultural identity defined in exclusively "Iraqi" (or indeed "Arab Iraqi") terms before the British contrived one in 1920, so has there never been a Syrian identity (let alone a "Syrian Arab" identity) as such before the French willed one into being during the 1930s. Indeed, what the French named "Syria" in 1936—a state carved out and cobbled together out of the Ottoman Vilayets of Beirut, Aleppo, and Damascus—displayed great difficulty transitioning from distinct multi-ethnic Ottoman administrative units to a single cohesive modern territorial state defined by a single identity and common bonds of national kinship.

Even some of the main avatars of Arab nationalist ideology, most prominently Michel Aflaq (1910–1989), the Syrian-Christian founder of the Baath Party, admitted to the contrived nature of the Arabism that he sought to promote among early twentieth-century Levantines and Syrians. In his nationalist manifesto, *For the Sake of the Baath*, Aflaq wrote that:

> Seldom were the terms "Arab" or "Arab identity" part of the national consciousness or the political lexicon of early twentieth-century Syrians, and rarely were such terms ever used. Indeed, Syrian political leaderships during the 1930s made use of the term "Syrian" as a sort of amulet, to evade negotiating the intricacies of their region's ethno-religious and racial mosaics. "Syria" was a regional term, and was intended to bring together disparate Muslims, Christians, Arabs, and non-Arab minorities, under the banner of a distinct national identity.[18]

It bears repeating in this sense that modern Syria, considered by many "the beating heart" of Arab nationalism, as a name and as a geographic entity remains before anything else a modern notion, the outcome of European geography and European conceptions of the Eastern Mediterranean. Isabel Burton, wife of famed British explorer Sir Richard Francis Burton, summed up the ethnic enigma of the Damascus Vilayet of the 1870s as one of various groups living

> together more or less, and [practicing] their conflicting worships in close proximity. [. . . But] in their hearts [the inhabitant of the State of Damascus] hate one another. The Sunnites excommunicate the Shiahs, and both hate the Druzes; all detest the Ansariyyehs [Alawites]; the Maronites do not love anybody but themselves, and are duly abhorred by all; the Greek Orthodox abominate the Greek Catholics and the Latins; all despise the Jews.[19]

Writing in a similar vein a mere thirty years later, another British traveler, Gertrude Bell, noted Syria to be "merely a geographical term corresponding to no national sentiment."[20] This observation was further confirmed by many Levantine contemporaries of both Bell and Burton, who claimed there to have never been a distinct Syrian entity; that what Europeans referred to as Syria was but a bevy of disparate groups and loose geographic entities brought together by conquest and ruled forcibly through terror and tyranny; in sum, "a society based on a despotism of brutal force modeled on that of the ruler."[21] "The tale of Syria was not ended in this count of odd races and religions," observed T. E. Lawrence in the early decades of the twentieth century. Albeit known by a single name, a European bequest, Syria is not one, but multiple entities, he noted, "each with its character, direction, and opinion," often "like twins disliking one another."[22] Yet the terms "Syria" and "Syrian" were alien to those upon whom they were foisted claimed Lawrence; "for in Arabic there was no such name, nor any name for all the country," thus indicating not only a lack of unity, but political incoherence as well.[23] In history, concluded Lawrence,

> Syria had been a corridor between sea and desert, joining Africa to Asia, and Arabia to Europe. It had been a prize-ring, a vassal, of Anatolia, of Greece, of Rome, of Egypt, of Arabia, of Persia, of Mesopotamia. When given a momentary independence, by the weakness of neighbors it had fiercely resolved into discordant northern, southern, eastern and western "kingdoms" with the area at best of Yorkshire, at worst of Rutland; for if Syria was by nature a vassal country it was also by habit a country of tireless agitation and incessant revolt.[24]

Heralding the disintegration of a Syria then still under construction, at a time when the current (Sykes-Picot) map was still on the drawing board, Lawrence warned that an Arab government in any future Syrian entity "would be as much 'imposed' as the [Ottoman] Turkish Government, or a foreign protectorate, or the historic [Muslim] Caliphate."[25] For, in his view, Syria then, not unlike Syria now, "remained a vividly coloured racial and religious mosaic," and any attempt at forming a unitary state where none was warranted "would make a patched and parceled thing, ungrateful to a people whose instincts ever returned toward parochial home rule."[26]

Only "Europeanized Syrians"—that is to say Arabic-speaking urban Christians and Jews—who were familiar with the languages and concepts of Europe, began describing the lands of their birth collectively as "Syria," and began viewing themselves as "Syrians," to be distinguished from Turks, Arabs, or Ottomans. Indeed, the name "Syria" stemmed exclusively from a European habit, European taxonomy, and European patterns of social and geographic classification. It derived from a designation prevalent in Greek translations of the Bible (the Septuagint) referring to the region known traditionally in Aramaic and Hebrew texts as "Aram"—that is to say "the land of the speakers of Aramaic." "Syria" was therefore deemed a more convenient appellation in Greek translation because in the times of the transmission "Aram" had been dominated by "Assyrians"—from whom the "Syria" toponym was ultimately derived. Arabs themselves never referred to that region as "Syria," and would not begin doing so until, at the earliest, World War I. Conversely, "modern Syria," with which the term "Syria" began being associated in the interwar period, was never a single entity, but many—namely the Ottoman Vilayets of Damascus, Aleppo, and Beirut. Some have also maintained that the term "Syria," in its classical European usage, was a referent to the place-name of those "speakers of Syrian"—that is to say the speakers of "Syriac," a dialect of Middle Aramaic once prevalent throughout what are today Lebanon, Israel, and Syria, and widely spoken at least into the eighth century of our era.

Therefore, Arabs and Arab nationalists who have ruled "Syria" since its independence in the middle of the twentieth century can be said to be newcomers to this name, and may only lay claim to it through semantic trickery and verbal embellishment. "*Shaam*" is the name that Arabs bestowed on "Syria" beginning in the seventh century—that is to say "Shaam" or "the North" in Southern Arabian languages, as opposed to "Yemen" or "the South" from an Arabian's geographic purview.

Even to this day, most users of Arabic languages opt for the term "Shaam" in reference to the country of Syria and its capital city of Damascus—even as the Arabized form of the noun "Syria" (*Suuriyya*) remains the official country name. Likewise, Syrian identity, or a sense of Syrian-ness as it were, had been alien to the Arabs of what became the Republic of Syria in the mid-1940s. Conversely, there had been a strong bent toward Syrian-ness among Levantine Christian expats in the New World and Europe, fleeing the vagaries and injustices of the late Ottoman period. But the Syria that emerges from the writings of those émigrés was distinctly Christian, and separate from the inchoate Arab nationalist concepts being sputtered in the early twentieth century. Indeed, the term "Syria" that those Levantine Christians were using in their literary works, correspondence, and political writings issued from the language and intellectual heritage of their pre-modern national churches, which were essentially "Syrian Churches" whose languages, as mentioned earlier, were Syriac.

One of those authors who researched and published extensively on the topic of Syria was early twentieth-century Lebanese nationalist and friend of Charles Corm's, Jacques Tabet. In his monumental *La Syrie Historique, Ethnographique, Religieuse, Géographique, Économique, Politique et Sociale*, published in 1920, Tabet argued that while, say, the "Armenian question" may be well known to European audiences concerned by the travails of the Middle East, the "Syrian Question" remains obscure, often wrongly conflated with what he termed the "Arab question."[27] Furthermore, claimed Tabet, Lebanon as a distinct entity should be viewed as the nucleus around which the "Syrian Question" is embedded. "Its impregnable mountains, which were never subjugated to any conqueror, have always served, since the remotest antiquity, as a haven and refuge to persecuted minorities; Christians overwhelmingly, but other smaller dissident Muslim sects as well."[28]

It was indeed the Lebanese, according to Tabet, who awakened Syria from its deep Ottoman slumbers. Thanks to the pugnacious independent character of Mount-Lebanon's inhabitants—its Maronites and Druze in particular—their communal and national coherence, their long tradition of independence, and most importantly perhaps the Maronites' own relationship with the Crusaders, their European successors, the special regime that was accorded Mount Lebanon in 1860—that is to say the autonomy granted the mountain under the *Règlement Organique*, a protectorate of a concert of European powers—and most importantly perhaps the intimate bonds of relationships that the Maronites cultivated with Western chancelleries in Beirut, were all critical assets that set the Lebanese apart from other subjects of the Ottoman empire.[29]

All that of course does not mean that there is no "Syria" as such. There has always been a "Syria," from classical antiquity until Ottoman times. But the "Syria" in question was at best a loose toponymic designation; a purely topographic concept and an amorphous one at that, strictly confined to European geographic usage and European obsessions with the Eastern Mediterranean as reflected in the Hebrew Bible and Christian Gospels.

Still, this European concept of "Syria" would be similar to the way one may refer to something approximating "the Balkans," or "the Alps," or "Anatolia," or "the Mediterranean" today. Eyebrows would be raised in discontent should analysts in our time venture to write about the Alps and the rest as some concrete coherent political entity. Yet, this is the kind of discourse dominating the debate on Syria, the finality of Syria, and the presumed uniformity of today's Syria. But in their majority, the Syrians themselves do recognize the diverse nature of their besieged country and have shown themselves to be keen on maintaining, protecting, and enshrining that diversity through constitutional safeguards.

From the preceding, one may deduce that the oft-heralded "end of Sykes-Picot," prevalent as it is in the literature of the early second decade of the twenty-first century, may not only be a way of heeding history, but may indeed end up being the more just and humane manner in which to manage the ethno-religious diversity of Syria, Iraq, and indeed the entire Levantine Near East. For, the main cause of the strife gripping the region in the early twenty-first century, reduced to its most simple form, pertains to "ethnic" or "ethno-religious" conceptions of identity pitted against the liberal "civic" parameters of selfhood that Sykes-Picot might have envisioned. Though this identity dichotomy may be a flawed and outmoded model from a post-ethnic and post-religious Western perspective, it is one that still has its adherents in the Middle East, where an organic, atavistic, often compulsory conception of identity poses a challenge to—and indeed spurns—the civic liberal patriotisms that are the hallmarks of the modern Western state. To put things in even simpler terms, the Middle East—and for our purposes now, today's Syria, Lebanon, and Iraq—are a bevy of peoples and ethno-religious groups who, for centuries, had defined themselves (and were defined by others) invariably as Assyrians or Alawites, Maronites or Jews, Druzes or Shi'ites, Kurds or Armenians, Greek-Orthodox and others. Yet inhibiting this diversity, unitary "national" notions spawned by Sykes-Picot (and the unitary "Arab" or "Muslim" conceptions of the Middle East) demanded that these peoples forget whom they thought they might have been, and begin referring to themselves as Syrians and Palestinians, Iraqis and Transjordanians, Arabs and suchlike; names, etymologically speaking, and conceptions of identity that were primarily a Western innovation and a reflection of Western typologies and Western ways of looking at the lands of the Eastern Mediterranean. Therefore, and albeit perhaps too sobering a reality, it may not be an indiscretion to keep in mind that the current ailing Middle Eastern state-system does not reflect a law of nature; indeed, it may be an aberration in the *longue durée* of the region's history, and its dismantlement, painful as it may prove to be, will perhaps not bode ill in the long run.

And so, although the present biography of Charles Corm may not be an exploration of what lies ahead for the "Arab Spring" and the future of the current Middle Eastern map and state-system, it is a research-based descriptive of a cultural and intellectual history that may elucidate the current Middle East, and—through the prism of the modern Levant and Lebanon—how it came into being. This biography may also serve as a reminder that a model for the future of the region may still be found in its "pre-modern" Ottoman and Franco-British Mandatory past—in the form of large commonwealths of varied identities—and that a single uniform "Arab" Middle East locked in its current map is neither sacrosanct nor a prerequisite for stability. Indeed, the modern Middle East of the past hundred years—that is to say, a state-system commonly defined as "Arab"—is an historical anomaly that could use a sober re-evaluation; an historical anomaly that stitched together a restive Ottoman mosaic of peoples, forcing fractious heterogeneous ethno-religious and linguistic groups into uneasy contrived "unions" which, it is now being realized, may have carried within them the seeds of their own destruction.

It is worth noting in this regard that at the outset of the Syrian uprisings of 2011, long before foreign *jihadis* came to sully what had initially begun as a noble call for freedom, a group of Syrian dissidents met in Antalya, Turkey, and issued a memorable statement reflecting the true face of their nation—and the Levant in general—and imagining a brighter future for themselves and their neighbors. "We, participants in the Syria Conference for Change," began the Antalya Declaration,

> affirm that the Syrian people are a composite of many ethnicities, including Arabs, Kurds, Chaldaeo-Assyrians, Circassians, Armenians, and others. The conference recognizes and asserts the legitimate and equal rights of all of these constitutive elements of Syrian identity, and demands their protection under a new Syrian constitution to be founded on the principles of civil state, pluralistic parliamentary democracy, and national unity.[30]

Unfortunately the Antalya Declaration had fallen on the deaf ears of a heedless world in 2011. It became dead letter. Yet in due course, it may still be revived. But such a revival may require more than feckless posturing by reluctant superpowers and empty slogans by truculent local actors. A new Syria in the image of Antalya is not a far-fetched fantasy; it is a reflection of a Middle Eastern reality. But for it to eventuate will require resolve, moral clarity, courage, and true leadership in a world awash in doctrinaires and politicians, but bereft of leaders.

And although it might not have gone as far as Kanan Makiya's 2003 suggestion that Iraq be non-Arab and withdraw its membership in the Arab League, the Syrian Antalya Declaration was equally earth-shattering, because it challenged the current "Arab Order" in Syria—and indeed, for all intents and purposes, it signaled the beginning of the end of that order: It made no mention of a distinct Arab identity for Syria (the Assads' favored trope of the past forty years, and one of the pretexts that they have used for maintaining themselves in power); it made no mention of the Golan Heights (conquered by Israel in 1967, and perhaps the most potent symbol and rationale behind maintaining the current regime in place); and perhaps more importantly, it made no mention of Palestine (the mother of all Arab causes, exploited to the hilt by the Assad regime, and again, one of the major pretexts for maintaining the Syrian people chained in voluntary servitude to their Alawite masters and their Arab nationalist facade).

And so, by shirking the symbols, affectations, and language that have kept in place an Arab nationalist order, in the name of an abstract ideology that scorned diversity—and by re-excavating and re-integrating the ethnic diversity of the Syrian people, and others—the Syrians of Antalya seemed to be signaling their readiness for a post-Arab era. This suggests that Makiya's vision may still be the only reasoned and peaceful—one may even argue the only humane and humanist—formula for the mosaic of cultures, languages, and ethnicities that is the Middle East; a living-formula valorizing the integrity of regional ethnic and cultural identities and acknowledging their sovereignty and autonomy.

WHERE IT ALL BEGAN, AND WHERE TO BEGIN ANEW?

For the past hundred years of Western and American interest in the Middle East, the region has been parsed from a purview that has often led to failures of interpretation, policy, analysis, and scholarship. These failures can only be corrected with a more honest examination of—and acquiescence in—the ethno-religious snarl that is the Middle East. Indeed, it is possible that no correctives may bear fruit unless a change is invested in the essentialist reductive language to which the Middle East is often relegated; namely the jargon conflating "Middle East" and "Arab World," using both interchangeably. Baghdad-born British historian Elie Kedourie (1926–1992) described this impulse some forty-five years ago as a "bore," and a "danger" to serious scholarship and sound policy on the Middle East. A century or more of Western interest in the Middle East, wrote Kedourie in 1967, has yielded a stale body of literature and analysis beholden to narratives and taken to biases of Arabs alone, to the neglect of other Middle Easterners; as if "others" in the Middle East and *their* histories mattered little, or were alien and inauthentic in the well-ordered, uniform, harmonious universe of the "Arab world."

Based on this prevalent notion of the "Middle East as Arab World," which Kedourie and others have questioned, Arabs, Arab nationalists, and their Western advocates have held all Middle Easterners to be Arab, even if only remotely associated with the Arabs, and even if alien to the experiences, languages, or traditions of Arabs. To wit, a Lebanese-born Arab nationalist ideologue and man of letters, Omar Farrukh, writing in the second half of the twentieth century, argued that it is irrelevant should Iraqis deem themselves a hybrid of Aramaeans, Persians, Kurds, Turks, Indians, and others; "they still are Arabs in spite of their racial diversity, because the overriding factor in their identity formation is the Arabic language."[31] Likewise, Farrukh stressed, the inhabitants of today's Morocco, Algeria, Libya, and elsewhere in Northern Africa may very well be a mix of Berbers, Black Africans, Spaniards, and Franks, "but by dint of the Arab nation's realities [sic], they all remain Arabs shorn from the same cloth as the Arabs of the Hejaz, Najd, and Yemen."[32]

Sati' al-Husri (1880–1967), a Turkish-speaking Syrian writer and spiritual father of Arab nationalism, who played a leading role in the elaboration of a compulsory Arab identity, famously wrote that:

> Every person who speaks Arabic is an Arab. Every individual associated with an Arabic-speaker or with an Arabic-speaking people is an Arab. If he does not recognize [his Arabness . . .] we must look for the reasons that have made him take this stand. [. . .] But under no circumstances should we say "as long as he does not wish to be an Arab, and as long as he is indifferent to his Arabness, then he is not an Arab." He is an Arab regardless of his own wishes, whether ignorant, unconcerned, recalcitrant or disloyal, he is an Arab, but an Arab without consciousness or feelings, and perhaps even without a conscience.[33]

This ominous admonition to embrace a domineering homogenized Arab identity is one constructed on an obvious historical revisionism and a brazen negation of the "other" as such; it tells the "other" bluntly, "you are whom I say you are, whether you like it or not!" Indeed, Husri was aware, even proud, of the fascistic impulses of this, his brand of nationalism. In fact, he bragged about the Arabism that he yearned for as one that had to exude totalitarian rigidity and regimentation in order for it to triumph: "We can say that the system to which we should direct our hopes and aspirations is a Fascist system," he famously wrote.[34] But this Arab identity is also one framed upon an assumed linguistic unity of the Arab peoples; a unity which a priori presumes the Arabic language itself to be a unified, coherent speech-form, used by all members of the Arab nation, as proposed by Husri. The irony here is that Husri himself was not a native "user" of Arabic; his mother tongue was Turkish, and until his dying day in 1967, the only form of "Arabic" that he used was a stilted Classical Arabic, heavily accented with Turkish.[35]

And so, Husri's advocating for the Arabic language as a foundational tenet of "Arabness" was problematic partly because, as mentioned earlier, Arabic is not a single uniform language that is common and mutually intelligible to all (300 million) presumptive members of Husri's putative Arab nation. Arabic is on the one hand a codified written standard that is never natively spoken—and that is accessible only to those who have had rigorous training and years of schooling in it.[36] On the other hand, Arabic is also a multitude of speech forms derisively referred to as "dialects," differing from each other and from the standard Arabic language itself to the same extent that French is different from other Romance languages and from Latin.[37]

Yet, Husri's dictum "you're an Arab if I say so!" became an article of faith for Arab nationalists. It also condensed the chilling finality with which Arab nationalists and their sympathizers have foisted their blanket "Arab" label on the mosaic of peoples, ethnicities, and language-communities that had defined the Middle East for millennia prior to the advent of twentieth-century Arab nationalism.[38]

But if Husri had been high-handed in his advocacy for a forced Arabization, his pupil Michel Aflaq (1910–1989), founder of the notorious Baath Party, promoted open cruelty and violence against those users of the Arabic language who refused to conform to his prescriptive overarching Arab identity. Arab nationalists must be ruthless with those members of the Arab nation who have gone astray from Arabism, wrote Aflaq:

> [. . .] they must be imbued with a powerful hatred, a hatred unto death, toward any individuals who embody an idea contrary to the idea of Arab nationalism. [. . .] An idea that is opposed to ours does not emerge ex nihilo; it is the outcome of individuals who must themselves be exterminated, so that their very ideas may in turn be also exterminated. The enemy of our ideology vivifies it and sends the blood coursing in our veins. Any action that does not call forth in us living emotions and does not make us feel the spasms of love [. . .], that does not make our blood race in our veins and our pulse beat faster, is a sterile action.[39]

Therein lay the foundational tenets of Arab nationalism and the Arabist canon of Middle Eastern history as preached by Sati' al-Husri, Michel Aflaq, and their cohorts: hostility, rejection, negation, and brazen calls for—*not* the mere suppression, but—the outright annihilation of the non-Arab "other."

Yet despite the dominance of such disturbing readings, the Middle East in both its modern and ancient incarnations remains a patchwork of varied cultures, ethnicities, and languages that cannot be tailored into a pure and neat "Arab" essence without distorting and misleading. Other models of Middle Eastern identities exist, and a spirited Middle Eastern tradition that challenges the orthodoxies and follies of Arab nationalism endures and deserves consideration, recognition, and validation.

Diversity, multilingualism, pluralism, and "linguistic humanism" have always been hallmarks of Middle Eastern lives—from the times of classical antiquity and into modernity and the age of nationalism—and Middle Eastern thinkers, chief among them Charles Corm, have been valorizing these multiple varied identities for centuries, despite the fact that their voices continue to be muffled and their ideas drowned in the muddy waters of uniformity and nationalist rigidity. A state-system mirroring this diversity could well have emerged after World War I were it not stymied by British colonial planners smitten as they were by uniformity and imperial oneness. Indeed, for all intents and purposes, and for all the modern Middle East literature on colonialism and Western imperial designs, it was in fact the British who drew up the modern map of the Middle East, to suit their own predilections and their own colonial interests, not the mixed ethnic makeup of the region.

The checkered Eastern holdings of the Ottoman Empire, which the British inherited alongside the French in 1918, were viewed by the British as a single, homogenous, exclusive preserve of Muslims and Arabs; a "land-bridge" area as it were to His Majesty's "crown Jewel," India. India was the lodestar, and the Middle East, preferably a single, uniform, Arab Middle East, was to be the "road to India." And so, it behooved the British and their colonial cartographers to contrive a single monolithic "Arab world" in what is to this day an inherently diverse, fractured, and fractious Middle East.

Unlike the British, and partly perhaps to spite them and scuttle their colonial designs, the French viewed the Middle East differently. The French were avid practitioners of a "minorities policy." Drawing on antecedents in Northern Africa (with the Berbers) and the Maronite Catholics in Lebanon, the French perceived the Middle East for the ethno-religious and linguistic mosaic that it really was, and indeed, they were contemptuous of the sloppy British conception of the region as a single entity. Robert de Caix, secretary to General Henri Gouraud, the first French High Commissioner in Beirut, wrote in a November 1920 diplomatic memorandum to the Quai d'Orsay in Paris that:

> The entire Middle East has been so poorly packed together [in the minds and plans of the British.] The resulting clutter is all the more legitimate reason for us [the French] to try and steer the minds clear of unitary political systems and, instead, to advance federalist concepts. [. . .] Federalism would be a great relief

for much of the notables of these lands, and a boon to the bulk of this region's disparate populations, who remain, to a very large extent, alien to all manners of [unitary] political life.[40]

This is largely why, in 1920, the French turned the Levantine Provinces that they inherited from the Ottoman Empire—what are today Lebanon and Syria—into five distinct, ethnically coherent, and largely homogenous states that were never defined as Arab states. Those entities were the State of Greater Lebanon (the precursor of what is today the Lebanese Republic), the State of Damascus (the southern part of what is today the Syrian Arab Republic), the State of Aleppo (the northeastern part of what is today the Syrian Arab Republic), the State of the Alawite Mountain (the northwest of today's Syrian Arab Republic), the State of the Druze Mountain (corresponding roughly to the Hauran district of today's Syrian Arab Republic), and the northwestern State or District of Alexandretta (ceded in 1939 to Turkey and becoming the Turkish district of Hatay).

Had the British not pushed for the dismantlement of these creations—which were ultimately the remnants of related Ottoman provinces—in favor of an artificially united Syrian state (or a unitary Iraq or Jordan for that matter), arguably sounder and less fractious entities could have emerged and conceivably endured into our times; states that may have very well remained at peace with themselves and their neighbors. Indeed, as mentioned earlier, Syria in its current configuration had no rationale for being and no precedent as a single, united, uniform entity resembling the Syrian Arab Republic of today. It had always, for millennia, been part of something else—in T. E. Lawrence's telling a "vassal," in turn, "of Anatolia, Greece, Rome, Egypt" and other larger entities.[41] Indeed outside of the coercive Arab nationalist ideology that had been its guiding principle for the past forty years, today's Syria never benefitted from a single, well-delineated, "Syrian" corporate identity shared by all of its ethnic and sectarian constitutive elements. It bears repeating that even the name "Syria" itself owes its etymology to Greek, not Arabic, origins, suggesting conceptual as well as political dubiousness. In fact, the precursor to the current Syrian Arab Republic did not come into being until 1936, when France had already become Britain's "junior partner" in the Levant. By 1940, France was no longer calling the shots in the Middle East; so, at the behest of Britain, a "United Syria" was granted independence from France in 1946, and became the "Syrian Arab Republic" in 1961; an improbable nation stitched together out of ethnically and culturally disparate Ottoman provinces, yet not without the protestations of this new entity's Alawite and Christian communities.

Indeed, the Alawite State that the French had established in 1920 would remain an autonomous administrative unit outside the Syrian state until 1942. And until 1944, a bevy of Alawite notables (among them one named Suleiman al-Assad) took turns passionately pleading with the French Mandatory authorities against attaching the autonomous State of the Alawites to a projected (United) Syrian Republic. The Syrians were too ethnically fragmented to warrant a single unitary state, argued Suleiman al-Assad. In a June 1936 memorandum addressed to the cabinet of French Prime Minister Léon Bluhm, Assad held that any future united Arab Syrian entity would put in place a regime dominated by fanaticism and intolerance toward non-Arab and non-Muslim minorities. He asserted that:

> The spirit of hatred and fanaticism imbedded in the hearts of the Arab Muslims against everything that is non-Muslim has been perpetually nurtured by the Islamic religion. There is no hope that the situation will change. Therefore, the abolition of the Mandate will expose the minorities in Syria to the dangers of death and annihilation. [Case in point, the] good Jews contributed to the Arabs with civilization and peace, scattered gold, and established prosperity in Palestine without harming anyone or taking anything by force. Yet the Muslims declared holy war against them and never hesitated in slaughtering their women and children. [. . . A United Syria] will only mean the enslavement of the Alawite people and the exposure of the minorities to the dangers of death and annihilation. [. . . The French] may think that it is possible to ensure the rights of the Alawites and the minorities by treaty. We assure you that treaties have no value in relation to the Islamic mentality in Syria. [. . .] The Alawite people [therefore . . .] appeal to the French government [. . .] and request [. . .] a guarantee of their freedom and independence within their small territory [in the State of the Alawites.][42]

Yet a mere four decades after Suleiman al-Assad's pleas, on November 16, 1970, his air force officer son, Hafez, seized power in Syria, claiming the country to Arabism, and ruling it under the auspices of a rigid Arab nationalist ideology, the Baath party, for the next three decades. Today, his son Bashar seems to be carrying his father's—*not* his grandfather's—mantle, is counted among the rare remaining relics of Arab nationalism, and is considered to be one of the most committed champions of Arab causes and a bulwark of a united Arab Syria. But are the Assads really the tried-and-true, dyed-in-the-wool Arab nationalists that they are making themselves out to be? Or is their conversion to Arabism—a departure from time-honored communal traditions—a sleight of political expediency?

Over the course of four turbulent "Syrian" decades, the Assad Dynasty managed to give this most improbable of states a patina of legitimacy and stability, mainly by co-opting and advancing a most extreme and sinister form of Arabism. They built schools, dams, hospitals, a third-rate economy, a rigid bureaucracy, an oppressive "security" and "intelligence" apparatus, a merciless prison and penal system, and an omnipotent, omnipresent military that acts as the regime's Praetorian Guard. The Assads also took pleasure erecting imposing ubiquitous statues of themselves. But they did precious little to forge a meaningful "Syrian" national identity, or deal with their country's intense regionalism, sectarian rivalries, and ethno-cultural differences. Nevertheless, they maintained themselves and their Alawite community—a mere ten to twelve percent of Syria's population—in power, and kept their contrived polity from rending by fabricating external enemies, inventing and foiling internal threats, and putting up elaborate shows of Arab nationalist engagements and overwrought pieties to Arab causes.

DOES AN ARAB MIDDLE EAST STILL MAKE SENSE?

By the second decade of the twenty-first century, this façade looks very likely to be crumbling, and the Assads' model is being shaken. Sunni Syria, Kurdish Syria, and perhaps at some point a Christian, Druze, and certainly Alawite Syria—which had all been blunted, marginalized, and despoiled over forty years of brutal Arab Baathism—appear to be reawakening. This may not necessarily entail an impending Balkanization or immediate fragmentation of Syria—especially in light of the Antalya Declaration, which appears to have committed to a form of Syrian "federalism" similar to the (still sputtering) Iraqi system. But at the same time, it is unlikely that the emancipation and political (as well as cultural and religious) reawakening of Syria's various ethnic and sectarian groups currently underway may lead to representative forms of government; at least not in the immediate aftermath of Assad's demise, should that eventuate, and certainly not under the auspices of the "Caliphate" established in the summer of 2014.

Still, a dynamic of change seems to have smitten the Syrians and shaken them out of their traditional inertia and resignation. The unitary monolithic Syria of the Arab nationalist may very well be breathing its last. Whatever emerges out of its charred remains might do well casting a glance at pre-Baathist Syrian history; at a "Syrian nation" that is a "multiplicity of nations," various entities, distinct and separate from the "Arab nation," composed of Arabs to be sure, but teeming with Levantine ethnic and cultural groups with histories and memories predating Muslims, Christians, Arabs, and Jews.

Lebanese thinker Antun Saadé (1904–1949), founder of the Syrian Social Nationalist Party (ca. 1932), advanced a unique conception of this "Syrian nation" as a crucible and synthesis of many cultures, civilizations, and ethnic, sectarian, and linguistic communities; a rich composite of Levantines, Canaanite Phoenicians and Hebrews, Aramaeans, Assyrians, in addition to Arabs and others. The Syrians, wrote Saadé, must

> completely do away with the myth that they are Easterners [read Arabs] and that their destiny is linked to that of the Eastern [or Arab] peoples. We, the Syrians, are not easterners. On the contrary, we are the fountainhead of Medi-

terranean culture and the custodians of the civilization of that sea which we transformed into a Syrian sea, whose roads were traversed by our ships and to whose distant shores we carried our culture, our inventions, and our discoveries.[43]

Saadé categorically rejected the claims made by Arabs or Arab nationalists of his generation over the geographic and conceptual notion of "Syria" and the "Syrian people," deeming them inherently Arab constructs. The Syrians are "Syrian" he claimed, not "Arab." Drawing on his belief in the interaction between biology and geography in molding the spirit and body of the Syrian people, Saadé recognized the diverse racial origins of his *Homo Syrius*; Syrian identity, he claimed, was a function of the racial fusion of multiple ancient civilizations: Canaanites, Akkadians, Chaldaeans, Assyrians, Aramaeans, Hittites, and Metannis."[44] But this hybrid Syrian crucible, in Saadé's view, had at best a negligible "Arab" component, one that did not warrant mention, let alone deserve the dominant place that it continues to occupy in many quarters.

Ill-favored as this view of the Middle East may seem to the keepers of the Arab nationalist canon, it is a story worth being retold and restituted. Acquiescence in diversity, not unlike yearning for unity, can be cathartic and can offer alternatives to authoritarian nationalisms. To paraphrase one of Charles Corm's companions, Lebanese thinker Michel Chiha (1891–1954), the Levant of Lebanon and Syria is "a meeting place to which peoples flock and assimilate regardless of their origins"; it is a "crossroads where varied civilizations drop in on one another, and where bevies of beliefs, languages and cultural rituals salute each other in solemn veneration."[45] Denying this reality, and insisting on approaching the Middle East through the blurred lens of Arabism and Arab identity alone, dooms observers, politicians, and academics alike to continued failures of interpretation, policy, and analysis of the region. As mentioned earlier, even Arabs and former Arab nationalists seem to be abandoning the failed models and narratives of Arab nationalism—and have indeed been doing so for close to a quarter century already. This is certainly not the result of the "Arab Spring." Indeed the "Arab Spring" itself might have been a symptom of more systemic changes under way. Perhaps Western analysts and policy-makers would do well following the lead of Middle Easterners abandoning the hackneyed language of old.

"I want to be different from you," wrote Syrian intellectual (and former Arab nationalist) Nizar Qabbani in the early 1990s;

> I want out of your hollow language and out of the silly worship of your idols. I want to set fire to your Scriptures, and to the language that you have forced upon me! [. . .] I want to free myself from the tyranny of your sands. [. . .] I reject you! [. . .] I want out of your poetry, out of your tedious literature. I want out of my voice, out of my writings, out of my place of birth!!![46]

Those were labored, painful words coming from one who was once among the most committed advocates of Arabism—his attestation, as it were, to the spuriousness and failures of the Arabist narrative, its legends, its standards, and its language. But Qabbani is not alone. As recently as June 2011, one of the Middle East's best-known Arabophone thinkers, the Syrian poet Adonis (b. 1930), living in exile in Paris for the past fifty years, published an "Open Letter" to President Assad of Syria, where he did not mince words about the cruelty and misery bred by Arabism. "Enough already, Mr. President," began Adonis's address:

> A culture that accepts the creed of Arab nationalists is one doomed to extinction. [. . .] A nation consumed by a need for "oneness" in thought, opinions, language, and belief, is a culture of tyranny, not singularity. [. . .] Arab nationalists have abused the hybrid cultural identity of Syria for far too long. They have submitted the richness of Syrian identity to a single linguistic, cultural, "racial," and "religious" Arabism, laying down the foundations of a uniform monolithic, one-dimensional culture. In sum, a resentful Arabism has presented us with a narrow, regurgitant, exclusivist culture built solely on negating, apostatizing, marginalizing, and annihilating the non-Arab "other"—indeed, Arabism is built on accusing the "other" of treason. Enough already, Mr. President![47]

Again, very powerful words and a devastating indictment of the coerced "oneness" of Arabism issuing from Adonis, himself an erstwhile advocate of Arabism. But like others of his generation, Adonis has had a change of heart: "Bury the ignoble face of Arab history, and lay to rest its dull heritage and traditions," he urged already during the 1950s and 1960s.[48] This ruthless assault on the sacred icons of a culture was Adonis's way of challenging Arab nationalist pieties, a way of slaying all elements of a previous existence and engaging new, dynamic, regenerated non-Arab and pre-Arab referents. "Bring along your axes and follow me," he pressed on in 1972:

> Pack up your "Allah" like a dying Arab Sheikh, open a pathway to the Sun away from Minarets, open a book to a child besides the books of musty pieties, [and] cast the dreamer's eye away from Medina and Kufa. Come along with me! I am not the only one.[49]

The 2011 upheavals rippling through the Middle East, the tenuous realities of its crumbling patrimonial geriatric Arab dynasties, the region's striking cultural diversity, and its remarkable intellectual and historical accretions, might very well be the charter of a new resurrected emergent Middle East—a new Middle Eastern state-order in the making, but one already dreamt up (and about) close to a century ago by Lebanese, Syrian, Israeli, and Egyptian "Levantines." The hybrid Levantine Middle East, at peace with its diversity and multiplicity, might not materialize for some time. But there is no doubt it is coming, its suppressors may, no doubt, be breathing their last, and its past advocates from a century ago deserve re-excavation and reevaluation in our time.

CHARLES CORM'S LEBANON IN THE TWENTY-FIRST CENTURY

> Located on the Western edge of the Syro-Mesopotamian quadrangle, Lebanon has the task of transmitting to the Western world the faintest pulsations of the Eastern and Arab worlds. And given its position on the shores of the Mediterranean, Lebanon also has the task of intercepting—before anyone else—the life ripples of the Mediterranean, of Europe, and of the universe, in order to cast them and retransmit them [. . .] to the nations of the hinterland, to these realms of sands and mosques and sun. Such is an element of an "Eternal Truth."[50]

This standard portrayal of Lebanon as a "mission" dictated by its unique geographic location came not from some zealous traditional Lebanese patriot of Charles Corm's persuasion, who would otherwise be expected to offer such kind and devout testimonials to the country's cosmopolitanism, diversity, and geographic uniqueness. But the above were the words of Kamal Jumblat, a Lebanese Druze chieftain, a one-time "Left-Wing" parliamentarian and committed Arab nationalist who spent a good portion of his adult life attempting to debunk the very image of Lebanon as elaborated by traditional Lebanese foes of Arab nationalism—that is to say, the image of Lebanon "the crossroads," the "hybrid intermediary," and the Middle East's "bridge to the West."

Yet going against his Arabist grain, Jumblat still portrayed Lebanon in terms reminiscent of Charles Corm's Young Phoenicians, as

> the birthplace of the first City-State, the first national idea, the first maritime empire, and the first representative democratic system [. . .] at a time when early humanity was still stumbling clumsily through its very first footsteps. Very near to this Mediterranean Sea, which radiated in the grandeur and reason of Sidon, Byblos, Tyre, Carthage, Alexandria, Athens, Rome, Constantinople, Beirut, and Cordoba [. . .]; here on this very unique spot in the world, where the Mountain and the Sea meet, frolic, and embrace [. . .] in a national consciousness that gave birth to the first independence movements in the East. [. . .] This national consciousness was incarnated in this homeland of humanism, receptive and open to all of the world's intellectual currents. In this country [Lebanon,] at once old and young, the Alpha and the Omega, this country to which the world owes values, ideas, Men, institutions, and splendor, [in this country, Lebanon,] we are justified in being optimistic and proud of who we are.[51]

This conception of Lebanese identity was generically referred to as "Phoenicianism" in the Lebanon of the early twentieth century, and as "Lebanonism" in more modern incarnations, beginning in the early 1950s. Exponents of both schools of thought were largely young Francophone poets, playwrights, businessmen, and diplomats, who ascribed to their loose association the sobriquet of *"Les Jeunes Phéniciens"* (or "The Young Phoenicians") and who wrote, published, and generally gravitated around the person of Charles Corm, and the guild of intellectuals and institutions that he had established.[52] In brief, those latter-day Phoenicians viewed the modern Lebanese people as a singular, unique, complete nation, descendants of the Canaanite seafarers of antiquity, unrelated to the more recently arrived Arab conquerors. They were described most exquisitely by their doyen, Charles Corm, as humanity's first teachers, first explorers, first inventors, and most notably perhaps, mankind's first and most exquisite humanists; long before England's Cromwell and America's Washington, wrote Corm,

> and long before the French Revolution and the giant leap forward for mankind that would result from it throughout Europe, the resounding cry of a Lebanese jurist, reverberating throughout the world, would hold that "according to natural law, all men are born free and equal." This was Humanism in its most exquisite unvarnished form [. . . issuing from] our very own Ulpian, this Magistrate from Lebanon, who would marshal dauntless audacity, inconceivable for its time, announcing from atop his pulpit as advisor to the [Roman] throne, the equality of all men down below, and Man's inalienable natural right to liberty. At a time when emperors and their empires, officially still avid practitioners of slavery, relishing the sight of tortured men women and children being devoured alive by wild beats in the State's sports arenas, our very own Ulpian would face down mighty Rome, shouting out his cry for moral justice, a cry which would soon become the collective cry of all of humanity for virtue and justice.[53]

And so, like their ancient Phoenician forefathers, today's Lebanese argued Corm, the "Young Phoenicians" of modern times, were skilled mariners, industrious traders, intrepid explorers, gifted teachers, inspired inventors, shrewd bankers, conscientious jurists, and subtle intermediaries who valued and practiced with aplomb linguistic, cultural, and moral humanism and fluidity. The *Revue Phénicienne*, a cultural and literary journal founded by Charles Corm in 1919, would become the Young Phoenicians' mouthpiece and their main political clarion. Its pages featured the works and thought of two future Lebanese presidents and a number of distinguished literati, diplomats, and businessmen—all of whom would become "distinguished" subsequent to their association with Corm and his journal.

An eminent "graduate" of the *Revue Phénicienne* was none other than Michel Chiha, a banker, poet, political thinker, constitutional scholar, and diplomat who arguably cut his intellectual teeth under the guidance of Charles Corm. Chiha was also the co-author of Lebanon's 1926 Constitution, which consecrated and codified the country's hybrid, cosmopolitan identity and its liberal cultural fluidity. Like Corm, Chiha was an exponent of multiple identities, advocating an expansive, syncretistic, humanist approach to selfhood, rather than one defined by "oneness" and cultural dogmatism. He wrote that a mere thirteen centuries of Arab domination of Lebanon (and the Levantine Near East) were not nearly enough to make the Lebanese oblivious to, or dismissive of, the fifty centuries that preceded the Arabs.[54] "Even if relying purely on conjecture," argued Chiha, "the blood, the civilization, and the language of today's Lebanese cannot possibly be anything if not the legacy and synthesis of fifty centuries of progenitors and ancestors" preceding and superseding the Arabs.[55] For Corm, Chiha, and their Young Phoenician circles, Lebanon was a diverse, multiform, polyglot, even a "bastardized" cocktail of cultures and languages; a conception of identity that valued composite, complex patchworks of ethnicities and historical memories; a millennial universe of varied civilizations, where peoples and times blended *without* dissolving each other, and where languages and histories fused *without* getting confused with one another.[56]

The importance of Charles Corm's Young Phoenicians dwelt not simply in their advocacy for a distinct Lebanese-Phoenician hybridity and multi-layered identity parameters. Their importance stemmed from their remarkable humanistic, elastic conceptions of identity, which, granted, opposed as they might have been to essentialist Arabism, they did not disown the Arabs, they did not bespeak hang ups toward the Arabs, and they did not shun the Arabs' rich cultural, linguistic, and literary patrimony. Indeed, although Charles Corm's intellectual language would remain French, he took immeasurable pride in the contributions that fellow Lebanese had made to the Arabic language and the revival of Arabic *belles lettres* (the *Nahda* renaissance) of the late nineteenth century. Interestingly enough, Charles Corm was also one of the first Lebanese intellectuals to have translated Kahlil Gibran's Arabic and English language works into French. There is also evidence in his unpublished papers that he had made multiple translations of the Arabic works of Saïd Akl (b. 1912)—then one of the youngest members of Corm's Phoenicianist circle—during the mid- to late 1930s.[57] Likewise, in *La Montagne Inspirée*, considered by many his *magnum opus*, Corm paid tribute to Maronite Bishop Germanos Farhat (1670–1732) who, in 1730, in a monastery of Mount-Lebanon, set up the Middle East's first Arabic-language printing press, paving the way for the *Nahda* renaissance movement to follow, and making the mass production of Arabic-language textbooks the first step toward mass literacy in the Near East. Corm also paid tribute to Nasif al-Yazigi (1800–1971) and Ibrahim al-Yazigi (1847–1906), two of the early pioneers of Arabic *belles lettres* in Mount-Lebanon, both of whose Arabic translations of the Bible were foundational to the revival of the Arabic language and, eventually, its simplification and modernization, making it fit for use as a modern (temporal) means of literary expression—not only Muslim cultic and ceremonial purposes. It should be noted that Ibrahim al-Yazigi's innovative linguistic and graphic contributions—namely his reduction of Arabic graphemes from 300 to 60 characters—were responsible for the development of the first Arabic typewriter, further contributing to mass literacy and greater access to learning. "After Farhat, we were blessed with the Yazigis," wrote Corm in *La Montagne Inspirée*, "two admirable pioneers, whose masterful voices restored a dead Arabic language, / Bringing it back to life, pulling it from beneath heavy sepulchral slabs [. . .] / And then we had Gibran, taking America by storm, / Bringing to the land, of the Mighty Dollar, higher spiritual norms."[58]

Inadequate as he might have felt about his Arabic language skills, Charles Corm still attempted to dabble in Arabic text. His own lone publication in Arabic, *al-Mouhjame*, or *The Lexicon* (1945), was a detailed 118-page glossary with explanatory notes for some 180 terms, names of personalities, and historical, geographic, and mythological references as occurred in the 1934 French edition of *La Montagne Inspirée*.[59] He had drawn up that glossary at the behest of the Arabic translator of *The Hallowed Mountain*, Fr. Stephan Farhat, in order to guide Arabic readers who might not have been versed well enough in Lebanese history and the events and personalities presented in Corm's *La Montagne Inspirée*.

Like Charles Corm, Michel Chiha, who was also strictly speaking a Francophone intellectual, was also passionate about the Arabic language and its preservation in the pantheon of Lebanese polyglossia—from his perspective, *and* Corm's, a splendid addition to Lebanon's vaunted cosmopolitanism. What both Chiha and Corm repudiated, however, was linguistic dogmatism, national rigidity, and cultural parochialism. Arabic is a wonderful language, wrote Chiha,

> the language of millions of men. We wouldn't be who we are today if we, the Lebanese of the twentieth century, were to forgo the prospects of becoming Arabic's most accomplished masters to the same extent that we had been its masters some one hundred years ago. [. . . How] can one not heed the reality that a country such as ours would be literally decapitated if prevented from being bilingual (or even trilingual if possible?) [. . . We must] retain this lesson if we are intent on protecting ourselves from spiteful [mono-lingual] nationalism, and its inherent self-inflicted deafness [to other languages]; an affliction that leads to assured cultural mutism.[60]

There is arguably no more exquisite a celebration of cosmopolitanism, and no more a forceful rejection of nationalist jingoism than the preceding. What's more, the Young Phoenicians' intellectual heirs abound in modern

Lebanon, despite a prevalent image of the country as a bastion of authoritarianism dominated by today's Hezbollah and likeminded maximalist company. To wit, the thematics of Franco-Lebanese author Amin Maalouf (b. 1949), member of the prestigious *Académie Française* and son of Rushdy Maalouf, one of Charles Corm's closest childhood friends, exude the cultural humanism and cosmopolitanism of the Young Phoenicians forebears of the early twentieth century. Indeed, Amin Maalouf's personal trajectory and literary characters often read like ideas and ideals from the Lebanon of Charles Corm and the Young Phoenicians; perhaps "more ideas and ideals than people," as noted one critic; but nevertheless "ideas and ideals" issuing from people—and Cormian people at that—no less real or compelling than the real thing.

Maalouf even brought elements of this, his supremely Lebanese experience—as imagined and yearned for by Corm—to the acceptance speech that he delivered at his induction into the *Académie Française* in June 2012. Sitting on the *Académie*'s chair number twenty-nine, a seat once occupied by Claude Lévy-Strauss, who, himself, had inherited it from Ernest Renan—one of Charles Corm's own intellectual heroes and an admirer of Lebanon and the Phoenicians in his own right—Maalouf, the "Phoenician guest" intruding on this company of "immortals" (as members of the *Académie* are referred to colloquially), pledged to bring to the legacy of this venerable French institution all that he had inherited from the land of his birth; his origins, his languages, his accent, his convictions, his doubts, and, more than anything else perhaps, his dreams of harmony, progress, and coexistence among contradictions and opposites.[61] Even the engravings on Maalouf's ceremonial sword illustrated "Phoenicianist" ideals and the idea of contacts and intellectual intercourse between civilizations: On one side the sword were featured an image of Marianne (symbolizing the French Revolution) grazing a Cedar of Lebanon, along with an engraving depicting the "Abduction of Europa," the Phoenician princess, by an oxen image of the Greek god Zeus; on the other side of the sword were etched the names of Maalouf's wife and three sons, along with two words, "exile" and "identity," taken from an Arabic poem by Maalouf's father and Cormian avatar, Rushdy.[62] And so, Amin Maalouf's academician's themes (or dreams) were not all that different from those advanced by the Young Phoenicians; the images of Zeus and Europa were a symbol of the millennial tradition of contacts and cultural intercourse between Phoenicia and indeed the East (as illustrated by the princess Europa) and the West (as illustrated by the god Zeus).

According to Phoenician tradition, and in a story recounted by the Greek Herodotus himself, Europa was a beautiful Phoenician princess. Her father, Agenor, who in the Phoenician language was called "Canaan," was according to Greek tradition a son of Poseidon and the nymph Libya. He ruled over Tyre, and fortune smiled upon him. But then, it seems, his luck ran out:

Smitten by the beauty of Agenor's daughter Europa—issuing from the Canaanite-Phoenician word "Erev," which means "where the sun sets," with the semantic connotations of "Evening" and "West"—Zeus assumed the form of a white ox, tempted Europa to climb on his back, and spirited her off westward, to the dark continent that would evermore come to bear her name. Europa's brother Cadmus along with his two siblings Phoenix and Cilix were sent off by Agenor to fetch their sister. All three eventually came back to Phoenicia empty handed. But Cadmus, we are told, taught the Greeks—and through them the whole of humanity—the simple Phoenician alphabet, through which all of mankind's intellectual heritage would come to dwell for all eternity.

It is based on this narrative that Charles Corm and his Phoenicianist cohorts, and after them Amin Maalouf and others, elaborated ideas and ideals of Lebanon-Phoenicia as the crucible, cradle, progenitor, and creator of values that are now associated with Europe and the West, but which were and remain Phoenician in origin. The very etymology of today's Europe—stemming from the Phoenician "Erev/Europa"—is perhaps a supreme symbol of this European (or Western) debt to Phoenicia (or the East); an "East-West intercourse" which Maalouf, and the Young Phoenicians before him, valorized and dreamt of and yearned for. Dreams and ideals that are perhaps being corrupted and abused in today's world, noted Maalouf in his acceptance speech; but dreams and ideals that are worth keeping and protecting and perpetuating. "A Wall is being erected on the Mediterranean," concluded Maalouf's address to the *Académie*:

> [a wall] tearing asunder the multiple cultural worlds that I have always called my own. I do not intend to step over that wall in order to move from one of my worlds into the next. This wall of hatred—between Europeans and Africans, between the West and Islam, between Jews and Arabs—I have every intention of subverting it and contributing to its demolition. This has always been my reason for being, my reason for writing. And I shall pursue this tradition of mine in your company [at the *Académie Française*], in the watchful shadow of our elders, and under the sober gaze of Claude Lévy-Strauss.[63]

This Amin Maalouf is supremely representative of a Cormian-Lebanese exercise that took flight in the early twentieth century. "This inflection that you hear" in my Lebanese rendition of the French language, began Maalouf's speech to the *Académie* in 2012, is an accent that precious few ever hear anymore in our France of today; it is certainly not the mode of speech in the confines in this bastion of French language and literature, the *Académie Française*.[64] Yet, asserted Maalouf, the "rolled 'R'" of his Lebanese-inflected French language had been the norm of all Frenchmen of times past: from the greats of seventeenth-century French literature like La Bruyère and Racine, to sixteenth-century precursors like Rabelais and Ronsard, to the very kings of France and the founder of the *Académie Française* himself, the Cardinal de Richelieu (ca. 1635), all of France spoke with rolled "R's" noted Maalouf. Therefore, he claimed,

> This rolled "r" is not coming to you from Lebanon; it is simply coming back. My [Lebanese] ancestors did not invent it. They simply preserved it in the form in which they had received it from the mouths of your forebears, [. . .] many of whom—like Volney, Lamartine, and Barrès, to name only those—visited us often. [. . .] Let me pause for a moment and reflect briefly on one of those Lebanese at heart: Ernest Renan. Renan wrote his "Life of Jesus" in six weeks, in one sitting, at the foot of Mount Lebanon. He had wished to be buried there, near Byblos, in the vault where his beloved sister, Henriette, lay. [. . .] People often attribute the ascendancy and influence of the French language to France's colonial era. That may be the case in many places in the world, but not in Lebanon. [. . . Our] romance is centuries old. The love story between the homeland of my birth and my adoptive country owes little to military conquest and much to the skilled diplomacy of King François I [. . .] who took special interest in the peoples of the Levant.[65]

Therefore, this Franco-Lebanese romance, claimed Maalouf, is ongoing and has been evolving since at least the sixteenth century. Yet, he noted, its true origins were much more removed in time, going back to an era when gods and men walked the earth together, and when the god Zeus, assuming the likeness of a bull, seduced a Phoenician princess named Europa and made off with her from the coasts of Tyre and Sidon to the continent that would become hers, bearing her name.[66] Later, as mentioned earlier, Europa's brother Cadmus, on his quest to find her and bring her home, transmitted to the Greeks the Phoenician alphabet, precipitating the development of the Greek alphabet (and with it Greek knowledge), and all that would follow in manner of human accomplishments. This was mythology of course, admitted Maalouf, but "mythology tells us stories that History itself might have forgotten; and this myth of the abduction of Europa in particular, is a written acknowledgement of a debt—the cultural debt owed by ancient Greece to ancient Phoenicia."[67] Amin Maalouf concluded the "Phoenician" segment of his speech by borrowing a description of Cadmus from the man he was replacing at the *Académie Française*. Claude Lévi-Strauss portrayed the Phoenician as "the civilizer, [the man who] had sown the dragon's teeth. And upon this land, scorched and burnt as it were by a monster's breath, we awaited the sprouting of men."[68]

And in this, Maalouf is hardly an outlier. His vision had echo in Rabih Alameddine's 2008 *The Hakawati*, another modern exemplar of the Lebanon of Charles Corm and the Young Phoenicians. A rich tapestry of distinctly Lebanese metaphor, *The Hakawati* related the story of the Lebanese Kharrat family, their Urfa-born patriarch Ismail, the illegitimate love child of a British missionary-physician (Simon Twining, "like the tea") and his Armenian housekeeper (Lucine Guiragossian). In sum, *The Hakawati* was the story of Phoenician Lebanon, told through the history of a family of "fibsters" and their patriarch, an Armenian-Lebanese, Turkish-speaking Anglican-Druze named Ismail Twining-Guiragossian "*hal kharrat*" (Anglice "that fibster" or "bullshit artist.") The colorful yarns that the *Hakawati*'s narrator spins and weaves tell the story of a quilt of boundless identities, embroidered with ancient memories of cultural exchanges and intellectual bartering, around the Mediterranean of the ancient world and the continents of modern times. Like Charles Corm's and Amin Maalouf's Lebanon, blending traditions and bending barriers, one of the *Hakawati*'s characters wrestles with his own relationship to multiple worlds and multiple traditions. His struggles pertained to his "Western" yearnings and affections on the one hand, and his "Eastern" roots and mainsprings on the other. The symbols of this anguish of the *Hakawati*'s were musical, and had to do with his character's vacillation between "Western" and "Eastern" musical instruments. He loved the *oud*, cherished it, was bewitched by it. At its sight, he ran in its direction, brushed his fingers lovingly against its "delectable wood" and "felt lost in its magic."[69] He was this instrument, its accomplice, its lover.[70] But he played it between "two wars, started taking lessons during the Six-Day War and gave them up during the Yom Kippur War, a period of seven years."[71] His musical nourishment was a diet of Eric Clapton, Deep Purple, and David Bowie, and his musical instrument the guitar, no longer the *oud*. Yet he still, from time to time, attempted to play "Eastern" music on his "Western" instrument. But the "guitar's sound proved awkward," even as his "fingers still remembered how to play."[72] He knew where the problem lay; so he resolved to unstring his guitar, took a steak knife to it, and proceeded to de-fret it, making it more like an *oud*; "without its frets, my guitar would sound better, more me," he concluded, bending the barrier, as it were, and like the Phoenicians before him, bridging the oceans between his "Eastern" soul and his "Western" yearnings.[73]

The last few pages of Alameddine's novel are particularly poignant, and in that sense deliciously Maaloufian and Cormian in their celebration of diversity and fluidity and cultural humanism. At one point, clasping the hand of his dying father, the *Hakawati*'s narrator proceeded with a drawn out detailed narration of his family's history as if to ward off death one last time, and buy his father one more night among the living. "Do you hear me?" asked the son:

> Do you hear me? I don't know which stories your father told you and which you believed, but I always wondered whether he ever told you the true story of who he is, [. . .] Did he? [. . .] Your grandmother's name was Lucine. It's true. I checked it out. Lucine Guiragossian. Your grandfather was Simon Twining.

> [. . .] See, you have English, Armenian, and Druze blood. Oh, and Albanian too. You're a man of the world. We always knew that [. . .] your grandmother died while your father was still a baby. Another Armenian woman raised him, Anahid Kaladjian. [. . .] She sent him away when he was eleven. He used to say that all he remembered was that she told him to go south, hide in the mountains of Lebanon, stay with the Christians.[74]

Clearly there is much poetic license in such imageries; yearnings perhaps for a bygone era. But yearnings, in the end, for things that were and can still be; not mere fantasy and imaginings and fanciful fairy tales, but rather the Lebanon of the Young Phoenicians as it really was.

In that sense, excavating the works and times of Charles Corm is an attempt in the direction of rehabilitating the pre-Arab nationalist Middle East mentioned earlier; a varied, pluralist, hybrid, ecumenical Middle East that, a hundred years ago, in their bid to shake off the yoke of Ottoman suzerainty, Charles Corm and his cohorts were trying to valorize and bring to bear. And so, it is in this post-Ottoman cultural, intellectual, and political milieu that the life and thought of Charles Corm will be probed.

For all intents and purposes Charles Corm the poet, the idealist, the businessman, and the aphorist was born an Ottoman. Yet he was the spirit and conscience of a timeless Lebanon. He was the luminary, trend setter, and mainstay of a society at a crucial turning point in its history; a society transitioning from four hundred years of Ottoman rule, into a French Mandatory period spanning a quarter century, and finally culminating in a choppy period of independent sovereign statehood beginning after World War II.

The Beirut of Charles Corm's birth in 1894 was the capital city of an Ottoman *Vilayet* (or a State) by the same name. Yet, it was a city (and a state) that many of Corm's elders—and later children of his own generation—deemed a bona fide "Lebanese province" unjustly truncated by the Ottomans in 1861, severed from a "natural, historical" Lebanese precedent. In 1921, bespeaking this general attitude among many Lebanese of the time—in the main Lebanese Christians—a representative of the League for the Defense of the Rights of Greater Lebanon—a Lebanese lobbying group based in Cairo—wrote to then French Prime Minister Aristide Briand that

> when [the Lebanese] speak of "Lebanon," they mean geographic Lebanon the way nature intended it, not this rocky skeleton that emerged out of the intrigues of 1860–1861. Neatly delineated by nature, Lebanon extends from the Litani River [near the gates of Palestine] in the South, to Nahr el-Kebir [abutting the Alawite Mountains] in the North, and from the Mediterranean in the West to the Orontes [River] in the East.[75]

This is a "Lebanon" that, in 1920, was justly restituted to its former "historical and natural" dimensions by dint of French magnanimity and Lebanese determination. It was the recovery of a repressed history, the redemption of a shattered geography, and the revival of a conquered country; an idea and a set of ideals cherished and pursued by the quasi totality of early twentieth-century Lebanese intellectual elites.[76] And so, on September 1, 1920, General Henri Gouraud, the High Commissioner of the French Republic, Governor of the French Mandated territories of a Levant recently wrested from the defeated Ottomans, would bring into being modern Lebanon. "Greater Lebanese," began Gouraud's solemn proclamation,

> I assured you a few weeks ago, at a crucial time in your history, that "the day is near that your ancestors had in vain hoped for, and that you, more fortunate than they, will no doubt see it shining through." Well, that day is now upon us! And so, before all the people gathered here, peoples of all regions once dominated by Mount-Lebanon; peoples, who had once lived as neighbors and who shall from this day forward be united under the auspices of a single nation, rooted in its past, eminent in its future. In the presence of the Lebanese Authorities, children of the country's most venerable families, representatives of all faiths and all rites, among whom I must greet with special veneration the great [Maronite] Patriarch of Lebanon, who has descended from his mountain sanctuary to celebrate this most glorious of days crowning his life's struggles. [. . .] At the foot of these majestic mountains, which in prevailing as the impregnable bulwark of your country's faith and freedom, have shaped your nation's strength; on the shores of this mythical sea, which has been witness to the triremes of Phoenicia, Greece, and Rome, and which once carried across the universe your subtle, skillful, and eloquent forefathers; today, this same sea is joyfully bringing you confirmation of a great and old friendship, and the good fortune of French peace. Before all of these witnesses to your aspirations, your struggles, and your victory, and in sharing your pride, I solemnly proclaim Greater Lebanon, and in the name of the French Republic, I salute her in her grandeur and in her power, from Nahr el-Kebir to the gates of Palestine and to the peaks of the Anti-Lebanon. It is in this Lebanon, with its Mountain, that the ardent heart of this nation beats. [. . .] Behold this beautiful country arising. Free, breaking away from the heavy hands that have for centuries tried to stifle it, this country will finally be able to employ, for its own development, the character and skill that you and your ancestors have often—way too often—deployed and expended abroad. You are now free to put your skills to the service of your nation. Renouncing this responsibility at this crucial juncture would amount to a crime against the homeland. [. . .] Behold, Greater Lebanese, the sacred lot of hopes and sacrifices that this solemn moment carries with it. [. . .] And so I shall be a traitor to the trust that you have put in me, and of which I am infinitely proud, should I fail to remind you that it is incumbent upon a free nation, wishing to become a great nation, to fulfill a sacred national duty. The first among your national duties, nay, the most sacred of them all, is Union; it is Union that shall define your greatness, just like your past ethno-religious rivalries had defined your weaknesses. Greater Lebanon was conceived to benefit everyone, and is in place to harm and disadvantage absolutely no one. [. . .] And so, saluting both our brotherly national flags, allow me to

join my voice to your own, loudly shouting with you, "Long live Greater Lebanon! Long live France!"[77]

This was the culmination of years of campaigning, lobbying, soliciting, and praying on the part of a number of—mainly Christian—Lebanese interest groups in France, in Lebanon proper, and elsewhere throughout the Lebanese diaspora, determined to bring back their lost autonomy. Not only that, but the clear references that Henri Gouraud—for all intents and purposes the representative of an occupying colonial power—was making to the ancient Phoenicians, the "subtle, skillful, and eloquent forefathers" of the modern Lebanese, was music to the ears of those Young Phoenicians of Corm's circle. A vernal twenty-six-year-old in the fall of 1920, Charles Corm had been present at the front porch of Beirut's *Résidence des Pins*, whence Gouraud proclaimed the establishment of Greater Lebanon. "I have just witnessed the birth of a new Lebanon," came at the time a dispatch from Maronite Patriarch Elias Peter Hoyek to his friend Camille Barrère, French Ambassador to Rome:

> I have just witnessed the proclamation of the establishment of Greater Lebanon, and I am still under the shock of profound emotion. I was deeply moved by this solemn moment in time, which gave France the opportunity to bring to fruition its noble millennial mission among us, and allowed the Lebanese to see their national aspirations fulfilled. It was due to the high energy and profound wisdom of General Gouraud that this question was resolved to the great satisfaction of your friends in Lebanon. "This is your man," you had told me in Rome, and I am pleased to tell you that you were not mistaken. In a profoundly religious country such as ours, General Gouraud, steeped in Christian values, is an exemplar. [. . .] With his valor he dominates the minds, and with his kindness he captures the hearts. Great is our gratitude to France for having chosen General Gouraud, to bring us proof one more time of the uninterrupted interest and deep affection in which it holds a country such as ours, which has for centuries remained faithful to France. [. . .] Your name for us, Mr. Ambassador, shall remain among the names of those Frenchmen who have contributed to the freedom and independence of Lebanon.[78]

Prior to the Paris Peace Conference of October 1919, which made the establishment of modern Lebanon a political reality in 1920, a series of memoranda issuing from a variety of Lebanese émigré groups from around the world attested to this general mood of Lebanon's "timelessness" and appealed to the "victors of the Great War" for the "restitution" of this "Lebanon in its natural and historical frontiers." One such memorandum read as follows:

> It is with profound trust in the justice of its cause that Lebanon petitions the Great Powers. Imperial France of 1861 sought autonomy and self-rule for the

Lebanese people; today, we have profound faith and conviction that victorious France of 1918 shall defend the legitimacy of the Lebanese desiderata.[79]

These desiderata were given a solemn official aura when Maronite Patriarch Hoyek, President of the Lebanese Delegation to the Paris Peace Conference, acting on behalf of the "Lebanese Government and its Administrative Council," and "representing the populations of all Lebanese cities and towns [and all outlaying regions,] requested reattachment to Lebanon," emphatically demanding

> the recognition of Lebanon's independence as proclaimed by both its Government and people on May 20, 1919; the restitution of Lebanon to its historical and natural frontiers and the recovery of territories that were torn from it by the Turks; the imposition of sanctions against the perpetrators or instigators of the atrocities and executions committed by the Turks and Germans in Lebanon, and the demand for reparations, which are crucial to the rehabilitation and re-population of a Lebanon that has been all but decimated by the systematic starvation campaigns organized by the enemy.[80]

This unique, timeless, revived Lebanon was also to be distinguished from whatever political entities may arise in its neighborhood, demanded the Maronite Patriarch in his address to the Plenipotentiaries of the Allied Powers present at the Conference. By way of an abusive and faulty interpretation of the language-nationality nexus, noted Hoyek, some have attempted to conflate Lebanon and Syria, or rather melt Lebanon into Syria; this is a grave mistake, affirmed the Patriarch:

> Lebanon's independence, as it was declared [by the Lebanese Delegation to the Paris Peace Conference] and as it was conceived by the near majority of the Lebanese, is not only an independence stemming from the collapse of the Ottoman authority! It is, above all, a complete and total independence vis-à-vis any Arab state that may come into being in Syria. [. . .] Without having to hark back to their Phoenician ancestors, the Lebanese have always constituted a well-delineated national entity, distinct and separate from neighboring groupings in terms of language, customs, trends, and westward-looking cultural orientation. And if a mere four hundred years of Arab occupation [. . .] have allowed the language of the conqueror to seep into Lebanon, it should be noted that many regions throughout Lebanon have preserved—and continue to safeguard to this very day—distinct accents and idioms, which, by themselves, suffice to revoke any national attribute that some may want to attach to the Arabic language. And this is to say nothing of the country's liturgical languages, which in and of themselves already distinguish Lebanon from its neighbors. [. . .] Indeed, Lebanon's independence vis-à-vis all neighboring governments, Syrian, Arab, or otherwise, is justifiable on the basis of many other considerations, the importance of which, I am sure, will not elude the Peace Conference.[81]

Remarkably, this is a narrative that the French Mandatory authorities embraced and promoted faithfully within the territories that evolved into Lebanon (ca. 1920) and Syria (ca. 1936).

Answering to concerns about the ethnic and religious imbroglio that was the post-Ottoman Levant, French High Commissioner Henri Gouraud revealed in an interview given to the French daily *Le Petit Parisien*, that a "unified Syrian entity" in what were then the States of Damascus, Aleppo, Alexandretta, the Druze and Alawite Mountains, in addition to Greater Lebanon, would be a folly and a recipe for conflict.[82] He expressed his confidence in the bright future of what he had envisaged to become a federation along the lines of the Swiss model. However, only Lebanon in his view possessed the basic ingredients of a "distinct peoplehood warranting a discrete sovereign statehood"; that is to say, only Lebanon had the benefit of a savvy political class, a sophisticated intellectual and cultural elite, a cohesive population with a strong sense of identity, and a long history of self-governance. Syria on the other hand, or "this fractious region unjustifiably designated under this name," remained in Gouraud's view a mirror image of its recent Ottoman past; a bevy of "intractable diverse racial, ethnic, and religious groups, in sharp opposition to each other, [. . .] making the idea of a unified Syria inconceivable for the time being."[83]

Gouraud's secretary, Robert de Caix, confirmed this attitude in a number of internal memos and correspondences with the Quai d'Orsay. Filing such a report from Beirut on February 4, 1921, de Caix wrote that outside of Lebanon, the Druze region of the Hauran, the Alawite Mountain, and the Turkish region of Alexandretta, each of which benefitting from their own distinct personality and aiming for independent statehood, one must recognize a certain propensity for unity in other parts of Syria, even if this unity were to be expressed one day in a federative form.[84] However, warned de Caix, this bent for unity is inchoate, far from unanimous, and remains mainly the sentiment of Sunni Muslims driven by religious solidarity rather than any sense of peoplehood similar to those of the Lebanese or the Turks.[85] Suggesting that the entire Middle East has been so poorly packed together by a British policy envisioning a unitary Arab state on the debris of the Ottoman Empire, de Caix wrote that

> the resulting clutter is all the more legitimate reason for [the French government] to try and steer the minds clear of unitary political systems and, instead, advance federalist concepts. [. . .] Federalism would be a great relief for much of the notables of these lands, and a boon to the bulk of this region's populations, who remain, to a very large extent, alien to all manners of [unitary] political life.[86]

However, Lebanon was to remain outside of this federative proposal. This was confirmed in a classified dispatch to Gouraud from French Prime Minister Aristide Briand, in which the latter advises caution in dealing with the Lebanese, taking heed of their distinct personality, and safeguarding their independence, "which France itself proclaimed [in September of 1920], and which we must very scrupulously respect."[87] Under no circumstances should France drown Lebanon's distinctness into the numerically superior Arab element of the region, concluded Briand's letter.[88] Nothing could have met more scrupulously and completely the desiderata of Lebanese intellectual and political circles at the time. Restoring peace to this ancient Near East, sprinkled as it is with the ruins of venerable civilizations, affirmed Henri Gouraud, and building French-style harmony among its disparate peoples is not an easy task. "But what a delightfully crucial task it is," he noted, and "one for which France is duly and supremely qualified!"[89]

The following chapters probe the life, the activities, and the achievements of one whose life's work had been to bring harmony to disparate peoples; to a busy, chaotic, often discordant universe. A Lebanese national poet possessed of a humanist mission and universalist impulses, Charles Corm was a man who touched off the first impetus, and provided the modern Middle East's first lesson and the first examples of a supremely humane and humanistic patriotism; a vision of his country, Lebanon, as a meeting place and homeland of choice for ideas, religions, ethnicities, and languages, where everything unfailingly led to universalist ecumenism—which was Charles Corm's own conception of a human life truly lived as human. Corm defined his understanding of humanism as the "supreme blessing of Mankind's, bestowed upon Mankind above and beyond all other riches"; humanism was to Corm a notion "so enamored of the truth, so impassioned by justice, so acutely sensitive to love [. . .] to the point that nothing of that which is human can be deemed alien."[90] And so Lebanon, claimed Corm—at least the Lebanon whose millennial history he zealously excavated and whose bright future he lovingly envisioned and charted—"can be legitimately claimed to be the supreme incarnation of this humanism."[91]

Human existence, alas, is fleeting, as Charles Corm's own frenetic meteoric life-journey had proven. Yet if we are to believe Charles Corm, the fortunes, effects, and accomplishments of a small people from the eastern Mediterranean, the Phoenicians of classical antiquity, are eternal, and seem everyday perpetuated in their modern Lebanese descendants—even as richer, brighter, more powerful civilizations tended to fall from memory and disappear. That is perhaps why, in spite of Lebanon's and the Middle East's changing fortunes, Charles Corm remains in the history of his country—as well as in the memories of those who knew him—a lodestar of optimism, and a paragon of the spacious liberal humanity and humanism that he came to valorize and live by. He was a faithful votary of an integral ecumenical kind of humanism, open to all peoples, receptive of all ideas, amenable to all intellectual currents, charmed by all artistic forms, and tempted by all social and political tendencies—that is, so long as the inspiration and ambition of this "ecumenism" remained the greater good of mankind at large.

NOTES

1. See for instance "La Terre Assassinée ou Les Ciliciennes," "Terre Assassinée."
2. On the ridicule that Lebanon's Phoenician legacy is systematically subjected to, often unfairly and by remorseless Arab nationalists, see for instance an August 2014 "journalistic duel" pitting two prominent Arabophone Lebanese commentators: Hazem Saghieh, who was at one time a leading Arab nationalist and analyst for the preeminent pan-Arab newspaper *As-Safir*, and Eli Khoury, a Lebanese intellectual and advocate on behalf of Middle East minority history and minority narratives. The "duel" (or editorials) in question exchanged barbs on who are the legitimate progenitors of the modern Lebanese (Arabs in Saghieh's telling, Phoenicians in Khoury's), and who are the allogenic conquerors (Arabs according to Khoury). For more detail, see the prologue of this volume; Hazem Saghieh's "ISIS and the Hazards of Our Abysmal Histories," *NOW*, Beirut, August 5, 2014, http://mme.cm/PM2U00, and Eli Khoury's "ISIS and the Hazards of Our Not So Abysmal Histories," *NOW*, Beirut, August 6, 2014, http://mme.cm/U22U00.
3. Charles Seymour, *The Intimate Papers of Colonel House*, Vol. 3 (Boston: Houghton Mifflin, 1928), 323.
4. Seymour, 323.
5. *Encyclopedia of Arabic Language and Linguistics*, General Editor Kees Versteegh (Brill, 2009), July 3, 2009.
6. T. E. Lawrence, *Seven Pillars of Wisdom* (New York and London: Anchor Books, Doubleday, 1991), 33.
7. Ephraim Karsh, *Islamic Imperialism: A History* (New Haven, CT, and London: Yale University Press, 2006), 7.
8. Karsh, 128.
9. Wheeler Thackston Jr., *The Vernacular Arabic of the Lebanon* (Cambridge, MA: Dept. for Near Eastern Languages and Civilizations, Harvard University, 2003), vii.
10. Thackston, vii.
11. Samar Farah, "So You'd Like to Learn Arabic. Got a Decade or So?" *Christian Science Monitor*, January 17, 2002.
12. Israel Gershoni and James Jankowski, *Egypt, Islam, and the Arabs: The Search for Egyptian Nationalism, 1900–1930* (New York: Oxford University Press, 1986), 220.
13. Bernard Lewis, *The Multiple Identities of the Middle East* (New York: Schoken Books, 1989), 53.
14. Kanan Makiya, "A Model for Post-Saddam Iraq," *The Journal of Democracy*, Vol. 14, No. 3, Washington DC, July 2003, 9–10.
15. Martin Kramer, *Arab Awakening and Islamic Revival* (New Brunswick and London: Transaction Publishers, 2008), 3.
16. Hazem Saghieh, *Wadaa' al-'Uruuba* [The Swansong of Arabism] (Beirut and London: Dar al-Saqi, 1999), 9.
17. Saghieh, 9–13.
18. Michel Aflaq, *Fi Sabiili l-Baath* [For the Sake of the Baath] (Beirut: Dar al-Talii'a, 1963), 93.
19. Isabel Burton, *The Inner Life of Syria, Palestine, and the Holy Land, Vol. 1* (London: Henry S. King, 1875), 105.
20. Gertrude Lowthian Bell, *Syria: The Desert and the Sown* (London: William Heinemann, 1919), 228.
21. Khairallah Khairallah, "La Syrie," *Revue du Monde Musulman*, Vol. 19, Paris, France, 1912, 16.
22. Lawrence, *Seven Pillars*, 333–34.
23. Lawrence, *Seven Pillars*, 336.

24. Lawrence, *Seven Pillars*, 336.
25. Lawrence, *Seven Pillars*, 336.
26. Lawrence, *Seven Pillars*, 336.
27. Jacques Tabet, *La Syrie Historique, Ethnographique, Religieuse, Géographique, Économique, Politique et Sociale* (Paris: Alphonse Lemerre, Editeur, 1920), 15.
28. Tabet, *La Syrie*, 15.
29. Tabet, *La Syrie*, 16.
30. The Voice of Freedom, Baghdad Times, *The Antalya Conference Urges Assad to Resign*, June 6, 2011,http://www.baghdadtimes.net/Arabic/?sid=75390, accessed September 16, 2013.
31. Omar Farrukh, *Al-Qawmiya al-Fusha* [Modern Standard Arabic Nationalism] (Beirut: Dar al-'Ilm lil-Malaayeen, 1961), 161.
32. Farrukh, *Al-Qawmiya al-Fusha*, 162.
33. Abu Khaldun Sati' al-Husri, *Abhaath Mukhtaara fi al-Qawmiyya al-'Arabiyya* [Selected Studies in Arab Nationalism] (Beirut, Lebanon: Markaz Diraasaat al-Wihda al-'Arabiyya, 1985), 8. See also Franck Salameh, *Language, Memory, and Identity in the Middle East: The Case for Lebanon* (Lanham, MD: Lexington Books, 2010), 9.
34. William Cleveland, *The Making of an Arab Nationalist; Ottomanism and Arabism in the Life and Thought of Sati' al-Husri* (Princeton, NJ: Princeton University Press, 1972), 127.
35. Franck Salameh, *Language, Memory, and Identity in the Middle East: The Case for Lebanon* (Lanham, MD: Lexington Books, 2010), 9–10.
36. Salameh, *Language, Memory, and Identity*, 10.
37. Salameh, *Language, Memory, and Identity*, 10.
38. Salameh, *Language, Memory, and Identity*, 10.
39. Aflaq, *Fii Sabiil al-Baath*, 40–41.
40. Robert de Caix, *Archives du Ministère des Affaires Étrangères (MAE)* (Paris, Volume 700, Carton 354, Dossier 7).
41. Lawrence, *Seven Pillars*, 336.
42. Matti Moosa, *Extremist Shiites* (Syracuse, NY: Syracuse University Press, 1988), 286–88.
43. Labib Zuwiya Yamak, *The Syrian Social Nationalist Party* (Cambridge, MA: The Center for Middle Eastern Studies, Harvard University, 1966), 89.
44. Yamak, *The Syrian Social Nationalist Party*, 83.
45. Michel Chiha, *Visage et Présence du Liban*, 2ème edition (Beirut: Le Cénacle Libanais, 1984), 49.
46. Nizar Qabbani, *I Reject you*, www.titanic-arwad.com/vb/showthread.php?t=16762 (29 July 2013).
47. Adonis, "Open Letter to President Assad: Man, His Rights and Freedoms, or the Abyss," *As-Safir* (Beirut, June 14, 2011), http://assafir.com/Article.aspx?EditionId=1870&articleId=1698&ChannelId=44050&Author=ادونيس.
48. Adonis, *Al-Kitaab, al-Khitaab, al-Hijaab* [The Scriptures, the Discourse, the Hijaab] (Beirut: Dar al-Aadaab, 2009), 27.
49. Adonis, *Waqt bayan r-ramaad wal ward* [A Lull Between the Ashes and the Roses] (Beirut: Dar al-'Awda, 1972), 11. (Emphasis in the original.)
50. See Camille Abousouan's "Présentation," *Cahiers de l'Est* (Beirut: July 1945), 3.
51. Kamal Jumblat, "La Méditerranée, Berceau de la Culture Spirituelle," *Les Années Cénacle* (Beirut: Dar al-Nahar, 1997), 99.
52. Salameh, *Language Memory and Identity in the Middle East*, 45.
53. Charles Corm, *6000 Ans de Génie Pacifique au Service de l'Humanité* (Beirut: Editions de la Revue Phénicienne, 1988), 113–14.
54. Michel Chiha, *Le Liban d'Aujourd'hui (1942)* (Beirut: Éditions du Trident, 1961), 49–52.
55. Chiha, *Le Liban d'Aujourd'hui*, 52.
56. Chiha, *Visage and Présence du Liban*, 49.

57. See for instance the following, untitled, undated poem of Saïd Akl's rendered in French by Charles Corm, with the simple title "Poème en arabe de Saïd Akl" (a Saïd Akl Arabic poem), signed "Traduit par Charles Corm" (Translated by Charles Corm):

Roulant sur ta poitrine brune mon visage, / Perds-toi avec ce visage, enivre-toi avec ce visage; / Notre volupté est dans un monde qui n'est pas né / et qui n'est pas même supposé par une inspiration / que l'inspiration n'a pas encore conçu; / Dans la profondeur de tes yeux / Il y a une supposition vaste de ce monde / Et un projet de ce monde, qui est genial. / Et nous sommes une éternité obscure, / aveugle envaissant une éternité lunaire. / Ou une symphonie qui n'est pas encore réduite par un musicien / et qui est errrante dans la stupeur des siècles. / Perds-toi avec moi. / Ni l'instant de nos plaisirs ne nous atteint / ni le lendemain de ceux qui parlent d'amour. / Nous sommes deux dieux du mont. / Notre amour est au-dessus de la mort / au-dessus de la sublime decomposition (fin) / Nous arrachons de notre essence une volupté / qui reste espérée jusqu'à la fin des siècles. / Ta beauté est une petite faute d'une pensée / qui avait l'intention de rester incréée. / Tu étais dans le monde de l'amour / une surprise, une exception, un hasrad / et j'étais dans ton sommeil un rêve tendre. (Beirut: Charles Corm Archives, not dated, but in the same pile of documents and a letter from Saïd Akl dated January 1937.)

58. Corm, *La Montagne Inspirée*, 65.
59. See Charles Corm, *Curriculum Vitae* (Beirut: Charles Corm Archives, November 27, 1948), 7.
60. Chiha, *Visage et Présence*, 49–52 and 164.
61. See Amin Maalouf, *Discours de réception et réponse de M. Jean-Christophe Rufin; Réception de M. Amin Maalouf* (Paris: Académie française, June 14, 2012), http://www.academie-francaise.fr/discours-de-reception-et-reponse-de-m-jean-christophe-rufin (accessed July 4, 2014).
62. "Amin Maalouf Reçu Jeudi à l'Académie Française" in *Le Monde*, June 14, 2012, http://www.lemonde.fr/culture/breve/2012/06/13/amin-maalouf-recu-jeudi-a-l-academie-francaise_1717909_3246.html.
63. Ibid.
64. Amine Maalouf, "Discours de Réception, et Réponse de M. Jean-Christophe Rufin," *Académie Française*, Paris, France, June 14, 2012, 1.http://www.academie-francaise.fr/discours-de-reception-et-reponse-de-m-jean-christophe-rufin.
65. Maalouf, "Discours de Réception," 1.
66. Maalouf, "Discours de Réception," 2.
67. Maalouf, "Discours de Réception," 2.
68. Claude Lévi-Strauss, *Tristes Tropiques* (Paris: Plon, 1995), 141.
69. Rabih Alameddine, *The Hakawati* (New York: Alfred Knopf, 2008), 145.
70. Alameddine, *The Hakawati*, 143.
71. Alameddine, *The Hakawati*, 143.
72. Alameddine, *The Hakawati*, 342.
73. Alameddine, *The Hakawati*, 343.
74. Alameddine, *The Hakawati*, 511–13.
75. Abdallah Sfer, *Memorandum de la ligue pour la déffense des droits du Grand Liban*, November 1921, Ministère des Affaires Étrangères (MAE) (Paris: Série E-Levant 1918–1940, Sous-Série Syrie-Liban, Carton 313, Dossier 27, Volume 127).
76. Elias Pierre Hoyek, President of the Lebanese Delegation to the Paris Peace Conference, *Les Revendications du Liban; Mémoire de la delegation Libanaise à la Conférence de la Paix*, October 25, 1919, MAE, Volume 266.
77. Charles Corm Archives; Text of Henri Gouraud's speech, September 1, 1920. Typewritten by Charles Corm. See also Adel Ismail, *Le Liban, Documents Diplomatiques et Consulaires Relatifs à l'Histoire du Liban* (Beirut: Éditions des Oeuvres Politiques et Historiques, 1979), Vol. XIX, 81.
78. Elias Pierre Hoyek, *Lettre de Mgr. Hoyeck*, MAE, Volume 126.

79. Union Libanaise, *Memorandum sur les aspirations des libanais de Buenos Aires,* February 1919, MAE, Volume 127.
80. Hoyek, *Les Revendications du Liban,* MAE, Volume 266.
81. Hoyek, *Les Revendications du Liban,* MAE, Volume 266.
82. André Leichtenberger, "Une Interview du Général Gouraud," *Le Petit Parisien,* Paris: June 7, 1922. See also MAE, Volume 133.
83. Leichtenberger, "Une Interview du Général Gouraud." See also MAE, Volume 133.
84. Robert de Caix, MAE, Volume 126, Carton 313, Dossier 27.
85. De Caix, MAE, Volume 126, Carton 313, Dossier 27.
86. De Caix, MAE, Volumes 290–92, Carton 417, Dossier 1.
87. Aristide Briand, *Lettre de Briand au Haut-Commissaire à Beyrouth (Très Confidentiel),* Paris, March 17, 1921, MAE, Volume 126, Carton 313, Dossier 27.
88. Briand, *Lettre de Briand.*
89. Leichtenberger, "Une Interview du Général Gouraud." See also MAE, Volume 133.
90. Charles Corm, "Déclaration de M. Ch. Corm," *Les Principes d'un Humanisme Méditerranéen* (Monaco, November 1935), 25.
91. Corm, "Déclaration de M. Ch. Corm," 25.

Chapter Two

Poet, Humanist

Charles Corm was an early twentieth-century Lebanese poet, entrepreneur, painter, philosopher, publisher, socialite, philanthropist, and patron of the arts. His intellectual trajectories, political activities, literary contributions, and commercial ventures were so broad and richly varied that one may safely brand him the consummate overachiever and polymath. Ambitious, precocious, restive, constantly seeking knowledge, and always eager to succeed and avail himself to the service of his country, Charles Corm burnt through the stages of his own life—and the life of a new nation he so cherished and helped bring into being—like a fleeting meteor.

In addition to his poetry, fiction, short stories, and plays, Charles Corm also left a wealth of political essays and aphorisms on art, music, history, and current events. Yet, in Middle East Studies circles and in the annals of modern Lebanese history, he is remembered best—often remembered exclusively—as the intellectual spark and *spiritus rector* behind the Young Phoenicians movement of early twentieth-century Lebanon; a national and cultural current that advocated for a millennial hybrid Lebanese identity and an independent Lebanon, distinct from the motley unitary political entities taking shape on the rubbles of a defunct Ottoman Empire. But Charles Corm was much more than a cultural figure or a notable man of letters—even though that alone would have still earned him immortality in the pantheon of modern Lebanese history.

HIS INTELLECTUAL CAPITAL AND HOME CITY

As a cultural and ethnic crucible of millennial existence, the Beirut of Charles Corm's birth in the late nineteenth century differed little from the bustling metropolis that is this Mediterranean port-city today. In 1894, the

Ottoman Vilayet of Beirut, and its capital city of the same name, were shaking off the grime and dust of the miseries wrought by the Druze-Maronite conflagrations thirty years earlier, even as they marched on to the drumbeat of a looming world war that was soon to consume a brittle Ottoman Empire, and with it the Province of Beirut and the autonomous Sanjak of Mount-Lebanon contiguous to it. Likewise, our times' city of Beirut, while attempting to suppress the memories of Lebanon's devastating 1975 civil war, maintains an intuitive foolish optimism, yet goes on teetering at the edge of raging wildfires engulfing a Middle East trying to reel back from a sizzling "Arab Spring" gone awry. Nevertheless, like Charles Corm himself and the Beirut of today, the city of his birth was "the spiritual beacon of the eastern Mediterranean."[1] It was feisty, resilient, modern, old, irreverent, conservative, libertine, seductive, warm, addictive, enchanting, and unforgiving all at once. In it cavorted, jostled for relevance, and feuded for influence nineteen different ethno-religious groups, each with their own distinct identity, each with their own special conceptions of their Vilayet, its capital city, and what may arise in their place as a tattered Ottoman Empire breathed its last.

In the Beirut of Charles Corm's birth, the enigmatic Druzes rubbed shoulders with the Maronite Catholics, the Melkites bickered with the Armenians, and all trafficked, feuded, and reconciled with Syriacs, Gregorians, Latins, Jacobites, and Israelites, alongside Arab Sunni and Shi'a Muslims. Yet each of these groups were at once Beiruti, Levantine, and Lebanese in their own way—each different and distinct from the other, yet all so much alike. From the hills of this Beirut one could hear the voice of Ezekiel lamenting the fall of Tyre, a Phoenician port-city standing sentry at the gates of the Mediterranean, trading with every other nation of classical antiquity, defining the very notion of humanity and the very history of mankind.[2] In Beirut, one could feel the roar of a river racing down the Lebanon ranges, heavy with the blood of Adonis, mingling with the sobs of a bereaved Venus. From Beirut, one can behold the stone of Abel, stained with his martyr's blood, or hear the sobs of Phoenician maidens weeping at the gravesite of King Ahirom, builder of Solomon's Temple. From Beirut, one can cast a gaze over at the snowcapped summits of Mount-Lebanon, throwing the crushing shadow of their fragrant cedar forests over a Mediterranean below, swarming with Phoenician triremes setting sail on to some new voyage, itching for some new horizon. Indeed, in this, Charles Corm's Beirut, one can be everywhere, in a thousand places and a thousand times all at once, setting out on a thousand journeys at one time, reading the history of mankind lain open over the span of seven thousand years, yet never leave the docks of this quaint Mediterranean harbor. It was in this enchanting city of millennial memory and promise and regrets, at once compassionate and cruel, that Charles Corm would come into the world.

Modern Lebanon, of which Beirut would become the capital city in 1920, is arguably the Middle East's only mountainous haven for minority populations where Muslims and Arabs were themselves—and until very recently—numerically inferior and culturally less dominant and indeed less invested in a Lebanese entity as such than the country's Christian communities.[3] Meir Zamir noted that by the time Lebanon was established in 1920, it had become for all intents and purposes a national homeland to the Middle East's largest Christian population. "Maronite political, economic, social and numerical dominance," wrote Zamir, was foundational to Lebanon's very existence, and "the Maronites were the driving force behind the Lebanese national movement; it was thanks to their efforts that the Lebanese state was established in 1920."[4] Others on the other hand, in the main Sunni Muslims but some Greek Orthodox Christians as well, remained for some time reluctant "Lebanese." Some, especially among the Sunnis, resented their incorporation into the nascent Lebanese state, which they had deemed artificial—as opposed to a larger, ostensibly more "natural" Syria, an overwhelmingly Sunni entity, which had been the lodestar of many Levantine Muslims. For the Sunnis, wrote Zamir in this regard,

> Their incorporation in Lebanon involved [. . .] a grave religious, cultural, political and economic crisis and a powerful emotional blow. For the first time in their history they were a minority in a Christian state. [. . .] For Muslims, the role of the state is to implement and defend the shari'a (religious law.) The Sunnis in Lebanon could therefore never fully identify with the Lebanese Christian state set up and guaranteed by a foreign Christian power.[5]

Still, geographically and demographically speaking, Lebanon was strikingly different from the countries of its neighborhood—Syria, Israel, Egypt, and the rest. Traditionally, and aside from the country's Sunni population, Lebanon's minority communities were never particularly enthralled with the idea of Arab nationalism and the notion that the Lebanese people were somehow, organically or emotively, beholden to their neighbors by bonds of Arabness, Arab culture, and Arab history. Indeed, rare were those from among Beirut's and Mount-Lebanon's minority populations—especially the Christians among them—who viewed themselves or were viewed by others as Arab. In fact the Maronite Catholics, although indigenous to the region and hailing from an ancient stock of Syriac-Aramaeans, considered themselves a sanctuary of Christendom—Western Christendom at that—in a Muslim-dominated East; a "little piece of France," as it were, on the seawalls of the Levant. Confirming this prevalent attitude of the times, a nineteenth-century French traveler depicted the proud Maronites, in the midst of "Ottoman barbarity," as "the sons of the elders of the masters of the universe"; children of ancient Phoenicia.[6] Other travelers wrote in the same vein that, elsewhere in the Ottoman Empire, the highlands and hillsides were like deserts, dreary and silent; [their] rocks bare, [their] soil almost barren. But here on the other hand, on this [Maronite] spot of Mount-Lebanon, life seems to pulsate more vigorously. And as one gazes over the crops covering the dizzying slopes of this mountain, it is almost unavoidable to not take heed of the robust, fearless breed of little children swarming about, growing up in these happy villages, eager to take on the toils and crafts of their forefathers. Here on this mountain, the Lazarist Fathers had established in the midst of these villages a number of schools where young Maronites were taught the rudiments of Classical Arabic, Syriac, French, and Italian. These fine institutes of learning are of particular importance to the Maronites. In these provinces of the Ottoman Empire, where despotism often wallows and drowns in ignorance, these colleges are a powerful and progressive harbor of civilization and learning. I can still recall with great emotion the thrills of a day I spent at the Antoura monastery. As I entered the grounds, I was overwhelmed by the beautiful courtyard of this place, shaded as it was by giant lush orange trees, giving way to an open-space terrace commanding a breathtaking view of the Mediterranean Sea below. There, some seventy to eighty young boys frolicked noisily, playing ball in the shade of those trees, their beautiful intelligent eyes animated, sparkling with passion. I could hear them quarreling and shouting in French—a scene that gave me pause, leaving me in awe, crouched behind a doorway, seized with profound emotion. This "little France," hidden in the confines of the Lebanese mountains, in the midst of a barbaric empire, touched me to the very depths of my soul, filling me with bewilderment and admiration. I had just crossed the Dog River below, having spent some time prior in the midst of motley Arab villages. Yet, here, at Antoura, I was suddenly back in the depths of my own childhood, engrossed in the games and pursuits of my youth, thousands of miles from Paris. Yes, here, I could hear my own school-bells ringing, calling students back to work. Here I could savor the sounds of my own language, in the shade of Lebanon's orange-trees, at a stone's throw from the Cedars of Solomon. [. . .] The times of the Crusades have long since gone away; but it seems to me that it is a question of national honor for us Frenchmen to never abandon these Christians of the Near East, children of an ancient race, reaching out to us, wishing to embrace us.[7]

In a sense, this was a description of Lebanon and the Lebanese as a challenge to their neighborhood; as a geographic, topological, cultural, and sociological oddity in an otherwise oppressive Ottoman dominion deemed homogenous and uniform. In Lebanon on the other hand, wrote French politician and historian Comte de Volney, already in 1784, it was easy to forget that one was in the midst of the Ottoman Empire, because people in Lebanon were quite different from others from among their neighbors.[8] As one of the most renowned among early Western travelers to the East, Volney provided an important anthropological portrait of the Lebanon of his times. Nothing was trivial and nothing was unworthy of being recorded in his travelogue. From people's habits, to peculiarities of language, food, and drink, to geographic details and agricultural methods, and from architectural features to local industries and weather patterns, nothing escaped Volney's flattering paintbrush when it came to Lebanon. It was "un pays délicieux" (a delicious country,) he wrote, and a "charming little province."[9] Maronites and Druzes seemed like the only human elements that inhabited Lebanon, or at least the only ones that mattered and merited mention in Volney's recollections, and his admiration of both communities was hardly concealed. He specifically referred to the Maronites as a distinct, majestic, and enterprising nation, and compared their attachment to their ancestral soil and their manifest esprit de corps to those of European nations. Conversely, Volney described the Ottomans as "pernicious and marauding," trying to stifle the autonomy and spiritedness of the Maronites. "The Maronite peasants," he wrote, indeed the

> [Maronite] nation in its entirety is agrarian; everyone of its members tills in his own hands the little domain that he possesses and holds dear. Even the [feudal lords] themselves live in that same manner. They all live in frugality, bereft of many comforts, but they do not live in penury. Needless to say, they lack many of modern life's luxury items. In general, the [Maronite] nation is modest, but none of its members are needy. And if one happens to come across paupers, chances are they originate in the coastal towns, not in the country [of Mount-Lebanon] itself. Private property [in Mount-Lebanon] is as sacrosanct as it is in Europe. Here [in Lebanon] the looting and injustice, so commonplace in the lands of the Turks, are nonexistent. One can travel through Lebanon by day and by night, in safety and confidence unknown in the remainder of the empire.[10]

In Volney's eyes, not only was physical Lebanon a geographical marvel to behold and a challenge to its neighborhood, it was more importantly a refreshing cultural, sociological, ethno-religious, and political oddity in the Ottoman dominions of the East. In that sense, Volney's narrative often referred to "Syrians," "Lebanese," and "Maronites," as if interchangeably, as a way to distinguish them from the dominant "Turkish" and "Arab" ethnos of his times.

In a similar vein, early twentieth-century Maronite Catholic jurist and political thinker Jacques Tabet used such terms as "Lebanese," "Syrian," *and* "Phoenician" interchangeably, but never in apposition to "Arab," and never to mean "Arab." Syria and Lebanon, he wrote in 1915, are no more Arab than they are Ottoman; indeed, they are nothing if not Phoenician, he claimed, and their

> history and geography attest to that undeniable reality. Today, their aspiration is to become once again their true selves and to live their own independence and specificity. [. . .Alas,] the Muslim element in Syria will only reluctantly consent its separation from Arabia. [. . .] This reluctance is born less out of feelings of Arab kinship than out of fears of sharing power with non-Muslims. [. . .] Yet this is by no means a feeling shared by all Muslims, across the board.[11]

Similarly, Michel Chiha wrote that,

> The Lebanese Mountain is a spiritual sanctuary. All of the ethno-religious minorities who live there [. . .] have found in these high mountains a refuge from oppression, and a haven for freedom. [. . .] The mystique of Lebanon is in the fact that its Mountain was gradually populated by restless people, by hunted people. [. . . The Lebanese] are a breed of mountaineer-navigators, markedly different form those nations that surround [them.][12]

Likewise, in a 1919 letter from the Buenos Aires chapter of the *Union Libanaise* addressed to then French Foreign Minister Aristide Briand, soliciting his support for the establishment of an independent Lebanese entity, one could read what amounts to a history lesson, beginning with the following comprehensive introduction:

> On the shores of the Mediterranean Sea, at the gates of this distant Orient, which has for so long transfixed the Superpowers' attentions, one can find in the midst of disparate peoples a small and steadfast nation, vigorous and determined, distinct form those who surround it: this nation is the Lebanese Nation. Its origins are quite removed in time. The Lebanese are in fact descended form the ancient Phoenicians; the latter, having extended their highly evolved civilization throughout their then known world, at a time long before today's great nations had ever come into being. Assembled in the framework of autonomous communities, the Phoenicians lived according to their own laws and their own customs, under the governance of their own local princes. Through their long history, they were subjected to the suzerainty of Rome and Byzantium, as well as to that of the Arabs, the Crusaders, the Sultans of Egypt, and the Ottoman Turks. Yet, they were able to preserve their own customs and national attributes.[13]

Thus, the ancient Phoenicians were depicted as the forefathers and progenitors of the modern Lebanese. They were conquered, ruled by Romans, Arabs, and Turks among others, yet their conquerors remained outsiders and were never able to intrude upon or alter their ethnic and cultural authenticity. Lebanese-American historian Philippe Hitti noted that modern presidents of the Lebanese Republic can recognize as ancestors and equals such counterparts as French high commissioners, Ottoman governors, Arab administrators, Crusader princes, Byzantine envoys, Roman potentates, as well as Assyrian, Babylonian, Egyptian, and Phoenician rulers.[14]

Along those same lines, a letter by another Lebanese diaspora lobby, addressed to the same French foreign minister argued that "the Lebanese do not belong to the same ethnicity as the Arabs," and that there was never any kind of ethnic fusion between them and the Arab conquerors; "as successors of the Phoenician Civilization, and as heirs to Greco-Roman culture, the Lebanese betrayed greater affinities to the [Mediterranean] West than to the peoples of the hinterland whom they have outpaced in culture and civilization by many centuries."[15]

Those were the realities and nomenclatures of the early twentieth century, when Arab consciousness as such, let alone Arab nationalism, were still inchoate concepts and notions utterly divorced form the Middle East's prevalent parameters of selfhood. And so, contemporary Middle Eastern events, peoples, and concepts, often anachronistically referred to as "Arab" in modern times, meant something entirely different in the late nineteenth and early twentieth centuries. And what some might have deemed prematurely "Arab movements" in 1914, wrote André Duboscq, "were no more than the expressions of local parochial visions that are hardly in concord with the varied identities of the Levant [. . .]; Yemen, Najd, Baghdad, and Syria are not about to march under a single banner, for the sake of Arab dominance and sovereignty."[16] This had echo with what was mentioned earlier by Lawrence of Arabia, noting the notion of an "Arab nation" or an "Arab people" as such to be spurious and imposed constructs, in a part of the world where identities are millennial, varied, elastic, diverse.[17]

Lebanon's distinction in the past hundred years of its modern political history has dwelt in the fact that it viewed itself—and was recognized by others—in those terms; as a mosaic of ethno-religious groups and a federation of minorities as it were, where the native Maronite Catholics, armed with a long history of strong association with Europe, namely and traditionally with Catholic France—the Elder Daughter of the Church—benefitted since the times of the Crusades from official French protection. And so, in addition to their clear sense of a distinct identity, it had been this strong association with France that differentiated Lebanon's Christian communities—at least in terms of their political behavior—from the rest of their coreligionists in other parts of the Middle East and the Ottoman Empire before the emergence of the modern 1918 state-system. Even post-revolutionary, anti-clerical secular France had remained committed to Lebanon's Catholics and supportive of their autonomist streak. But Lebanon's uniqueness was evident in many other respects as well.

Various Emirs (or mountain princes) from Lebanon, beginning with the Druze Maanid Dynasty of the early 1500s and throughout the country's four-hundred-year history as an Ottoman province, strove to maintain autonomous control over Mount-Lebanon and its surroundings, often extending their dominions all the way into Palestine in the south, and to the gates of Damascus in modern-day Syria to the east. Speaking of the Maanid Fakhreddin II, who ruled Mount-Lebanon from 1584 to 1633, Lebanese historian Kamal Salibi described him as "the leading champion of Lebanon and the exemplar of the national leader who embodied the true spirit of the Lebanese nation and its lofty aspirations."[18] Indeed, argued Salibi, "the legend of Fakhreddin" in modern Lebanon is "more eloquent than reality itself":

thanks to his unmatched statesmanship, Fakhreddin was able to remove his country from the restricted context of the Ottoman universe and throw it open to the outside world. He was also able to occasion fundamental affinities attaching the disparate regions of Lebanon together and creating bonds between their religiously and communally diversified inhabitants. This community of interests outlasted Fakhreddin himself, and over time, gave birth to a coherent and visible Lebanese entity. And so, if some should argue that Fakhreddin was not the initiator of the notion of a Lebanese state—which would of course be a faulty assessment—one cannot doubt the fact that this Prince laid the foundation of the Lebanese entity that emerged after him. And this very entity could in turn be seen as the inspiration behind the "Lebanese idea" that was outlined by the legend that emanated from the name of Fakhreddin.[19]

As with regards to the political geography of the Lebanon assembled during the sixteenth century by Fakhreddin, Salibi noted that:

> Fakhreddin inherited the principality of the Shuf from his father in 1584. In 1591, he was entrusted the dominions of Gharb, Jurd, and Metn, in addition to the Shuf. He proceeded to seize Sidon in 1592, the Bekaa in 1594, Beirut in 1598, and Kesrouan in 1605. However, prior to taking hold of Kesrouan, he had wrested Safed form the Wali of Damascus. In 1610 he began campaigning to expand his authority to Acre and Ajloun, East of the Jordan. [. . .] In 1618, he annexed the districts of Byblos and Batrun [. . .] and in the following year he took the Sanjaks of Lattakieh and Jabla. [. . .] By 1631, Fakhreddin was in full control of a large part of geographic Syria, including parts of Palestine [. . .], Palmyra [. . .], and Antioch.[20]

Those were the dimensions of the "historical Lebanon" of which spoke the Lebanese desiderata and a number of Lebanese intellectuals in the early twentieth century—among them Charles Corm's circle—as they campaigned for the establishment of Greater Lebanon.

Aside from historical antecedents—some going back to Fakhreddin in modern times, others to the Phoenicians of classical antiquity—there were also momentous developments in the early to mid-nineteenth century, which compelled the Maronite intelligentsia of the early twentieth century to insist on the establishment of a "Greater Lebanon." The Egyptian invasions of the Levant by Muhammad Ali's son, Ibrahim Pasha, during the 1830s were a turning point for Mount-Lebanon's population, and for the Maronites in particular, who had been privileged under Fakhreddin II's rule, but who came to lose some of their entitlements by the middle of the nineteenth century. The Egyptian forays into the Levant translated into a brief—albeit positive—change of fortunes for the Maronites. During those times, the Egyptian viceroy—an Albanian by ethnicity but an Egyptian with strong autonomist impulses—attempted to create buffer states between his dominions south of the Sinai, and Istanbul in the north—the seat of Ottoman authority—so as to buttress his sovereignty and independence vis-à-vis the Ottomans. Thus, and as an upshot of their invasion of the Vilayets of Beirut and Damascus, the Egyptians disarmed the Druze inhabitants of Mount-Lebanon and empowered their historical rivals, the Maronites. This emboldened the latter and spurred them to begin expanding their areas of influence and domination—which had traditionally been confined to the central and northern portions of Mount-Lebanon—southward, into the Druzes' historical heartland.

But when Ibrahim Pasha's troops withdrew in 1840, a struggle for power and control ensued between France on the one hand (the Maronites' traditional protector) and the Ottomans and their British sponsors on the other, in an attempt to fill the vacuum left by the departing Egyptian legions. This resulted in a protracted Maronite-Druze civil war, reaching a pinnacle in 1860, and ending with the systematic butchering of more than 14,000 Maronites in Mount-Lebanon and surrounding regions. Those events of 1860, referred to colloquially by the Christians of the Levant as "*Mdébih es-Sittiin*" (or the massacres of 1860), bolstered the Maronites resolve to establish an independent, Christian-dominated state in what they now controlled of Mount-Lebanon.[21] This was aided by the French landing an expeditionary force in the Beirut Harbor, lending moral and military support to their Lebanese Catholic (Maronite) protégés, and seeking to help them establish an autonomous province in their new area of influence, with a Maronite "governor" at the helms of its government. The Ottomans, with the support of Britain, France's traditional rival in the Levant, objected to this projected (exclusively) Maronite canton, and instead advanced the idea of a special "power-sharing" régime for Mount-Lebanon—the *Règlement Organique*—which bestowed upon the mountain province (*Sanjak*) an autonomous status (as *Mutasarriflik*) investing it with self-rule by a Christian (albeit a non-Maronite) Ottoman subject, who by tradition had been an Armenian.[22] This arrangement would remain in place until the outbreak of the Great War and the Ottomans' full entry into that conflict in 1915.

Although not meeting the totality of the Maronite and French demands, the *Règlement Organique* regime accommodated some of the stipulations for a semblance of Maronite autonomy, without instigating the ire (or concerns) of Mount-Lebanon's Muslim neighbors, nor stirring the misgivings of the Ottoman sovereigns and their British allies. And so, in 1861, the *Mutasarriflik* of Mount-Lebanon, under the *Règlement Organique* regime, came to represent Lebanon's ethno-religious communities proportionately (albeit privileging the Maronites), and became a forerunner of sorts to the modern Republic of Lebanon. In this *Mutasarriflik*, the Christians—not to say the Maronites—came to constitute an overwhelming majority of the population, perhaps justifying their political and cultural dominance, and inaugurating an era of peace and self-assurance, which ushered in a relatively lengthy period of prosperity and stability and freedom for the Mountain's population—

validating a popular adage of the times, boasting that "happy is the one who owns but a shed large enough for a single goat on Mount-Lebanon."

But Ottoman authorities abolished this autonomous province in 1915, and they set out to exact revenge on the inhabitants of Mount-Lebanon, namely the Maronites among them, in retaliation for their open cooperation with the French who were now the Ottomans' World War I archrivals. This triggered widespread Maronite migrations, further compounded by the Ottomans' institution of the draft[23] and the mobilization of Mount-Lebanon's resources for the war efforts, triggering widespread deforestation, soil erosions, draughts, loss of arable land, and ensuing famines and devastations, all of which contributed to the destruction of one-third of the Mountain's population by the end of the war in 1918—some three hundred thousand victims by some estimates.

This traumatic experience would remain seared in the memory of early twentieth-century members of the Maronite political elites—among them Charles Corm and his own Young Phoenicians—who would now in earnest begin lobbying the French for the establishment of a "Greater Lebanon," restituted as it were "in its natural and historical frontiers."[24] The new entity that "Lebanese" activists were now calling for had to be one unconfined to land-locked mountainous regions—easy prey as the *Mutasarriflik* of Mount-Lebanon had been to blockades and systemic starvation schemes. Hence a new Lebanon would emerge on the debris of the Ottoman Empire; an expanded *Mutasarriflik* as it were, endowed with coastal cities and western seaports—like Beirut, Tripoli, and Tyre, open to Mediterranean trade and an uninterrupted exchange of goods, peoples, and ideas—and an eastern fertile plain in the ancient Bekaa Valley—the "Granary of Rome" in classical antiquity, which would remain the new Lebanon's "breadbasket" come what may. This new (restituted) Lebanon, in the vision and yearnings of the times' Maronites, was reflective of the Maanid principality of the seventeenth century, and its Phoenician antecedent, "in its natural and historical frontiers."[25] No longer would Lebanon be starved to death vowed the Maronites of 1918, and so a "Greater Lebanon" would be inaugurated in 1920 with that objective in mind. It is against this background that the life, works, and national ventures of Charles Corm's ought to be explored.

FAMILY BACKGROUND AND EARLY INFLUENCES

Exuding sincerity and conviction, sometimes rhetorical, often lyrical, Charles Corm wrote with spontaneity, innocence, optimism, courage, and determination about this era of modern Lebanon and the birth of a new republic, which owed much to his efforts. Infusing his literary production—which always maintained lofty universalist values—with a distinct sense of national and cultural commitment, Charles Corm was in many ways an innovator and a trailblazer, setting a certain tone and providing mood, momentum, and rhythm to those who would follow, rendering themes inspired by his own worldview and his own conceptions of Lebanon and Lebanese history into standards of humanism and ecumenism. In all, Corm's literary production throughout the first half of the twentieth century was one infused with vernal passion and enthusiasm, inspiring faith in a bright destiny and a confident future; for Lebanon in particular, for the Middle East as well, but for the world at large in more general terms. In that sense, one touches in Corm's work elements and contours of Lebanese life, Lebanese history, and Lebanese landscapes unfolding with both precision and symbolism. To wit, we witness Lebanon's intermingling mountains and seas reading Corm's work; we walk alongside him on the shores of port-cities like Byblos, Tyre, Sidon, and Beirut; we climb the snow-covered mountain hamlets—the source as it were of Lebanese history; we explore the traditional Lebanese home and hermit's hut; and we pass in review all the relevant stages of Lebanon's millennial history. Yet, much more is reveled in and revealed in Corm's work; political, linguistic, and educational themes bearing local relevance to be sure, but also possessing universal civilizational and spiritual dimensions pertinent to places, peoples, times, and events far removed from the immediacy and specificity of Lebanon. It is quite natural for Lebanon and the Lebanese to radiate humanity and humanism, wrote Charles Corm in 1949, in a conference paper inspired by the Lebanon Exhibit that he had set up ten years earlier at the 1939 New York World's Fair. In this, his *6000 Years of Peaceful Contributions to Mankind* lecture, Corm told his audience that

> it is quite natural for Lebanon to go on being human (in spite of the world's periodic delirious descents into collective acts of self-destruction). [. . .] In a beautiful country such as Lebanon, one has little merit remaining human, humane, and humanistic. [. . .] On the shores of this Mediterranean Sea, this sea of eternal renewal, at once old and wise and young at heart, a civilized sea that is a nurturer of nations and a sensible and thoughtful foster-mother who never despoils what she embraces, a sea that whispers lovingly, at the foot of our happy mountains, a thousand melodies and a thousand shimmering wonders [. . .] In these parts, in Lebanon, the human spirit is a mirror image of the landscape. Between our sea [. . .] and the ranges of our ever-benevolent "Alps," the human spirit—provided it is left to its own devices unhindered—sets itself aloft, uplifted by our summits, nourished with dreams and endless horizons, christened with pure unsullied azure-blue skies, and hemmed in by halos of bright stars. [. . .] In these parts, in Lebanon, the human spirit is the living image of these very surroundings that spawned and amplified it, and which continue to seduce it, exalt it, and glorify it. [. . .] Here in Lebanon, the human spirit is at once the simple and complex synthesis of all that is grand and magnificent in this universe.[26]

This is Lebanon's and the Lebanese's "mission and ambition" in Corm's telling: heirs to an eternal calling of benevolence and a dual nature of both peaceful magnificence and fearless initiative; undaunted, steadfast, secure in the highlands, building a temple and a citadel; intrepid sailors descending from their high places to answer the call of the sea, to take to the uncharted oceans and swarm unexplored continents, contributing to the edification of a nobler, loftier human civilization.[27] "Such is the mission of the Lebanese individual; such is his Humanism" in Charles Corm's vision.[28]

Born on March 4, 1894, to Lebanese modernist painter and doyen of religious art, Daoud Corm (1850–1930), and his wife, Virginie Naaman, Charles Corm received a traditional Catholic education in Beirut, at one of the Levant's most-illustrious Jesuit institutions. His father, Daoud, was a native of the Mount-Lebanon village of Ghosta, although his family lived in the highlands of Ghazir, overlooking the Bay of Jounié and the Mediterranean below. Heir to a well-to-do family of scribes and clerks, Daoud's male relatives held high positions in the courts of the Maanid and Shehabi dynasties that ruled Mount-Lebanon from the early sixteenth century to the middle of the nineteenth. Charles Corm's paternal grandfather, Sham'un al-Chidiac (or Simon the Clerk/Archdeacon, an Arabic corruption of the French "*Archidiacre*"), whose real surname had been Hkayyim ("the Little Sage"), was the cousin of Emir Bashir Shehab's court priest in Beiteddine, the seat of the principality of Mount-Lebanon since the seventeenth century.[29] Historian Philip Hitti referred to Bashir Shehab, also known as "Bashir the Great," who ruled Mount-Lebanon from 1788 to 1840, as "the second architect of Greater Lebanon."[30] Although an anachronism—Greater Lebanon was established in 1920, some seventy years after Bashir's death—this encomium was on account of Emir Bashir's independent spirit, his courage, and his determination to maintain Lebanon as a distinct entity separate from the Ottoman Empire. According to Hitti, this awe-inspiring, bushy-eyebrowed, towering prince with the imposing figure commanded the respect of even enemies who might otherwise be expected to slight him. Among the well-known Lebanese popular legends celebrating the character and stature of Bashir the Great, illustrating the respect that he commanded among foes and friends alike, is one that took place during his last exile to Istanbul in 1840. Legend had it that when the defiant Bashir, then a "prisoner" of the Ottoman Sultan, would enter the court of his captor, whose design it had been to humble an unruly vassal in his exile, the Sultan's courtiers would instinctively rise to their feet to greet him, in spite of the Sultan's express instructions not to do so. Even the Sultan himself, it is said, could not escape Bashir's imposing presence, and might have caught himself a few times just ahead of genuflecting before his vassal.

It is worth noting that Emir Bashir was a native of Ghazir, the Corms' ancestral home, was believed to have been baptized by the village's Capuchin friars, and received his primary education at the Ghazir Jesuit Seminary, where Daoud Corm himself had become a teacher some twelve years after Bashir's death, in 1862. But before Daoud Corm, Daoud's own father, Sham'un (who had not yet become a "Corm"), held the position of clerk and private instructor to the Emir's children. Sham'un was believed to have been the child prodigy of his times, a rare talented polymath and a gifted polyglot who would be enlisted foreign-language instructor to the Emir's two young boys even as he was still barely a teenager himself. The young princes, many years senior to Sham'un, were often defiant and contemptuous of their adolescent teacher, who reportedly lost patience with them one day and ended up slapping the most impertinent of the boys, the eldest of the Emir's sons, in the face. When confronted by a furious Bashir, and when censured for having dared lay his hand on the heir to the throne, Sham'un was reported to have told the ruler of Mount-Lebanon that if faced with a similar situation he would not hesitate striking the recalcitrant pupil again. Sham'un claimed that it was his duty to "not condone the Emir's children in error, but rather tutor and educate them so that they may one day become worthy of inheriting their father's mantle."[31] Bashir, reportedly impressed by Sham'un's audacity and rectitude, shot back "by God, you are truly one valiant spirited steed!"[32] He also rewarded Sham'un with a hefty purse of gold coins and a permanent appointment as court clerk and instructor, which Sham'un would occupy for the next eighteen years.

From that day on, the nickname "spirited steed"—which translates into the dialectal Lebanese "Corm"—stuck to young Sham'un and ended up replacing his Hkayyim surname and his al-Chidiac court title. Many years later, Sham'un Corm would wed Marie Hani, the maid of honor of Prince Bashir's second wife, begetting three sons, among them Daoud Corm, Charles Corm's father.

Daoud Corm himself, like his own father before him, was a child prodigy and gifted artist in his own right. Family legends have it that the stones, rocks, and trees of the backwoods and vineyards of his native Ghazir served as the principal canvas for young Daoud's early paintings and sculptures.[33] In 1862, at the tender age of twelve, Daoud Corm was discovered by the Jesuit friars of his neighborhood, and was enlisted to teach painting at Ghazir's Jesuit College, the forerunner of the Beirut Université Saint-Joseph, Charles Corm's alma mater, and where the young Belgian Jesuit Henri Lammens had incidentally completed his novitiate—before moving to Beirut and subsequently becoming Charles Corm's own mentor and professor at the Jesuit College. In Ghazir also, in 1861, and in the neighborhood of that same Jesuit College where Daoud had become a teacher and where Henri Lammens received the rudiments of his training as philologist and historian, Ernest Renan had seemingly found the perfect retreat where the early manuscripts of his monumental *La vie de Jésus* began taking shape. In 1861, Renan was also in the thicket of his *Mission de Phénicie* excavations, which would in time lead to the rediscovery and restitution of Phoenician history to its Lebanese heirs. At a stone's throw from the Jesuit College, Renan shared a small house with his sister and personal assistant, Henriette, and the cataloguer of the *Mission de Phénicie*, Édouard Lockroy.[34] Maurice Barrès, who relayed accounts of Renan's stay in Lebanon in his *Une enquête aux pays du Levant*, relied to some extent on the recollections of the son of one of Renan's companions, Henri Gaillardot, who reported that Lockroy roamed quite extensively the village of Ghazir, befriending many of its residents, enchanting them with his enthusiasm for their country and its landscapes:

> [Lockroy] was the one responsible for the stage effects at the Jesuit College's production of the "Saint Agapitus Tragedy." It should be noted that the Jesuit College at that time was still in Ghazir; the Jesuits had not yet moved to Beirut. Indeed, they only transferred to Beirut when they saw that the Americans were establishing their own institution of high learning there. You must know their predilection for school plays. Renan, in a frock coat, came to watch their play. [. . .] All the stage effects were Lockroy's work, if I remember well! [. . .] Oh yes! Renan fostered good relations with the Jesuits [. . .] and made use of their knowledge of archaeology.[35]

There are no explicit accounts of possible encounters between Ernest Renan and the young Daoud Corm here, nor even between the latter and Renan's talented engraver, Lockroy. But it is not far-fetched that such encounters might have taken place in the close quarters that is Ghazir, a traditional Mount-Lebanon village where everybody knew everybody else, and everyone got involved in everyone else's business. And so, it seems feasible that just as Jesuit friars were to happen upon the young talent of Daoud Corm, so could have Lockroy—the drifting troubadour who spent a good portion of his Ghazir sojourn roaming Daoud Corm's haunts, Henri Lammens's classrooms, the village's quaint streets, its terraced orchards, and its Jesuit rectory. Many decades following Renan's *Mission de Phénicie*, the fondness and special affection that Lebanese nationalist intellectuals from Charles Corm's circle held for Ernest Renan bore witness to possible past personal encounters.

In that sense it is worth mentioning that in the 1930s Charles Corm had, at his own expense, restored Henriette Renan's Amchit burial ground, turning it into a place of pilgrimage and remembrance, and a site of cultural value and historical significance. The Renans had resided in Amchit in early 1860 as Ernest had undertaken his *Mission de Phénicie* before moving to Ghazir. Henriette had quickly fallen in love with the picturesque beauty of this coastal town north of Beirut. With its pleasant Mediterranean climate, its vestiges of Phoenician and Roman temples, its twenty-four churches (some dating back to the fourth century and earlier), its ancient Phoenician harbor wedged under a striking promontory, Amchit brought much needed comfort to Henriette and Ernest Renan during their stay in Lebanon. And so it had become Henriette's wish, who had fallen ill in 1862, to be buried in Amchit, opposite the church that had become her sanctuary and home parish—on the site of "the most beautiful place on earth," to use Ernest Renan's own words.[36] Her being there, wrote Maurice Barrès, sleeping for all eternity in the company of strangers, was a moving tribute to Lebanon: "This gentle soul gambled everything she had to remain close to the labors of her beloved brother; her dust now lay melded for evermore in this ancient land, the secrets of which she had come to uncover," and to which she finally succumbed.[37]

The Renans' had found a pleasing syncretism in Amchit, similar to the themes of their own agrarian life in Brittany. The vista of oak trees, carobs, and pines running along a Phoenician coast beating its foam against the foothills of the Lebanon; a bevy of peaks hurling into the heavens heaps of villages and convents and churches; a pinkish blueish Beirut shimmering in the horizon; and the endless rustle of the sea set against the snowy slopes of the Lebanon overhead, all lent an air of immortality and harmony intoxicating the senses, making Amchit Henriette Renan's final resting place of choice. Still, before Charles Corm refurbished it, Renan's tomb had been a nondescript anonymous crypt within the Tobia family mausoleum—the Renans' hosts in Amchit. It consisted of four simple walls barely two meters high, sitting in the shade of an old stocky oak tree, almost filling the sky above it.[38] Henriette Renan's headstone was nameless, settled in the company of her deceased Lebanese hosts, Tobia Schalhoub Callab (d. 1836) and Michel Bey Tobia Schalhoub Callab (d. 1856). Ernest Renan had intended to send a stone and epitaph from France to replace the "placeholder," but none ever arrived.[39] And so, Henriette's resting place would remain obscure, uncelebrated, concealed, as if abandoned, in the company of strangers, until Charles Corm restituted it and bestowed upon it a name. Today this simple tomb is an important national monument and a charming destination for tourists and pilgrims alike drawn to modern Lebanese history. And although the site may be an important "hermitage" benefitting from the state's national conservation laws, protected and maintained by the Lebanese Ministry of Culture's directory of antiquities, it is not unlikely that it would have remained an unremarkable ordinary—even a forgotten—spot had it not been for Charles Corm's sensitivity and devotion and sense of history and decency. Likewise, the fact that today one of the major reading rooms of the Beirut Jesuit university's *Bibliothèque Orientale* bears Ernest Renan's name, is also attributable to Charles Corm's personal efforts and diligent sense of history.

Going back to Charles Corm's father, Daoud, the Jesuits of Ghazir had become so impressed with his talent that they pressed him to pursue a traditional formation at Rome's Royal Academy of Fine Arts. He went there in 1870, after a few days' walk from Ghazir to Beirut. And while in Rome, he resided in the Vatican's Maronite Seminary where he befriended the future Patriarch Hoyek, one of the *other* "architects" of what would become the state of Greater Lebanon in 1920. Daoud ended up spending five years in Italy, benefitting from Roberto Bompiani's mentoring, frequenting fine arts institutes besides the Royal Academy—namely the *Academia di San Luca*—and most importantly perhaps, spending an inordinate amount of time visiting churches, museums, and art galleries, and feverishly and voraciously copying the works of the great masters of the Renaissance—Michael Angelo, Raphaël, and Titien—who would remain his major influences and his pre-eminent points of reference. Daoud's reputation and talent even won him the privilege of painting the official portrait of Pope Pius IX, who subsequently bestowed upon him the Knight Commander's Cross of the Order of St-Gregory the Great—one of the five Orders of Knighthood of the Holy See.

In 1871 Daoud Corm returned to Lebanon, settling in Beirut where he would spend his time fulfilling mounting commissions to paint the period's luminaries and political and religious leaders, from Beirut, to Damascus, to Cairo and Istanbul. Among his most famous works of that era—which essentially told the "story of the Levant" through the faces of its period dignitaries—were the portraits of the Emir Bashir the Great (not dated), Hussein Faouzi Pasha of Damascus (1885), Emir Hassan Pasha of Egypt (1890), and the Khedive Toufic Pasha of Egypt (1891). This was also a period during which Daoud was to dedicate himself to religious paintings and murals, which would subsequently come to grace many of Lebanon's churches and monasteries—chief among them his painting of *Le Sacré-cœur de Jésus* (1880), which currently sits in Saint-Joseph's Church of the Jesuit fathers in Beirut. Of note is also Daoud Corm's participation in various international expositions, namely representing Mount-Lebanon and the Vilayet of Beirut at the Versailles world's fair (1889), and the famous *Exposition Universelle de Paris* (1900).

At the turn of the twentieth century, Daoud Corm founded one of Beirut's first bookshops and art supplies stores; the famous *La Maison d'Art*, which provided paper goods and office surplus inventories to local businesses, schools, and universities, and catered to the era's literati, painters, and photographers. *La Maison d'Art* would ultimately become the Vilayet of Beirut's first art studio, contributing to the formation of a generation of future Lebanese artists and painters, among them Habib Srour, Mustapha Farroukh, César Gemayel, and most notably perhaps a young Kahlil Gibran. Naturally, among Daoud Corm's students would also figure prominently his two young boys, Charles and Georges. Charles would ultimately handle the administration of *La Maison d'Art* (ca. 1913), turning it into a veritable library and office supplies and furnishings store, and eventually the Middle East's first photocopying center—similar to, say, today's Staples and Office Depot stores in the United States. Before the break out of World War I, *La*

Maison d'Art under Charles Corm's direction had become the Middle East's exclusive agent and sole distributor of Photostat and Rectigraph copying machines.[40]

EDUCATION AND LIFE OF A HUMANIST NATIONALIST

It was in this familial atmosphere of culture, art, learning, spirituality, ardent ambition, and religious fervor that Charles Corm would receive his early education. But his formal schooling would begin at the turn of the twentieth century, at the Beirut campus of the same Ghazir Jesuit college—now the *Petit College* of Beirut—where his own father Daoud had once been both pupil and instructor in the early 1860s. Among Charles Corm's friends and classmates in those days one could count eminent Lebanese literati and national figures such as Joseph al-Saouda, Michel Chiha, and Hektor Klat, with perhaps most notably Riyad al-Solh (a future prime minister of the nascent Lebanese Republic), and Emile Eddé (a future president of Lebanon under French Mandate). Indeed, when Charles Corm's father passed away in 1930, his remains were (temporarily) interred in the Eddé mausoleum of the Beirut Maronite Cemetery, near the plot where Charles Corm in later years built his own family's crypt—to which his father and mother would later be moved, and where his own remains are resting today. "They were friends during their lifetime, and they remained friends and neighbors in death," remarked Charles Corm's son David during a visit to the cemetery in the summer of 2012.[41]

It is worth noting here that Charles Corm's family crypt remains the Maronite Cemetery's only unmarked gravesite today. It was Corm's intention, as he wrote in his *curriculum vitae*, to achieve "through the sheer architectural simplicity and anonymity of a mortuary monument bereft of epitaph, something consistent with the dignity of a Christian death."[42] In its current appearance, Charles Corm's gravesite today remains both anonymous and simple; yet it is precisely its simplicity and anonymity that beckon and appeal to the visitor; something Charles Corm certainly did not intend, but an outcome that is in line with his fascinating personality, charming and magnetic as it was even in death.

As a pupil, Charles Corm was precocious, curious, sharp, engaging, and "exquisitely bewitching" as described him former classmate and poet Youssef Ghsoub (1893–1972). He was a charming, garrulous, and tireless orator, Ghsoub recalled, passionate for his own ideas, fascinated by those of others, committed to debating thoughts, philosophies, principles, as well as artistic, historical, and literary predilections, whatever their sources.[43] Most of all, remembered Ghsoub, Charles Corm was fearless, elegant, gentle, never offensive or discourteous, even when advancing ideas seemingly impious or dissenting from accepted norms. Indeed, when one disagreed with Charles Corm, one could never shirk him or wave him off. He had an enchanting, soothing air to him, his voice and demeanor grabbing hold of his interlocutors, ensnaring them, casting a spell over them, leaving them craving for more, despite inherent disagreements.[44] His admirers were many, wrote Ghsoub:

> In the schoolyard we were in awe of his fearlessness and the freshness of his provocative thinking. Even as kids, he advanced his views with conviction and intensity and power—especially when presenting some controversial idea. Yet he was never heavy-handed, never discourteous, never rigid. His friends and interlocutors never avoided him; to the contrary, they all flocked to him, besieged him during recess. Often times they would purposely say something contentious to provoke his anger so as to bask in whatever retort he may present; a retort, which as everyone expected, always came nimble, witty, eloquent, forceful. Yet, he never lashed out, never hurt anyone's feelings, never humiliated anyone, never put down those who disagreed with him. [. . .] It is due to these qualities that Charles Corm's friends and admirers were many, even back during our school days.[45]

Even his critics, those committed Arabists who did not share Charles Corm's Phoenicianist predilections, were unable to resist his charm. They were unanimous in their recognition of the genius, the singularity, the enormity, and the fantastic aura that surrounded Charles Corm, his talent, his creativity, and his encyclopedic knowledge. On the day after his death, on the morning of Friday September 20, 1963, the editor of the cultural page of Lebanon's leading Arabic daily, *an-Nahar*—not a rabid fan of Charles Corm's by any stretch—wrote the following in his tribute:

> Charles Corm is no more. This Phoenician whom we all knew very well, whom we had heard about as children without ever seeing his face, has passed away. The imposing personality that was Charles Corm burst onto our universe, uttered his word, then retreated to the top of his skyscraper. Fearful, appalled, superstitious, or despaired, he entombed himself on the summit of his Beirut tower. No one took the pain to find out why; whether the reasons for this self-imposed isolation stemmed from despair, asceticism, or narcissism, no one knew exactly. [. . .] Yet, Charles Corm's poetry remained the stuff of dreams, kissed by the mystical, the mysterious, the nostalgic, the fairytale. As Lebanon's cantor *par excellence,* Charles Corm exalted his country's ancient glories like no other, distilled from the past the primordial elements upon which to inaugurate a better present, founded on memory, issuing from a dream.[46]

Yet, the *an-Nahar* editorial could not help qualifying its praise, engaging a common hoax of the times, alleging an eccentric Charles Corm had, in his final days, taken to living like a vampire, moving in the twilight and resting by day, "sleeping in an empty coffin, shunning daylight and cutting himself off from the rest of the world, burrowing deeply inside a dreadful, mysterious, fantastic tower; a cross between a cloud and a mental institution."[47]

But there was no doubt of Charles Corm's genius, "a charming human being and an impactful solid writer," as described by Jean Gaulmier; more genuine and classy and delicate and inspired than the noise makers and upstarts of his generation; he was a writer with class and grace and style; a subtle spirit who "rooted poetry in the history and the energy of a people, becoming in short the prototypical national poet."[48] But Lebanon had become entangled in an Arab nationalist web by the time of Charles Corm's death, and Charles Corm would not deviate from his Phoenicianist principles, from his beliefs that the Lebanese were heirs to the Canaanites of classical antiquity, not the newly arrived Arab conquerors of more recent times. And for this, the Arab nationalist component of Lebanese society never forgave Corm, and took every opportunity to denigrate his work and besmirch his reputation, leading to such inanities as the claims that he had become a recluse, a misanthrope, a madman, and a vampire who prowled in the shadows and shunned the light of day, sleeping in a coffin.

It was perhaps not untrue that Charles Corm slept during the day and remained awake at night. It was indeed in the stillness of night that he found solace and mustered the inspiration to write. He was Lebanon's "Book of Genesis" to those who knew him; a man in constant movement, antsy, tireless, busy, "engrossed in his library, his lifeline the scent of books," devoted, reverential, relentless, spellbound, and spellbinding, "beholden to two vices only: Lebanon and books."[49] So his hours of creation often came when others slumbered. Rare are those gifted minds who don't find inspiration at nighttime. Still, Corm tried to adhere to his demanding work timetable, keep the schedule of his *Amitiés Libanaises* cultural salons intact, mostly on Saturday evenings. But illness had gotten the best of him in the final months of his life, making it nearly impossible for him to remain in the public eye. So, except for a few of his closest friends, like Youssef Ghsoub, Saïd Akl, Hektor Klat, and Fouad Ephrem Boustany, who visited him regularly, Charles Corm had indeed disappeared in the confines of his *Maison Blanche*.

As for the rumor alleging he slept in a coffin, its origins may be easy to explain. In 1931, after the passing of his mother, Virginie, Charles Corm decided to have the remains of his father, Daoud, moved from the Eddé family mausoleum, where they had lain since 1930, to the nearby Corm family crypt, the construction of which Charles had in the meantime completed.[50] His son David relates his father having been deeply troubled by the sight of cockroaches scurrying forth from around Daoud Corm's casket during the inhumation ceremony. This scene and the reality that it brought home—that is, that no matter what, a beautiful life will always end in decay—haunted Charles Corm for many years to come. He could not reconcile himself to the idea that he or his loved ones would one day come to such an end. To use Charles Baudelaire's chilling image in "Une charogne," Charles Corm could not fathom the prospects of ending up like a pile of putrescence,

> [...] a superb cadaver, / Blossoming like a flower. / [With] the blow-flies [...] buzzing round that putrid belly, / From which came forth black battalions / Of maggots, which oozed out like a heavy liquid [...] —And yet you will be like this corruption, / Like this horrible infection, / Star of my eyes, sunlight of my life, / You, my angel and my passion! / Yes! thus will you be, queen of the Graces, / After the last sacraments, / When you go beneath grass and luxuriant flowers, / To rot out among the bones of the dead.[51]

If postmortem decay was an inevitability that could not be halted, Charles Corm still had the intention of preventing it from seeping out of the world of the dead and into that of the living. He could not imagine his loved ones seeing him in that condition, so he set out to circumvent that inevitability, to have a hermetic stainless-steel casket custom-made for him, in the United States, and have it shipped to his home in Beirut. This is the casket holding Charles Corm's ashes today.

By our times' standards, the (not so exceptionally curious) act of commissioning a customized coffin for one's own funeral seems innocuous—indeed sensible. This is so especially for someone wishing to spare his family the stress and grief of planning a funeral in times of great sorrow. But in Lebanon the imagination often runs wild with what may or may not be deemed orthodox or normative practice. Only the creepy, the macabre, it seems, would venture to plan their funeral during their lifetime. Furthermore, a stainless-steel casket, not unlike Charles Corm's (experimental) avant-garde home furnishings of the 1920s, which prompted the ire of "elegant" Beirut then, must have surely been judged idiosyncratic during the 1950s and 1960s, prompting charges that this "peculiar metal casket" had indeed been some cryptic bed where the eccentric Charles Corm (and his wife) laid at night. Yet that metal "bed," from the day it arrived in Lebanon in the late 1940s until it received Charles Corm's remains in September 1963, had been consigned to a storage shed behind the gardens of the Corm property, not his bedroom.[52] In fact, as youngsters playing "Cowboys and Indians," David and Hiram Corm have vivid memories of having repeatedly used that shed and its contents, including the casket that had still been in its shipping container then, as one of the hiding places of their childhood games.

But it might have been true, as the *an-Nahar* editorial speculated, that Charles Corm had grown disappointed with the Lebanon of the 1950s and 1960s, perhaps prompting him to seek refuge "on the summit of his Beirut tower."[53] As will be analyzed in more detail later in this chapter, the Lebanon that Charles Corm had warned against during the 1930s, namely in "The Saga of Agony" of his *La Montagne Inspirée*, had indeed come to pass. But being disappointed with Lebanon's political class, and being a "recluse," are not the same thing. Indeed, judging from the events of the times, Charles Corm might have been justified shunning Lebanon's degraded political culture. But a "recluse" he certainly was not. And both his consoling and caustic pens remained hard at work, lovingly praising that which merited acclaim, sharply decrying that which merited reprimand. The following is an explicit case in point: on April 2, 1949, two months before the UNESCO's General Assembly was to convene in Beirut, Charles Corm issued a summons and a challenge to Lebanese (as well as leading world) political figures to move away from resentful nationalism and base opportunism, and to espouse the practice of humanistic politics and compassionate human relations. The indictment he issued was in the form of a lecture delivered at Saint-Joseph's University, commemorating the golden Jubilee of Pope Pius XII's ordination into the priesthood. Written in a Biblical poetic style, consisting of verses aligned one next to the other to resemble rhythmic prose, the lecture-poem was both an arraignment and an act of faith; at once a denunciation of the savagery, deceit, immorality, and abandon that Man was capable of, and a celebration of the benevolence, decency, and humility of Mankind. *Je Cherche un Homme* (I am Searching for a Man), the title of Corm's lecture, was a reminder of Diogenes the Cynic's strolls among his fourth-century BC Athenian contemporaries, in full daylight, holding a lamp, "searching for an honest human being." Like Diogenes, Charles Corm advocated for a life of honest labor, self-reliance, independence, happiness in contentment, and zeal for personal integrity and reform—all the while shunning vice, profligacy, and extravagance.

A cosmopolitan at heart, and a man who valorized and lived by the basic principles of decency and humility, Charles Corm had become disheartened by the ostentatious and morally hollow lifestyle of his Lebanese contemporaries, and was deeply troubled by the corrupt social values and venal political institutions of the "modern" society that Lebanon was veering into during his lifetime. Most importantly Charles Corm's *Je Cherche un Homme*, was an indictment of then Lebanese President Bechara el-Khoury, the problematic constitutional structure that he had helped establish for post-independence Lebanon, his involving the nascent nation in the first "Arab-Israeli conflict" of 1948, and the strains that that adventure had placed on the Lebanese social fabric, its delicate political equilibrium, its fledgling economy, and ultimately its civil peace—issues that would in time lead to Khoury's resignation, and eventually the break out of the Lebanese Civil War of 1958.

In distressingly poetic prose, Corm began his *Je Cherche un Homme* by introducing himself as the unfortunate child of dark ominous times,

> a child destined to the slaughterhouse. I am a madman who seems capable of having peace with his brothers only through fire and by the glint of the sword,

only through ruin and war. Oh, and war, alas, I have already waged two of them. They were hideous! Yet, I am hard at work readying myself for a third war, very likely to end up being far more hideous and more cruel than whatever came before it. I have confined the Boundless, the Eternal, to the petty peddling of the marketplace; I have reduced the treasures that the Eternal had bequeathed, to the cheap gold of my drawers; I have impounded the Dawn for the sake of the wretched Twilight. And my hand, which was once the exquisite tool of human wisdom; my hand, which was the sower of seeds; the hand with which I once built, bequeathed, written, and loved; this hand with which I once blessed, anointed, and absolved, has now been rendered a ghastly heap of hate. [. . .] And so to save myself from myself, to save myself from "the other," I am searching in the dead of night, in vain I am searching for a man. And my captains are not unlike myself; not unlike my brother, my neighbor. They are brainless heads; they are soulless brains; they are heartless bodies; they are hearts that have lost their fire; lost their conscience; lost their humanity. And so I take refuge cowering into my sorry carcass, at the bottom of my barrel,[54] in my bitter solitude. I am Diogenes the madman, a fool on the run, returning to his first state of nothingness, surrendering to decay. Strapped by arrogance, deriving from my foolish pride the basest kinds of servitude, I am left without ideals, I am left without a flag. [. . .] Subjected to anarchy, handed over to the herd, I am left without a lodestar, I am left without a lamp. [. . .] I am broken, decayed, reeking of death. Ah yes! To save myself from the horrors of my fate; to save my country and my home, to save my body and my soul, to save along with myself all of those who look like me, all of those who tremble and suffer under the most hideous of yokes, to save myself and save others, who are, like me, riveted by fear and tormented by ghosts, I keep searching in the dead of night, in vain I keep searching for a man![55]

The Lebanon that Charles Corm had campaigned and labored for throughout the 1920s and 1930s, the resurrected Lebanon-Phoenicia of classical antiquity, the Lebanon of "6000 years of pacifism and peaceful contributions to mankind,"[56] the harbor of peace and freedom, the haven of skillful cultural intermediaries and eloquent cosmopolitan polyglots who were at home in several cultural settings, who wielded multiple languages and practiced multiple cultural rituals, that Lebanon of Charles Corm's had surrendered to an Arabist narrative under the leadership of Bechara el-Khoury. It had now begun to get confused with its Arab neighbors, reduced to a single, monistic identity, defined by a single language and a single cultural ethos. This was the state of affairs that Corm's *Je Cherche un Homme* was lamenting. But as noted earlier, nothing ends in despair with Charles Corm, even in the darkest of times. And those were times of which he had already warned during the 1930s, most notably perhaps in the grimly prescient "The Saga of Agony" of his *La Montagne Inspirée*, where in spite of the collective despair gripping Lebanon, Charles Corm celebrated an impending redemption: "I hear better times approaching," he wrote in 1932:

And then I hear the coming of our finest hour, / Descending upon our desolate countryside, / Like a great rebuilding and a re-adjustment, / After the collapse and crumbling / Of the most exquisite of mountains / Those sanctuaries of the loftiest sentiments; / I hear Time approaching, / From the yonder, from beyond the stars, / Gliding forth / Like a ship / In full sail; / Like a new Dawn emanating from the bosom of God; [. . .] Like a new solstice / On the horizon, / Doing justice and order, over again, / For Lebanon![57]

And so in the midst of anguish and gloom, as Lebanon was veering in the direction that Charles Corm was dreading, a voice of hope called out to him, conveying the notion that nothing is lost, that hope still lives on, and that, as that voice implored Corm,

You are not doomed, so long as you listen to me. For, on this terrible path, where your afflictions have led, even when you opt to run away from me, my Grace will always follow you. [. . .] Do not forget, my child, [. . .] that without freedom there is no dignity, and therefore no progress and no happiness. Without freedom, joy crumbles in the most abject of ways, and distress fills the heart. Without freedom, you are nothing but a vile unfeeling robot; a castoff, a non-entity, a dreadful tool, a bowed mangled servant worn out by shame and bitterness. Without freedom, your native soil is no more than a graveyard. Without freedom, your life is no more than a tomb. Without freedom, even your loving heart is no more than the cesspool of a devilish monster reeking of filth. [. . .] Remember, child, that in order for you to rid humanity of the weight of its calamity, there is no redeeming Grace besides my Compassion. [. . .] I am Love, I am Life, I am Peace and Happiness. My narrow path is boundless, infinite. I am everywhere, and I am in your heart. You can reach me, you can join me, with no more than a lonely teardrop trickling down a sad eye. You can touch me, in the softness of grass, in blooming flowers, in fragrant cedars, atop your majestic mountains, in the blue skies and on the clouds, on the migrant's sails where the smile of a stranger's gaze shines upon you like a star. I am there. And everywhere. I am always your Providence, always your Remedy. I am always your Savior. [. . .] My day will come. I have all the time in the world. I am Time timeless. You can count on me, eternally. Let go of your fears. Let go of your demons. Take heart. Be happy. You were searching for a mere mortal, you were searching for a man; you have happened upon and recovered your God.[58]

This insurgency against the opportunistic Lebanese of his day, which had characterized much of Charles Corm's "nationalist" poetry and political writings, would continue for some time. For he was particularly loathe to the sloganeers and propagandists who had taken the helms of Lebanese politics since Independence, turning Lebanon into a marketplace and a menagerie of corruption and nepotism and extortion, instead of the beacon of culture and freedom and humanism that he had dreamt. In this, he was in agreement with his friend and colleague—and to a certain extent a mentee of his—Michel Chiha, who had at one time become a supporter of Bechara el-Khoury, but who had previously been a "disciple" of his junior, Charles Corm, and who had three decades earlier issued his own indictment of Lebanon's "unprincipled politicians" in Corm's very own journal *La Revue Phénicienne* (The Phoenician Review). "We only dream petty dreams," wrote Chiha in 1919;

> We claim descent from the ancient Phoenicians, but what have we preserved of their virtues? They bequeathed Rome their purple dye! Fearless mariners, they sailed the frenzied oceans of antiquity carrying "The Idea" as their sole guiding light! And what about us? Look around you. Behold the nation of sedentary merchants that we have become. We buy in order to sell. But what do we generate? The arts and sciences elude us; therein dwells our main weakness in modern times. We are in want of ideas, I tell you; and therein lie our incompetence and our weakness. [. . .] Only five men constitute the foundation of a nation: the priest, the judge, the physician, the soldier, and the merchant. All five of those men must die in order to safeguard the precepts of their nation. The priest must die rather than contravene his faith; the judge must die rather than betray his conscience; the physician must die rather than flee before an ailment that he could otherwise alleviate or cure; and the soldier must die rather than betray his country. This leaves us with the merchant! Do you see the dilemma one faces in the case of the merchant? Can you tell under what circumstances the merchant must meet death? [. . .] Aye, the merchant hasn't the faintest idea how he must live, as long as he does not know when is the appropriate time for him to die. This ultimately means that none of us will ever be able to accomplish anything grandiose, so long as we do not have before us the everlasting law of sacrifice. For this, we are indeed a nation of merchants. And as such, the bones of our departed forefathers remain warmer than our very own lives.[59]

But this was the discourse of Phoenicianists of Corm's generation, disappointed as they were by the excessive concessions that many Lebanese Christians were making before an unchecked irredentist Arabism. "The greatest tragedy of a people" emerging from the hardships of occupation, wrote Corm in a heavily censored essay in 1919, is to witness its longed-for autonomy and its right to self-determination be removed from its custody; it is to see its inalienable national rights be surrendered to the will and base designs of another nation, an Arab nation.[60] What is it exactly that associates the Lebanese with the Arabs, and demands that their fate be tethered to that of the Arabs, he wondered?[61] What are those characteristics that the Lebanese are assumed to have in common with the Arabs?

> What meager affinities can one invoke, in our and the Arabs' dissonances, to justify the raising of a common national edifice incorporating us to them? What kind of contrived edifice will this be that will not eventually crumble upon both our heads and bury us both in the process? The experience of the great powers, and against all forms of justice, seems to be dictating to us an eventual unity with the Arabs. [. . .] And so, in a few centuries—perhaps even

much earlier, maybe in a few years—always true to ourselves, always ever the whiners and the complainers, always ever the indolent lot, we may end up claiming that "our afflictions are the Arabs' fault." Why, no, they are not! Our afflictions will always be of our own making; our fault, and ours alone; and we shall always have over our heads the swords of the tyrants that we so rightly deserve. The Lebanese and the Syrians are not Arabs, in spite of what is being concocted in Damascus today, with the formation of the alleged "Syrian Congress." What is it exactly that is deemed Syrian in the person and the ideas of [the Hejazi prince] Feysal? What is the idea behind all the declamations of late about "an Arab awakening, an Arab honor, an Arab civilization, an Arab circle, an Arab flag, an Arab army, an Arab police, an Arab liaison officer and suchlike?" What has remained of Syria in the midst of all of this meddlesome and invasive Arabism? The Allies have been professing to the four winds of their victory that they do not fancy any territorial conquests in the East. Yet they have already laid claim to chunks of territories to be allocated to newly improvised "friendly" mini-states. They tell us that they wish to resurrect, among other things, the "Arab empire." Why, that is all fine and well! We do not see transgression in such a noble enterprise. However, let the Allies resurrect Arabia in Arabia proper, not in Syria, and not at our expense. [. . .] We [Lebanese] pride ourselves on being a peaceful nation, yet we are nothing if not a nation of shopkeepers. We refuse to cast our gaze beyond our storefronts. Never mind that our house may be on fire—that is fine, business is good at the perfume outlet, and that is all that matters! Never mind that our wheat-fields are being sacked—that too is fine, we can't be bothered while picking roses for Sybarite's pleasure bed, even though in due time that bed of roses may become our funerary couch! Not all of us who have dared look the Arab menace straight in the face ended up confronting it head on. Most of us withdrew from the battlefield and took to the Lebanon mountains. We are well entrenched there, today, we think. Yet, we shall lose our well-guarded perch in due time. [. . .] And what is nibbling at Lebanon now will soon fester and, in no time, will spread its ulcer to the entire Mediterranean coast. [. . .] And so long as we continue fornicating for the vile gold of cameleers, so will we have well earned the Arab's heel on our neck, and the world's contempt. So, get up, and let us face the future together. [. . .] Let each one of us, to the extent that he is capable, contribute his little ear of wheat to the common sheaf; let each one of us bring his small brick to the national edifice. It is with common efforts like this that the obscure masons of the Middle Ages built their nations' soaring cathedrals. [. . .] On with it, then! Let us work, so that even if we were to die before ever succeeding, we shall at least have comfort in our achievements, however modest. And we shall have hope that after us, and through us, the task at hand will endure, will remain, and will progress. And we shall have eternal hope that one day, in spite of all adversity, our labors will be rewarded.[62]

Charles Corm was twenty-five years old at the time he penned that essay; yet, in his prognosis he gave evidence of wisdom and foresight and vision beyond his years. He was expressing these views at a time when the Christians of Mount-Lebanon and the former Ottoman Vilayet of Beirut were clamoring for the establishment of a distinct "Lebanese" state, while an inchoate (albeit intrusive) Arab nationalism was calling for the creation of a single Arab kingdom on the remnants of former Ottoman provinces. Lebanese jurist Paul Noujaim wrote in this regard that

> as a motley crew of political currents jostle and joust over the political future of geographic Syria, the Lebanese Nation, zealous for its independence, remains steadfast in its rejection of all notions and all attempts of attaching its territories to any of those of its neighbors. [. . .] Therefore, the Lebanese Nation demands the establishment of an independent political entity in tune with Lebanon's geographic position, and compatible with its historical accretions.[63]

Indeed, and as noted earlier in this chapter, Lebanon may have been the only former Ottoman province to have benefitted from a distinct corporate identity that could be argued to have been an expression of both a people's will and favorable geographic circumstances. While some may still justifiably claim that there is much that makes the populations of the other former Ottoman Vilayets alike (that is to say the populations of the states of Beirut, Damascus, Aleppo, and the Sanjak of Jerusalem), there is equally as much that sets them apart and renders the flowering of a single distinct national consciousness among them a near impossibility. Only Lebanon—or rather what became Lebanon in 1920—had the requisite human, geographic, and intellectual climate to bring into being a distinct "Lebanese identity" as such. In this regard, and in a preface to René Ristelhueber's *Traditions françaises au Liban*, French statesman and historian Gabriel Hanotaux wrote that

> Mount-Lebanon never actually reaches the highest of altitudes; yet it remains the loftiest of pinnacles in the universal history of mankind. From the times of Solomon to Renan's own days [in the mid- to late nineteenth century,] the gentlest noblest of human wisdom has dwelt in the shadow of Lebanon's millennial cedars. Those simple peasants of Mount-Lebanon, who have jealously safeguarded their freedom, their religion, and their lineage by making their stand *here*, alongside those stubborn cedars, while others around them bowed down to their conquerors; those farmers [. . .] stem from a family-tree as old as their magnificent cedars.[64]

Yet, noted Corm, no sooner had the Lebanese rid themselves of the Ottoman yoke than they had to contend with a new kind of imperialism; an Arab one this time. Why should the Lebanese consent to becoming an addendum to a planned Arab state, he wondered? What peculiarities do they share with Arabs? What commonalities could they appeal to in order to build, "out of their diverse backgrounds," a single national edifice that would not end up collapsing on their heads and consigning their specificity to the grave?[65]

Corm was adamant in his rejection of the Arabist vision of an exclusively Arab Middle East emerging out of centuries of Ottoman rule. But he was equally critical of a fledgling Lebanon and the Lebanese lack of "republican" traditions. Blunted by centuries of servitude, and lacking the "Latin World's reliance on institutions, and the Anglo-Saxons' self-controlled individualism and collective discipline," the Lebanese collective, argued Corm, was deficient in matters of public life, institutions, and national responsibilities and obligations.[66] They lacked both "reliable government" and a "national collective upon which government could rely."[67] But this deficiency, he claimed, is reparable. What is challenging, however, and what may eventually cause irreparable damage to the Lebanese collective, are the Arab intrusions from the East, and the Arabs' attempts at folding Lebanon—and indeed the whole of the erstwhile Ottoman provinces of Damascus, Beirut, and Aleppo—into a budding Arab collective. "The Arabs would do better tending to their Arabia" rather than initiating another era of Arab colonialism in the Levant, he wrote in his massively censored 1919 essay.[68]

But again, despite his strident criticism of post-Ottoman Arab expansionism into the Levant, Charles Corm reserved his harshest invective to the Lebanese themselves. In 1933, with the publication of *La Montagne Inspirée* close to a decade before independence, he seemed to be (once more) forecasting what had perhaps appeared inescapable from the outset; possibly a Lebanon being swept away by a nascent wave of Pan-Arabism, and the tragedy that Arab nationalism was bound to dispense in its wake. In *La Montagne Inspirée*'s "Le Dit de l'Agonie" ("The Saga of Agony"), and with disturbing perspicacity taking the space of a single strophe summarizing perhaps the entire political history of modern Lebanon, a thirty-nine-year-old Charles Corm wrote:

> In rich covenants, struck under arches festooned with laurels, / I can hear the bloody hoisting of a thousands gallows. / [. . .] I can hear the shameful wicked sound of gold changing hands, / Sinful gold, with which one buys clients and friends, / Pontiffs and poets, / Hideous gold for which one sells brother, father, and mother, and even one's own infant offspring; / That wretched gold that buys you Persian rugs and cosmetics, / Silk stockings and good-time girls, / The gold that buys judges and juries, conscience and character, / Gold for which you would sell your very soul, your own country, and all the human race; / Alarm bells in smoldering homes, / Horizons in retreat, / Walls tumbling down,/ And the rising reign of debauchery.[69]

The Lebanese must begin their healing process by admitting their own deficiencies and taking stock of their own failings, wrote Charles Corm; "we must burst out of our graves if it is resurrection that we are after."[70] Again, Corm was especially critical of the opportunism and the lack of scruples among Lebanon's ruling elites, who, to his sense, were "driven by self-interest and personal ambition rather than by dedication to public service and the common good."[71] This aversion for the unprincipled mercantilism of

Lebanon's political classes would remain seared in Corm's memory, from his earliest dabbling in writing until the day he died, keeping him away from politics and firmly grounded in his idealism. Though his widow, Samia Baroody, admitted to his interest in politics, she maintained that his affections were for "national service" not "political office" per se.[72] Yet many of his friends and disciples would have loved to see him occupy a political position. Lifelong admirer and "disciple" Lebanese poet Saïd Akl (1912–2014) wrote in his elegy of Charles Corm that,

> it is a stain of dishonor on Lebanon and the Lebanese that this remarkable patriot was never afforded the opportunity to take the reins of government. Try to imagine Charles Corm, even for a brief moment in time, as the Governor of the Province of Beirut; as the Minister of Public Education and Fine Arts; as the Minister of Foreign Affairs; try to imagine Charles Corm as President of the Lebanese Republic. [. . .] Yes! And why not? Let them be offended those who should feel offended by the audacity of such a thought! That is how things should have been, and I stand by what I say. Alas, Charles Corm has left us before we drove him to fulfill our innermost desires. [. . .] Still, to my sense, Charles Corm shall remain the only true President of the Republic of Lebanon; the only consummate, authentic, Lebanese that I know; the only man who is truly worthy of carrying in his heart the real ambitions of Lebanon; the only creative intellect of this land, spawning a most exquisite and most refined genius, dedicated solely to the service of Lebanon.[73]

Yet, Charles Corm could hardly have imagined himself in the company of the very same corrupt politicians that he had spent his life excoriating. But he was—and he would remain until his final days—thoroughly engaged in the well-being of his country and fully active in the service of his countrymen. He had high hopes, grand ideas for post-Ottoman Lebanon, and was possessed of great energy to put his plans into action. As a young man, he regretted not being able to join the French forces in the European theatre of the Great War. When friends of his in the French community of Beirut came to bid him farewell at the outbreak of the war, he told them that he would join them, that, in time, he would be shipping out with them; he tried to enlist as a volunteer, but was turned down—tears of regret streaming down his face.[74] He remained in Beirut, but dreading the shame of having to don Ottoman regimentals—instead of wearing a French army uniform that he'd been so keen on showcasing—he became a deserter, leaving Beirut for the safety of Mount-Lebanon, where many "draft dodgers" of his generation, Beirutis and Mount-Lebanese evading service in the Ottoman army, had taken refuge.[75] For four years atop his perch on Mount-Lebanon, young Charles Corm worked the land and skirted the famine that the Ottoman war efforts had precipitated. At that time many of the inhabitants of this former autonomous *Mutasarriflik* had been reduced to scavenging and subsistence living, and as a result became—albeit reluctantly—full participants in the devastation of their country's natural resources. Bound, at least in principle, by the autonomous status of Mount-Lebanon—an Ottoman Sanjak then guaranteed autonomy by a concert of European powers—Istanbul never directly invaded the Lebanese countryside; at least not in the initial phases of the Great War. Instead it marked the recalcitrant inhabitants of Mount-Lebanon for certain death "not by exterminating them en masse, but rather by adopting a more humanitarian system of mass-murder; killing them slowly by way of a well programmed starvation."[76] And so, overnight, wrote Charles Corm, Mount-Lebanon was blockaded, its lifelines to the Mediterranean and the Bekaa Valley—once "the granary of the Roman Empire"—cut off, and its wheat and flour supplies depleted, inaugurating a grim era of horror and infamy culminating in the death of over one hundred and fifty thousand Lebanese men, women, and children by war's end.[77] "I bore witness to this devastation firsthand," wrote Charles Corm:

> I saw firsthand the famished chew on decaying cadavers in Beirut; I witnessed firsthand an octogenarian burying with his own gaunt hands the emaciated body of a grandchild. I have seen with my very own two eyes the municipal garbage-wagon, right here in Beirut, piling up atop heaps of rubbish the dead children of Mount-Lebanon strewn about on city sidewalks, in order to dump them in freshly dug mass-graves; human trenches from which emanated the abominable desperate cries of those who had not yet been drowned by death. One wonders what the task would have been for a Lady Macbeth before such an ocean of blood and mud and utter devastation.[78]

But, as noted Charles Corm, the bruised Lebanese did "not go gentle into that good night."[79] Charles Corm clandestinely fought against this devastation. If he were not able to fight his war against the Ottomans by traditional means, he rendered himself a "peasant soldier," struggling against an occupier by other means.[80] In 1916, he founded "The Lebanese Trestles," a traveling theatre where he produced and acted in French-language plays written by a select group of his Lebanese friends; the purpose of this exercise was "to help raise the morale of those despaired by the oppression and the devastation wrought by the War."[81] In the same vein, Corm founded two nighttime homeless shelters in 1917—Asiles de Nuit—in a working-class district of Ashrafiyyé not very far from the location of today's *Maison Blanche*. Those shelters served as a refuge to those Lebanese fleeing the starved Mountain in search of employment and sustenance in the capital.[82] Also in 1917, Corm organized a number of "Flying Work Camps"—Camps Volants de Travail—in the Kesrouan highlands of Mount-Lebanon, one of the hardest hit districts of the mountain, utterly devastated by famine and devoured by migration. The purpose of those work "laboratories" had been to try to maintain as many Lebanese as possible on their properties—preventing abdication and exodus and certain death by starvation on the sidewalks of Beirut—by working the land and producing whatever foodstuffs possible out of the Mountain's remaining meager resources. As a result, tons of grape jelly and other preserves were produced from the harvests of Mount-Lebanon's abandoned vineyards and orchards. The products were distributed to the needy of Beirut and the villages of Mount-Lebanon often free of charge, providing sustenance and livelihood to peasants and their families who might have otherwise died of hunger.[83]

These activities did not go unnoticed or unpunished by the Ottoman authorities who arrested Charles Corm in 1917, and incarcerated him for several days before he managed to escape, taking to the Mountains, where he would remain in hiding (and still operating his clandestine "Flying Work Camps") until the end of the war. Charles Corm's "crime" had been not only helping his countrymen defy death in those times of national hardship, but also bearing witness to the devastation that the blockade of Mount-Lebanon had wrought on the population. He did so by chronicling the ravages in a personal memoir, and an accompanying sketchbook, which were later published in *Les Miracles de la Madone aux Sept Douleurs* (*The Miracles of Our Lady of the Seven Sorrows*, 1949).

Throughout this time, holed up in the Kesrouan highlands, Charles Corm's eyes would remain riveted to the Mediterranean, awaiting the triumphal return of his French friends and liberators. Finally, on October 1, 1918, "the Turkish army got routed from Lebanon," and by October 8, the first French vessel entered the Beirut Harbor.[84] This was Charles Corm's providential sign and his clue that salvation was at hand. He subsequently spent an entire overnight racing down the Mountain, in the direction of Beirut. Once there, trembling with emotion, he jumped aboard the first French vessel that he came across and proceeded to "hug and kiss those beloved uniformed strangers," dearer to his heart than his own parents.[85] A few days later, as Beirut festooned itself in France's tri-colors and cedar-encrusted flags to receive a highly decorated Allied commander, Charles Corm stood on one of the city's thoroughfares watching with great emotion

> column after column of soldiers marching in formation. Suddenly, a small battalion of the French cavalry emerged, with riders rearing their horses, their bravery barely contained, throbbing with audacity and manly valor. They had fire in the belly! They breathed flames into the crowds. By God, those were the long-awaited saviors; our much-needed protector-gods. The entire crowd of spectators quivered. I felt my own legs buckling from under me. My voice was growing faint, choked, as if something passionate, moving, loving, was grasping at my breast, embracing me, snuggly cuddling me.[86]

This was what the future looked like for Charles Corm; Lebanon rising from the ashes, with the benevolent assistance of France. To him, France was

Lebanon's savior, its redeemer and mender; a friend, not a colonial occupier—at least not in the classical sense of the images conjured up by such terms as "occupier" and "colonizer." Indeed, Charles Corm's French interlocutors from the early twentieth century suggested that it was France itself that had once been a Phoenician colony, and therefore could not possibly be a colonizer of its mother country.[87] "In a colony, the colonized receive the occupiers as masters; in Lebanon we are received as long-awaited friends," noted one Frenchman from Corm's recollections.[88] The French port-city of Marseilles, he claimed, had once been the Phoenicians' doorway to the lands of the Celts, long before it became in modern times France's window to the East.[89] "Say what you will," added Corm's French friend, "you are not a French colony, and we are not your colonial masters [. . .]; Algeria is a colony; Lebanon is not."[90] And from the East to the West of the Mediterranean lake, the ebbs and flows of the centuries have continuously thrown France and Lebanon in each other's embrace.[91] "And so, you have come back to us," retorted Corm; "and we are scarcely surprised to see you back, because we already knew you in our hearts, and by heart, and through the words of our forefathers who never despaired of waiting, and never tired from speaking of this day."[92] Yet Lebanon still had much to learn from France, noted Corm:

> Lebanon has yet to learn the principles of becoming a nation; a zealous and proud nation, like France, worthy of donning the colors of freedom and liberty. In sum, we have to learn how to become a "second France," dignified and confident in its staying power and its grit, united, strong, tenacious, just like France had been in the face of invaders. We need to learn how to honor the thousands of our own who died from hunger, and whose corpses are still lining the roads of our mountains. [. . .] We must learn how to build a modern state, a modern seaport, a great Lebanese homeland where, on the right hand of our ancestors, France would occupy another place of honor. And only France could help us in this arduous building process, because, in the course of the centuries, we have both equally shared in the same great ideas adorned with Civilization and Liberty.[93]

Charles Corm was big on words, passionate in hope and in vision. He was equally eloquent and eager in action, possessed of boundless energy, always standing ready to implement principles and ideals that he held dear. Even as a teenager, in a country torn by the Great War, he never shied away from responsibility. In addition to the homeless shelters and the clandestine farming camps that he ran during the war, Charles Corm founded national youth organizations (L'Association Nationale de la Jeunesse Libanaise, 1918, and the Conférences du Cercle de la Jeunesse Catholique, 1911) and a post–World War I relief organization (Le Ravitaillement Civil de Beyrouth, 1918) which grew out of his 1917 Camps Volants de Travail. It is worth noting that these associations, in particular the latter relief organization, might have served as early models of governmental and non-governmental administrative units to benefit the nascent Lebanese state. To wit, the Ravitaillement Civil de Beyrouth operated some fifty warehouses and distribution centers, and employed hundreds of salaried operators and staff members. Later on, as an adult in peacetime, Charles Corm established and contributed to the establishment of dozens of civil service, governmental, and non-governmental agencies, among them environmental protection agencies (La Société des Amis des Arbres and the Cooperative de la Protection des Paysages, 1934).

THE HUMANIST WHO PLANTED TREES

Some of Charles Corm's labors during the Great War, especially as illustrated in his clandestine Camps Volants de Travail, would by 1934 evolve into full-fledged governmental agencies—namely, Lebanon's first "environmental protection agency," the Les Amis des Arbres (The Friends of the Trees) association. Corm's Christmas 1919 *Revue Phénicienne* essay, "Rendre la Terre au Paysan" ("Giving the Land Back to the Peasant"), was perhaps a prologue to this association. In this essay, he delivered an allegorical message of love and life, calling for communion with the land and rediscovery of its magic, reflecting on its harmony and generosity, and urging the prevention of its willful destruction. The essay spoke also of the selfless act of creation and the defiance of death and destruction that is working the land. In that sense, one may argue that Charles Corm might have been Lebanon's Henry David Thoreau; the country's first naturalist and environmentalist who saw in the protection of the ecology and wildlife of one's nation an exquisite act of patriotism and humanism. Again, as with all of his endeavors, whether political, artistic, literary, or humanitarian, the great galvanizer for Charles Corm was the Great War, the atrocities he was witness to, and the lessons of hope and endurance and optimism that he drew from them.

And so would Corm become a "humanist who planted trees," a man who defied death and desolation simply by living, and by giving life. And so would he willingly, openly, altruistically "plant" on land that wasn't his own, on land that might have belonged to someone else—most probably to no one at all—or land that might have possibly fallen from a people's memory, or that had been the property of immigrants and exiles who lost touch with it and let it lay fallow. Incidentally, the conservationist spirit that was Charles Corm is an inheritance that might have been passed on to his son Hiram. An avid naturalist in his own right, who sports straw fedoras festooned with wild flowers and aromatic herbs, Hiram keeps seedlings and greeneries of all kinds in pots and flower beds on the *Maison Blanche* grounds, tends to them lovingly all year round, and treks them in his car, around the Lebanese countryside, planting them randomly wherever he passed, in forests and on the sides of country roadways, thus, in his own way, magnifying and dignifying his native land, reforesting it and proliferating its fauna, keeping his father's legacy alive, and, in a true winnower's movement and a selfless act of love and creation, practicing the gospel that Charles Corm himself had preached in his 1934 Friends of the Trees Program.

Fulfilling the lumberjack's exhortation in *La Montagne Inspirée* to "plant cedar trees,"[94] the program of Charles Corm's Friends of the Trees Association maintained that the very life and livelihood of Lebanon dwelt in its agriculture and its magnificent landscape—its principal source of wealth, as it were, "glorified in the Biblical tradition," and incumbent upon the Lebanese to restitute and protect.[95] "Without having to define it, the mere title of the 'Friends of the Trees' association is a complete program in and of itself," came Corm's description of the organization in its official preamble.[96]

The Friends of the Trees Association was an ecological and environmental protection agency par excellence, because, as Corm himself put it, being "Friends of the Trees" was perforce being friends of water and natural resources; friends of nature, friends of wildlife, friends of healthy living, and "in sum, friends of life itself."[97] All this, in Corm's telling, amounted to being friends of Lebanon tout court; Lebanon, which had been famous throughout its history for its forests and majestic cedars, whose brooks, springs, and waterfalls had been glorified in the Biblical narrative, but which had since World War I begun a dreadful (almost inexorable) descent toward deforestation.[98] Consequently, the Friends of the Trees Association, under Charles Corm's leadership, undertook the task of launching a "national environmental salvation" project, in which all Lebanese citizens were urged to take part and become full active participants. This was so because "trees and water are inseparable," claimed Corm, and "without trees, water resources will simply run dry," just as "without water resources, no trees, and indeed no crops could ever be sustained."[99] This would ultimately lead to the "death of the nation," he argued; a potential calamity which necessitates immediate action so as to "protect and upkeep Lebanon's remaining forests, embark on a large-scale reforestation drive, and create a National Heritage Reserve" to revive Lebanon's millennial native natural industries including timber, mulberry, vine, and olive trees.[100] Corm also called for the revival of Lebanon's citrus industry, "a fabulous modern enterprise from which our neighbors [in the *Yishuv* in British Mandatory Palestine] currently draw immeasurable benefits."[101] Lebanon is therefore summoned to follow suit, urged Corm, and through cooperation, method, and discipline, the Lebanese were called upon

> to mold their minds and their souls to privilege and love trees; to obtain the direct and immediate support of the press and state institutions to guarantee the

success of this worthy endeavor; to establish the necessary regulatory agencies (for instance, to devise a Forestry Code, Ranger Services, and Floriculture Legislation); to constantly monitor adherence to the Codes in effect, and report to the authorities and the press any and all violations likely to harm forests and the environment in general; to nurture the concept of respecting nature among school-age children; to embark upon large-scale reforestation campaigns and inform the state of land-owners wishing to develop forests and woodlands on their otherwise barren estates; to hasten the official surveying, demarcation, and supervision of unchecked public forests, national parks, and natural trails; [. . .] to draw well-detailed official forestry maps covering the entire country; to provide for easy access to seedlings, good quality seeds, and other supplies so as to aid in sustaining effective state-of-the-art nurseries; to improve conservation methods and responsible use and exploitation of forests and natural resources [. . .]; to declare national holidays celebrating trees and other natural reserves in order to increase awareness, encourage preservation, and spur the creation of protected national heritage reservations and symbolic nurseries and forests (sacred groves and the like); to maintain contact and close cooperation with likeminded associations, especially those from countries around the Mediterranean basin.[102]

In sum, even back in 1934, some forty years before the United States itself established its own Environmental Protection Agency, Charles Corm had been in the avant-garde of Lebanon's ecological movement; a pioneer of Lebanese "Greenpeace" as it were, four decades before the Greenpeace movement of the 1970s had come into being. Again, his aim was a simple one; an act of creation and renewal, and a selfless altruistic expression of humanity and humanism. The momentum to this "environmental" campaign was set on May 5, 1935, a date on which Charles Corm had launched Lebanon's first "Tree Day" celebration; a national "festival" of sorts, remnants and analogues of which are still extant, observed and ritualized annually in modern-day Lebanon.[103] The brochure and promotional materials announcing that May 5th event contained a poem titled "The Example," which Corm had clearly written for the occasion, intended to set the tone for the future, incarnating the motivation behind this environmental protection society. As an ode to Lebanon's wildlife and both its ecological and human offerings (with the obligatory mention of the Phoenicians), Corm's inaugural poem read as follows:

> Beautiful trees, how I long to be like thee:
> Not only a massive trunk, rugged and crude,
> Armored with a sturdy hull and a solid attitude:
> Beautiful trees, how I long to be like thee!
> [Like thee] to the very depths of the ashes of those departed beloveds,
> And into the dimmed riches or our sainted origins,
> Firmly pushing my delicate roots on,
> [Like thee] to the very depths of the ashes of those departed beloveds!

So as to bounce back higher, skyward, and into the splendor of daylight,
And to sink even deeper, bravely, into the pitch of my toils,
Securing my strongest bonds to the ground below,
So as to bounce back higher, skyward, and into the splendor of daylight!
[Like thee] against the vain clamor of a mad destiny,
When the storms howl and the lightening rages on,
Like thee, stoic, I long to stay, serene and wise and strong,
[Like thee] against the vain clamor of a mad destiny!
[Like thee] light and evergreen, filled with breeze and azure blue,
Shaking off my dusts to the breeze of a cloud,
Waving my living limbs quivering with the leaves,
[Like thee] light and evergreen, filled with breeze and azure blue!
And with arms wide open, ever welcoming to all,
From the break of dawn to the soft sunset, reaching out,
Hurling skyward, toward the zenith, an ever vertical soul,
And with arms wide open, ever welcoming to all!
Through endless miracle, unimaginable and real at once,
Drawing out of the dark soil, where decay and mold lie,
The brilliance and the fragrance of the purest of flowers,
Through endless miracle, unimaginable and real at once!
Tender, cheerful, upright and proud, sensitive, and serene,
And so as not to drain my ever-gushing verve and zeal,
In the fleeting winds my branches will remain few,
Tender, cheerful, upright and proud, sensitive, and serene!
From the early spring buds, to the ripe summer fruits,
Nourished through the sturdy clay, and the gliding open air,
Anchored in my past, soaring skyward into space,
From the early spring buds, to the ripe summer fruits!
Like those brave Phoenicians, moving far beyond the seas,
Their genius molding the fate of early Humanity,
Filling the far-flung skies with aromas and seeds,
Like those brave Phoenicians, moving far beyond the seas!
So as to give hope, for evermore a brighter future,
We must always tap into the ancient blood of our fertile land,
For an ever-new April, regenerating the world,
So as to give hope, for evermore a brighter future! [104]

No doubt Charles Corm's endeavor had immediate national interests and trappings—bringing healing, renewal, well-being, and prosperity to Lebanon and the Lebanese. Yet the universalist dimensions of his act—as was the case with his deeds and temperament in general—went beyond the narrow, the national, and the self-interested. It was, as Corm himself would have called it, "humanism in deeds." It was not without reason that Saïd Akl had yearned for a Lebanese President of the Republic in the image of Charles Corm, the only President that would have been the "consummate, authentic Lebanese [. . .] worthy of carrying in his heart the real ambitions of Lebanon," dedicated to the service of both Lebanon and the greater good of Mankind. [105]

But, to Saïd Akl's chagrin, Charles Corm would remain true to his poetic (and patriotic conscience), and would never enter the political fray. This decision was perhaps best encapsulated in Corm's 1919 "Nationalist Musings" of *La Revue Phénicienne*, and the impassioned poem of "The Saga of Agony" mentioned earlier, and which documented with disturbing accuracy the impairment and utter decay that was Lebanese political life. That is probably why the *Je Cherche un Homme* lecture mentioned earlier would strike a sensitive chord in 1949, and beyond, spurring a deluge of letters of support and admiration—chief among them perhaps Hektor Klat's telegram from Sao Paolo, where he had been serving as Lebanon's Consul General at the time, and where he reminded his friend that "no doubt you shall find the man that you are searching for, in your own mirror."[106] Alas, Charles Corm never looked in the mirror, and never took heed of his friends' claims that the man (of the hour) that he was looking for, had all along been himself.

CHILD-POET AND HUMANIST

Although his earliest and best-known publications date back to 1919 (inaugurated namely with the launching of the short-lived iconic *La Revue Phénicienne*), Charles Corm did not become a full-time writer until 1934, on the day of his fortieth birthday, when he decided to liquidate all his business assets, abscond all commercial activities, and cease being Lebanon's "Mr. Ford." By then, wrote Asher Kaufman, Corm had become a very wealthy man, and was no longer concerned with earning a living; his aim had now become to mainly work in the service of his country, vaunting its grandeur, excavating its history, and trotting out its bequests to mankind.[107]

It was at the tender age of sixteen, in late 1911, that Charles Corm completed his secondary education at the Jesuit petit college of Beirut and began considering a future "conquest of America." His French formation and his infatuation with French culture notwithstanding, the pursuit and realization of the "American dream" still baffled and captivated the adolescent Charles Corm. Yet, at the same time he had been pulled since a very early age by the lure of art and painting—perhaps goaded in that direction by the general mood of his household, compelling him to follow in his own father's footsteps. And so upon graduating high school, young Charles would resolve to dedicate himself full-time to sating an innate (possibly a familial) artistic appetite.

Yet, he was uneasy at the thought of having to rely on parental largesse to subsidize his creative passions. He therefore set out to jump into the business fray before indulging his artistic affections. This took him to Paris where he spent a few fleeting months soaking in the city's charms and rubbing shoulders with the bohemians of the *belle époque*. Pre–World War I Paris left a lasting impression on the wide-eyed adolescent Charles Corm, and it was the city's Symbolism, Expressionism, Modernism, and Art Nouveau that grabbed hold of his affections, dominated his emotions, and persuaded him that the life he had long fancied for himself—the life of an artist—was indeed the life that he was destined for, whatever he may end up doing beforehand and in order to get to his calling.

And so, Charles Corm the artist was to be overruled by Charles Corm the pragmatist in Paris, even if only briefly, and even if for purely practical reasons. So he elected to trade in his painter's brushes and his dreams of Henri Matisse for the work-apron and streamlines of Henry Ford; industry and wealth production as it were, before artistic creation. Thus, in mid-July 1912, reluctantly perhaps, but driven by vernal ambition and verve, Charles trekked from Paris to Le Havre in Normandy, and crossed the English Channel into the southern coast of Britain. From there, he boarded the Royal Mail Steamer *Olympic* at the Port of Southampton and headed to New York, where he would remain and operate a successful import-export business on Broadway Avenue, until the outbreak of the Great War.

Charles Corm, a proud product of French Jesuit missionary education and the child of a Beirut that relished the language and ways of France, would undergo a happy cultural and linguistic transformation on the streets of Manhattan. There, in the vastness of the Big Apple, attending the same Broadway plays night after night for months on end, the adolescent Charles Corm would come to gain near-native fluency in English—a language that he did not know prior to his arrival in America.[108] It was also during this brief stint in the New World that a vernal, baby-faced, eighteen-year-old Charles Corm—who in 1912 looked more like a high-school sophomore than a serious entrepreneur—would secure a meeting with the founder of the Ford Motor Company. A number of unparsed documents in Charles Corm's Beirut Archives reveal him to have "pestered" Henry Ford's assistant for nearly a month, sitting at her desk day after day, imploring her for a meeting with her famous inventor-industrialist boss. Out of exasperation or pity—or perhaps succumbing to Charles Corm's tenacity and charm—the reluctant assistant was alleged to have finally consented, granting the persistent teenager from Mount-Lebanon his wish.

Even Henry Ford himself was reportedly smitten by Charles Corm's charisma and determination. Barely minutes into their meeting, a cheeky young Corm had already begun "buttering up" the American tycoon, talking him into importing Ford motorcars to Lebanon. "Lebanon?" queried a puzzled Henry Ford. "*Where exactly is* Lebanon?" he asked quizzically. When young Charles proudly pointed to a barely visible speck on a wall map, a spot where the Ottoman Sanjak of Mount-Lebanon would have been,[109] an amused and incredulous Henry Ford quipped, "son, do you even have roads in Lebanon?" "You give me the cars, sir, and I'll build the roads!" countered the undaunted young Charles Corm. Intrigued by his visitor's bewitching audacity, Henry Ford was said to have agreed to name the adolescent Charles Corm the Near East's "Exclusive Agent for Assembly, Sale, and Distribution" of Ford automobiles, tractors, and agricultural machinery. And so would Corm travel back to Beirut on the eve of the Great War, clutching in his coat pocket a document bearing Henry Ford's signature; a piece of paper and a signature that may very well have ended up being dead letter had the adolescent Charles Corm not followed through, but nevertheless a document that still changed the course of his life, and with him the course of modern Lebanese history.

At its height, Charles Corm's commercial ventures, all folded into the *Société Générale* brand name, counted dozens of Ford automobile showrooms and a number of Firestone, John Deer, and McCormick-International Harvester subsidiaries, assembly shops, and distribution centers sprawling from Turkey to Transjordan and Mandatory Palestine, and from Damascus to Baghdad and Teheran. As mentioned in the Prologue, Corm's holding companies employed hundreds of Turks, Lebanese, Syrians, Iraqis, Transjordanians, and Palestinians—Jews, Christians, and Muslims alike—contributed to the livelihood of thousands of families, and expanded the infrastructure and networks of roads, railways, and bridges in countries that had not yet come into being at that time.

But commerce and wealth creation were not Corm's only achievements in modern Levantine social life. In 1921, at the tender age of twenty-seven, in the bustle of his commercial activities—and while he was still serving as commissioner of the Lebanon post-war relief organizations—he would contribute to the founding of Lebanon's first modern public library, the *Bibliothèque Nationale de Beyrouth*, to whose collection his friend Prince Albert I of Monaco (an amateur oceanographer and lover of the Mediterranean) would contribute some 50,000 volumes. Charles Corm was also a founding member, along with Albert of Monaco, of the Mediterranean Academy; a learned society that encouraged and produced scholarship on Mediterranean civilizations. Still engaged in the demands of his post-war relief project—a program that brought moral, material, and financial assistance to Lebanese victims of the Great War—Corm headed the Committee of the Friends of the Beirut Museum; a commission of private donors, intellectuals, and cultural figures who drew up the blueprints of what would become the Beirut National Museum. In 1934, Corm inaugurated and began hosting, in his Beirut home and the former Ford Motor Company Headquarters (at a stone's throw from the museum that he brought into being), the iconic *Amitiés Libanaises* cultural salons. Before long, this intellectual society would become a trendy and much-coveted weekly "gathering of the minds," to which flocked a number of eminent local and international political, cultural, and intellectual figures—among them Pierre Benoît, Paul Valéry, Charles

Plisnier, and F. Scott Fitzgerald among others; figures whom an adolescent Charles Corm had no doubt encountered a quarter century earlier during his brief stay in Paris. The *Amitiés Libanaises* forum was also home to a number of Lebanese literati, politicos, and aspiring authors, who, hard as they might have tried, seldom escaped the spell of their host's charm and infectious energy.

Even Israeli scholars (or at least members of the pre-State *Yishuv* community) had also taken part in these activities in the Beirut of the 1930s and 1940s.[110] This was still during times of greater "innocence" in the Levant, when the resentful (barbed) borders of an emerging Middle Eastern state-system had not yet been finalized, and when the animosities between Muslims and Jews had not yet exploded in armed conflict. Nevertheless, Charles Corm would always remain outside the petty disputes of the region's competing nationalisms, and as mentioned earlier, his business emporium, cultural exchanges, and cordial collaborations reached across borders and bypassed ethnic, religious, and political barriers. And so, his *Amitiés Libanaises*, bringing together Muslims, Christians, Jews, and others, was a natural order of things for him; a reflection of his own humanism and his ecumenical temperament—in literary, artistic, commercial, and human endeavors alike.

To wit, Eliahu Epstein—a representative of the Jewish Agency who had somewhat of a "second home" in Beirut—was a friend of Corm's and a bit of a fixture at the *Amitiés Libanaises*.[111] In correspondence between Corm and Epstein during the late 1930s, there figure a number of invitations that Charles Corm had extended to Jewish archaeologist Nahum Sloucshz and sculptor (and friend of Marc Chagall) Chana Orloff, suggesting they present their work at the *Amitiés Libanaises* and a number of other Beirut cultural venues. Naturally, Corm was particularly interested in Slouschz's work on the Phoenicians, and in Orloff's personal ties to a number of French and European artists whom Corm admired greatly, whom he had encountered earlier in his youth, and who were often hosted at his gatherings.[112] Other scholars and intellectuals of the *Yishuv* took part in these gatherings; among them were Zionist leader and diplomat Victor Jacobson, who had business interests in Beirut, and who lectured in Beirut on the Biblical relationship between King Solomon and the Phoenician King of Tyre, Hiram, the builder of Solomon's Temple. Of note among *Yishuv* visitors to Beirut were also the Hebrew poet Haim Nahman Bialik and author Rachel Ben-Zvi—both having been personal friends of Lebanese-Jewish community leader Joseph Farhi.

Yearning for those interrupted weekly gatherings of the *Amitiés Libanaises*, Lebanese author Rushdy Maalouf (1914–1980), father of Francophone novelist and member of the *Académie Française* Amine Maalouf (b. 1949), noted in his 1963 elegy of Charles Corm that although the meetings of the *Amitiés Libanaises* had become sparse in Charles Corm's final days, the legacy that they and he left behind, "like the Cedars of Lebanon, never ceased to lavish glory and grandeur on the altar of Humanism that is his Lebanon."[113] Charles Corm was "our first teacher," wrote Maalouf; he was Lebanon's "national school," its "national museum," its "national torch and beacon," and the "fountainhead and spring eternal of its humanism."[114] Charles Corm, asserted Maalouf,

> was the first one to show us *how* to love Lebanon; *how* to chant and rhapsodize Lebanon, *how* to vaunt and defend Lebanon, and how to become masterbuilders of this Lebanon of his yearnings; Humanists, Cosmopolitans, Ecumenical friends and allies to mankind, yet steadfast in our love and affection for our homeland.[115]

Maalouf further noted that it was not unusual for artists, intellectuals, and cultural and political figures visiting Lebanon for the first time to have Charles Corm and his *Maison Blanche*[116] on their itinerary of peoples and places to see: "they visited Lebanon seeking out Charles Corm the way some of us may visit France to see Da Vinci's *Mona Lisa*, or the way we may visit Athens to see the Acropolis."[117] This is the veneration that many, Lebanese and foreigners alike, held for Charles Corm, and it is still this mystique of Charles Corm's that haunts the walls and halls of his now-muted *Maison Blanche de Beyrouth*.

Charles Corm was a universalist humanist who loathed sectarianism and resentful nationalisms built on the rejection or marginalization of the "other." He believed in Lebanon as an exemplar of religious toleration and coexistence between various ethnic and cultural groupings. Nevertheless, he was also a devout and committed Christian, proud of this component of his identity, and to the bitter end, invested in Lebanon's role as one of the last remaining strongholds and havens of Eastern Christendom in the East. Stemming from this, Corm petitioned the League of Nations in 1937, with the assistance of his old friend Robert de Caix,[118] advocating for the transfer of 30,000 Assyro-Chaldaean refugees from Iraq to Lebanon—given the discriminatory policies, large-scale massacres, and forced population movements that they had been undergoing at the hands of successive Turkish and Arab governments since the early twentieth century.[119] Corm's petition was not lent the support he thought it deserved in Geneva, and was to remain dead letter. But this was a period that, in many ways, turned out to be a prelude to the tempests that would grip Lebanon throughout the 1940s and 1950s.

As mentioned earlier, the Lebanon-Phoenicia that Charles Corm had made battle for was sacrificed on the altar of the 1943 National Pact—a "constitutional agreement" brokered between Lebanon's Sunni and Maronite communities, represented by then President of the Republic Bechara el-

Khoury and Prime Minister Riyad al-Solh, appointing an "Arab face" to an otherwise diverse multi-cultural Lebanon in return for conceding a tenuous Christian majority rule. The National Pact was intended to guarantee the security, cultural rights, and political representation of the non-Muslim components of Lebanese society, without encroaching on the Arabist references of Lebanese Muslims who were otherwise more interested in becoming part of a Syrian (Arab) state than a (Christian-dominated) Lebanese one. Political power was therefore to be divided proportionately between Christians and Muslims, with a six-to-five ratio in favor of Christians. Likewise, civil service, diplomatic appointments, and positions of leadership in the armed forces were also subject to this six-to-five ratio. This guaranteed the participation of the various communities in government. But as mentioned earlier, it conceded an "Arab face" to Lebanon—and for all intents and purposes it signaled the nullification of the Lebanon that Charles Corm and his circle had yearned for. Indeed, the National Pact was one of the major catalysts behind Charles Corm's 1949 *I am Searching for a Man* lecture excoriating Bechara el-Khoury for signing off on such an agreement. For it was the 1943 National Pact that paved the way to the sectarianism that was to grip Lebanon in the decades to come, and it was the National Pact that turned the influx of some 300,000 Arab refugees from British Mandatory Palestine in 1948 into the spark that would inflame inter-Arab rivalries and Arab-Israeli hostilities, all making battle on Lebanese soil.

In that sense, Charles Corm predicted the "unmaking" of Lebanon; reluctantly so perhaps, but he knew that momentous changes were looming on Lebanon's horizons. He made his prediction most saliently perhaps in his 1949 *I am Searching for a Man*. Yet, there were traces of the "prophecy" elsewhere. In a manuscript titled *La Terre Assassinée ou les Ciliciennes* (The Murdered Homeland or the Cilicians), and published posthumously in 2004, Charles Corm, in a memorial to the Armenian Genocide, handed out an indictment of aggressive irredentist nationalism, and offered a celebration of humanism and compassionate nationalism as he dreamt them and wished them to be practiced in Lebanon. Corm's indictments were against "Turkish nationalism" in *Les Ciciennes*, yet implicitly he was lamenting what had happened to Lebanon since 1943 and the forced Arabization of his Phoenician heritage. Said one of the leaders of the Armenian refugees in *Les Ciliciennes*, on the road of exile:

> It is here, in Lebanon, since time immemorial, that every minority, whenever mistreated and whenever abused, elsewhere in the Near East, has found sanctuary, has found safe refuge, from murder and tyranny. Even Druze and Shi'as, even Muslims themselves, when persecuted by majorities among them, have always found peace, freedom and security, in the shadow of the Lebanon! And so, here are we, us the Armenians, ever since the persecutions of 1875, and during the massacres of Red Abdulhamid, in 1895, then in 1915, and later in

1916, 1917 and 1918, and to this very day [in 1939?] it is always there, near the hearth of the Lebanese homeland, that a brotherly welcome has been granted us! Without hesitation, always with devotion, the Lebanese have given their exquisite friendship. They have given us convents, they have given us churches, they have given us happy hearty homes, mountains impregnable, and lands arable; they have given us charming climes, and beautiful skies; most importantly perhaps, they have given us, unhindered freedom, to move about and grow! And so, in the embrace of the Lebanon, we shall dwell in the Lord![120]

A pleasing image of Lebanese hospitality and humanity and generosity to say the least, but—as some of the Armenian exiles clamored—an image that carries within it the seeds of Lebanon's destruction; "if the Lebanese are truly what you say they are" quipped some Armenian voices,

their mountain must be cursed! If they open their doors to every new comer, they must be crazy for sure! If they are so generous, then it must not be long before they become exiles in their own homeland! [. . .] And if their country is truly a sanctuary, where they truly live their Gospels, like wolves the foreigners will soon put an end to that! We are better off seeking refuge elsewhere![121]

Although no date can be ascertained for *Les Ciliciennes*, the tone and language of its conclusion certainly point to the 1940s and even the 1950s, and could very well have been written today describing Lebanon's challenges in the twenty-first century. Indeed, Lebanon in our times has become a "sanctuary" for hundreds of thousands of refugees; a theatre for regional conflicts; a harbor for violence and terrorism; and a homeland whose own children are exiles—both internally and externally.

LET THERE BE LIGHT OVER THE MOUNTAIN

If any sort of judgment can or should be leveled at Charles Corm the poet and the humanist, it ought to be done through a close scrutiny of his literary work. In that sense, investigating Charles Corm's life and cultural production without a thorough analysis of his texts remains a mere sketch, an abridgement of an otherwise monumental corpus. Therefore, in the following section, a selection of annotated critical translations of three representative works of Charles Corm will be provided. Although not exhaustive by any stretch, the purpose of these samples is to introduce the reader to the span of Charles Corm's work in poetry, short stories, and aphorisms—not its totality, but a sampling. And so, in a sense, like this biography itself, which remains at best a furtive glimpse into a vastly complex life-story, there is only so much that can be broached of Charles Corm's monumental oeuvre in the span of a single biographical volume.

The themes of the poetry culled from Corm's *La Montagne Inspirée* (*The Hallowed Mountain*, 1933) may seem at first glance patriotic in nature, specific to Lebanon and early twentieth-century Lebanese history. However, its scope and outlook, namely its focus on humanism, syncretism, and an intercourse of ideas and peoples, is universalist in its breadth and its capacity to reach those molded by different experiences and affected by different circumstances.

Likewise, the short story titled *Conte de Pâques* (*Easter Story*, 1915–1918), written by a twenty-one-year-old Corm, in the thicket of the famine that devastated Ottoman Mount-Lebanon during the Great War, may have resonance and find meaning among those touched by the horrors, the destitution, and the dispossession wrought by war—as much during the early decades of last century as during the early decades of our own.

Those readers socialized in the West and who may be familiar with the horrors of World War II and the dreadful conditions of ghetto life—as intrinsic riggings to the machinery of the Nazis' systematic destruction of European Jewry—will no doubt recognize some striking similarities in *Conte de Pâques*. "Who, after all, speaks today of the annihilation of the Armenians"[122] is a sentence attributed to Adolph Hitler, alluding to war crimes committed by the Ottomans in the early decades of the twentieth century; crimes that had all but fallen from historical memory by the time Hitler himself had embarked on his own extermination campaigns. But the devastations rained on the Armenians during World War I were by no means random or limited to the Armenians alone. Many of the Ottomans' former subject peoples—the Armenians perhaps chief among them—who dared raise their voices for "national" recognition and self-determination in the run up to the Great War were dealt with swiftly and cruelly by spiteful Ottoman authorities intent on protecting the integrity of their tenuous, crumbling empire. Charles Corm's *Conte de Pâques* is the story of one such "national" group who defied the Ottoman suzerain. The narrative provides gripping, devastating testimonials on both "perpetrators" and "spectators" of "ghetto life" in Ottoman Lebanon a good quarter of a century before Hitler's "Final Solution." As Corm's 1915–1918 story suggests, although unprecedented in its "irrational rationality" and the horrors that it perpetrated, the Holocaust might not have been unique in its intent and finality; it had precedents and early exemplars, and it is not farfetched that the recalcitrant Levantine Ottoman dominions during World War I might have provided Hitler's Germany with a suitable template.

Yet, one discerns no grudges, no acrimony, and no calls for revenge or retribution in Corm's *Easter Story*; only dignity and grace and charming humanity, and most of all perhaps uplifting resilience and will to survive. Indeed, these qualities seem to populate Corm's work as a whole, where he is always able to derive hope and draw light out of the darkest direst of times.

That, to him, was the precondition and condensation of "being human": a way of "bursting out of one's own twilights, repelling the darkness [. . .] defying death, and propagating and procreating far beyond the grave."[123] Rancor and resentment drain the human spirit, wrote Corm in *La Montagne Inspirée*,

> but love quenches the soul; / For, the more loving we can be, the more joyous we become; / For, to a tender dazzled heart, loving one's enemy is even more thrilling than a beloved's embrace! [. . .] And loving one's enemies, wicked as they may be, / is a way of thwarting evil, / A way of gleaning light, from the shadows of night.[124]

Besides its lyrical value as a saga of survival and an exalted ode to humanism, Corm's *Easter Story* provides a vital historical framework, and arguably a rationale, for the establishment of Greater Lebanon in 1920: a state far exceeding the dimensions that the Maronites of Corm's generation might have been entitled to, but one then deemed imperative to the security and survival of a hunted down and traumatized community, barely re-emerging from the throes of death.

Finally, the selections of short poems, aphorisms, reminiscences, and fantasies of *Contes Érotiques* (*Erotic Tales*, 1912), written by a vernal seventeen-year-old Charles Corm, invoke "lived memories," often sublimated pubescent yearnings that Corm might have held for women he encountered in Lebanon, and during his first trips to Paris, London, and New York between 1911 and 1914.

In all, Charles Corm's corpus reflects the profound impact that World War I (and later World War II) might have had on him personally and on his worldview. Wars and the devastation that they wrought taught Charles Corm the value of tolerance and humanism, put him in touch with the absurdity of violence and the futility of resentful nationalism, and made him realize that only a spacious, humanist, hybrid, universalist "patriotism," bereft of all manners of orthodoxy and chauvinism—religious, linguistic, and national alike—could offer a panacea to the Levant's volatile inter-identity quarrels, and give the Lebanon that he dreamt of respite from its endemic ethnic dissentions.

In a sense, Charles Corm's lifelong literary, intellectual, commercial, and humanitarian work was intended as an act of defiance and confrontation directed at orthodoxy—*all* orthodoxy, whether in politics, art, architecture, historiography, or literature. But his work was also a summons to the inherently pacifist impulses of the Lebanese people as he saw them, and namely a valorization of their much disputed and debated claims to a Phoenician ancestry.

As time moves on ever further from the day *La Montagne Inspirée* was first published, wrote Élie Tyane in 1935, and as the tempests that had vigorously shaken the souls of those who came into contact with that sublime poem's verses in 1934, Charles Corm's *Hallowed Mountain* goes on acquiring new meanings and added gravitas.[125] Besides being an "ode" to Lebanon's ancient glories and an optimist vision of its days to come, the poem, argued Tyane, was above all a confirmation of Lebanon's high moral values and a restitution of the country and its people to their true selves and their true history. "Long had I stayed in awe of this book," wrote Tyane,

> unable to write or utter a single commentary on it, crushed and eclipsed as I was by the enormity and loftiness of the emotions taking hold of me as I ran through its pages, breathless, thunderstruck, euphoric. Today, however, with my soul finally composed, reasonably collected before the hallowed image that *La Montagne Inspirée* evokes, I feel myself ready to bear witness, not so much to the inherent beauty of this work, as to filial piety that it exuded, conferring upon it an almost sacred aura.[126]

But, as we saw earlier, Tyane's wonderment before the exalted lyricism of *The Hallowed Mountain* was not an exception; it had become the prevailing emotion of most of those who came into contact with that epochal work. An energizing blast of energy and warmth "reminiscent of a Victor Hugo and an Alphonse de Lamartine" runs through the pages of *La Montagne Inspirée*, boasted a 1934 editorial in Lebanon's leading French-language journal, *La Revue du Liban*.[127] Reading Charles Corm, wrote *La Revue du Liban*, one feels as if possessed, inflamed, entranced, and carried away on a breathtaking journey through the millennia, breathing love and nostalgia. Like many other Lebanese poets, Charles Corm drew divine inspiration from Lebanon's mountains; yet, he remained so different from all those who came before him, and possibly all those who may follow, because,

> nowhere, at any time in its history, has Lebanon been graced with a moving, tormented, passionate national cantor such as Charles Corm, and nowhere have we heard in Lebanon national inflections as vibrant and as powerful as Charles Corm's! *The Hallowed Mountain* is truly a landmark of our literary history [...] worthy of the widest audiences possible. Indeed, one feels it is the duty of the Lebanese government to disseminate this work and make it required reading in Lebanon's national schools.[128]

La Montagne Inspirée was written in the style of a *chanson de geste*, a mediaeval French narrative genre of "heroic deeds" composed in verse and intended for oral recitation. The *chanson de geste* was often a narration of a nation's legendary events, celebrating national heroes, boasting their heroisms and great deeds on the battlefield, and taking pride in the defeats meted out on their otherwise superior enemies. *La Montagne Inspirée* fits snugly into that quintessentially French literary genre—one might even argue a distinctly "Christian" literary genre, given that the "first" *chanson de geste* that set the tone for that poetic medium was the eleventh-century *Chanson de Roland*, which many scholars believe to contain references to the First Crusade.

In line with such epic stories of a nation's exploits, Charles Corm's *La Montagne Inspirée* is divided into three "Cycles," French "*Dits*," "Sagas," or "Tales"; the Tale/Saga of Anticipation, the Tale/Saga of Agony, and the Tale/Saga of Remembrances. *La Montagne Inspirée*'s first Cycle (or Tale) of Anticipation had already been published, some fifteen years prior, on September 1, 1920, on the day that General Henri Gouraud had proclaimed the establishment of Greater Lebanon. This "Tale of Anticipation" reads like a charming procession of verses, each of which a passionate cry of joy, a canticle intoned by a people and an allegorical Lebanon finally redeemed and delivered, grateful to their liberator. Reading the power, the profound emotion, and the freshness of this first cycle of *La Montagne Inspirée*, one feels as if almost before a vision of a Biblical David, beautiful in his youth and his eagerness and passion, dancing deliriously before the Ark of the Covenant, singing the song of Victory, shouting out a solemn hallelujah celebrating the fulfillment of a Prophecy, the work of Destiny.[129] This cycle then ends with a salute to General Gouraud, Lebanon's redeemer, and in Corm's telling an epitome of beauty, elegance, and power, comparable to Venus of Milo and Nike of Samothrace; a contemporary carrier of beauty, elegance, and power that only a bruised, unbowed, French war hero—Lebanon's millennial friend and protector—can condense and bring to bear in modern times.

The poem's second cycle, the "Tale of Agony," takes the reader into the year 1932, painting a disturbing apocalyptic canvas lifted straight out of Dante's Inferno.[130] To Charles Corm's idea of a restored, resurrected Lebanon, reclaimed to its Phoenician heritage, reconnected to its Greco-Roman and Christian past, the Arab nationalists of the 1930s, those disciples of Sati' al-Husri's coercive Arabism, sounded spiteful roars of fury, issued sharp impeachments of Charles Corm, his distinct brand of patriotism and his ardent celebration of Lebanese particularism. Nationalism to them, the one that mattered, was the one that devoured others in its path, erased their cultural vestiges, and suppressed their passions and their memories. But Charles Corm's frustrations were not directed at those zealots of Arab nationalism who came from the outside; rather his disappointments were with those local Lebanese surrogates of Arab nationalism. His "Saga of Agony" was therefore addressed to them, to those merchants of corrupt ideas, trading an ill-earned gold, signing shady pacts of abdication in the shadow of "bloody gallows" blotting out Lebanon and sacrificing it on the altar of alien ideologies.[131] It was both inconceivable and unconscionable to Corm that some Lebanese would chime in with the Arab nationalists, at the expense of Lebanon, renouncing, for the greater good of the Arabs, their own Lebanese history and their own Phoenician heritage; a legacy which had once made Lebanon a splendid space of liberty and free exchange of ideas and peoples and traditions.

But, like the "Saga of Anticipation" before it, the "Saga of Agony" does end on a positive high note, sounding the joyous bells of redemption, announcing the coming of the "Saga of Remembrances," happy recollections of a past and a millennial history redolent with the sounds and fragrances of Lebanon. To exult the beauty of her beloved, the Shulamite girl of the Song of Songs simply said that "his appearance is like Lebanon"—and this, in one of the pinnacles of poetry. No other comparison would have been deemed as complete, or would have captured the Shulamite's feelings. Those were the very same imageries that Charles Corm's *La Montagne Inspirée* attempted to convey.

In many ways, *La Montagne Inspirée* was a book that went way beyond the realm of poetry, strictly speaking, wrote one reviewer in 1935; "it is a manifesto! a summons to the Lebanese youth" and an exhortation for them to draw faith and hope and energy from the living fountainhead of their proud lineage.[132] Even the Anglophone press of the times had its say, with a November 1934 *Domestic and Foreign Research* review hailing *La Montagne Inspirée*[133] a "remarkable poetic composition of stirring religious strains [...]; Epopoeia of sublimely inspired lyricism, setting forth the contributions of Phoenicia to this world civilization, from the remotest times to our days." In this same vein, Eliahu Epstein's editorial in the *Palestine Post* of February 24, 1935, titled "Lebanese Renaissance," perhaps merits being reproduced in its quasi totality. Not only because it concisely encapsulated Charles Corm's thought, but also because it spoke to the intimacy with which Epstein himself understood Charles Corm—and indeed the bond of friendship that the two of them shared. "*La Montagne Inspirée* is more than a mere collection of poems," wrote Epstein:

> It is an enthusiastic expression of an "idée mystique" of the author, the idea of Lebanese renaissance. Charles Corm is a Lebanese patriot who preaches all through the pages the revival of the old Phoenician civilization. His dreams are like those of Astarte and Baal. His heroes are Hiram, Fakreddin, Emir Bechir, Youssef Karam, the emigrants and the peasants of the mountain. He is inspired by Byblos and by Ras Shamrah who speak to his mind and heart, in a more compelling voice than the cultures under which the Lebanese lived and developed since Phoenician days. Lebanon to him is not merely a part of the Arab world. He speaks of the Lebanese tongue, which is the old Phoenician. He speaks of "our leaders" which to him are not the present leaders, but the heroes of old, to whom he would like to hark back, for the revival of that brilliant age which made Lebanon a power in the world, and his ancestors were the bearers of culture; when Tyre and Sidon, and Byblos were metropolises from which

emanated knowledge and learning to the far-flung corners of the world. Corm is not a new name. He is the director of the *Revue Phénicienne,* one of the founders of the *Association des Gens de Lettres* of Beirut, and the promoter of *Les Auteurs Libanais de Langue Française.* There can be but little doubt that one of the factors which inspired the new Phoenician aspirations was the Zionist movement which has encouraged them to dream of reviving their own culture and traditions. Corm writes prose and poems. They are a mixture of the epic, sometimes weaved into lyric emotions. He recalls the greatness of the old Phoenicians whose Kings built the garden of Semiramis and the temples of the Near East; of the Phoenician colonies in Africa. Has the greatness of the Phoenicians been dimmed, he asks, because they were merchants and sometimes forgot that independence must be defended even by blood? We may expect more from the pen of Charles Corm. He is not only an able poet, but a man who battles for his ideas.[134]

In sum, *La Montagne Inspirée* was stirring and exhilarating to both those who knew Charles Corm personally, and those who did not; to Lebanese invested in and sensitive to Corm's themes, and to foreigners who were not. To the Lebanese, *La Montagne Inspirée* was a veritable epopee, the stuff of legends, evoking in living poetic form all the hopes, the emotions, the disappointments, and the yearnings and memories of a people. Indeed, if there were such a thing as a book repository for the spirit of a nation, Charles Corm's *La Montagne Inspirée* had to be it; "a kaleidoscope of emotions," wrote Albert Naccache, "wonderfully depicted; a book that bewilders at first, then grabs hold of your heart, parading before you cavalcades of the most diverse of centuries and the most contradictory of events, where Lebanon is restituted in all its glory and all its splendor."[135] Charles Corm is sometimes "too realistic" in his depiction of historical events, often "too brassy" in formulating his thoughts and his imageries, "yet he remains an idealist to a fault, supremely principled"; an incarnation and confirmation of all that is great and graceful in Lebanon.[136] The brassiness of Corm's poem can perhaps be summarized in the three simple words that he casually bandied at the beginning of each cycle: "Traduit du Libanais," or "translated from the Lebanese language." Thus, he disclosed, although the poem might have been written in French, its soul and inspiration, and indeed its internal language, remained fundamentally Lebanese. Therefore, while wielding all the languages of mankind, often with the intimacy of natives—as is the case with French—the Lebanese still breathed, clasped, sensed, and spoke a *sui generis* Lebanese language. And so ends Corm's "symphonic epopee" with the disclosure that "even these sweet words, / Stolen from France's lips, / With impassioned affection / Quivering in my heart, / Still taste on my lips, / Where my smiling sorrow sits, / Still taste of a Lebanese kiss."

The excerpts of *La Montagne Inspirée* produced herewith, "The Saga of Anticipation" and "The Saga of Remembrances," are renditions of the original French "Le Dit de l'Enthousiasme" cycle. This "Le Dit de l'Enthousiasme" chapter may also translate roughly into the "Epic" or the "Tale of Enthusiasm"—with the term "enthusiasm" here being in anticipation of the establishment of Greater Lebanon, under the auspices of French High Commissioner Henri Gouraud. The poem is therefore a celebration of the euphoric moment that September 1, 1920, represented for Lebanese patriots of Corm's persuasion—the date at which Gouraud declared the establishment of the new state.

A graduate of the prestigious St-Cyr military academy, and the heroic leader of France's Fourth Army during the Great War, General Henri Gouraud sustained life-threatening injuries during the 1915 Dardanelles Campaign. He subsequently lost his right arm and right eye, and had only limited mobility in his right leg. He would nevertheless go on to command the Western Front for the remainder of the war, and would gain renown for his distinguished service, his heroism, and his agility as a war strategist. After the war, Gouraud was rewarded with the command of the French Army of the Levant, and would eventually become the first French High Commissioner to the States of the Levant—the name commonly used in reference to the former Ottoman territories that fell to the Allies after the Great War. Consequently, out of the disparate former Ottoman Provinces of Beirut, Damascus, Cilicia, and Aleppo, Gouraud would inaugurate the creation of five new states: the State of Damascus, the State of Aleppo, the State of Greater Lebanon, the State of the Alawite Mountain, and the State of the Druze Mountain. Subsequently, in 1936, the States of the Druze Mountain, the Alawite Mountain, Aleppo, and Damascus would be stitched together to form a Syrian Federation, which would come to constitute the nucleus of a formerly non-extant Syrian state—today's rending Syrian Arab Republic. Only the State of Greater Lebanon would remain outside of the new Syrian entity, and would continue functioning as an independent—albeit not always sovereign—republic.

This poem of Corm's "Saga of Anticipation" is, therefore, both a celebration of the establishment of Greater Lebanon in 1920 (and later the Lebanese Republic in 1926), and a tribute to Henri Gouraud himself; a maimed war hero who would bring unity and redemption of body and soul, and who would breathe health into the mutilated "Lebanese nation." Thus, on a bright day on September 1, 1920, standing imperiously before local and foreign dignitaries expressly gathered for this momentous occasion, Gouraud would declare the birth of modern Lebanon as follows:

> [B]efore all the people gathered here, peoples of all regions once dominated by Mount-Lebanon; peoples, who had once lived as neighbors and who shall from this day forward be united under the auspices of a single nation, rooted in its past, eminent in its future. [. . .] At the foot of these majestic mountains, which

in prevailing as the impregnable bulwark of your country's faith and freedom, have shaped your nation's strength; on the shores of this mythical sea, which has been witness to the triremes of Phoenicia, Greece, and Rome, and which once carried across the universe your subtle, skillful, and eloquent forefathers; today, this same sea is joyfully bringing you confirmation of a great and old friendship, and the good fortune of French peace. Before all of these witnesses to your aspirations, your struggles, and your victory, and in sharing your pride, I solemnly proclaim Greater Lebanon, and in the name of the French Republic, I salute her in her grandeur and in her power, from Nahr el-Kebir [in the North] to the gates of Palestine [in the South] and to the peaks of the Anti-Lebanon [in the East.][137]

Charles Corm was present on that portentous day, and he must have taken frenzied jubilant notes documenting its goings on—as his own euphoria can barely be contained in the poetic recollections of *Le Dit de l'Enthousiasme*. Here, Corm celebrates not only the "rendering whole" of a dismembered nation, but *also* the exquisite act of "restoring," "rehabilitating," and "re-mending" an "assassinated nation" by a "mutilated" war hero no less. Hence, the different body parts that Corm invokes and gives voice to throughout the poem, recall the parts of a formerly dismembered Lebanon now being lovingly restored to its former self. But those very same tattered body parts that Corm brings back to life are also the limbs of Henri Gouraud himself.[138]

The Hallowed Mountain (1933)
The Saga of Anticipation

The heart spoke:
A famed maimed old man has come
To unshackle my mutilated nation

The arm spoke:
With his one remaining arm[139]
He has brought back to my embrace
My dismembered cities!

The brain spoke:
Beirut shall, again,
Be the capital of my thoughts and yearnings![140]

The eyes spoke:
I can make out, in the distant light,
My ancient Phoenician coastline!

The ears spoke:
We shall again hear,
Without shame or fear,
The old motherland's name!

The mouth spoke:
I shall eat, again,
The native bread of my forefathers' plains[141]

The lungs spoke:
Our harbors can finally breathe
The boundless air of the open seas![142]

The feet spoke:
Again and with firm steps
We shall march toward the future,
With heads held up high!

The bones spoke:
Again will we rest
In the reclaimed peace
Of our ancient graveyards!

The blood spoke:
I am surging out from my veins
And coursing to the summit of my soul!

The soul spoke:
I was once immortal,
He brought me back to life![143]

And so, old Lebanon,
Like an ancient cathedral
Whose old statues
Had fallen silent
Since the Middle Ages,
Has suddenly surged back to life!

And so, the graceful outlines
The modest sculptures
And the candid paintings
Of its glowing stained-glass windows,

Once more set ablaze the golden hues
Of once obscure contours,
Along the edges of moldings
And the threshold of frames,

Suddenly coming alive
In their alcoves
And along the ledges
And entablatures,

And within the cusps of stones
Shaking off their dust
And their past quietude,

From the outer sanctuaries
To the sanctums of chapels,
And from the high altar to the flying turrets,
They all told me, with a blushing glow,

This simple and solemn plea,
Stalled between a smile and a tear:

The poet spoke:
The muse has come back!

The gardener spoke:
The laurels are green once more!

The shepherd boy spoke:
I shall have more than just one lamb!

The poacher spoke:
Never again will I steal!

The lumberjack spoke:
I shall plant Cedar trees. [144]

The woodworker spoke:
I shall raise new altars!

The carpenter spoke:
I shall arm battleships!

The emigrant spoke:
We are finally coming home!

The sailor spoke:
The sea has no more wrinkles!

The street-porter spoke:
There are no more burdens to bear!

The blacksmith spoke:
We shall forge new canons!

The shoemaker spoke:
Our old hiking-boots

No longer befit our routes!

The architect spoke:
*The path on which we walk
Has never been clearer!*

The tailor spoke:
*I sized him up
To the glory of his battlefields!*

The smuggler spoke:
There are no more boundaries!

The merchant spoke:
Business is great!

The indigent spoke:
It matters little to go hungry!

The doctor spoke:
*Only too much happiness
Is now the cause of death!*

The lawyer spoke:
All plaintiffs are reconciled!

The peasant spoke:
*A liberated homeland
Is newfound paradise!*

The maidservant spoke:
I am now a princess!

The princess spoke:
*I am now a servant
To all my countrymen!*

The convict spoke:
I shall sin no more!

The nun spoke:
We are no longer needed!

The little girl spoke:
*In my dream I saw him sleeping,
And I was kissing him!*[145]

The young maiden spoke:

I will be married soon!

The old lady spoke:
Freedom is a fount of youth!

The old man spoke:
I shall die without regrets!

The atheist spoke:
I believe in God;
May he protect us all!

The songster spoke:
The hymns of Lebanon,
Which had been sobs and tears,
Are joyful again!

The musician spoke:
The spirits of Lebanon
Are true symphony!

The painter spoke:
When I try to paint him,
My brushes quiver
And the colors go pale! [146]

The goldsmith spoke:
I shall emboss with gold
The iron of our swords!

The sculptor spoke:
Venus of Milo!
Nike of Samothrace!
General Gouraud! [147]

The Hallowed Mountain (1933)
The Saga of Remembrances

We Have Shaken this Planet

If I dare remind my countrymen
Of our Phoenician forefathers,
It is because, back in their heyday,
Long before we ever became
Mere Muslims and Christians,
We were a single nation
At the forefront of History,
United in a single glorious past.

Today, having grown
Into what we have become,
And by virtue of all our modern creeds
—which are all praiseworthy—
We owe it to ourselves
To love one another
The way we did when we were still
Splendid humanist pagans.

[. . .]

We have stirred up this planet,
Labored it to its core,
Plowed its continent,
Molded their laws and lore;
Yet our language has fallen,
In the stillness of night,
Buried, silent, quiet,
And we've remained alive!

Never have we buckled
Under the weight of fate,
Never have we bowed
From calamity's weight
Without feeling a rush
Of blood coursing in our veins,
Heralding redemption,
Proclaiming the return
Of the ancient spirit,
Of the ancient glories,
That propelled our forbears.

Many were the nations that charged our land,
This tiny plot of land,
Which quelled them in the end!
We have witnessed the passing
Of peoples and of Ages,
Yet withstood and endured,
In the glistening horizon,
Steadfast on our peaks,
Peaceful, sober, wise,
Since the early dawn of time!

Many were the Magi,
Poets, Popes, and Princes;
Many were the gods,
Pompous kings and tyrants,

Who have filed at the foot
Of our rugged mountain!
O Ramsis, Aserhaddon,
O Barkuk, Caracalla,
Transcending all your crimes,
Outlasting all your horrors,
The mouth of Nahr-el-Kalb [148]
Has kept but broken shards
Of your gory passage,
On its quiet peaceful shores.

There's never been a nation,
Anywhere on this earth,
Equally small as ours,
With proud destinies like ours,
With fortunes such as ours,
Destined for even more
Glories and good fortunes . . .

Our apanage as a people
Is our restraint and poise,
Our weapons and coat-of-arms
Have been, for six millennia,
To think! . . and to love!! . .
To always bear in mind,
That all else comes to naught!!

For, rancor drains the spirit,
And love quenches the soul;
For, the more loving we can be,
The more joyous we become;
For, to a tender dazzled heart,
Loving one's enemy
Is by far more thrilling
Than a beloved's embrace!

[. . .] Loving one's enemies,
Wicked as they may be,
Is a way of thwarting evil,
A way of gleaning light,
From the shadows of night.

The Hallowed Mountain (1933)
The Saga of Remembrances

Grief, Good Grief!

Grief, good grief!

O unspeakable grief! . . .
Once upon a time, our grand-parents spoke
Syriac at Ghazir,
Syriac, where the Phoenicians' flair,
Their vigor and finesse
Are still extant today;

Alas, no one now,
Can fancy finding shades
Of our grandparents' footsteps,
In the shadow of old vines;
The bygone language of yore,
Is choked for evermore,
In our muzzled scrawny throats.

And now our Mountain,
Ever kind to her sons,
Beholds its splintering skies
Riven by the sounds,
Of foreign Western tongues;
It is a bitter clash
That ails and torments her
With quarrels and heartaches.

For, languages like Italian,
Like English and Greek,
Like Turkish and Armenian
Clutter and jam her voice,
While she willingly yields
To the sweet tyranny
Of the language of France.

Yet, I know that in London,
In Paris and in Rome,
Our writers can never hold
The station they deserve,
That everywhere they go,
Despite their humanity,
They shall always remain
Outside the human race.

For, a people is orphaned
When it hasn't a tongue;
And the languages of others
Are borrowed outer cloaks,
In which one seems dubious,
Shameful, lifeless, frail,
Obnoxious and strange!

For, a man without his language
Is like an intruder
On someone else's feast,
Even when turning up
With the best of intentions,
Loaded with gifts and zeal;

Yet, these foreign-sounding words,
Which are taught to our children,
To us are not that strange;
For, it seems that our hearts
Can still recall remembrances
Of having fashioned them
And styled their graceful sounds!

Indeed, it is they
Who disowned their lineage;
Uprooted from us,
Torn from our embrace,
Embellished by exile,
They now disown their race
Like beloved ingrates.[149]

The Hallowed Mountain (1933)
The Saga of Remembrances

O Spirit of my land

O spirit of my land,
I miss your ancient glories,
Your treasures and your feats,
You inspiring stories,
I miss your high deeds...
I miss your golden years,
Your benevolent prestige!

O spirit of my land,
I miss your boundless wealth,
Whence mankind drew out once
Oceans of abundance;
I miss the high seas
That once carried your ships,
Your benevolent missions,
And your children's ambitions!

No, no, my mother tongue,
You aren't a fallen corpse

In the abyss of time!
I still can feel your verve,
Swelling up in my veins,
Rising like springtide,
Surging up like a wave!

And I still can hear
Your sparkling silver springs
Churning up from the past,
Whispering to my soul.
[. . .] And I still can feel your blazing breath
shimmering over these Eastern shores!

In all of nature's shudders,
Which molded the spirit
Of my distant forefathers,
It's still your warm voice,
And it's still your whispers,
That move about the Eastern skies!

Your soft and graceful inflexions
Still slip their ancient drawl
In all the modern languages
Swarming on our shores;
Your sparse and scattered caresses,
Still flow in my veins
And cuddle with my soul!

And I still can feel your faithful fingers,
Gently knock on memory's door,
Awakening my heart,
With flashbacks of ancient glories,
Filling my soul with joy!

For, even as I write
In someone else's language,
And even when I speak
In someone else's tongue,
It's still you in my voice,
My sainted mother's voice,
Snug like a lover's warmth!

For, Man here below,
In spite of having learnt
His brute oppressor's tongue,
Has kept the looks, the tone,
Has kept the pitch, the pulse,
Of his forefathers' inflections,

Of his old ancestors' voice!

Exiles and vagabonds,
Through all their ports of call,
Still bring along their language,
Still cling to their old brogue,
Still pilfer its perfumes,
Still tinge it with the hues,
Of their first mother's voice!

From one universe to the next,
In spite of time and space,
The languages of mankind
Still seek each other out...
So, let their sounds embrace,
Let their melodies mingle,
Let their clamors entwine!

For, even these sweet words,
Stolen from France's lips,
With impassioned affection
Quivering in my heart,
Still taste on my lips,
Where my smiling sorrow sits,
Still taste of a Lebanese kiss.

MIRACLES OF OUR LADY OF THE SEVEN SORROWS

The following short story was first published in 1949, as part of a collection titled *Les Miracles de la Madone aux Sept Douleurs* (*The Miracles of Our Lady of the Seven Sorrows*). Named for the Beirut *Mater Dolores* Church (in the Ashrafiyyé district) very near to where Charles Corm grew up and was schooled, this collection of "miracles" tell stirring stories of suffering, redemption, and salvation, and are in a sense a celebration of the human spirit, and the triumph of light and hope against darkness and despair. The book *The Miracles of Our Lady of the Seven Sorrows* contains four short stories: a "Christmas Story," a "New Year's Story," a "Palm Sunday Story," and an "Easter Story." All four narratives, written in the style and with emotions reflective of traditional Christian devotional literature, were penned (or, at least, were outlined) during the Great War, by a young Charles Corm profoundly stirred by the calamities that he was witness to—even though his chronicles were published at a much later date. And so the stories are essentially Corm's own personal recollections of the atrocities, devastations, and tragedies suffered in times of conflict. All four "memoirs" are dedicated "To all mothers; all of whom suffer in times of war, for the sake of their children." Charles Corm provided the pencil and charcoal-on-paper illustrations of the *Easter Story*; drawings which were reproduced from a notebook in which the young poet had kept a diary of images and drawings commemorating the war.

It should also be mentioned that the "Seven Sorrows of Mary/The Madona" (Lat. *Mater Dolorosa*) are popular Roman Catholic devotional prayers and meditations over the Virgin Mary's sufferings. The Beirut church by the same name lay in the Ashrafiyyé district where Corm grew up, where he later built the Ford Motor Company headquarters, and where he is buried today, in the Ras el-Nab' Maronite Cemetery where parts of the events of *Easter Story* also take place. Furthermore, the church of the Madonna of the Seven Sorrows was Charles Corm's own parish and the chapel of the Jesuit college (the Université Saint-Joseph) that he attended as a young man. His father, Daoud Corm (1852–1930), as mentioned earlier a pioneer of modern Lebanese religious art, is credited with the murals and other paintings inside the church. At the age of 78, Daoud Corm was reported to have produced one of his most impressive masterpieces; the painting of Saints Sergius and Bacchus astride their horses. The work was a feat of artistic and technical dexterity at once. Being frail and unable to reach the top of his three-meter-high canvas by ladder, Daoud Corm is believed to have asked that the work be turned on its head, and he completed it thusly, by painting its top half upside-down. He died a short time thereafter, on June 6, 1930.

THE MIRACLES OF OUR LADY OF THE SEVEN SORROWS: EASTER STORY (1919)

Some of the events of this story take place in the high mountains of Batroun,[150] in one of the poorest villages of northern Lebanon. Like a bundle of dry wood bearing down on the hunched back of an elderly woman, the village consists of twenty or so flat-roofed homes piled up on the spine of a solitary peak, mingling with the gaunt limestone of surrounding mountains.

Proceeding from the Beirut-Tripoli coastal road, the village cannot be reached except by taking the only rocky exit leading up to it; an exit that wiggles its flaky snake-like skin in between the green coastal hills above the port-city of Byblos.[151] From there, one needs upwards of a nine-hour ascent through the tangled, bushy, circuitous foothills of Batroun, which would then begin an abrupt climb through receding goat-trails that often get lost in the crumbling rubble of majestic peaks towering overhead.

Before reaching the village, there whispers a silent brook, hidden timidly under the gravel of a pine grove buried in a canyon dropping to the foot of the village. A half-hour later, we are at Elché.

Well before reaching the meager vineyards surrounding the village, the visitor is often greeted by a swarm of children, sturdy and carefree, besieging strangers in their midst with their large sunny eyes, bickering like some warriors from Homer,[152] trying to outdo one another offering visitors the hospitality of their neat and modest little hovels.

It was there, in this little lost corner of the world, that in 1902, Morcos Hanna Morcos, who had just returned from a long exile in Mozambique, rich but still proud of his native village, would set out to construct a castle of sorts; an inordinately fantastic structure in its dimensions; a place where he had intended to spend the remaining years of his adventurous life, quietly, tending to the spare dregs of his weary days and the needs of his beloved countrymen.

Morcos wore a thick black mustache that went all the way back to his ears, forming two giant hooks almost snaring his bushy eyebrows. He took great pleasure proudly stroking and smoothing them with his big hairy hand, whose pinky finger, in addition to a motley rings, was adorned with an impressive diamond. On his broad chest, swelled up with confidence and redundant with optimism, hung two huge golden chains, each holding a timepiece the one fancier than the other, each bedecking one pocket of his lavish coral-buttoned vest. A number of multicolored pens, which he could never use given that he could neither read nor write, graced the little breast-pocket of his jacket. Finally, a pair of big flashy reading-spectacles, for which his sharp eyes had no need at all, rested like a proud conqueror astride his prominent nose.

As the fruit of his thirty-years of hard labor in the African jungles, he had brought back with him a thick well-padded purse, overflowing with bank notes. And in order to prove that what he had stashed in that purse was real currency, real Pounds Sterling, and that he had plenty of them to spare, he took great pleasure lending parts of his hard-earned fortune, free of interest, to the notables of Byblos—among whom he had dwelt for some time, and with some ostentation, as he awaited the completion of the work on his dream mountain-castle.

But before Morcos was able to finish installing his roof trusses and sheathing, and cover them with the prized Marseille red tiles, and long before he could complete the monumental internal staircase that was to lead up to the mansion's first floor, most of his debtors, now less willing to pay him back his monies than to ply him with nebulous promises, no longer had qualms openly declaring themselves bankrupt.

And so good old Morcos would now begin cursing the day he had returned to the homeland, complaining and railing loudly about everything and everyone around him; pulling his hair in despair at the mere thought of having to waste what had remained of his fortune on costly liens and endless lawsuits—that may or may not retrieve even a portion of what he had already lost. But like any and all the brave folk of this impregnable mountain, Morcos could not imagine himself resigned to his misfortune. Looking at the bright side, he kept consoling himself with the notion that his castle was almost half finished, and that it was already the talk of the town, from Jounié to Tannourine.[153] And so, all he had left to do now was to count his blessings, cut his losses, and go ahead and complete that castle once and for all already. Gathering up all the courage he could muster, and entrusting the liens owed him to lawyers as devious as his deadbeat borrowers were deceitful, Morcos decided to go back to South Africa, vowing to amass another fortune to allow once more a triumphant return to Elché, and the completion of the construction he had pledged to finish. This time around, he convinced himself, he would not lend a single penny to anyone, and he would spend his hard-earned bread solely to cover the costs of completing his sumptuous pink Ehden-marble staircase, and finishing his Marseille red tiled roof—both feats that would compel the admiration of the entire mountain, spanning a radius of some twenty leagues or more.

Morcos was so certain that he could soon return to the country with a new fortune in tow, that he left sweet Martha, his young bride, behind in Byblos, along with their newborn Farid. But time had passed so quickly, and the money that he had left behind for Martha to provide for herself and their little boy was depleted in a few years' time. Tired of waiting much longer, and anguished by the lack of news coming from Morcos, Emm-Farid[154] set out gradually to sell off her jewelry and home furnishings, so as to afford raising her young boy on her own, bereft of the support of a husband and father.

Behind the towering powerful and colorful trait of character that was Morcos Hanna's had lain the modest figure of sweet Martha—that is, at least until her husband had vanished. Martha was diffident, quiet, her character drawn out in a faint, discrete watermark. But ever since she found herself alone, raising her young boy on her own, fighting with great love and determination for his sake and hers all the adversities of life, the faint watercolors that had defined her self-effacing personality soon began revealing themselves in glowing bolder vigor, displaying hidden virtues that would come to leave a profound imprint on her own destiny, and on the drama that was being played out in the life of her household.

She ended up selling off, for next to nothing, the mahogany piano that glitzy Morcos had bought her on their wedding day; a beautiful instrument that no one knew how to play anyway. Then she sold off the buffet, which had been stocked up with cumbersome and unnecessary serving dishes. Then it was the turn of the lush green and gold armchairs that once graced the living-room, soon to be followed by her linen-cabinet, her lingerie and Morcos's brand new wedding-suit, which he had worn only once. Finally, getting to the end of her rope, Martha picked up the barest of necessities, carried her little one on her back, and headed out on foot, up to Elché, where she reluctantly resigned herself to living in the cellar of her husband's unfinished castle—that structure's only room that could provide a roof over her son's and her own head. And as a memento from the days of her fleeting opulence, she had kept but a few security vouchers and written pledges from deadbeat borrowers, along with a promissory note valued at 500 pounds gold signed by a reluctant village-mukhtar.[155] And by the time she found out from Lebanese natives of Tartej[156] returning home from Transvaal that Morcos had died half mad and in most abject poverty, the war of 1914 had already broken out.

During normal times, and save the obligatory—albeit few—vines and fig-trees strewn about, here and there, around the modest properties of the Lebanese countryside, the people of Elché, like most of the mountaineers of the Batroun district, had made their living from the tobacco industry. A rare few fistfuls of arable land, often torn with great effort from the nooks and crannies of the rocky terrain, and preciously maintained with much skill and sweat and patience on superimposed terraced fields, over time became the ideal setting for tobacco farming, somehow insuring the always frugal, often austere, livelihood of those hardworking brave villagers.

Even Martha would end up planting and caring for hundreds of tobacco plants, grown in the flowerbeds that Morcos had reserved for the Capetown carnations that he had intended for the entrance of his dream castle. A little patch of potatoes, with a little bed of lentils, mint, and parsley, formed the basis of the vegetable garden to which Martha would tend devoutly.

Wheat, barley, and corn, grew only with much difficulty in the bitterly cold high altitudes of Mount-Lebanon, and so, the villagers got in the time-honored habit of buying their grains and wheat stocks from faraway Jounié, which in turn imported those staples from Syria or Egypt. Martha herself often went down to Jounié, and brought back—lugged on her back—her seasonal wheat supplies, which she would stop over to grind on her way back to the village, at a mill near the River Adonis. But the events that were about to grip Europe, a thousand leagues from Lebanon, were going to have their tragic effect on the poor people of the Mountain, making life for Martha more difficult and more perilous by the day.

Ever since Turkey entered the war on the side of the Triple Alliance, its main fixation had become the repudiation of Lebanon's independence and the punishment of its people, longtime friends of the Western powers.[157] Unable to massacre the Lebanese en masse, the Turks set out to instate so-called war effort measures and wartime austerity laws whose sole mission, it seems, had been to starve out the people of Lebanon and annihilate them.

Busy with its own war effort and the hostilities that it was enduring on its own territory, France was unable to lend effective support to her Lebanese friends,[158] who found themselves squeezed in between a Syrian interior blockaded by the Turks, and a Mediterranean coast sealed off from all contacts or exchanges with the outside world. Meanwhile, Allied warships patrolling the high seas beyond the Lebanese coastline had the limited aim of establishing a modest intelligence service, more or less clandestine, and were therefore reluctant to land either troops or supplies to come to the aid of the besieged populations of Lebanon. In turn, the Ottomans took advantage of the situation by expelling the country's main religious and political leaderships, summarily executing sizeable batches of vocal patriots, and exterminating the rest of the population by way of a systematic, well-orchestrated, long-drawn government-actuated famine.

All grain harvests and foodstuffs were thus confiscated by local agents of the Turkish government, who would overnight become the administrators of Turkish "high deeds" on Mount-Lebanon. Only a tiny minority of local Turkophiles was maintained and pampered and replenished, and indeed fattened during those times. And it was this very same local minority of quislings, in connivance with the tyrants, who set up the "black market," thus raking benefits on the corpses of our martyrs.[159]

Based on statistics collected by the Austro-Germans, nearly 300,000 Lebanese perished from hunger between 1915 and 1918—that is to say about one-third of the country's population. No other country on earth has ever had to pay such high and ignominious a blood tribute to the war effort.

Going back to Elché, the inhabitants of this little hamlet, not unlike the other villagers of Batroun and Byblos, were forced by the famine to sell off all that they could dispose off: To wit, entire buildings and their furnishings were sold off to petty shopkeepers in Tripoli and Beirut;[160] upstarts who got promoted overnight to the rank of major businessmen. For a rotten crumb of bread, Lebanon's proud farmers were despoiled and depleted of their dearest possessions. Restaurant owners in the bazaars of Tripoli, most of whom at the beginning of the war ran vile decrepit little taverns selling chickpeas and beans to street-porters and dock-workers, were suddenly buying entire villages with vineyards and orchards spanning towering hillsides on the Lebanese mountains. In some villages, they even went so far as purchasing wholesale cemeteries. Fleeced of their resources, and half dead, the peasants of Mount-Lebanon would now begin flocking to Beirut, the "big city" of their day, hoping to feed themselves from the leftovers of its municipal garbage dumps. City sidewalks, private doorsteps, and church courtyards down to the last and least accessible of public spaces were all literally littered with the dead and dying—some of whom often spending upwards of two entire months in the hunger-throes of unimaginable suffering before finally breathing their last.

The Beirut Municipality, under the close watch of the Turkish Vali[161] and the executioners of the occupying Ottoman army, soon began heaping dead bodies up onto municipal carts, dumping them into the sea. At times, the waves, having vomited one too many cadavers onto the shore and all the way into the Beirut harbor, the Ottoman authorities resigned themselves to changing practice, beginning to dump the corpses directly on the coastal sands south of the city. And Beirut, having of all times had this curious specialty of populating its blue skies with flocks of white doves, often raised by mellow peaceful local lunatics, would soon witness its horizons obscured by clouds of crows, noisily flocking to the spoils.

Jamal Pasha,[162] who often came to spend some time in the wonderful world of the capital city, partaking of its sumptuous orgies, was reportedly outraged one morning at the sight of dark clouds of black birds croaking furiously over his head. He therefore rebuked the Beirut municipal services, which later resolved to dig out new ditches in the cemeteries of Beirut's outskirts, and prepare fresh mass-graves to receive new heaps of the freshly dead.

The old Maronite cemetery of the Medawar quarter was at the time deemed too small and overcrowded to contain all the villagers expiring on the city streets. The new cemetery of Ras el-Nab' was therefore chosen instead; it was still relatively empty at the time, given that it had only recently been donated to the community by Archbishop Chebly of Beirut, who later died in exile in Adana.[163]

"*I'm hungry! . . . I'm hungry! . . . I'm hungry! . . .*" Shrunken and shriveled skeletons, bellies up atop heaps of city garbage dumps, unable to move even to beg for a scrap of food, could still be heard beseeching passers-by for help, for a crumb of bread. Utterly reduced to an abominable skeletal state, passed out as if entranced by the stench of the vermin emanating from their own decomposing bodies, excreting this god-awful hideous hallucinating smell that seems to imbibe this city by day and by night. Some, having already succumbed to their bodies' and their souls' devastation, seemed to have (beforehand) spat up their entrails, dragging them behind them in the filth and the dust of the city streets before collapsing atop the municipal garbage dump; their last hope for a scrap of food.

Bellies swelled up by putrid gazes, sheared shriveled and perforated skins, monstrous gory human waste, feculent and turbid wounds, tortured and gnarled by famine, expired souls, ambulant cadavers, wholesale mass despair. That, in brief, is what had become of the best, the healthiest, the purest, the strongest, the most gentle, the most beautiful, benign, noble, and brave from among the peoples of this assassinated Mountain . . .[164]

Haven't we seen all too many of those scenes back in those days? Haven't we encountered such dreadful sights as if they were the most normal and banal in the world? Innocent babies, rendered to the status of hideous fetuses by famine, still suckling their dead mothers' worm-eaten breasts, until the dreaded municipal dumpster-carts came to sweep them all helter-skelter, and ditch them into ghastly mass graves? . . .

Of course, poor Martha had done her best to spare her son that bitter cup and dodge the general calamity gripping the country. Farid was already twelve-years of age when the war had broken out. And Martha would manage things, through a series of ingenious ploys, until 1917, saving her son from guaranteed starvation. Having remained alone with him in Elché, even after many waves of villagers had already abandoned their homes in search of livelihood, Martha was finally constrained to follow suit. She ended up abandoning the cellar and selling the iron of its reinforced concrete to Miniyé[165] profiteers who had come to retrieve the metal when the unfinished castle had finally been demolished.

Martha moved down to the coastal town of Fidar,[166] where she got temporary employment with a group of woodcutters.[167] And when all the forests had been felled down and depleted to the benefit of fueling the Ottoman railroads, Martha landed herself a housekeeper's position at a nearby inn by the River Adonis.[168] Farid, who was pushing 15 years of age by that time, did his best to help his mother with her work, but the inn soon closed its doors, and both mother and child found themselves on the streets again, destitute, without employment, clutching the Mukhtar's 500 pound promissory note—which Martha had kept hidden, attached around her neck alongside her scapular.

The Mukhtar had become a millionaire by that time, managing the Ottoman Government's food warehouses. And Martha, by dint of insistence and supplication, managed to snatch from him the payment of the debt owed to her. But the Mukhtar, now a wily profiteer, agreed to pay her only after having made a few re-adjustments of his own to the original bill. And so, instead of giving Martha her 500 pounds gold in full, he gave her paper banknotes, and attached to this payment a new onerous ransom: He demanded that she use the money he'd just given her to purchase from his own stockpile a qantar[169] of wheat, at black market prices. This came up to five pounds per rotol.[170] She agreed, and set out with Farid, dragging the qantar of wheat to the Nahr el-Kalb mill.[171] But the Mukhtar's wheat had already been adulterated with sand and gravel, to the point that even after having sifted it, Martha's qantar yielded a mere thirty-five rotols of wheat—instead of the one hundred she had paid for. In other words, Martha was defrauded by the very same Mukhtar who was supposed to protect her, and she ended up paying upwards of fifteen pounds per rotol instead of five—once more depleting whatever little money she had left in her possession.

At any other time, 500 pounds gold would have bought an entire farm and a dozen small orchards in Lebanon; yet they yielded Martha less than a hundred kilos of bad wheat. And such meager pittance is hardly long lasting. Soon, Martha and Farid found themselves scrambling again for ways to keep the specter of death away from them. Martha no longer dared looking her son in the face, as Farid became more emaciated by the hour, gnawed as he'd been by hunger, helplessness, and the terror of death drawing ever nearer by the day.

—*"Go to Baabda,"*[172] said Martha to her son one morning; *"go see our friend Nessib Bey. I hear he is so well off these days that I doubt there would be a thing he wouldn't do to lend us a hand. Remind him of the times he'd spent at our house in Byblos; how he'd pass the hours smoking hookah with your father, designing all these grand business schemes together. Show him all of our ration vouchers, and ask him if he would at least give us one quarter of our allowed quota. Awaiting your return, I will try to go work in the onion fields of the Deir el-Jose monks; this should allow us to pay our friend Nessib Bey for whatever amount of wheat he will have given you."*

And so Farid would set out for Baabda. But it wasn't until after long and humiliating supplications at Nessib Bey's doorsteps that he would be granted an audience with his father's "friend."

—*"Oh, your dear father! . . . Oh, your dear mother! . . . Dear friends of mine! . . . Of course I will help! . . ."* pretended Nessib Bey, with much histrionics. [. . .] *"Of course I shall help! However, at present, all I have in my silos is the lousy grubby kind of stale wheat, which is unworthy of your dear mother, and which has moreover been allocated for the troops. Come see me next week. I want to make sure that you are treated like the dear friend that you are, and I insist on giving you only the best wheat in my possession; the one I reserve for my own family. Come back to see me next week!"*

Farid waited a week, then two, three, and four, only to find himself eventually booted out of the property by Nessib Bey's orderlies; Nessib Bey who suddenly no longer had time to spare for the son of a friend to whom he had owed much.

The little odd jobs that unfortunate little Farid had managed to cobble together here and there in Baabda no longer squelched his searing hunger. In desperation, he decided to head down to Beirut, to try to seek out employment there, any employment there. But Farid was so worn-out and bone-weary by fatigue and hunger that he fell flat on his face several times along the way. He resolved to remain in place, motionless, just for a short while to gather up some strength, and he began begging passersby for anything they might hand him. But he ended up collapsing from exhaustion and starvation on a sidewalk near Beirut's Café des Glaces[173] at the corner of the Place des Canons.[174]

The utter slaughter to which waves of cattle succumb daily, with utmost deliberation and brutality, in the slaughterhouses of Chicago, offer a privileged spectacle of death by comparison to the wicked savagery of the mass killings by hunger meted out on the inhabitants of Mount-Lebanon cramming the streets of Beirut.

Death by starvation is not dying only once and for all; it is dying horribly; it is dying a tortured, ulcerated death, tearing at one's throat and chest and heart and loins; it is dying endlessly, all the time, multiple times, every minute of every day, and every week for several months.

Farid was now, no doubt, facing this terrible end.

Seeing her son having tarried much longer in Baabda than she had expected, Martha set out to go look for him. But he was nowhere to be found. And so she began running frantically from one village to the next, from Hadath, to Wadi Chahrour, to Chiaaah and Bourg el-Brajneh where someone finally mentioned to her having perhaps glimpsed a small street-vendor fitting Farid's description. Unkempt, disheveled, panting, and with her mouth frothing with dust and foam, Martha desperately clung to people on the streets, begging passersby, invoking all the saints, and screaming her little boy's name out-loud, through the countryside, lest he would hear her. The insatiable voracious hunger already strangling her could no longer cause her pain, now that both her heart and her eyes—whose sole nourishment had been the sheer presence of her beloved little Farid—were more famished than ever for a mere glimpse of him.

By dint of drinking water, and drinking water some more, thus dosing the fires searing her charred heart, and no longer being able to eat anything besides the unhealthy wild grasses torn along the roadsides as she was roaming the streets aimlessly, her belly began swelling up and weighing her down as if it'd been carrying lead, and her loins were rendered burning embers, embedded like red hot irons inside her back....

But the most horrible of all her encounters, as she ran desperately across the deserted countryside that was in this new season beginning to anoint itself with new scents of orange blossoms, was her constantly stumbling against the carrion stench, leaping out at her from the shadow of some green bush, scratching her in the face like a heart-wrenching reminder of the probable fate awaiting her own beloved child....

Then one day, as she had collapsed and lain exhausted before a small spring in the town of Choueifat, she felt as if surrounded and overtaken by those cruel smells of death. Soon enough, she realized that she had been in front of the remains of a beautiful young woman, already in a state of decomposition, and whose one-year-old baby was ceaselessly kissing her head swarming with flies....

—*"Ya waladi! Ya waladi! Ya Farid! Yaaa Farid!"*[175] she cried out staggering away in horror. Words emanated from her as if torn from her chest, crumbling in her parched throat, falling in fragments, carrying with them into the void little pieces of her heart.

She finally dragged herself all the way down to Beirut. But when she saw the scenes of the doom and damnation of an entire people filling the streets with their moans, and when she came upon heaps of the dead and half-living piled up together, being readied to be ditched outside the city walls, she fell straight down in the direction of Caracol el-Abd, and kept on crawling on her stomach, perhaps for days on end, in the direction of the sands south of the city, then in the direction of the Karantina, north of the Beirut Harbor, in order to scratch and dredge around the mass graves, looking for some vestige of her lost child.

But all in vain; it was all in vain. And all the heroic efforts of a poor soul in agony would do nothing except drain and exhaust Martha's heart further, and deplete her completely of what had remained of her energy, until she blanked out and got ever closer to the looming eternal twilight beckoning to her. As for Farid, he too had also bit the dust, for many, many weeks now, hardly able to get back up on his feet again.

Meanwhile a banana peel, the skins of a few peanuts, and empty bean pods thrown out the window of the Café des Glaces sustained Farid for another week. Then one day, around noon, a caravan of some five camels laden with Sidon oranges made their way through the Place des Canons—which, at that time, had not yet been paved. A springtime shower of sleet and rain had turned the streets into a quagmire of soft frozen mud. One of the camels slipped into this tide, fell over, and dropped its load of oranges onto the mud, causing torrents of fruits to roll from all sides all over the square, and toward the curb where Farid lay. For Farid this was like a God-sent celestial manna. He braced himself unto the pavement, and gathering all the strength that his drained body could muster, he crawled onto his chest until he got ahold of a single solitary orange. Grasping it while it dripped with mud and dung, he brought it closer to his chattering teeth. But suddenly, the Bedouin leading the caravan pounced upon Farid, snatching the orange from his hand and kicking him toward the wall of the café where the boy would fall again unconscious.

That same evening, paralyzed, lifeless, cataleptic, Farid was carried away with piles of corpses, hauled over onto the municipal truck and driven off to the nearest mass grave.

It was the evening of Good Friday. The terrified and tongue-tied city of Beirut seemed to be slumbering under heavy darkened skies. Yet the smothered hearts of its people were hardly dreaming; rather they were ruminating sinister nightmares.

At the very same moment that Farid was being thrown into the common grave of Ras el-Nab', Martha was awoken and shaken to the depths of her soul by a sudden commotion. Unconcerned by any of her surroundings, she began rowing with both her arms and legs in the filth that the city had become, in the direction of the Jesuit college chapel, to ask the Madonna of the Seven Sorrows to return her disappeared child to her.

It took her an entire day before she finally made it to her destination. But the church was bolted shut, guarded by a Turkish sentry. Determined to somehow enter the sanctuary, Martha leaned back against one of the church's outer walls, and recalling in her mind's eye the altar where the Blessed Virgin had her compassionate arms stretched out to the faithful, revealing her pierced mother's heart, she cried out to her:

—*"Mary! Mary! Save my child! Give my son back to me! . . . Have mercy on him! Have mercy on my Farid, Mary, in the name of your own Son! . . ."*

Then Martha felt an inexplicable jolt running down against her back as she leaned on the edge of the church door. It was as if all of the University buildings had suddenly begun convulsing in response to the call of her heart; as if telling her that the Blessed Virgin had heard her plea.

What happened next was so outrageous, so implausible, that the reader is urged to check the facts for himself before reaching a conclusion.

The custodian of the Maronite cemetery of Ras el-Nab', Salim Feghalé, who is still living, and who is now married and raising a beautiful family residing in the very lodge of this very same cemetery, where anyone can go visit him today, relates lying down for the evening in the alcove to the left of the cemetery's entrance gate. It was a balmy, muggy evening, with nary a breath of air, nary a noise, and nary a movement disturbing the stillness of the night. The cemetery's common grave, though covered as it was with a film of sand, overwhelmed the entire neighborhood with its offensive stench, and prevented Salim Feghalé from sleeping that night. Suddenly, shattering the first-light of that quiet Easter Sunday, Feghalé reported having heard a scream rising from the back of the cemetery, from behind the young olive trees, the area marking the common grave. He ran to the window to look in the direction of the scream, and felt as if his eyes and ears were being torn from his face and hung onto the howl that had pierced the darkness of early dawn.

Then, there was a voice that would have passed for almost human had it not emitted a timber of a wild monstrous sound, like the throttling of an inverted bark, like a cry from beyond the grave. Then Salim saw something moving at the edge of the pit, something rolling in the sand, then collapsing, then standing up half-way, staggering, then bolting through the front gate and out of the cemetery, running up toward the hills of Ashrafiyyé, panting a disgusted breath, shaking off long bony arms as if revolted by something it might have brushed against.

It was Farid.

Salim never found out whether the resurrected boy was ever reunited with his mother—whom Salim himself never had the pleasure of meeting. But Salim nevertheless did run into Farid, on multiple occasions after the war, and he realized that this ghost of the dark days of yesteryear was now leading a normal existence, without anyone even fathoming what living hell he had actually returned from.

Salim even remembers one day coming upon a person with an uncanny resemblance to Farid, at a hardware and building supplies store. The ghost was inquiring about the price of Marseilles red-tiles, and the cost of their transport from Beirut to Elché.

The last time that Farid and Salim would meet again was following a procession of the Congregation of the Children of Mary, at the Jesuit chapel, gathered before the bleeding (and always generous) heart of Our Lady of the Seven Sorrows.

EROTIC TALES (1912)

Charles Corm prefaced this collection with a plea that, in his words, was at once "immodest and respectful." Incidentally, he also dedicated the collection to the woman who would be his wife one day, *and* to French erotica author Pierre Louÿs. The plea and dedication read as follows:

> Let him the first among men who has never experienced the ecstasy of carnal love, / Let him cast the first stone. / Here are the little white pebbles / That I have tossed along the way, / A little Tom Thumbling of Love, / In the thicket of forests of big cities. / I would not venture to say / That the ogress of Pleasure / Has eaten me whole yet, / However, I will say the following: / I am no longer able / To find my way / To the footprints that may lead me back / To the home of Childhood.

Dedication:

> An immodest and respectful tribute / To the one who will be my wife. / To Pierre Louÿs, / Whom I love very much, and who does not know me.

Erotic as they may seem at first glance, these texts of *Contes Érotiques* ultimately prove to be profoundly spiritual; an adolescent's tributes as it were to his life's first encounters with love, perhaps some of it "imagined" or "fantasized" love, but certainly lyrical hymns testifying to Corm's love of country.

The opening poem in the series, *Phoenicia*, which Corm billed "the opening prayer," appears to have been written between 1911 and 1912 (the manuscript itself is dated 1912). However, some of its references may suggest a later date—or perhaps later edits and minor re-writes that the author might have played around with. Although prepared for publication by Charles Corm during his lifetime, and subtitled *"Variations sur le mode sentimental"* (*Variations of the Sentimental*), the text of the *Erotic Tales* would remain unpublished and in manuscript form until 2011. The collection plots the trajectory of young Charles Corm's growing pains, his "puppy love" as it were, and his reluctant departure from childhood. The *Phoenicia* selection is clearly the story of his first love, perhaps his early adolescent's sexual experience. Yet *Phoenicia* seems to also be Corm's ode to Phoenician Lebanon, arguably his first and only love—as the conclusion of the text may reveal. Notwithstanding the erotic nature of the recollections recorded herewith, their sexual references remain surprisingly subtle, discrete, mystical, even at times prudish, often confusing the reader as to whether the author was extoling a beloved woman or a beloved homeland. Either way, the style and symbolisms of the text, throughout *Erotic Tales*, brim with Biblical imagery culled from both Christian and Hebrew traditions. This rhetorical device, often wedding the Judaeo-Christian ethics and heritage (into which Charles Corm himself was socialized) to Pagan Canaanite-Phoenician allegory, pervaded his literary production. Both monotheistic "puritanism" and Pagan "sensuality" are valorized in Corm's work, even as an adolescent. Moreover, Judaeo-Christian monotheism and Phoenician Paganism, with the latter having alluded to the idea of a "compassionate" deity, are essential elements (in Corm's telling) of the liberal compassionate humanism that he advocated, and which was the bequest of the Phoenicians that he admired and deemed progenitors of the modern Lebanese. Youthful and clumsy in its innocence as this particular poem may appear, its Phoenician themes are unmistakable. This is all the more remarkable given Corm's age at the time that this adolescent supplication was written. Even at seventeen years of age, Charles Corm had already mastered the stylistic, thematic, and emotive hybridity (again, a fundamental Phoenician characteristic in his telling) which he would continue practicing and advocating later in life, as an older seasoned man of letters, and as doyen of modern Lebanese *belles lettres.*

The Opening Prayer, *Phoenicia* (1912)

She stands erect and bare before my ecstatic eyes. The sun coats her with caresses. Her perfectly harmonious outlines stand out against the dark background of old Phoenician curtains. Her feet tread an ancient carpet of Asia; a red carpet; red with the blood of souls poured out in tribute to her.[176]

On a tripod next to her, an old inlaid silver incense burner quietly consumes itself. Spirals of fragrant smoking incense curl up lovingly around her youth.

Like the ascending outlines of burning incense enshrouding her, the outlines of my imagination enfold her as well, in sly searing words: imperfect exaggerated words, like the outlines of the burning incense…

Her hair is a sea whose copper-colored waves come crashing on the sunny beach of her shoulders.[177]

Her forehead is a mirror reflecting light; her forehead is a cultic cry!

Her eyebrows are two black comets, two curved swords, and two triumphal arches.

Her eyes are two vistas. Her eyes, between the streams of eyelashes, are two lakes of damp shade reflecting an internal moonlight.

Her pupils are two large black grapes.

Her cheeks are two downy peaches, with hints of rose petals.

Her aquiline nose is a miniature hallowed hill.[178]

Her thin translucent nostrils, quivering and delicate, are two wings of a butterfly.

Her tiny plump ears are seashells that carry the mysteries of a voice;[179] they are homes peopled with melodies; they are temples where my prayer goes to kneel.

Her lips are Cupid's drawn bow, whence a word is on the verge of being discharged, to strike me in the heart. Her lips are triumphal banners, blood-soaked and happy. Her lips are smiles.

Her teeth are white Carrara marble surrounding the pool that is her mouth.

In the pool that is her mouth, wiggles the little goldfish that is her sweet tongue. Her tongue is a bountiful bit of jam.

Her chin is sexed up with a dimple that seems to be a nest for a kiss.

Her tender neck is round like the collar of a fresh alcarazas.[180]

Her throat is bathed in milk and ticklish amber.

Her armpits are retreats for blonde foam and fragrant shade.

Her arms are a stirring gesture. Her arms are a soaring ascent. Her arms are wings!

Her folded elbow is like a living handle for the vase that is her body.

In the crease of her elbow a blue dipping beckons the red lips.

Her hands are the rare flowers of an outlandish hothouse.

Her slender fingers awaken like the rays of a star.

The fingernails of her hands are like delicate mica.

At the root of her fingernails, I was surprised to find a silver crescent.

The fine grain of her skin is the celestial manna.

Her delicate and firm breasts are twin siblings. Her white, soft, and round breasts, like two full moons, never make like quarter-moons.

Her breasts are quilts to lull the sleep of heroes and of gods.

The tips of her breasts are blooming buds, buttons of ruby, crimson candy.

Her smooth belly is a shield of shivering pearl.

And the navel is in the middle, like a mouth made for silence, like a lock for the mystery below.

Her pubis is a gentle slope . . .

And her secret, in the foam, is a source of intoxication and perfume. Her pink secret is rebounded like an apple. Her beautiful secret is a ripe fruit in a divine orchard.

Her dear secret fills my caressing hand, and its frizzy hairs exhaust the eager energy of my fingers.

In the middle of the secret, two small vertical lips emerge, even and crimsoned. They open and they close, as if silently whispering troubling and mysterious invocations. More so than the lips of the mouth, the lips of the secret are beautiful indeed!

More so than the mouth of the face, the lips of the secret have a tongue erect and mischievous, although it only leaves the temple when beckoned by the supplications of love.

Her hips curve up, like pure amphora. Her hips drip with freshness, like the falling snow. Her hips are slippery, like the glaze of fortresses.

Her slender legs are the pillars of heaven. Her elegant legs are like leaping gazelles.

Her knees are little sachets of benzoin soap; little honey cakes.

Her calves are molded in a nervous alabaster; subtly, they go thinner as they drop to the neck of her foot.

The neck of her foot, veined with emeralds, deserves the most beautiful necklaces of the most beautiful necks.

Her arched foot is the most precious ornament in the world. Her little delicate impressionable foot, is worthy of musk, nard, and myrrh, and Magdalena's humiliated hair.[181]

Her toes are carved in coral and carmine, in nougat and fondant.

Her tiny toenails are glistening droplets of holy water.

And the soles of her feet are made to walk all over the life of humans.

Proceeding to the back of her "legs," her hamstrings are a resting place for the bewildered eyes.

Past the globes that home in on the earthly pleasures, one happens upon a narrow valley, where another mouth smiles like a grenadine flower falling onto a bed of violets, or like a golden ring in a fold of velvet.

Then the valley widens, revealing her loins, rising again, safely, between the plains of her majestic back, and along her spine, like a beautiful path leading up to the horizon.

And on the left and right sides of her back, her light shoulder-blades unfold upon her torso, like exquisite fans.

The back of her neck...

And I'm back, safe and sound, thank God, to her hair, whose braided strands are like the heavy clusters of an immortal vine.

It is there, under the Lebanon skies, which flood you in a shower of lights; it is there, on the holy land, which holds you piously before the enchanting Mediterranean sea cradling your dreams; it is there, in the breath and in the skies of an ancient East, nostalgic and outdated, that, trembling, I recalled the eternal landscape of your beloved body. And it is in memory of our beautiful love that I drew these clumsy arabesques.

May you forgive me should you deem them unworthy, if only in memory of our beautiful love, O child of my race, O daughter of Lebanon, O Phoenicia.

NOTES

1. Maurice Barrès, *Une Enquête aux pays du Levant* (Paris: Librairie Plon, 1924), 33.
2. Paul Morand, *Méditerranée, Mer des Surprises* (Paris: Éditions du Rocher, 1990,) 206.
3. Meir Zamir, *The Formation of Modern Lebanon* (Ithaca and London: Cornell University Press, 1985), 5–6.
4. Zamir, 5.
5. Zamir, 126.
6. Vicomte de Vogüe, "Voyage au Pays du Passé," in *Le Voyage en Orient; Anthologie des Voyageurs Français dans le Levant au XIXème Siècle* (Paris: Robert Laffont, 1985), 778.
7. Charles Reynaud, "Catholiques et Français, Toujours!" in *Le Voyage en Orient,* 771–72.
8. Jean Raymond, "Le Liban: Terre Traditionnelle de Liberté; Textes Commentés, Tirés des Récits des Voyageurs Occidentaux du 16ème au 18ème Siecles," *Cahiers de l'Oronte,* No. 7 (Beirut, 1967), 16.
9. Raymond, 14.
10. Raymond, 16.
11. Jacques Tabet, *La Syrie; Historique, Ethnographique, Religieuse, Geographique, Economique, Politique et Sociale* (Paris: Alphonse Lemerre, 1920), 29.
12. Chiha, *Visage et Présence,* 147 and 166.
13. A 1919 memorandum from the Buenos Aires chapter of the *Union Libanaise,* MAE, Levant 1918–1940, Syrie-Liban, Volume 17, Serie E. Carton 313, Dossier 27.
14. Philippe Hitti, *Taarikh Lubnan* [*The History of Lebanon*] (Beirut, Lebanon: Dar al-Thaqafa, 1985), 4–5. Note this is the Arabic translation of Hitti's English language *Lebanon in History,* and will be referred to herewith under that title, not *The History of Lebanon.*
15. A 1921 memorandum from the *League for the Defense of Greater Lebanon's Rights.* MAE, Levant 1918–1940, Syrie-Liban, Volume 17, Serie E. Carton 313, Dossier 27.
16. André Duboscq, *Syrie, Tripolitaine, Albanie* (Paris: Librairie F. Alcan, 1914), 5.
17. T. E. Lawrence, *Seven Pillars of Wisdom,* 33.
18. Hitti, *Lebanon in History,* 4–5.
19. Kamal Salibi, "Fakhreddin al-Thani w al-Fikra al-Lubnaniyya" [Fakhreddin II and the Lebanese Idea]. *Les Dimensions du Nationalisme Libanais* (Kaslik, Lebanon: Editions de l'Université Saint-Esprit, 1970), 110–11.
20. Salibi, *Les Dimensions,* 107–8.
21. For more on this and the Maronites' desiderata following World War I, see the introduction.
22. See for instance Daoud Pacha (1861–1868), Franko Pacha (1868–1873), and Ohannes Pacha (1912–1915).
23. Maronites and other Christian communities were initially, and under the regime of the *Règlement Organique,* exempt from service in the Ottoman army.
24. See for instance the memorandum of *Union Libanaise,* dispatched to the Quai d'Orsay from Buenos Aires in February 1919, outlining the desiderata of the Lebanese diaspora. (Paris: MAE, Levant 1918–1940, Syrie-Liban, Volume 17, Serie E. Carton 313, Dossier 27.) After giving the Quai d'Orsay a drawn-out lesson in Lebanese history, the *Union Libanaise* memorandum requests French assistance in the "restitution of Lebanon in its natural and historical frontiers."
25. See for instance the following *Union Libanaise* memo. (Paris: MAE, Levant 1918–1940, Syrie-Liban, Volume 17, Serie E. Carton 313, Dossier 27.) "The Lebanese are in fact descended from the ancient Phoenicians; the latter having extended their highly evolved civilization throughout their then known world [. . .]; they were subjected to the suzerainty of

Rome and Byzantium, as well as to that of the Arabs, Crusaders, the Sultans of Egypt, and the Ottoman Turks. Nevertheless, they were able to preserve their own customs and national attributes. [. . .] Those Lebanese raise their voices one more time, before the Great Powers of the world, to request what is scarcely excessive. They demand their independence before anything else, [. . .] and the restitution of their territories to their natural and historical frontiers."

26. Corm, *6000 Ans de Génie Pacifique au Service de l'Humanité,* 15–16.
27. Corm, *6000 Ans de Génie Pacifique au Service de l'Humanité,* 18.
28. Corm, *6000 Ans de Génie Pacifique au Service de l'Humanité,* 18.
29. Corm, *La Montagne Inspirée,* 131. It should be noted that the surname "al-Chidiac," which is the common Arabic term of "church deacon," is actually the corruption of the French "archidiacre" or "archdeacon." This is clearly a reflection of the Corms issuing from a line of church and court officials.
30. Hitti, *Lebanon in History,* 142.
31. Corm, *La Montagne Inspirée,* 131.
32. Corm, *La Montagne Inspirée,* 131.
33. Corm, *La Montagne Inspirée,* 131.
34. Ernest Renan, *Mission de Phénicie,* Third Fascimile Edition (Beirut: Editions Terre du Liban, 1998), 846–48. See also Maurice Barrès, *Une Enquête aux Pays du Levant* (Paris: Librairie Plon, 1924), 54–55.
35. Barrès, *Une Enquête,* 54–55.
36. Barrès, *Une Enquête,* 50.
37. Barrès, *Une Enquête,* 50.
38. Barrès, *Une Enquête,* 49.
39. Barrès, *Une Enquête,* 50.
40. Charles Corm, *Curriculum Vitae* (Beirut: Charles Corm Archives, November 27, 1948), 1.
41. Conversation with David Corm at the Ras el-Nab' Maronite Cemetery of Beirut, July 2012.
42. Corm, *Curriculum Vitae,* 4.
43. Youssef Ghsoub, *Shaarl Qorm; Sawt Lubnaan al-Madwiyy* [Charles Corm; The Resounding Voice of Lebanon] (Beirut: Charles Corm Archives, ND), manuscript, 1. See also *Al-Hikma* (Beirut: The Hikma Institute, Volume 11, Number 9, December 1963), 451.
44. Ghsoub, 451.
45. Ghsoub, 451.
46. Unsi El-Hajj, "Charles Corm," *an-Nahar,* Beirut, September 20, 1963.
47. El-Hajj, "Charles Corm."
48. Charbel Tayyah, "L'idée de Dieu et la "spiritualité" dans l'œuvre de Charles Corm," *Al-Manarat; Revue de Sciences Religieuses* (Jounié, Lebanon: Congrégation des Missionnaires Libanais, Vol. 31, No. 1, 1990), 190.
49. Jamil Jabr, "Charles Corm and Lebanon," *Al-Hikma,* Vol. 11, No. 9 (Beirut, September 1963), 450.
50. See above for details.
51. See Charles Baudelaire's "Une charogne" in *Les Fleurs du Mal,* where he writes:

Rappelez-vous l'objet que nous vîmes, mon âme, / Ce beau matin d'été si doux: / Au detour d'un sentier une charogne infâme / Sur un lit semé de cailloux, / Les jambes en l'air, comme une femme lubrique, / Brûlante et suant les poisons, / Ouvrait d'une façon nonchalante et cynique / Son ventre plein d'exhalaisons. / Le soleil rayonnait sur cette pourriture, / comme afin de la cuire à point, / Et de rendre au centuple à la grande Nature / Tout ce qu'ensemble elle avait joint; / Et le ciel regardait la carcasse superbe / Comme une fleur s'épanouir. / La puanteur était si forte, que sur l'herbe / Vous crûtes vous évanouir. / Les mouches bourdonnaient sur ce ventre putride, / D'où sortaient de noirs bataillons / De larves, qui coulaient comme un épais liquid / Le long de ces vivants haillons. / Tout cela descendait, montait comme une vague / Ou s'élançait en pétillant; / On eût dit que le corps, enflé d'un souffle vague, / Vivait en se multipliant. / Et ce monde rendait une étrange musique, / comme l'eau courante et le vent, / Ou le grain qu'un vaneur d'un movement rythmique / Agite et tourne dans son van. / Les formes d'effaçaient et n'étaient plus qu'un rêve, / Une ébauche lente à venir / Sur la toile oubliée, et que l'artiste achève / Seulement par le souvenir. / Derrière les rochers une chiene inquiète / Nous regardait d'un oeil fâché, / Epiant le moment de reprendre au squelette / Le morceau qu'elle avait lâché. / —Et pourtant vous serez semblable à cette ordure, / À cette horrible infection, / Étoile de mes yeux, soleil de ma nature, / Vous, mon ange et ma passion! / Oui! telle vous serez, ô la reine des grâces, / Après les derniers sacrements, / Quand vous irez, sous l'herbe et les floraisons grasses, / Moisir parmi les ossements. / Alors, ô ma beauté! dites à la vermine / Qui vous mangera de baisers, / Que j'ai gardé la forme et l'essence divine / De mes amours decomposés!

52. Conversation with David Corm, July 2012.
53. El-Hajj, "Charles Corm."
54. Diogenes, having made virtue of poverty, was reported to have lived in a ceramic barrel—perhaps the barrel that Corm is making allusion to here—and to have repudiated and mocked authority. This is perhaps best illustrated in a famous encounter with Alexander the Great during which the Macedonian asked Diogenes (who had been lazing in the sun) if he needed anything, and to which the philosopher replied, "Yes, stand out of my sunlight." At this, a pleased Alexander was reported to have exclaimed, "If I were not Alexander, then I should wish to be Diogenes," causing Diogenes to quip, "and if I were not Diogenes, I should also wish to be Diogenes."
55. Charles Corm, *Je Cherche un Homme* (Beirut: Charles Corm Archives, ND). See also *La Revue du Liban* (Beirut: October 26, 1963).
56. This is the title of a lecture that Charles Corm delivered on June 7, 1949, as the UNESCO's General Assembly was convening in Beirut.
57. Corm, *La Montagne Inspirée,* 36.
58. Corm, *Je Cherche un Homme.*
59. Michel Chiha, "Entretiens de Patrice," *La Revue Phénicienne* (Beirut: Éditions de la Revue Phénicienne, August 1919), 91.
60. Charles Corm, "Méditations Nationalistes," *La Revue Phénicienne* (Beirut: Éditions de la Revue Phénicienne, September 1919), 174.
61. Corm, "Méditations Nationalistes," 174.
62. Corm, "Méditations Nationalistes," 174–79.
63. Paul Noujaim, "La Question du Liban; Étude de Politique Économique et de Statisque Descriptive," *La Revue Phénicienne* (Beirut, Éditions de la Revue Phénicienne, Volume 1, Number 2, August 1919), 66.
64. René Ristelhueber, *Traditions françaises au Liban* (Paris: Librairie Félix Alcan, 1918), v–vi. Emphasis in the original text.
65. Corm, "Méditations Nationalistes," 174.
66. Corm, "Méditations Nationalistes," 174–75.
67. Corm, "Méditations Nationalistes," 175.
68. Corm, "Méditations Nationalistes," 175.
69. Corm, *La Montagne Inspirée,* 31–2.
70. Corm, "Méditations Nationalistes," 175.
71. Corm, "Méditations Nationalistes," 175.
72. "Charles Corm as I Knew Him; An Interview with Samia Corm," *Al-Hikma* (Beirut: The Hikma Institute, Volume 11, Number 9, December 1963), 454.
73. Saïd Akl, "Charles Corm," *Al-Hikma* (Beirut: The Hikma Institute, Volume 11, Number 9, December 1963), 458.
74. Cédar, "Les Impressions d'un Jeune Phénicien d'Aujourd'hui," *La Revue Phénicienne* (Beirut: Éditions de la Revue Phénicienne, July 1919), 30. Cédar is one of the pen names used by Charles Corm.
75. Cédar, "Les Impressions," 30.
76. Charles Corm, "Rendons le Sol au Paysan" [Let Us Give the Land Back to the Peasant], *La Revue Phénicienne* (Beirut: Éditions de la Revue Phénicienne, Christmas 1919), 271.
77. Corm, "Rendons le Sol au Paysan," 272.
78. Corm, "Rendons le Sol au Paysan," 272.
79. Corm, "Rendons le Sol au Paysan," 272.

80. Corm, "Rendons le Sol au Paysan," 270.
81. Corm, *Curriculum Vitae*, 2.
82. Corm, *Curriculum Vitae*, 2.
83. Corm, *Curriculum Vitae*, 2.
84. Cédar, "Les Impressions," 31.
85. Cédar, "Les Impressions," 31.
86. Cédar, "Les Impressions," 31.
87. E. Le Veilleur, "Les Propos d'un Français" [In the Words of a Frenchman], *La Revue Phénicienne* (Beirut: Éditions de la Revue Phénicienne, August 1919), 82. E. Le Veilleur is one of the pen names used by Charles Corm.
88. Le Veilleur, "Les Propos d'un Français," 83.
89. Le Veilleur, "Les Propos d'un Français," 82.
90. Le Veilleur, "Les Propos d'un Français," 83.
91. Le Veilleur, "Les Propos d'un Français," 82.
92. Le Veilleur, "Les Propos d'un Français," 83.
93. Le Veilleur, "Les Propos d'un Français," 83.
94. "Le bûcheron m'a dit: Je vais planter des cèdres!" See Corm, *La Montagne Inspirée*, 17.
95. Charles Corm, *Programme de l'Association des Amis des Arbres* [*Program of the Association of the Friends of the Trees*] (Jounié, Lebanon: Missionaries' Press, 1934), 1.
96. Corm, *Program of the Association*, 1.
97. Corm, *Program of the Association*, 1.
98. Corm, *Program of the Association*, 2.
99. Corm, *Program of the Association*, 2.
100. Corm, *Program of the Association*, 2.
101. Corm, *Program of the Association*, 2.
102. Corm, *Program of the Association*, 2–3.
103. See for instance the (once) world-renowned annual Bikfayya Flower Festival, which was inaugurated in 1935, and for a time, before the Lebanese Civil War of 1975, attracted participants representing a number of European nations, including France. The Bikfayya Flower Festival featured floats covered with flowers parading through the village's main street, accompanied by marching bands and street performances, all culminating in the election of the year's three "beauty queens": the Queen of Flowers, the Queen of Fruits, and the Queen of Sports. The festival was interrupted during the Lebanese Civil War, and was re-launched in 2013.
104. Charles Corm, "L'Exemple," *Société des Amis des Arbres du Liban; Fête de l'Arbre* (Bhamdoun, Lebanon: May 5, 1935), 3.
105. Akl, "Charles Corm," 458.
106. Hektor Klat telegram from Sao Paolo, May 29, 1949 (Beirut: Charles Corm Archives, May 29, 1949).
107. See Asher Kaufman's *"Tell Us Our History"; Charles Corm, Mount-Lebanon, and Lebanese Nationalism*, in *Middle Eastern Studies*, Vol. 40, No. 3, May 2004, 1–28.
108. Multiple anecdotes about this can be found in Charles Corm's unpublished private papers. It is important to note here that Corm's only spoken languages at the time were vernacular Lebanese and French; he also knew and made use of Classical Arabic, but that was never a spoken language. See also "Charles Corm, le visionnaire," in *L'Orient-Le Jour* (Beirut, September 24, 2009), 16.
109. As mentioned earlier, a distinct independent Lebanese entity had not yet come into being at that time.
110. Charles Corm Archives; see for instance letters between Corm and Eliahu Epstein, dated January 25, 1938; February 22, 1938; March 3, 1938; April 26, 1938, etc.
111. See earlier in this chapter Epstein's review of Charles Corm's *La Montagne Inspirée* in the *Palestine Post*.
112. Charles Corm Archives; letters from Eliahu Epstein dated May 6, 1935, and January 25, 1938. In the 1938 letter, Epstein informs Corm that Nahum Slousch was currently "out of Jerusalem but is expected back next week. On his arrival I shall discuss with him the matter in a more definite fashion and will let you have details."

144 Chapter 2

113. Rushdy Maalouf, "Yabisat Arza" [A Cedar Tree Has Died], *Al-Hikma* (Beirut: The Hikma Institute, Volume 11, Number 9, December 1963), 463.
114. Maalouf, "Yabisat Arza," 463.
115. Maalouf, "Yabisat Arza," 463. Emphasis in the original.
116. Short for *Maison Blanche de Beyrouth* (The Beirut White House), which was the name under which Corm's residence (and the former Ford headquarters) was known locally.
117. Maalouf, "Yabisat Arza," 463.
118. Robert de Caix was General Henri Gouraud's secretary during his tenure as French High Commissioner to the States of the Levant from 1919 to 1923.
119. Corm, *Curriculum Vitae*, 5.
120. Charles Corm, *La Terre Assassinée ou les Ciliciennes* [The Murdered Homeland or the Cilicians] (Beirut: Editions de la Revue PHénicienne, 2004), 131–32.
121. Corm, *La Terre Assassinée*, 132.
122. Quoted in Kevork Bardakjian's *Hitler and the Armenian Genocide* (Cambridge, MA: The Zoryan Institute, 1985). It first appeared in Louis P. Lochner's *What about Germany?* (New York: Dodd, Mead & Co. 1942), 1–4.
123. Corm, *La Montagne Inspirée*, 47.
124. Corm, *La Montagne Inspirée*, 104.
125. Élie Tyane, *Lumière sur la Montagne* (Beirut: Éditions de la Revue Phénicienne, 1935), 7.
126. Tyane, *Lumière sur la Montagne*, 8.
127. See E. M., "La Revue du Liban et de l'Orient Méditerranéen," Paris, February 1934, in *Extraits de la Critique* (Beirut: Éditions de la Revue Phenicienne, 1935), 3.
128. E. M., "La Revue du Liban et de l'Orient Méditerranéen," 3–4.
129. Tyane, *Lumière sur la Montagne*, 12–13.
130. See further details earlier in the chapter.
131. Corm, *La Montagne Inspirée*, 31–32.
132. Jeanne Arcache, "La Bourse Egyptienne," Alexandria, February 8, 1935, in *Extraits de la Critique* (Beirut: Éditions de la Revue Phenicienne, 1935), 6.
133. Charrier, "Domestic and Foreign Research," New York, November 25, 1934, in *Extraits de la Critique* (Beirut: Éditions de la Revue Phenicienne, 1935), 4.
134. Eliahu Epstein, "Lebanese Renaissance: La Montagne Inspirée by Charles Corm," *Palestine Post*, Jerusalem, February 24, 1935, in *Extraits de la Critique* (Beirut: Éditions de la Revue Phenicienne, 1935), 8.
135. Albert Naccache, *L'Orient*, Beirut, January 14, 1934, in *Extraits de la Critique* (Beirut: Éditions de la Revue Phenicienne, 1935), 8.
136. Naccache, *L'Orient*, 8.
137. Adel Ismail, *Le Liban, Documents Diplomatiques et Consulaires Relatifs à l'Histoire du Liban* (Beirut: Éditions des Oeuvres Politiques et Historiques, 1979), Vol. XIX, 81.
138. See the *Easter Story* selection in this chapter for a better understanding of Ottoman Lebanon during the Great War, the hardships suffered by its inhabitants, and consequently the rationale that drove Charles Corm and others from his generation to campaign for the establishment of a *Grand Liban* (the "Greater Lebanon" entity celebrated in this poem), and acclaim the French colonial officer (General Henri Gouraud) who brought that Lebanon into being.
139. This is a clear reference to Henri Gouraud.
140. The French original is "Capitale de ma pensée," which in Corm's telling refers to the famed Beryte of classical antiquity and Roman times. It should be noted in this regard that by the third century AD, the Romans had named Beirut "*Beritus Nutris Legum*," that is to say, "Beirut the City of Law." That sobriquet was earned on account of the city's famous law school, and its reputation in forming some of the Roman Empire's most illustrious jurists and magistrates. This Beirut, in Corm's telling, a shining beacon of knowledge and the main intellectual capital of antiquity, was the worthy capital of the new republic that Gouraud was bringing into being.
141. See *Easter Story*.
142. As mentioned earlier, this part of the first cycle of *La Montagne Inspirée* may be dedicated to the French High Commissioner and the role that he played in the establishment of

Greater Lebanon. To the Phoenicianists of Corm's persuasion, this new state was the culmination of their dreams of statehood, which began with the events of 1860 in Mount-Lebanon; a series of conflicts and civil wars that culminated in large-scale massacres and forced immigration of Lebanese Christians. Of course, the agonies of the 1860s preceded Corm's birth by a good fifty years. But he'd heard stories of the massacres during his childhood—as would have any child of his generation, socialized in the Christian environments of Mount-Lebanon and Beirut. Most importantly perhaps were the memories of the Great War, and the near decimation of the population of Mount-Lebanon—due to famines and blockades that the Ottomans had imposed on the mountain, amputating it from the Mediterranean coast and the fertile hinterland of Eastern Lebanon, once considered the "Granary of Rome." These memories were still fresh in the minds of children of Charles Corm's generation. That is partly why the events of September 1, 1920, were such an auspicious occasion for Corm and his Young Phoenicians. And that is why it was crucial for them to have an independent Greater Lebanon restituted to its Mediterranean harbors, breathing the "boundless air of the open seas." This was important certainly because, in their view, it restored Lebanon to its "natural and historical frontiers." But more importantly perhaps, Greater Lebanon provided an outlet to the Mediterranean and meant that the country would never again become amputated from the rest of the world, from Mediterranean Europe namely, and would therefore never be subjected to the horrors of hunger—described later in Corm's *Easter Story*.

143. Again, the reference here is to the redeemer of Lebanon, General Henri Gouraud.

144. The Biblical cedars of Lebanon are not only the national emblem of the modern Republic of Lebanon; given their Biblical significance, they populate the logos, regalia, and symbols of the Maronite Church—the "national church" of which Charles Corm was a member, and a community that was instrumental in the establishment of the modern state of Lebanon, transposing its own motifs, symbols, and narratives onto those of the nascent state. More importantly perhaps, cedar wood, prized for its strength and durability, was a crucial component of the Phoenicians' shipbuilding industry, and ultimately the fundamental ingredient in the growth of their maritime empire. Planting cedar trees, in Charles Corm's telling, meant rekindling the glories of the Phoenician forefathers and bringing them back to life. See also earlier section on The Humanist Who Planted Trees and, in Corm's telling, the importance of "planting" in the life of a nation.

145. This bespeaks not only the affection that many Lebanese of the time held for Henri Gouraud and his "act" of establishing modern Lebanon; this is also powerful testimony of the "love story" that bound some Lebanese, namely the Maronite Catholics among them, to France.

146. In other words, no human endeavor, no words, and no art forms can adequately express the exquisite generous act of "creation" that was France's formation of modern Lebanon. And therefore, no act of "recognition" or "gratitude" emanating from the Lebanese, genuine and delicate as it may be, can fittingly repay the French.

147. The image of the figures of Venus of Milo, the Winged Victory of Samothrace, and General Gouraud, all three of which charmingly maimed and disfigured, is as exquisite as it is moving. Each of these figures may be visually defective or fragmentary; yet in the power and glory that they inspire, they each are in their own right a pinnacle of perfection. The Venus of Milo, considered by many an epitome of beauty, is a representation of Aphrodite, the Greek goddess of love and fertility, and in her own right a "life-giver." Born on the island of Cyprus, a renowned Phoenician possession, Aphrodite is simply the Greek rendition of the Phoenician Astarte, whose chief worship centers were namely in Cyprus, but also at Byblos (Gebal, modern-day Lebanon) and Ashkelon (modern-day Israel). The transition of the cult of Astarte-Aphrodite from Phoenicia to Greece is attested to by Herodotus, and by inference the "act of transmission" from East (the Phoenicians) to West (Europe) is a theme that is recurrent in Corm's work. In the end, from Corm's perspective, Venus of Milo, the Winged Victory of Samothrace, and General Gouraud were all three the product of Mediterranean (and therefore Phoenician) intercourse and exchange of ideas, goods, and values. Corm's choice of Venus of Milo in this final image of the poem was as historical as it was aesthetic and emotive in its inferences. Likewise with the Winged Victory of Samothrace—which in its current rendition (like Henri Gouraud himself) is an amputee, yet seems well-equipped and ready to take flight. And just as Nike of Samothrace is the greatest masterpiece of Hellenistic sculpture in Corm's

telling, so was the maimed Henri Gouraud an epitome of French beauty, elegance, and heroism; conveying not only victory and triumph against great odds, but also the dynamism of energy, motion, and creation—in this case the energy, motion, and "creation" of modern Lebanon.

148. Nahr el-Kalb or the "Dog River" (the Lycus River of classical antiquity), which meanders some thirty-one miles through the gorges of Mount-Lebanon before emptying in the Mediterranean ten miles north of Beirut, carries significant historical relevance. See for instance Corm's *Easter Story* for more detail. For forty centuries, conquerors and armies that have processed along the Lebanese coast, from classical antiquity to modern times, have often left their markings on monuments that they erected along the banks and at the mouth of the Dog River. Some of those conquerors included Nebuchadnezzar, Marcus Aurelius, Napoleon III, and in more recent times French High Commissioner General Henri Gouraud. The conquerors mentioned by Corm, Ramsis, Caracalla, Asarhaddon, and Ramsis, who are also memorialized at the Nahr el-Kalb corridor, left behind them a particularly bloody trail.

149. Following a drawn-out cry lamenting the loss of Lebanon's "authentic, native" language (be it Phoenician or Syriac-Aramaic), Corm concludes by reconnecting with a suddenly rediscovered "Lebanese language." Indeed, even in the darkest hours of despair over the "loss of language," Corm recognized and revealed a hidden vigor to his ancestral tongue, which he claimed to have fused and infused the modern languages currently spoken in Lebanon. It is worth noting here that Corm is not merely discharging fanciful linguistic romanticism and naïf hope in the imperishability of his language. To the contrary, he seems to exude confidence in the claim that his native language, the language of the Phoenicians, was still pounding vigorously in his veins, and suffusing his voice, in the form of spoken Lebanese. To him, a national language was like a timeless, warm, hallowed maternal voice, surging up from a distant past, reverberating in the present, emitting shudders of national pride and tales of forebears and glory. Therefore, even when they seem to acquiesce in their proverbial polyglossia, Lebanese nationalists of Corm's generation still yearned for an "authentic" national language and recognized its endurance and its latent essence in their modern idioms. Their touted multilingualism was, in Corm's words, simply a palliative, a borrowed outer garment, and an artifice meant to ward off the dominance of any single intruder language. Yet, the "Lebanese language" that Corm spoke of—both an "internal" emotive language *and* an actual living one—impregnated, metabolized, and transmuted the *other* languages currently in use in Lebanon; namely Arabic, which like other idioms, Corm viewed to be an intruder on pre-existent *sui generis* speech forms. Although written in French, and in the French mediaeval poetic tradition of the *chanson de geste*, chronicling local heroic exploits, *La Montagne Inspirée* was, as stated by Corm, "traduit du Libanais"—that is to say "translated from Lebanese. The introduction of each of the poems' three "cycles," or "sagas," presented them as French translations of an original Lebanese, thus suggesting that although "speaking in tongues" as it were, and sounding as if uttering French, Italian, or Arabic for that matter, the linguistic reservoir of the Lebanese people remains a single authentic ancestral "Lebanese" language, a progeny of the ancient Phoenician tongue.

150. Batroun is both the name of a northern Mount-Lebanon district, and the coastal capital of that district. The port-city of Batroun itself was a famous Phoenician harbor in classical antiquity, given mention in the works of Strabo, Pliny, Theophanes, and others. It sits on a promontory just north of Byblos, another Phoenician trading-town, considered by many the world's oldest continuously inhabited human settlement, the home of the earliest systems of alphabetic writing (see for instance Maurice Dunand's *Byblia Grammata*, Paris: Paul Geuthner, 1945), and a major papyrus and "writing" trading center—hence its classical toponym "Byblos," a name from which the word "Bible" is derived. The highlands of the district of Batroun are famous for their Greek Orthodox and Maronite churches, attesting to the appeal of their rugged terrain to hunted-down minority communities. The coastal city itself is home to the "Puy du Connétable" Crusader castle, upon which Fakhreddin II, the seventeenth-century Druze Prince of Mount-Lebanon, built a fort to preserve his autonomy from Ottoman suzerainty, and guard his Beirut-Tripoli coastal trade routes.

151. See above note on the Phoenician port-city of Byblos, a UNESCO World Heritage Site. Also known colloquially in Lebanon as Jbeil, a distortion of the original Canaanite Gebal/Geval (for "the well of the god El/Al"), Byblos was a major center of archaeological discover-

ies during the late nineteenth and early twentieth centuries, illuminating much of what we know today about the Phoenician inhabitants of ancient Lebanon and their contributions to Mediterranean civilization. It is natural for Charles Corm, one of Lebanon's most eloquent cantors of Phoenician glories, to have chosen Byblos as one of the settings in a tale of trials, desperation, hope, and renewal.

152. This is a clear reference to Homer's *The Illiad* and its conception of the notions of masculinity and the ideals of honor, bravery, nobility, and duty—especially as concerns the protection of homeland and family. Describing the ruggedness and nobility of Lebanon's highlanders, likening them to "some warriors from Homer," and bestowing upon them qualities instilled by both society and topology, from a very young age, are part of a trope dominating Corm's corpus. In this story in particular, nobility and dignity and grace—human and humanist values *par excellence* in Corm's worldview—are used in juxtaposition to the indignities and horrors suffered during World War I.

153. Two major towns of Mount-Lebanon delineating its extremities from the eastern highlands (Tannourine) to the western port-cities (Jounié). Tannourine teeters on the edge of valleys and gorges, and is dotted with ancient Maronite monasteries. It is distinguished by its ruggedness, its inaccessibility, and its isolation high up in the mountains. Jounié on the other hand, dominating one of Lebanon's major Mediterranean seaports, symbolizes openness, fluidity, movement, and access to the Mediterranean world. The interconnectedness between "mountain" and "sea" is a theme dear to the hearts of young Lebanese nationalists of Corm's generation, who saw themselves as proud descendants of the ancient Phoenicians, a breed of mariners-mountaineers. It is therefore not surprising that Charles Corm should use those two emblematic Phoenician towns in his narrative.

154. "Emm-Farid" literally means "the mother of Farid." It is an honorific title, its prefix the feminine form of the more common masculine "Abu." Both "Emm" and "Abu" are prefixed to a proper noun, usually the name of a first-born male offspring. Thus, in patriarchal Middle Eastern socieites, titles like Emm-Farid and Abu-Farid become the honorifics or nicknames of the proud parents of a male child, often replacing the parents' own birth names.

155. A *mukhtar* (Ar. "the chosen one") is ordinarily a village elder who represents a country's central authority in rural areas, often taking on the role of mayor or town manager.

156. Tartej is a hamlet of Mount-Lebanon situated in the Byblos district.

157. See earlier historical overview of modern Lebanon, and the dismantlement of the *Mutasarrifiyya* by the Ottomans at the outset of World War I.

158. This is in reference to the *Règlement Organique* regime, which France had helped broker for an autonomous Mount-Lebanon in 1861, providing the Mountain's population a measure of political freedom and protection from Ottoman meddling and molestation. This special regime was guaranteed by a concert of European powers—Russia, Prussia, France, Britain, and Austria—and granted Lebanon legal autonomy, which yielded a relatively long period of peace and stability—that is until the Ottomans stripped the autonomous province of its special status at the outset of the Great War and proceeded to punish and subjugate its populations in retaliation for their "collaboration" with the European intruders—namely France. Given that the *Règlement Organique* had emerged in the midst of devastating wars and massacres in mid-nineteenth-century Mount-Lebanon, and had the purpose of alleviating the suffering of the mountain's population, many early twentieth-century Lebanese of Corm's generation came to expect France and its European allies to rush once more to Lebanon's rescue during the dire hours of World War I. France was, of course, preoccupied with its own tragedies on its own devastated home-ground, and Lebanon as a result had to wait until the post-war peace settlement to regain France's attention.

159. See Charles Corm's report in "Rendons le sol au Paysan," *La Revue Phénicienne*, December 1920.

160. Beirut and Tripoli were two major Ottoman metropolises—with Beirut as capital of the *Vilayet* by the same name. Although diverse and cosmopolitan population-wise, like most of the Ottoman Empire's mercantile port-cities hugging the Mediterranean (Alexandria and Izmir for instance), Beirut and Tripoli remained overwhelmingly Sunni, dominated by Sunni merchant classes that were close allies and accomplices of the Ottoman establishment. Even the most modest of Sunni shopkeepers in those two cities were able to amass vast fortunes during

the war years, often purchasing foreclosed farmlands and Christian properties at rock-bottom prices, overnight becoming formidable landed proprietors in their own rights.

161. Lebanon as a distinct political entity did not exist in those days. Neither did Syria, Palestine, and the rest of the modern states of the Levant for that matter. Instead, Beirut was the capital city of an Ottoman *Vilayet* (State) by the same name, ruled by an Ottoman *Vali* (Governor). Likewise, Syria and Israel in their current modern configurations did not exist. What is today Syria consisted of two *Vilayets*; the *Vilayet* of Damascus (which included parts of what are today Israel and Jordan) and the *Vilayet* of Aleppo (which included parts of modern day Syria and Turkey). The Beirut *Vilayet* stretched over the coastal region of what are today Lebanon, Syria, and Israel, and included Latakia in the north (in what is today Syria), as well as Haifa and Akko in the south (in what is today Israel), and large swaths of what is today the Republic of Lebanon. Mount-Lebanon, where some of the events of this story take place, benefited form an autonomous status, as a *Sanjak* guaranteed by a concert of European powers, and ruled by an Ottoman Christian and aided by an Administrative Council of local (Lebanese) politicians. This would remain the case from 1861 until the Ottoman's entry into the Great War, at which time the special autonomous regime of Mount-Lebanon would be revoked, and retribution would be meted out against the Mountain's Christian populations—peoples then deemed treasonous by the Ottoman authorities due to their European, namely French, sympathies, and their autonomist impulses. This is a theme alluded to throughout Corm's narrative.

162. Jamal Pasha, commonly referred to in Lebanese history books as *al-Saffah* ("the Butcher"), was a member of a "Triumvirate" of Pashas who ruled the Ottoman Empire during the First World War. He was the effective Governor of the *Vilayets* of Damascus, Beirut, and Aleppo during the war, and is believed to have been the perpetrator of the Armenian and Assyrian Genocides, as well as the systematic starvation of Mount-Lebanon, as described here by Charles Corm.

163. Peter Chebly (1871–1917) was Maronite Archbishop of Beirut and President of the Lebanon Congress of Bishops. He was also the rector of one of Beirut's most prestigious Maronite-Catholic schools (the College de la Sagesse), and a vocal opponent of Ottoman rule over Lebanon. He was banished to Adana—along with large numbers of the Maronite intelligentsia—by the Ottomans at the beginning of the Great War. The land that he donated for the Ras el-Nab' cemetery was part of the endowment of the Maronite Archdiocese of Beirut. What became the Maronite Cemetery of Ras el-Nab', where Charles Corm himself is buried today, lies in the Ashrafiyyé district of East Beirut. It abuts the neighborhood's Jewish cemetery and sits on the eastern side of the Damascus Road, which cuts the city of Beirut in half, and which was once the major artery linking the Ottoman *Vilayet* of Beirut to the *Vilayet* of Damascus— hence its name "Damascus Road." Damascus Road was therefore a bustling commercial nerve center, used in Ottoman times by coaches and grain traders traveling between the two main Ottoman provinces of the Eastern Mediterranean, and connecting cosmopolitan Beirut (and its Western legacies and ostentations) to the sleepy, rural Ottoman interior in the east. Peoples of all faiths and religious and ethnic backgrounds, Jews, Christians, and Muslims, mainly merchant families, but also laborers and members of less fortunate social classes, took residence along the eastern and western sides of the Damascus Road. The relevance of this artery to Corm's *Easter Story* is in that it witnessed the demise and utter devastation of one particular Lebanese community (namely the Christian community), while other communities (namely the Sunnis, who were associates and often accomplices of the Ottoman authorities) would survive and thrive during the Great War. These events of modern Lebanon's history were foundational in molding young Charles Corm's worldview, and contributed to his subsequent intellectual and political activities on behalf of an independent, neutral, and diverse Lebanese entity, distinct and dissociated from the intrigues and the foul politics of identity, resentful nationalism, and selfish irredentism that gripped the Eastern Mediterranean following the demise of the Ottoman Empire.

164. Note Corm's earlier description of the children of the Mountain as "sturdy and carefree, besieging strangers in their midst with their large sunny eyes, bickering like some warriors from Homer, trying to outdo one another offering visitors the hospitality of their neat and modest little hovels."

165. A Sunni coastal merchant-town just north of the Tripoli harbor.

166. A coastal town south of Byblos.

167. Many of the inhabitants of Mount-Lebanon had been reduced to scavenging and subsistence living during that period, and as a result became—albeit reluctantly—full participants in the devastation of their country's natural resources. The Ottoman authorities had confiscated all of the country's capital and assets, assigning them to the war effort. In the process, they decreed and enforced a systematic "deforestation campaign" to feed the "fuel shortages" that the Ottoman armies were suffering on the war fronts. The corvée-like "woodcutting" assignments to which some inhabitants of Mount-Lebanon were appointed contributed to large-scale deforestation of the countryside, which in turn profoundly disrupted the country's ecosystem and further contributed to landslides, loss of arable land, crop failures, and generalized penury and famine. In this segment of the *Easter Story*, Martha seems to have been left with no choice but becoming a participant in this general devastation, if only to earn her wretched daily bread.

168. Not very far from Fidar.

169. Qantar is a common unit of mass in the Middle East, arguably a remnant of the Islamic "Kintar," which comes form the Roman "Centarius" (a unit of 100). One qantar equaled 100 rotol, and approximately 40 kilograms.

170. A rotol comes up to one hundredth of a qantar, which meant that Martha would have ended up giving her entire 500 pounds back to the Mukhtar.

171. Nahr el-Kalb (the Dog River, the ancient Lycus River) is some twenty miles south of Byblos. Like most of the Lebanese towns and villages where Corm's *Easter Story* is staged, the Dog River carries significant historical relevance. For some forty centuries, conquerors and armies that have processed along the Lebanese coast, from classical antiquity to modern times, have often left their markings on monuments that they erected along the banks and on the mouth of the Dog River. Some of those conquerors included Ramses II, Nebuchadnezzar, Marcus Aurelius, Napoleon III, and in more recent times French High Commissioner General Henri Gouraud. Legend has it that in ancient times a wolf guarded the mouth of the river, which sits at the foot of a steep mountain gorge wading deep into the Mediterranean coast, howling whenever conquerors approached, thus alerting the highlanders overhead. More importantly, at least from Charles Corm's perspective, Nahr el-Kalb was a symbol of Lebanese resilience and tenacity, figuring prominently in his *La Montagne Inspirée*, where he proudly writes:

> Many were the nations that charged our land, / this tiny plot of land, which quelled them in the end! / We have witnessed the passing, of Peoples and of Ages, / yet withstood and endured, in the glistening horizon, / steadfast on our peaks, peaceful sober and wise, since the early dawn of time! / Many were the magi, poets and princes; / many were the gods, pompous kings and tyrants, / who have filed at the foot of our rugged mountains! / O Ramsis, Asarhaddon, O Barkuk, Caracalla, / transcending all your crimes, surmounting all your horrors, the mouth of Nahr al-Kalb, has kept but broken shards / of your gory passage, on its quiet peaceful shores.

172. Currently the seat of the presidency of the modern Republic of Lebanon, Baabda was the capital of the *Sanjak* (autonomous province) of Mount-Lebanon, which the Ottomans had revoked at the beginning of the Great War.

173. The Glass Café (Leb. *'Ahwet le-'Zééz*) was an iconic downtown Beirut coffeehouse dating back to Ottoman times. There are many Glass Cafés throughout Lebanon (in Sidon, Tripoli, and the Gemmayzé district of Beirut for instance), owing their names to their large glass façades. But the one mentioned by Charles Corm in *Easter Story* refers to the original Glass Café near Martyrs' Square, which owes its renown and historical relevance to its very location. It is situated in a central area of downtown Beirut, which is called "Martyrs' Square" in reference to Lebanese patriots who were executed near that very location by the Ottomans on May 6, 1916. Corm must have been marked by the gory images of those days, as his home was literally at a stone's throw from the square in question. His choice of this location as stage for his story was certainly to accentuate its relevance as a place of suffering and martyrdom—and perhaps eventually redemption and salvation. Yet, Martyrs' Square did not become a memorial only to those patriots executed by the Ottomans in 1916. It was also the final resting place of

thousands of peasants from Mount-Lebanon, flocking to the city of Beirut in search of food (or salvation), and who probably breathed their last on that very location. It should be noted that Martyrs' Square is also referred to as the Tower's Square (Leb. *Séėhit el-Birj*) in reference to the Tuscan-style palace and tower that Emir Fakhreddin II, prince of the autonomous Ottoman province of Mount-Lebanon during the seventeenth century, had built on that location, making Beirut the capital city of his dominions—which extended from the Mediterranean in the West, to the gates of Damascus in the East, and to Akko in the south. Fakhreddin's palace and its lush gardens were subsequently destroyed by the Ottomans, and their stones were carted away to prevent the monument from ever being rebuilt. But the name "Tower's Square," and its significance remained—although it would be given new contents and trappings by the Ottomans in later years. During the Russo-Turkish wars of 1768–1774, Catherine the Great was reported to have dispatched an armada laden with heavy canons to the Beirut Harbor, in an attempt to occupy the Ottomans with an additional war front and weaken their hold on the Crimea. The campaign to dislodge the Ottomans from Beirut failed, but that particular battle ended up being one of the costliest for the Ottomans, and one during which they sustained heavy losses. In 1773, the Ottoman governor of Beirut, Jazzar "the Butcher" Pasha, decided to commemorate those events by erecting cannon-towers on that very same location, affixing a new historical event to a pre-existing name. The plaza earned a new sobriquet in the process; the "Place des Canons" (or Canons' Square), which was often used interchangeably with "Tower Square." Thus, the famous Glass Café (*'Ahwet le-'Zééz*), with its towering iconic glass windows, would come to represent a symbolic and actual "looking-glass" through which pivotal events of modern Lebanon's history would play out, get witnessed, and recorded. It should be noted that Charles Corm grew up at a stone's throw from the Glass Café, on the western edge of the Damascus Road (mentioned earlier), near a street that now bears the name of his own father, the painter Daoud Corm. Young Charles witnessed firsthand the devastation wrought on Beirut and its children during the Great War. He was an ambulant Glass Café in his own right, roaming the streets of his ravaged city and countryside, bearing witness to their tragedy, recording their desolation, and chronicling their humbling and their utter destruction. The characters of Corm's *Easter Story* were real; people he'd witnessed, touched, and many times comforted. In a way, he was unlike the patrons of the real Glass Café; Ottoman officials and sympathizers from among Lebanon's Sunni ruling classes, who remained heedless to the suffering reigning outside their hangout's stone-deaf windows. In a way, Charles Corm's *Easter Story* was as much an indictment of war and a celebration of human resilience, as it was an indictment of indifference—a human failing as much as resilience might have been a human virtue and a symbol of the triumph of the human spirit.

174. Today's "Martyrs' Square" in the heart of downtown Beirut, it was known as the "Place des Canons" (or Canons' Square) in Ottoman times. It was the site of utter devastation and death during the Great War, due mainly to food shortages caused by large-scale confiscations by the Ottomans, and compounded by swarms of locusts overtaking the countryside and allied ships blockading the littoral.

175. This is Martha crying out for her son, in dialectal Lebanese, using the sorrowful vocative "ya." It is difficult to translate its emotions into English, especially when emitted by an afflicted mother. Although the plaintive "Ya" of Corm's text can be rendered "My son! My dear son! Oh Farid! . . ." it does not captivate the emotion, the grief, and the despair evoked by a mother bemoaning the loss of her child. It is a plaintive cry, similar to that of the Madonna of the Seven Sorrows, muffled and dignified and stirring at the same time. That is why, although writing in French, Corm opted to produce this mother's lament, with its raw and dignified emotion, only in the language in which it was expressed; in Lebanese.

176. The imagery of the red of "the blood of souls" here twined to the red of "an ancient carpet of Asia" seems to suggest the "color purple" or the crimson-red of the Phoenicians. This "red," what eventually became the "color of royalty," was one of the Phoenicians' most-prized industries, and arguably the best-guarded trade secret of the ancient world. It made the Phoenicians rich and famous, and became both a source of admiration and envy among the peoples of classical antiquity.

177. One cannot help evoking the Phoenicians, or picture them braving the waves of the ancient world, when Corm's language blends crashing waves and seas with the reddish brown

color of copper. Both maritime trade and "riding the waves," as well red-dye industries, were notable Phoenician trademarks.

178. This is an explicit nod to Maurice Barrès's *La Colline Inspirée* (The Hallowed Hill) novel, published in 1913. Barrès's earlier work, often swelling with youthful energy and patriotic devotion, left an indelible mark on Charles Corm's own literary production. Indeed, Corm's elaboration of Phoenicianism in later years (ca. 1916–1919), culminating in the publication of *La Montagne Inspirée* in 1933, another obvious allusion to Barrès's *La Colline Inspirée*, speaks to some Barrèsian impact. Incidentally, the First Cycle of *La Montagne Inspirée*, titled "The Saga of Enthusiasm" (*Le Dit de l'Enthousiasme*), was dedicated to Maurice Barrès. Written in French, but "translated from Lebanese" in Corm's telling, it read "En mémoire de Maurice Barrès, qui a su nous comprendre parce qu'il nous a aimés" (In memoriam, to Maurice Barrès, who was able to understand us [Lebanese] because he loved us). As mentioned earlier, the references to Barrès in many of Corm's literary production, were certainly not fortuitous. They bespoke the "ancient spirit" of "ancient forefathers," which were foundational in Barrès's *La Colline Inspirée*, and likewise in Corm's own attachment to the Lebanese mountain, where still lives the ancient Phoenician spirit. Mount-Lebanon was the repository of Lebanese identity in Corm's telling; it is the origin and extension of Lebanese selfhood, and fulfills the mystical desires of a poet on a quest for the absolute.

179. The "mysteries" of the "human sound," and its endurance and eternal life in alphabetic writing, is a prevalent theme in Corm's work. In *La Montagne Inspirée* and elsewhere, as well as in his public lectures and journalistic output, Charles Corm always celebrated the Phoenician alphabet, deeming it a stunning accomplishment, the pinnacle of humanism and human achievement. To wit, *La Montagne Inspirée* describes alphabetic writing and its place of honor in the pantheon of human creation as follows:

> Today, no one would fathom holding / The invention of writing, to be the greatest miracle of all, / One whereby human genius, raised us up mere mortals / To the status of Creator, God, / With a simple sleight of hand! / For, the simple act of writing, breathes life into otherwise fading words, / Granting them plain form, and an eternal face; / Indeed the act of writing yields a lucid image / To the sounds of our words, / And assigns a high altar to our fleeting thoughts! / [. . .] For, the simple act of writing, / Is like gushing out of one's own empty twilights, / It is an act of defiance against nothingness [. . .] / For, when God set out to redeem his own sinful creation, / The Word became flesh, so as to defy death, / Likewise, when our ancestors, spawned the miracle of writing, / The word was given form!

180. The word "alcarazas" here refers to the fresh water, wine, or Arak (anised alcohol) clay pitchers common in rural Mount-Lebanon. The French alcarazas used by Charles Corm is a loan from Spanish with origins in the Arabic "al-Karraz," which itself issues from the Aramaic "Karzé." In its nominal form, the Aramaic word "Karzé" means sermon. Its transitive verbal form connotes "consecration" and "dedication," by way of "sermonizing," "pouring libations," and "throwing holy water." Hence the later Arabization of "Karzé" from the Syriac noun "Karruz" (predictor, announcer, herald-making consecrations, by way of holy water), connoting the container of holy water.

181. Charles Corm's beloved is clearly worthy of baby Jesus here, the innocent recipient of fragrant "musk, nard, and myrrh" as a newborn, and the consort and friend of prostitutes and sinners in his adult life. Namely, the image that comes to mind here is that of the "Sinful Woman" of the New Testament, anointing Jesus's feet with perfume, and wiping them with her hair. "Let him who is without sin among you be the first to throw a stone at her," says the evangelist John (in John 8:7) describing Jesus and his reaction to puritans and practitioners of phony virtue. Corm's Preface to the collection of poems from which *Phoenicia* is excerpted likewise reminds those of us who may be quick with judgments of their own to "Let him, the first among men, who has never experienced the ecstasy of carnal love, cast the first stone."

Figure 1. Charles Corm at the publication of *La Montagne Inspirée* (Beirut, 1934). Charles Corm's Archives and Private Papers, Beirut, Lebanon.

Figure 2. Charles Corm as a 13-year-old (Beirut, 1907). Charles Corm's Archives and Private Papers, Beirut, Lebanon.

Figure 3. Charles Corm, Commissioner General of the Lebanon Pavilion at the New York World's Fair (New York, 1939). Charles Corm's Archives and Private Papers, Beirut, Lebanon.

Figure 4. Charles Corm (Beirut, 1962). Charles Corm's Archives and Private Papers, Beirut, Lebanon.

Figure 5. Charles Corm, self-portrait. Charles Corm's Archives and Private Papers, Beirut, Lebanon.

Figure 6. Charles Corm and the 1925 Ford Model T in front of his Haifa Ford dealership in British Mandatory Palestine (Haifa, 1928). The storefront signs read "Charles Corm and Company" in both Arabic and Hebrew in addition to English. Charles Corm's Archives and Private Papers, Beirut, Lebanon.

Figure 7. Charles and Samia Corm atop the Empire State Building (New York, 1939). Charles Corm's Archives and Private Papers, Beirut, Lebanon.

Figure 8. Charles Corm signing the *Book of Nations* at the New York World's Fair (New York, 1939), with his wife, Samia, at his side, and under the watchful eye of Commissioner General of the French Pavilion, Marcel Olivier. Charles Corm's Archives and Private Papers, Beirut, Lebanon.

Figure 9. Inauguration of the Lebanon Pavilion at the New York World's Fair, with New York City Mayor La Guardia (New York, 1939). Charles Corm's Archives and Private Papers, Beirut, Lebanon.

Figure 10. Samia Corm putting the finishing touches on traditional Lebanese costumes in preparation for the "Lebanon Day" at the New York World's Fair (New York, 1939). Charles Corm's Archives and Private Papers, Beirut, Lebanon.

Figure 11. Charles Corm and the 1925 Ford Model T in front of his Jerusalem Ford dealership in British Mandatory Palestine (Jerusalem, 1928). The storefront signs read "Charles Corm and Company" in both Arabic and Hebrew in addition to English. Charles Corm's Archives and Private Papers, Beirut, Lebanon.

Figure 12. Charles Corm's austere, nameless, burial site, as he designed it; Ras el-Nab' Maronite Cemetery, a stone's throw from his home in the Nazareth Quarter of Ashrafiyyé, and very near to where the "miracles" of his *Easter Story* took place (ca. 1963). Charles Corm's Archives and Private Papers, Beirut, Lebanon.

Figure 13. Daoud Corm's portrait of Sham'un/Semaan al-Chidiac Hkayyim, grandfather of Charles Corm and court clerk and instructor in the Court of the Emir Bashir the Great, ruler of Mount-Lebanon (ca. 1890). Charles Corm's Archives and Private Papers, Beirut, Lebanon.

Figure 14. Self-portrait by Daoud Corm, Charles Corm's father, pioneer of Lebanon's modern painting, and teacher and mentor to renowned Lebanese artists such as Kahlil Gibran, César Gemayel, and Mustapha Farroukh (ca. 1900). Charles Corm's Archives and Private Papers, Beirut, Lebanon/

Figure 15. A closeup view of the *Maison Blanche de Beyrouth*, the headquarters of Charles Corm's *Société Génerale* business emporium until 1934. It would later become Corm's family residence and the main venue of his *Amitiés Libanaises* cultural salons; cherished weekly gatherings which were attended by a veritable who's who of Lebanese and international intellectual personalities, including Pierre Benoît, Charles Plisnier, Eliahu Epstein, Michel Chiha, Saïd Akl, and Amin Rihani among others. Charles Corm's Archives and Private Papers, Beirut, Lebanon.

Figure 16. Charles Corm's *Maison Blanche de Beyrouth*, the Middle East's first skyscraper; designed by Corm himself and built in 1928, it would remain Lebanon's tallest urban structure until 1968. The *Maison Blanche de Beyrouth* served as the headquarters of Charles Corm's business emporium, including his Ford Motor's affiliates until 1934, and became his family home until his death in 1963. Today, the building houses the Charles Corm Archives and a fifty-thousand-volume private library, the remainder of Charles Corm's book collections, a good portion of which was lost to fires and looting during the Lebanese wars of 1975–1990. Charles Corm's Archives and Private Papers, Beirut, Lebanon.

Chapter Three

Entrepreneur, Patriot

We stood, yesterday, in the high-ceiled Lebanon Pavilion, awed by the antiquity of the exhibits. Lovely murals, showing the Phoenicians building the first boats of Cedar; the hill scenes and the places famous in Scripture slowed our steps and smooth-edged the fuss and fury. [. . .] Something in the ageless stare of the white marble statues of the ancient heroes of Lebanon dimmed the immediate greatness of the Great. [. . . Then] we stood before the Cedars of Lebanon. "These cedars, [. . .] felled by heavy snows, are from the 480 surviving cedar trees of Lebanon, some of which date back to Solomon's time, 3000 years ago." We saw them, then as through a mist, imagination carried us completely out of the World of Tomorrow. [. . .] Presently we were aware of a little man who stood beside us, a little, dried up man, with bright little eyes. [. . .] "These trees," we translated, "stood on the hills of Lebanon. Solomon may have walked beneath their shade, and Sheba's Queen." The little man winked. "Sheba," he told us in an extraordinarily deep and resonant voice, "did walk beneath them." [. . .] "Now," the little man muttered, "therefore command thou that they hew Me cedar trees out of Lebanon." Never [. . .] had we heard human voice so rich, so warmly narcotic. "My servants shall bring them down from Lebanon unto the sea," the voice gravely intoned, and we knew a vague uneasiness. The little man moved away. Slowly he passed through the shadowy door into the brightness of the sun. We asked the girl at the little book counter about the little man; who he might be. "What little man?" she wanted to know. We turned to point. The little man was gone.

Meyer Berger
"At the World's Fair"
New York Times

August 18, 1939

"Little men" it should be mentioned, like "pixies," "elves," and "leprechauns" were common features at international expositions during the 1920s and 1930s. To wit, the 1934 Chicago World's Fair, the most attended and most extravagant international exposition of its day, boasted a "Live Two-Headed Baby" exhibit and a "Believe It or Not Odditorium," both of which, along with semi-nude burlesque dancer Sally Rand's shows, raised the Fair's profile, gave it renown, boosted exhibit attendance, and increased revenues. And so, it may not have been unusual for the *New York Times* excerpt above to have inquired about a "little man" roaming the Lebanon Pavilion, as the 1939 New York World's Fair did feature some of the "low minded entertainment" exhibits that were customary at the time.

But then again, what if there were a "little man" at the Lebanon Pavilion? Who was he? Who would he have been? Could it be that he was, with his "rich, warmly narcotic" voice, Charles Corm himself? Weren't those words with which Corm was frequently described by those who knew him? By those who saw him wrapped in halos of bright stars whenever he entered a room and whenever he uttered a word?[1] Or was this "little man [. . .] with bright little eyes," who quoted Scriptures in a celestial "resonant voice" before disappearing as mysteriously as he had appeared "into the brightness of the sun," an angelic apparition? A heavenly lover of things Lebanon? A bard from the Land of the Cedars? Whatever the case, the style, the tone, the structure, the content, the imageries and the literary techniques with which Charles Corm and the Lebanon Pavilion of the 1939 New York World's Fair were referred to in American media and diplomatic circles were in line with the passage above; they all spoke of a man of extraordinary talent and charm, and of a Lebanon exhibit of exquisite mythical beauty. Grover Whalen, the President of the New York World's Fair 1939–1940 Corporation, noted that as an indication of the profound impression that the Lebanon Pavilion had left on the American public, the mayors of twenty-seven American towns named Lebanon had sent Charles Corm their personal congratulations on the occasion of Lebanon Day on September 1, 1939.[2] "May I take this opportunity," wrote Julius Holmes on behalf of Whalen, "of conveying to you [Charles Corm] my personal admiration and appreciation for the high principles which you have here proclaimed in harmony with the theme and purpose of this International Exposition, which is dedicated to the spirit of peace and goodwill among the nations of the world."[3]

As Lebanon's messenger of amity and friendship and light, like a blazing meteor setting the twilight aflame before dissipating in the neighborhood of stars, an enterprising, ambitious, sensitive Charles Corm, wedding humanism to entrepreneurship, and patriotic duty to poetic charm, would bring forth to the 1939 New York World's Fair a dazzling image of his Lebanon; an image imbued in the spirit of benevolence, pacifism, and goodwill—the exemplar and embodiment of his life's work and the vision he bore for his country and his countrymen.

And so, dovetailing the spirited activities of his press (the Éditions de la Revue Phénicienne), his bustling cultural and literary salons (*Les Amitiés Libanaises*), and the punishing rhythm of his writing, publishing, and public-speaking commitments, Charles Corm undertook almost on a whim (as had been the habit of this enterprising cultural and corporate pioneer) to represent Lebanon at the 1939 New York World's Fair. At forty-five years of age, Corm was still youthful, energetic, bursting with zeal, and ever committed to serving his people and flying his nation's banner. But his years of uninterrupted work—burning the candle at both ends as it were—had taken a toll, and behind his tough spirited exterior, Charles Corm was brittle, his health was ailing, and it was against the strong advice of his physicians that he would still go on to furrow oceans on yet another lengthy transatlantic trek to the New World. Yet woes of health were the least of the challenges testing and expecting this overachiever's endeavors.

As we shall discover in the following narrative of Lebanon's participation in the 1939 New York World's Fair, the demands of building a Lebanese national pavilion at this international extravaganza were not only budgetary matters relating to finances and cash resources—which, archival evidence shows, Charles Corm will have shouldered anyway—nor did they pertain solely to issues of vision and planning.[4] Putting on display, at an international forum, a country still under French Mandate, and for all intents and purposes a subordinate republic still untrained and untried in the global limelight, required at the very least the minimal attributes of statehood. From sovereignty, to a diplomatic corps, to the central mechanisms allowing for the normal functioning of political, economic, social, cultural, and international affairs, all these details were lacking in the case of Lebanon. Yet the country that Charles Corm came to put on the international stage turned out to be a resounding success. And the diplomatic and logistical minutiae that he overcame in order to put together such a sumptuous show were overcome as a result of his own labors—and arguably his labors alone. He was certainly the official face of Lebanon and its diplomatic and cultural representative. But so also were the behind-the-scenes planning and housekeeping matters his own handiwork. From drawing up the blueprints of the Lebanon Pavilion taking into account American regulations, labor laws, and the Fair's own architectural specifications; to commissioning artwork, crafts, and replicas of artifacts on three continents; to shipping the décor, accessories, and other trappings of the Pavilion from Beirut, Paris, and Brussels, and seeing them through American customs; to hiring building contractors and supervising architects and engineers in New York; to obtaining the necessary construction and occupancy permits, ascertaining that the minutest details of electrical work, plumbing, and ventilation are observed; to passing inspections, maintaining the Pavilion itself, and hiring its personnel; all of this was the responsibility and liability of Charles Corm, and the expenses for this whole enterprise came largely out of Charles Corm's personal checkbook.[5]

LEBANON'S PLENIPOTENTIARY TO THE WORLD: A RATIONALE FOR CORM

By 1938, barely five years after the publication of *La Montagne Inspirée*—what was at the time hailed by many as a work that defined the canon of twentieth-century Lebanese literature—Charles Corm's reputation had become larger than life.[6] To the Phoenicianist component of Lebanese society—both at home and in the diaspora—his name was well nigh synonymous with Lebanon itself; a condensation of grandeur, grace, wisdom, and beauty. He was considered to be the epitome of the Phoenician archetype: skilled cultural intermediary, industrious entrepreneur, fearless adventurer, intrepid pioneer, eloquent orator, and exquisite weaver of national energy and pride.[7] In that sense, no one could have possibly cast a more charming image of Lebanon's face abroad than Charles Corm, and no one more than he could have been a more eloquent ambassador of Lebanon to the world—and namely to the New World and the New York World's Fair 1939–1940.

By the account of those who knew him, all by himself, Charles Corm was the kind of individual akin to the very foundations upon which nations arise, histories get written, and societies get built.[8] Wrote his friend Assaad Younis in 1934, "Charles Corm in our day mined the thickets of time and space the way the Phoenicians of yore tamed the intractable oceans of antiquity; he did so to uncover precious buried truths about his seafaring forefathers, and lay them bare, offering them like divine oblations at the feet of his countrymen, so that they may take pride in their lineage and bask in the glory of having graced Mankind with gifts and triumphs everlasting."[9] Charles Corm does not sing the glories of the Phoenicians, argued Younis, for the sake of bombast or empty bravado, nor to please our sense of vanity and arrogance and national hubris;

> nay, his mission is loftier and his ambition nobler than that; his aim is to awaken our slumbering souls and shake us out of our indolence, as if to tell us that the descendants of those giants of antiquity, who dazzled and dizzied the world with their accomplishments and who conquered the earth as skilled and benevolent teachers to mankind, those modern descendants of giants cannot be ignorant uncouth trifles. [. . .] Indeed, the nation that gave birth to Humanity's greatest thinkers, titans like Thales of Miletus, the doyen of the Seven Sages of Greece, or Archias, the teacher of Cicero, or the jurists Ulpian and Papinian, authors of the Roman Codex of Justinian, or Saint-Augustine, the beacon of the Catholic Church [. . .]; a nation such as this is truly worthy of admiration

and must command our respect. [. . . This is] the edifice upon which Lebanon's national and literary renaissance are framed; [. . .] erected singlehandedly by Charles Corm, layered one stone at a time, one boulder at a time, with skill, determination, enthusiasm, majesty and grace.[10]

That was at least the view of those Lebanese who swore by the Phoenician narrative of their young country's history, and the charming incarnation of that narrative flowing from the inspired quill of its poet laureate.

To the Arabist component of Lebanese society on the other hand, things were otherwise: Among them, Corm was adulated as he was heckled, revered as he was reviled, and admired as he was contested. To be sure, his person was respected and extended the dignity it commanded and deserved, and indeed many Arabists—among them Amin Rihani (a Maronite) and Takieddine al-Solh (a Sunni Muslim who served briefly as Prime Minister of Lebanon in the early 1970s)—were close lifelong friends of Charles Corm's.[11] Still, they were not particularly enthralled with his ideas of Lebanon as a unique presence in the Middle East, as a distinct non-Arab entity in the midst of an Arab sea, and as a progeny of the Phoenicians of classical antiquity rather than the Arabs of more recent times. Rihani deemed Lebanon a parcel of a putative Arab space, and the "Phoenician message" emanating from Corm's pen "could not have appealed to him in its entirety," wrote Asher Kaufman.[12] Indeed, Kaufman notes that Rihani might even have "scoffed at Corm's tendency to 'phoenicianize' every rock and tree in Lebanon," always detecting some Phoenician remnant in every nook and cranny of the country's highlands and seashores.[13] Likewise, Takieddine al-Solh was at times resentful of Charles Corm's Phoenician convictions and even exploited their relationship in order to divert his friend from the Phoenicians and guide him into the fold of Arabism. Solh went so far as admitting the obvious in agreement with Corm; that is to say, he conceded the Phoenicians were indeed the ancestors of the modern Lebanese—for physical Lebanon of today had unquestionably been their homeland, and the country's Mediterranean seafront their cultural space and commercial playground. But Solh could not swallow that bitter pill without a sedative. Countering archaeological evidence revealing otherwise, he brandished a classic Arab nationalist pretense fancying the Phoenicians ancient Arabs. He claimed that the children of the Arabian Peninsula had during classical antiquity "launched many waves of invaders, conquerors, and teachers throughout the world," and that the Phoenicians, "by the account of most historians were tribes that issued out of these waves, from the areas of today's Shatt al-Arab or Bahrain," and should therefore be deemed ancient Arabs.[14]

The preceding is, of course, the claim *not* of "most historians," as argued Solh, but of one historian in particular; Herodotus to be exact, "the father of historians" (or "the father of lies" depending on the source), a fanciful chronicler the factuality of whose accounts is questioned by modern scholarship.[15] Moreover, the idea of Arabs or proto-Arabs bursting out of the Arabian Peninsula and establishing civilizations throughout the Levant and the Middle East remains a mere theory based on no known historical record and no credible archaeological evidence. To wit, none of the Arabian epigraphic or oral literatures contemporaneous of the times noted by Solh make mention of such migrations. Rather, as a theory, this idea of early Arabs surging out of their deserts in ancient times and civilizing the world is modeled on a more recent event, the seventh-century Muslim conquest, "retrojected" into a distant past "to fit an unknown situation."[16]

Historical inaccuracies and omissions notwithstanding, there were at times unmistakable hints of condescension in Solh's appeals that Corm acquiesce in his assigned Arabness; an attitude reminiscent of Sati' al-Husri's much anthologized claim that it is irrelevant what kinds of identities users of the Arabic language may arrogate themselves, for they are in spite of themselves Arabs, regardless of their own wishes.[17] Wrote Solh in one instance, in a text addressed to Corm and titled "The Perplexed Mountain" (a clear pun on *The Hallowed Mountain*):

> I do not blame you should you forgo aspects of Arab history that might have endeared Arabism and the Arabic language to you; I do not blame you because in the confines of the Western institutes that you frequented in your youth, you encountered only that which made you repulse Arabism and the Arabic language; I do not blame you because you were made to repudiate the language of your country, the language of your people, and the language of your mother and father [. . .]; I do not blame you because I know very well the hand that undertook your formation and education, and oversaw your boyhood and your youth, when you were still malleable and vulnerable and susceptible to the ideas that were being hammered into you; I do not blame you because I can still see how this cunning Machiavellian hand might have taken control of your head and directed it astray, towards the dark corners of Arab history [. . .] so as to make you despise the Arabs [and overlook] the light that emanated from them. And so, you were raised in ignorance, to be unfamiliar with the Arabs—and man, as the saying goes, is the enemy of that which he does not know.[18]

Aside from the patronizing tone of this text, infantilizing an otherwise worldly, cultured, sophisticated adult—a successful business magnate and an accomplished poet to boot—Solh's arguments may be easily turned on their head and applied to his own reticence vis-à-vis the Phoenicians. Isn't it conceivable that Corm could have also raised the possibility of a hidden "Machiavellian hand" of a different kind, and with an opposite agenda, having taken hold of Solh's own head, directing it astray, so as to make him despise the Phoenicians and overlook "the light that emanated from them?" But Corm never engaged his philosophical adversaries on that level. To the contrary, he had great admiration and affection even toward those who opposed him. He was especially fond of Takieddine al-Solh, who hailed from Sidon, one of the leading city-states of the Phoenician Decapolis and a place which Corm considered to be the fountainhead of Phoenician culture and the birthplace of its benevolent maritime empire. Speaking of Sidon and its sister city Tyre, French novelist Paul Morand, the biographer of Coco Chanel, a fan of the Mediterranean and colleague of Corm's from the *Congrès de l'Académie Méditerranénne*, and a frequent feature at his *Amitiés Libanaises*, wrote in 1938 that

> Sour and Saïda were once the entire history of Mankind; the very essence of the Mediterranean spirit and the wellspring of science. [. . .] Art, industry, and trade were all born and raised on these two promontories, two thousand years before Christ. Cedar wood, destined to the ceilings of Solomon's Temple in Jerusalem and the fleets of Pharaoh, it is on this very spot, from these shores, that you have set sail once to brighten the world and set it alight.[19]

It is no wonder then that Corm's body leaped forward and his soul fluttered with eagerness and joy as he ran to embrace Solh the moment he found out that he was a Sidonian: "Now I know the secrets of my yearning for you, ever since the minute I laid eyes on you," exclaimed a visibly elated Corm; "you are a true Phoenician of ancient venerable stock; by God, look at your face! Aren't those the features of a proper timeless Phoenician?"[20]

Going back to Corm's alleged disregard for, even his loathing of, Arab culture in Solh's telling, it should be noted that, contrary to Solh's claims, Corm knew the Arabic language and Arab history well, and indeed was well versed in both classical and popular Arabic literature, as well as the canon of modern Lebanese *belles lettres* as written in Arabic, in addition to French and English.[21] Admittedly, the history of the Arabs and their proud literature did not figure prominently alongside the Phoenicians, who naturally enjoyed pride of place in the narratives of Lebanese history as woven by Charles Corm. But the Arabs did get honorable mention, alongside Greeks, Romans, Crusaders, Turks, and others still, whom Corm deemed important, but who remained mere passersby and transient invaders in his view, who got ultimately transformed and assimilated into the Phoenician-Lebanese family. To wit, at one point in *La Montagne Inspirée*, urging the dormant language of the Phoenicians to arise and tell the modern Lebanese their true history, Corm wrote:

> Oh language of my land, do tell us our history, / Tell our humbled children, to take heart in their past, / Tell them they have much, so much to be proud of, / Glories upon glories, and triumphs that shall last! / Oh language of my land, give us back our courage, / Make us believe again, in ourselves, and our forebears, / Keep us in our rank, keep our audience for us, / At the banquet of

the gods! / [. . .] Tell us how in the grooves, of our mountains' hamlets, / In the shade of our vines, we danced a joyous "dabké," / Tell us how our boys, with roses in their hair, / Pranced in Pyrrhic sword-dances! / Tell us how our townsmen, tell us how our villagers, would spend long sleepless nights, / Listening to the tales, of Antar, Sitt-el-Bdour, and Harun al-Rashid; / And how our lively teens, haunted by victory, jostled for the Djérid.[22]

Not only does the preceding demonstrate Charles Corm had nary a compunction recognizing Arab and Muslim flavors to Lebanese social and cultural patterns, he seemed to revel in them—albeit maintaining, not unreasonably, the Phoenicians' rank and audience "at the banquet of the gods," and recognizing those Phoenicians as the Lebanese first forefathers.[23] Moreover, Corm's mention of the tales of the pre-Islamic Arabian knight-poet Antar, the deeds of Abbassid Caliph Harun al-Rashid, and the traditional Arab, Persian, and Turkish *Djérid* martial games suggest some—not to say a profound—grasp of classical Arabic literature, Arab popular culture, and Muslim traditions in general. Indeed, Corm's work, without restraint, spoke with pride of the endeavors of nineteenth-century Lebanese literati in the *Nahda* renaissance and advancement of Arabic *belles lettres*: It is the Lebanese, he wrote, "with their masterful toils, / Who, pulling it from beneath heavy burial stones, / Raised the Arabic language, and brought it back to life."[24] The fact that among Corm's lifelong friends one could count Amin Rihani, May Ziyadé, Elias Abou-Shabké, Eliya Abou-Mady, and most famously perhaps Kahlil Gibran—all of whom were pioneers and titans of the Arabic *Nahda* movement—must speak to our author's amity and sincerity, and the esteem that he held for the Arabic language. It should be noted that these Lebanese contributions to the revival and modernization of the Arabic language—during the late nineteenth and early twentieth centuries—were extoled and given center stage at the exhibits that Charles Corm put together at the New York World's Fair.

Further debunking Takieddine al-Solh's dubious accusations, it would be worth mentioning that many of Charles Corm's childhood friends and classmates, who frequented the same Jesuit institutions as he, rather than having succumbed to the same "cunning Machiavellian hand," grew up to become eloquent Arabists, skilled users of the Arabic language, and some even committed Arab nationalists. Among those it suffices to mention Youssef al-Saouda (a Lebanese nationalist who wrote almost exclusively in Arabic), Youssef Ghsoub (an Arabophone journalist, poet, and teacher of Arabic), Hektor Klat (a brilliant bilingual Arabic-French translator and poet), and most importantly perhaps Riyad al-Solh, a cousin of Takieddine's and an erstwhile Ottomanist turned Arab nationalist, who in 1943 would become Prime Minister of Lebanon and co-architect of the country's famed National Pact.

The fact that Charles Corm chose French over Arabic as his literary medium was his way of heeding history, geography, and the demands of Lebanon's unique cultural mission at the crossroads of continents and civilizations. Lebanon, in the telling of cultural anthropologist Selim Abou, had since "the early dawn of history [. . .] always practiced some form of bilingualism and polyglossia; one of the finest incarnations of intercultural dialogue and coexistence."[25] More recently, Fouad Ajami noted that one needed not be old or nostalgic to recall with affection a multi-cultural Lebanon where eighteen different communities jostled and feuded for power and influence and relevance; where Lebanese beholden to the creed of Arab nationalism met their match in "Lebanese who thought of their country as a piece of Europe at the foot of a splendid mountain [. . . and who] savored the language of France."[26] And so, it might not have been an especially noxious kind of malice that steered Corm away from the Arabic language and into the embrace of French. His "partiality" for French was a reflection of the special affection that he held for the language itself and the culture that spawned it, and the intimacy with which he wielded both. After all, and for any number of reasons, authors may write in a variety of languages—other than ones judged to be their exclusive appanage—without earning denunciations of the kind Solh felt Corm had deserved. To wit, Samuel Becket is not deemed any less Irish (nor a hater of the Gaelic and English languages) for having written in French; nor is Vladimir Nabokov any less Russian (nor indeed a Russophobe) for having written in English. Moreover, there is no evidence in Corm's published work or private papers to suggest that he was capable of hate—let alone was he capable of loathing Arabism and the Arabic language per se. He guilelessly believed in Lebanon's unique personality, and he did not consider that personality or the Lebanese identity to be Arab; a prerogative that he practiced with neither hostility nor resentment. Indeed, a difference with a distinction exists between repudiating an imputed Arabness deemed alien to one's beliefs, and outright hating the Arabs and the Arabic language as Solh suggested. Simply put, wrote Corm's Arabic biographer Jamil Jaber, with his extensive knowledge, his high morals, his humanism, and his exemplary patriotism,

> Charles Corm is a national school all to himself. At a time when Lebanon's identity was still being contested, Charles Corm came forth with his *Hallowed Mountain*, emerging as a beacon of historical verities incarnating Lebanon's true self and true identity. The Lebanon that Charles Corm brought back to life was not merely this small speck of geographic space in a vast endless universe; Corm's Lebanon was a homeland for love and benevolence, and a meeting place of civilizations, religions, and peoples at the crossroads of the ancient world's three continents; Corm's Lebanon was the Lebanon of Adonis coming back to life, surging forth more vigorous and more spirited with each new Spring. [. . . In that,] Charles Corm was the author of the first truly Lebanese

act of faith, issuing a challenge to six thousand years of history and conquests, intoning the first hymn inspired by Lebanon's immortality.[27]

Salah Labaki concurred, chiming in that

> the man exudes charm and purity of heart. In his soul dwells a paradox of extreme enthusiasm and unbounded goodness, as if he were a whiff emanating from the pages of Scriptures. His passions are noble, his style pure, his words winnowed with love, and his lines brimming with resolve, youthful energy, humanism, and peace. Charles Corm is Lebanese through and through, from head to toe and to the depths of his soul. [. . .] His poetry is simply the portrayal of that which has been conveyed to him by the melodies of Lebanon's valleys, the choirs of its mountains, and the flickers of its starry nights, [. . .] about aged traditions and venerable ancestors, and naval fleets surging forth, bridging distance, linking Lebanon to peoples and countries beyond the horizons.[28]

In other words, Charles Corm's flaw was simply having painted an image of his beloved country with a palette of colors flowing out Lebanon's mountains and valleys, and the whispers of its Mediterranean shores—rather than drawing inspiration from distant deserts to its east. His crime was being an inveterate, committed, Lebanese nationalist, who was infinitely proud of Lebanon's topography, its traditions, its specificity, and its polyglot openness, who believed in a Lebanese-Phoenician filiation, and who postulated—based on history, geography, personal conviction, and emotive fervor not unlike that of patriots and nationalists of other stripes—that the modern Lebanese were indeed descendants of the ancient Phoenicians. To suggest that advocating for Phoenicianism somehow means loathing Arabism and offending the Arabic language infantilizes Arab nationalism itself and casts it in the light of an insecure, resentful doctrine; it also misinterprets Phoenicianism, caricatures Charles Corm, and, as we saw earlier, denudes Corm's nationalist creed of its inherently humanistic impulses. "As long as the children of Lebanon find the source of their inspiration at the highest heights of their cedars, it matters little that languages are many and varied in their cultural universe," wrote Youssef al-Saouda; and so, "it is our prerogative and privilege as Lebanese to sing to the Ages in the languages of Horace, Shakespeare, and Hugo."[29] In line with this, and addressing Arabic, English, French, Italian, Greek, Armenian, and many other languages, all still in use in Lebanon, Corm famously noted in *La Montagne Inspirée* that

> even these foreign-sounding words, which are taught to our children, / to us are not all that alien; / For, it seems that our hearts can still recall remembrances / of having fashioned them and styled their graceful sounds! / [. . .] Uprooted from us, torn from our embrace, / Embellished by exile, they now disown their race, / Like beloved ingrates.[30]

And so, from Corm's perspective and the perspective of others belonging to his school of thought, French was no more a foreign language (nor a colonial throwback) in Lebanon than were Arabic, Turkish, or English. Likewise, Arabic itself is no more Lebanon's "authentic" or "native"—or for that matter its "exclusive"—language than are Syriac, Italian, Greek, or Armenian. In this regard, Abou wrote that the French language (or early Latin variants of what later became French) entered Lebanon and the Eastern Mediterranean littoral at the time of the first Crusades, around 1099.[31] Centuries later, the establishment of the Maronite College in Rome (1584) and the liberal enlightened policies of then Mount-Lebanon's Druze ruler, Fakhreddin II (1572–1635), allowed the Maronites to further strengthen their religious, cultural, and linguistic ties to Rome and the rest of Europe—France in particular. This unleashed a wave of missionary work to Lebanon, and eventually led to the founding of schools tending to the educational needs of the Christian—namely Maronite—communities of the region. Although foundational courses in Arabic and Syriac were generally taught at those missionary schools, European languages including French, Italian, and German also became part of the regular curriculum. French, therefore, can be argued to have had an older pedigree in Lebanon than might have suggested Solh in his indictments of Corm's affinity for the French language. And contrary to the classical norms in the expansion and transmission of imperial languages—the spread of Arabic included—which often entailed conquests and cultural suppression campaigns, the French language can be said to have been adopted willingly by the Lebanese, through centuries of cultural intercourse and "seduction," not colonialism and "subjection."[32] That much may not be said with regards to, say, Greek, Persian, Latin, Arabic, and Turkish, all of which belong to the long linguistic repertoire of Lebanon, but none of which can be said to have been native idioms or ones adopted willingly.

At any rate, Lebanese Arabists suspected (not without reason) that the Lebanon that Charles Corm would end up putting on display at the New York World's Fair would come to be a reflection of his vision of his country rather than their own. And so, Corm's nomination in 1938 as Commissioner General of the Lebanon Pavilion (by then President Émile Éddé) would come to be fought vehemently by those who objected to his worldview and his unique conception of Lebanon and Lebanese history. Even Corm himself, for a variety of reasons, was initially reluctant to accept the nomination; he vacillated, and even resigned his assigned position a number of times before finally acquiescing, eventually taking on the responsibilities entrusted him, and forging ahead with the plans and designs of the Lebanon exhibit.[33]

On October 1, 1938, by Presidential Decree No. 3302, and against strong objections issuing both from opponents at home and arrivistes in the diaspora coveting the position for themselves, Charles Corm was appointed Commissioner General to the New York World's Fair 1939–1940, thus becoming the first official representative of the Republic of Lebanon in the United States.[34] This appointment would also carry with it all the prerogatives, privileges, and responsibilities incumbent upon a diplomat—from holding a diplomatic passport and benefitting from diplomatic immunity, to performing official duties and affairs of state, to the building of the Lebanon Pavilion itself and projecting the country's formal aura, to shouldering the financial burdens of international taxes, tariff duties, and other charges accrued to the United States for articles and services used for the Lebanon exhibit.[35] As we shall see, Lebanon's participation in the New York World's Fair was a long-fought battle, and the challenges that Corm would encounter along the way were many and varied. But he was the man for the job.

Still, and bereft of the requisite state resources and institutional support, Charles Corm would conceive, design, and execute, almost single-handedly, what would become, on April 30, 1939, the "Lebanon Pavilion," one of the New York World's Fair's most charming and deeply moving cultural exhibits; "a museum of history and a temple of art," as described in the promotional literature, press releases, and news stories of the time.[36] More importantly, for the first time in modern history, representatives of Lebanon, festooned in national costumes, and flying a fluttering Lebanese national flag, were able to parade alongside more powerful nations on April 30, 1939, and process with pomp and fanfare around the Fair's Court of Peace, en route to a Lebanon exhibit that was to become at once a visual and legal representation of their country to the world.

Although hastily put together, the Lebanon Pavilion was so impressive an attraction that New York City's firebrand mayor, Fiorello H. La Guardia, would declare it the event's most delightful exhibit, and would use it as part of his publicity campaigns in an effort to promote the Fair as a whole and boost attendance to its individual exhibits. In one particular instance, during a promotional trip to Chicago, addressing a group of some seven hundred local businessmen, La Guardia took a swipe at that city's own 1933 World's Fair and its supposed indebtedness to burlesque dancer Sally Rand[37] for its success and claim to fame: "We have the Aquacade in our Fair," he boasted, "the most beautiful performance ever staged and one stripped of even the slightest semblance of vulgarity. We pride ourselves that our Fair will not be remembered for any hootchy-kootchy dance—and a fan means nothing to us."[38]

World Fairs were ordinarily reflections on past and contemporary human developments, seldom attempting to charter or forecast a future course. The New York World's Fair of 1939, on the other hand, took upon itself the responsibility of pioneering and projecting a picture of life in the future.[39] In that sense, this was a Fair intended to comfort and inspire, wrote the *New York Times* in August 1939, with not even "one inch [. . .] that is depressing or that leaves the visitor with a sense of hopelessness."[40] And the Lebanon put on display by Charles Corm came to fit snugly into that vision. Come to the New York World's Fair, Mayor La Guardia was reported to have told his Chicago audience, where we don't have Sally Rand's fans, but where you will find "hamburgers and frankfurters sold for a dime each," and where "the Pavilion of Lebanon" looms large.[41]

Curiously enough, La Guardia chose to trot out not some of the technological or scientific cornerstones of the Fair, which was after all his own brainchild and an international exposition expressly designed to showcase some of the world's greatest achievements. He noted that the Fair proposes to be "the last word in the application of the genius of man: progress in the development of science, of transportation, of the mode of living, of medicine."[42] Yet it was "soul" over "matter" that mattered most to the mayor. He did not, for instance, publicize the full-size replica of the Mayakovsky Station of the Moscow subway system, the pride and joy of Soviet Socialist city planning and recipient of the Fair's 1939 Grand Prize; nor did he tarry long on the impressive, car-based city model presented by General Motors' Futurama, an eloquent incarnation of the Fair's "World of Tomorrow" theme. Instead, an uncelebrated, little-known country on the eastern shores of the Mediterranean, its message of pacifism and humanism, and its displays as both museum and educational institution, became La Guardia's sales pitch. He noted that "Two of the [Fair's] most inspiring exhibits are those of Lebanon, an independent country with a history of 6,000 years behind it, and of Iceland, an independent country which can take some of the conceit out of the younger nations."[43] Lebanon mattered in La Guardia's telling because it gave hope to visitors, and it was a fine incarnation of what was to him the "soul" of the Fair. In the Court of Peace, on the northern end of the Corona Park fairgrounds, alongside the Hall of Nations where Corm's Lebanon took center stage, visitors were in the presence of a bevy of nations, said La Guardia, all happy nations, happy to be here, standing together,

> side by side, with the exception of one nation (Germany). And the representatives of all these governments sit down around the conference table in friendly fashion. If they did the same thing in Europe they would not be calling each other names and making faces at one another. But here, in the New York Fair, we have a great demonstration of nations living in peace with each other. And in the evening, in the Court of Peace, we find steam, water, gas and electricity—the elements used for war purposes abroad—combined in a great spectacle of beauty. [...] You are not human if you are not gripped by that sight.[44]

To be merely included in this lot of nations coexisting side by side—let alone to be acknowledged and singled out as a nation "with a history of 6,000 years behind it," putting on display a "most inspiring exhibit"—was a big nod of approval that was no small feat for a "Tiny Republic" barely coming into existence; a country whose name kept being misspelled in the American media reports of those days, and an exhibit that, in contravention of what had been put on display by other participants, had a cultural, historical, and largely didactic locus, rather than the cavalcades of technological, scientific, and economic achievements as paraded by others.[45]

Still, Corm's Lebanon garnered admiration incommensurate with its size and international renown at the time. In his introductory remarks at the dedication ceremony of the Lebanon Pavilion, E. F. Roosevelt, the Fair's Director of Foreign Participation spoke of the great privilege that it was for him, for New York, and for the United States in general to welcome Lebanon and its charming exhibit to the Fair. He also noted that Charles Corm, in an affectionate gesture of friendship, and with the help of twenty Lebanese-American girls dressed in Lebanese national costumes, offered New York City a thousand seeds of Lebanese cedars. Roosevelt concluded with the hope that the seeds, when planted, will flourish and grow like the friendship between Lebanon and the United States, and like the children of the Lebanese community transplanted and flourishing on American soil.[46] Later, representing Grover Whalen, President of the New York World's Fair, Julius Holmes spoke fondly of the country of Lebanon, the Lebanese people, and Charles Corm himself, and he expressed the high regard and appreciation that he and the Fair's organizers had for the noble principles that Corm was putting on display in New York: "your people have endured through the ages," said Holmes,

> [and they] left the mark of their high cultural attainments indelibly stamped upon the pages of the world's history; and, as your ancestors, the ancient Phoenicians carried the torch of civilization and progress throughout the then known world, so today, the people of Lebanon are to be found in the fore, wherever freedom and human progress exists. An indication of profound impression made by your people on this country, is the fact that there are in the United States twenty-seven towns named Lebanon, and from each of these towns the Mayors have sent to your Commissioner General their congratulations upon this occasion. Today, as we are on the brink of what may prove to be one of the greatest tragedies in history, the example of the Republic of Lebanon should stand as a beacon of hope to the whole world. [. . .] May I take this opportunity of conveying to you my personal admiration and my appreciation for the high principles, which you have here proclaimed in harmony with the theme and purpose of this International Exposition, which is dedicated to the spirit of peace and goodwill among the nations of the world. I salute you people of Lebanon, with a word in your own language—AHLA WA SAHLA. ("You are welcome in our hearts.")[47]

These pronouncements, liberally and formally extoling Lebanon's "substantial and beautiful contribution to the New York World's Fair," inspired and moved those in attendance to tears, prompting Corm to cable both Roosevelt and Holmes from his hotel near Central Park, on that very same evening of July 13, 1939, thanking them for honoring Lebanon on its official dedication day, and extending on behalf of the President of the Republic of Lebanon and the government and people of Lebanon his "deep gratitude and wholehearted thanks."[48] Furthermore, although the General Rules and Regulations of the New York World's Fair strictly prohibited awarding prizes or bestowing special honors on individual exhibitors, it was decided that some recognition was in order to representatives of foreign governments who had left a special mark, and who made exceptional contributions to the spirit of the Fair.[49] Charles Corm was *that* special Commissioner General who would come to be officially recognized for his "splendid assistance toward insuring the success of the Fair."[50] He became the recipient of the Golden Medal of Merit of the State of New Jersey, and the Gold Medal of New York City "for services rendered to the American people." Corm was also designated "Honorary Citizen of New York City" by Mayor La Guardia; a special honor bestowed on a rare few foreign dignitaries, and one that was voted unanimously at the General Assembly of New York City's Municipal Council in the winter of 1939.[51] Finally, on Thursday October 19, 1939, at the Lagoon of Nations near the Fair's southern gates, Lebanon was honored "with a Special Symphony of Fountains," accompanied by a light and water show integrating the Lebanese national colors, and set to the music of the Lebanese national anthem and an Oriental air by Czech composer Gabriel Sebek.[52] With this, Charles Corm's Lebanon can be said to have held its own in the parade of nations, putting its best foot forward on a major international stage, and making a name for itself when no other Middle Eastern states at the time—no Syria, no Iraq, no Palestine, and no Israel to speak of—had the wherewithal to brandish their distinct and independent personalities in like manner, nor earn the recognition of other sovereign nations in such a memorable international forum.

A WORLD OF NATION-STATES THROUGH WORLD'S FAIRS

World's Fairs are not trivial, whimsical, or improvised affairs, and they are not born out of nothing. They are the outcome of the industrial revolution, and they began taking shape in Europe during the first half of the nineteenth century. In their heyday World's Fairs were occasion for important global displays of national opulence and might, where nations were afforded the opportunity to parade, in an international forum, power, technological innovations, scientific discoveries, achievements in the arts, architecture, urban planning, and other such manifestations of cultural pride and national ingenuity. World's Fairs also afforded participants and host countries alike opportunities for international visibility, cooperation, and the boosting of trade and tourism. In many ways, the preparations, pageantry, and costs involved in putting together a World's Fair during the nineteenth and early twentieth centuries, *and* the fame and fortune that were often drawn from them by participants and organizers alike, can be compared in our times to the prestige and financial windfalls that often accompany hosting such awe-inspiring international spectacles as the Olympic Games.

Some of the most famous World's Fairs include the 1851 Great Exhibition of Hyde Park in the United Kingdom, Chicago's 1893 World's Columbian Exposition, the Paris *Exposition Universelle* of 1900, and the 1929 Barcelona Universal Exposition.[53] Many of the innovations on display at these international forums have since become iconic representations—and indeed essentials—of our modern world. To wit, the Centennial Exposition of Philadelphia in 1876 introduced the telephone, ushering in a new era of communication; the 1893 Chicago World's Fair introduced electricity, and the Louisiana Purchase Exposition of St. Louis in 1904 heralded the advent of the automobile and the beginnings of a new age of transportation. Likewise, such common ingredients of modern life as the escalator, the diesel engine, talking pictures, and magnetic recording technology—not to mention *Art Nouveau* and the Eiffel Tower itself, the world's most-visited national monument—all had their beginnings at the Paris *Exposition Universelle* of 1900. Similarly, avant-guard modernist architecture, and the iconic Bauhaus and Barcelona chairs, which came to define what is referred to as "popular classics" in the modern home and office furnishings of today, had their launch at the 1929 Barcelona Universal Exposition. Likewise, sanitation, modern-city infrastructure, urban planning, and extensive use of street lighting were some of the hallmarks of the 1893 Chicago World's Fair—at that time symbols of "American Exceptionalism" no doubt, but today the physical foundations of modernity, urban development, and the ideal "state of the art" archetype of modern living.

It is within this context that the New York World's Fair, and Lebanon's participation in it, must be placed. Held in the Borough of Queens' Flushing Meadows–Corona Park, the 1939–1940 New York World's Fair is still, to this day, considered to have been the most ambitious and extravagant international exposition ever held in the United States. Its inspiration had been Chicago's 1933–1934 "Century of Progress" event, and New York's intent was to surpass Chicago's successful exhibition, with the aim of shaking the local and national economy out of the torpid aftermaths of the Great Depression, and re-energizing trade, industry, the arts, and international understanding at a time when the winds of a second world war were beginning to gather steam on an old continent tending to festering wounds and seething rivalries. But the New York World's Fair of 1939 was up against more serious challenges than the global; challenges issuing from New Yorkers and Americans in general, who were strongly opposed to the building of what they deemed a symbol of decadence and profligacy at a time when austerity would have been the decent practice. And so, it was against great odds and vicious criticisms that La Guardia would carry on with his project; a project that would require, throughout its lifespan, continuous publicity, marketing, and public relations exploits to keep visitors filing through its gates.

The actual construction of the Fair—what would ultimately become the Flushing Meadows–Corona Park Fairgrounds—began in 1936, on what had initially been a colossal municipal dump. Commemorating the one hundred fiftieth anniversary of the birth of the United States under a Federal Constitution, and the inauguration of George Washington as its first President, in its first capital city on April 30, 1789, the Fair was a festival for the "average man" celebrating the past, the present, and the future.[54] What it placed on display were the achievements of a century and a half of American life—and more broadly the achievements of the modern world—in science, industry, politics, the arts, and literature. It brought forth "every interest and activity of mankind, government, means of production, means of transportation, means of communication, means of distribution, business administration, shelter, clothing and cosmetics, sustenance, health and public welfare, education, recreation, arts and religion."[55] Moreover, the 1939 New York World's Fair presented foreign governments with an opportunity of establishing contacts with large audiences of tourists, politicians, diplomats, students, and foreign dignitaries, hence fostering new friendships and honing the building blocks of international cooperation and cross-cultural goodwill and understanding. This was a project that mobilized "thousands of architects, engineers, designers, artists, contractors, and trades people, [who worked] around the clock, to transform the Corona Dump into [the global festival that] the New York World's Fair" became.[56]

It was this kind of industry, ambition, determination, and above all a quest for an international role and a serious standing for Lebanon among the nations, that animated Charles Corm and ignited his desire to "go to the Fair." As mentioned earlier in the Prologue, Corm was particularly fond of international exhibitions and trade shows, and had indeed attended the Barcelona Expo in 1929, where he was left in awe of the masterwork of architect Ludwig Mies van der Rohe at the German Pavilion. Indeed, van der Rohe's work turned out to be a complement of Corm's particular predilection for simplicity and purity in architectural form. Of special interest to him was van der Rohe's fondness for the free-flowing, open spatial concepts, wedding structures of minimal framework to materials such as glass, steel, and animal skin. It should be noted that both Corm's office and home interior design and furnishings would come to reflect this penchant for open spaces, and the particular sensitivity that Corm had developed for the Bauhaus styles encountered at the Barcelona Universal Exposition. In that sense, Charles Corm was the child of his times and indeed a "Young Phoenician" at heart; an impavid pioneer, a subtle and sensitive intellect, a worldly man of taste, an elegant artist engaged in the trends and styles of his era, and a savvy businessman who knew with profound perspicacity the importance of a country's international reputation in its quest for legitimacy in the eyes of its own peoples, its colonial administrators, and its irredentist neighbors; hence the crucial importance of representing Lebanon as such, at least from Corm's own purview, as a distinct entity at this global extravaganza that was the 1939 New York World's Fair.

The Fair, which sprawled over twelve thousand acres of Flushing Meadows–Corona Park, was the second largest American expo of all times, featuring exhibits from some fifty-seven countries from around the world, and visited by upwards of forty-four million people.[57] The *Book of Nations* (1939) described the New York World's Fair as the "Living Geography of the World," representing "the collaboration of [. . .] nations intent on advancing self-interest by furthering the sum total of international understanding; [. . .] a testimonial to the inherent friendliness among men."[58] This was an event on a global scale, intended to bring back the United States—and the world at large—from the dreary days of the Great Depression, and forestall a sense of despondency that was beginning to grip Europe with Hitler's ascent to power, and with the winds of a new international conflict blowing across the continents.

In that spirit of tenacity and hopefulness, on July 6, 1937, the United States Senate would pass a bill appropriating three million dollars (the equivalent of fifty million dollars based on the 2013 Consumer Price Index) of federal money to finance the New York World's Fair.[59] This was in addition to the thirty million dollars expended by participating governments, another thirty million dollars spent by non-governmental exhibitors, twenty-six million dollars pledged by New York City, seventeen million dollars appropriated from concessionaires, and six million dollars contributed by New York State.[60] These monumental expenditures issued out of an act of political and economic skill and foresight, intended to ward off a looming global conflagration and marshal a new kind of national and international enthusiasm, cooperation, and positive optimism—where none might have been warranted. This is how important this global event had been, to New York, to America, and to the world certainly. But for our purposes, the Fair was obviously a golden opportunity for Charles Corm himself to put on display a certain image of Lebanon that he had wished to project to the world; an independent, sovereign, restored Lebanon, issuing a message of peace and hope and humanism to the world; "6,000 years of peaceful activities in the service of mankind," as the exhibit came to be referred to colloquially and in media reports and official promotional materials of the time.[61]

The inaugural ceremonies of the New York World's Fair took place on a hot Sunday afternoon, on April 30, 1939. They were presided over by President Franklin Delano Roosevelt, with more than 200,000 people in attendance.[62] As mentioned earlier, this opening date coincided with the sesquicentennial anniversary of George Washington's inauguration, in New York City, as the first President of the United States. In his opening remarks, tracing the history of his country, from its founding to the investiture of its first president—taking his oath of office on April 30, 1789—all the way to the present day, in 1939, on the grounds of Flushing Meadows–Corona Park, President Roosevelt marveled at America's accomplishments, the American miracle as it were, and its evolution from a minor revolutionary state (and a former colony to boot) to the world's most enduring, prosperous, liberal, and dynamic republic. The New York World's Fair, noted President Roosevelt, in the tradition of America's ethos of openness and representative government, is proud of the participation of "most of the nations of the world," under the optimistic theme of "The World of Tomorrow."[63] All people of good will, who shall come to visit this World's Fair in New York, continued Roosevelt,

> will find that the eyes of the United States are fixed on the future. Our wagon is hitched to a star. But it is a star of good-will, a star of progress for mankind, a star of greater happiness and less hardship, a star of international good-will, and, above all, a star of peace. May the months to come carry us forward in the rays of that hope. I hereby dedicate the New York World's Fair of 1939 and declare it open to all mankind.[64]

It is no small wonder that a youthful, optimist, and ambitious Charles Corm would be drawn to these themes of the New York World's Fair. For, those values incarnating what the United States stood for, were the very same ones that nourished the energy of Charles Corm, fired up his spirits, and fed his imagination, in the tradition of his industrious Phoenician forefathers. It is this spirit of goodwill, pacifism, and generous bequests to mankind that would come to imbue the motifs that Corm would place on display in the Lebanese Pavilion of the New York World's Fair. And it is in this same spirit of openness to the other, one of the building blocks of Phoenician Humanism as portrayed in the body of Charles Corm's own work, that Mayor La Guardia would welcome the international community to his city's exhibits. "I bid you welcome," he said in his inaugural remarks, noting that "in a city of seven and one-half million people, coming from every land and every country, and children of these people who have come from every country in the world, live here together in peace and harmony."[65] It is in this "city of today" he concluded, that we greet you and welcome the globe into "the world of tomorrow."[66]

Like La Guardia—who would become a friend and admirer of Charles Corm's, conferring upon him the title of honorary citizen of New York City and offering him the city's ceremonial key[67]—Charles Corm was a work glutton, a polyglot, an iconoclast, and an upright, charismatic, and committed crusader on behalf of his country.[68] He was involved in everything and appeared to be everywhere at once. A clever showman, a keen reader of human characters, theatrical, sometimes flashy, Corm's lodestar had always been efficiency, honesty, fighting corruption, and keeping his country's highest interests always a priority.

The greatest tragedy in a people's life, wrote a youthful Charles Corm in 1919, was for it to be denied its rights to freedom and self-determination, and to see those inalienable national rights be squandered and surrendered to the will and base designs of resentful irredentist nationalisms.[69] Corm was expressing these views at a time when the Christians of Mount-Lebanon and the former Ottoman *Vilayet* (State) of Beirut were clamoring for the establishment of a distinct Lebanese Republic, while at the same time an inchoate Arab nationalism was calling for the creation of a single Arab kingdom on the remnants of former Ottoman provinces—Lebanon included. Lebanese jurist Paul Noujaim (penname Jouplain) summed up the situation of those times as follows:

> [. . .] as a motley crew of political currents jostle and joust over the political future of geographic Syria, the Lebanese Nation, zealous for its independence, remains steadfast in its rejection of all notions and all attempts at attaching its territories to any of those of its neighbors. [. . .] Therefore, the Lebanese Nation demands the establishment of an independent political entity in tune with [Lebanon's] geographic position and compatible with its historical accretions.[70]

As mentioned in the preceding chapters, Charles Corm was wary of independence without sovereignty for Lebanon; a new legal existence with a new kind of statehood replacing Ottoman authority with Arab domination.[71] Indeed, Corm spurned the notion trotted out by some of his contemporaries of a future Lebanese state beholden to an Arab collective and perhaps even tied to a future Arab state. He was ill-prepared to consign the specificity and diversity of the Lebanese to a single, unitary, and uniform Arab edifice.[72]

But Corm's grievances were not limited to Arab nationalist irredentism. He was likewise critical of his own compatriots and their deficient grasp of "republican" values. Subjected for many centuries to "Eastern" despotism and foreign rule, and want of the individualism and discipline valorized by the West, Charles Corm deemed the Lebanese of his day unprepared for self-rule and sovereignty,[73] and unable to administer and safeguard their collective identity.[74] But this flaw, he believed, could be rectified. However, what in his view might have been more problematic to the Lebanese collective was Arab nationalism and its attempts at folding Lebanon—and indeed the whole of the former Ottoman provinces of the Levant—into a proposed Arab state. And this, he fought zealously. Yet, his ardent patriotism remained innocuous, benevolent, and conscientious. And as a matter of both temperament and principle, Charles Corm was loath to the militarism, bitterness, and irredentism practiced by contemporary movements, in the Middle East and elsewhere.[75] "The Arabs would do better tending to their Arabia," rather than initiating another era of Arab colonialism in the Levant, he wrote in a 1919 essay that had been massively censored by the French Mandatory authorities.[76] Little did he know that his forebodings would become a self-fulfilling prophecy in the Lebanon of the second half of the twentieth century.

At any rate, there was a special kind of honesty, commitment, and principled patriotism that animated Charles Corm. This brutal honesty had perhaps been the basic ingredient in the complicity and friendship that had developed between Corm and Fiorello La Guardia. For, in early 1937, deep in the thicket of preparing for the World's Fair, La Guardia showed how he was equally unafraid (as Corm) of following his own moral compass and pursuing his commitment to his own ethical principles, jarring as they might have been to the criteria of "political correctness" of his times. La Guardia instigated an international incident in an address to the American Jewish Congress in New York in 1937, when he called Adolph Hitler a fanatic and a danger to world peace, suggesting this rising world leader be made into a central figure at the upcoming New York World's Fair's "Chamber of Horrors." Little did La Guardia know that his prescience—viewed at the time as bombast and aspersions cast upon a major head of state—would come to haunt the world in the years that followed.[77]

As it turns out, this was the same kind of subtle perspicacity, determination, energy, moral courage, and overall temperament that animated Charles Corm. It was also this same kind of openness and the quest for harmony and principled pacifism that Corm would put on display at the Lebanon exhibit; "6,000 years of peaceful activities in the service of mankind" as the Lebanon Pavilion became known colloquially.[78] In this spirit, a panoramic mural of Lebanon, viewed from the sea, greeted visitors entering the Pavilion. Above the mural, figured with lapidary brevity, the Lebanon epigram of the times, as imagined and longed for in Corm's pacifist yearnings: it read "NO ARMY, NO NAVY, NO AMMUNITIONS, NO INTERNAL DEBT . . ." This was the Lebanon that Corm had brought to New York, and this was the image of the country, and both its mission and ambition, as he'd imagined them and as he wanted them broadcast to the world—"the country's four virtues," as described in a July 20, 1939, *New York Times* article.[79]

"Lebanon loves, believes, hopes, and works" read those Lebanese virtues at the exhibit, reflecting the kinds of ethos expounded in Charles Corm's *La Montagne Inspirée* where, a mere decade earlier, he had written that:

> The wealth we rest upon, no one can take away, / Bottomless wellsprings and mines without end, / Bubbling with ruby, smoldering underneath, and beading on our brows; / Our appanage as a people, is endurance and poise; / Our armor

and coat of arms, for the past six thousand years, / have been to think, to build, and to love, / And to know that beyond that, all else will come to naught. [80]

If only for this mindset, proclaimed the *New York Times*, the pavilion of the Republic of Lebanon has been a resounding success, "although most of its 4,000 to 5,000 daily visitors could not have found the country it represents on the map."[81]

LEBANON'S AMBASSADOR TO THE NEW WORLD

And so, ever the ambitious charismatic visionary, Charles Corm decided to return to the United States in 1939. A quarter century following his first encounters with America, and five years after he had absconded all commercial activity, and therefore all contacts with the Ford Motor Company and its American homeland, this time, accompanied by his young bride, Samia Baroody, and (coincidentally) with the winds of *another* war blowing through Europe and soon to engulf the entire globe,[82] a still-youthful and antsy optimist in spite of his ailing health, Charles Corm would pack up his native skies and set sail to the New York World's Fair.

Already in 1933, paying homage to Lebanon's enterprising expat communities and its intrepid mariners peacefully and skillfully sailing through the ages, Charles Corm wrote that a Lebanese worth his salt never travels without carrying in tow with him bits and fragrances of the land of his birth; the homeland he'd left behind:

> Exiles and vagabonds pack up their native skies, / and carry them along, through all their ports of call; / They pilfer their perfumes, tinge them with tints and hues, / of memories from home![83]

And so would Charles Corm, in the tradition of his forefathers, roll up his native Lebanon and carry it to America. Representing a small, fledgling republic at a World's Fair—indeed at one of the largest international exhibits of its kind to date—was no small feat; not least because Lebanon in 1939 was still under French Mandate, and was viewed by the French as a colonial chattel to be answerable to the whims and will of its colonial masters. In fact, save for Lebanon itself, none of France's "Colonial Possessions" were represented as distinct autonomous entities at the New York World's Fair. Many held exhibits to be sure, but they were all on display at the "French Colonies" Pavilion, authorized and regulated by the French government, and expressly marked as French dominions and crowning achievements of France's *Mission Civilizatrice* (or Civilizing Mission).[84] The same applied to Great Britain and its colonial possessions. And so, Algeria, Tunisia, French Indo-China (today's Vietnam), and Tahiti were all under the marquee of the

"French Colonies" exhibits. Even Cameroon and Syria (both technically speaking Mandates, not colonies per se), and Morocco (a protectorate), would not be accorded the right to their own pavilions. But Lebanon and France evinced special affections toward each other, and the Lebanese in turn, and in the person of Charles Corm, upheld French values, held the French to higher standards, and expected from them much in return. "In the thicket of the Great War," wrote Corm in 1919,

> hunted down by the Turks, and betrayed by the Arabs, I squandered my small fortune and my old father's life-savings to go into hiding; not so much to dodge military service as to avoid the shame of having to don an Ottoman military uniform. And so a deserter I became, taking sanctuary in the remote caves of Mount-Lebanon, my searching eyes riveted to the deserted high seas below, at times comforted to see go by a beloved solitary vessel flying France's tricolor flag. And with what unspeakable joy, at such a sight, my arms would stretch out to the horizon of deliverance, the echoes of my exhilarated cheers of joy and anguish bouncing back from the distance, my body rising skyward, erect among the rocks, like a suddenly resurrected slab of marble jutting out of the ruins of an ancient Temple.[85]

When the French finally came to Lebanon's rescue on October 8, 1918, writes Corm, Lebanon and the Lebanese willingly submitted to France's desires, like a bride on her wedding night.[86] And so, on that day, having spent an entire overnight prior racing down the slopes of Mount Lebanon to be the first at Beirut Harbor, to kiss the flag of France, "the mother of all sacred liberties," the flag whose folds, in Corm's direst hours of doubt, still lapped at his soul, the way it now flutters against Lebanon's azure blue skies, a young Charles Corm eagerly hopped aboard the first French vessel he saw docked and proceeded to

> hug and kiss those beloved uniformed strangers, dearer to me than my own parents; elated, jubilant, bordering on delirium, I felt the blood of my arteries erupting in joyful song, echoing triumphantly within me. [. . .] That night I slept peacefully, but not before having said a passionate prayer—even though I can no longer recall the last time I had prayed—asking God Almighty to safeguard France, and to keep her always; always strong, always great, always grandiose.[87]

Of course those events of October 8, 1918, are reported in traditional Middle East Studies literature as the Franco-British occupation and partitioning of former Ottoman provinces, and the beginning of the French Mandate period over Lebanon and Syria. But not so from Charles Corm's perspective! No "partitioning" of previously "whole" cohesive entities ever took place— to the contrary, France and Britain in reality stitched together smaller fractious Ottoman administrative units, shaping them into what became Iraq,

Syria, Palestine, and the rest—and France's "occupation" was in truth a "liberation" of Lebanon and its restitution to its "historical and natural frontiers."[88] Furthermore, the League of Nations Mandate regime assigned to France and Britain—a euphemism for colonialism by the reasoning of most period historians—was instead instated at the behest and with the approval of the Lebanese, not in spite of them nor to their detriment according to this Cormian (and indeed Lebanese) version of history.[89] Nor, it should be made clear, was Corm's Francophilia unconditional or complacent. In a 1919 open letter addressed to French High Commissioner Henri Gouraud, an associate of Charles Corm's, the poet Jacques Tabet, on the pages of Corm's *La Revue Phénicienne*, was already laying down his group's unyielding commitment to Lebanese sovereignty and their expectations from the French Mandate and its official representatives. "We have put our hands in yours," said Tabet to Gouraud,

> only because we are confident that you will lead us to the fulfillment of our sacred dream [of liberty and sovereignty]—a dream that you have exalted as well. Yet, to date, nothing has been done in this direction, and I hasten to acknowledge that [for a variety of valid reasons] this goal remains unattainable for the time being. What we need at this juncture is a pair of skilled and spirited hands to pull our country out of the decay to which it was subjected during the war years, and ready our people for the roles it wishes to play. This is our understanding of your mission among us. [. . .] We shall not erect obstacles to your noble endeavors, and we shall assist you to the best of our abilities every step of the way. However, just as much has been given you, much is expected of you in return.[90]

As we shall see below, this is the tone in which many Francophile Lebanese, ordinarily expected to yield to France's colonial appetite, defined their position vis-à-vis the Mandatory authority and interpreted the relationship—as they saw it—between ruler and ruled. Hence the unbounded pride in Corm's temperament and demeanor as representative of a distinct, independent sovereign nation at the 1939 New York World's Fair—even though he might have been a proponent of French influence and presence in Lebanon during the early 1920s. Indeed, reflecting the prevalent attitudes of his times, many of Lebanon's Christians would for a long time remain avid advocates of French oversight and protection of Lebanon, largely for fear that their newly established state devolve into an appendage to some larger Arab entity in the works. Such apprehensions are confirmed by a wealth of unpublished papers, memoirs, diplomatic correspondence, and official internal memos and exchanges between the French and Lebanon's Christians. The following is quite telling in this regard: On September 1, 1921, Beirut commemorated the first anniversary celebration of the establishment of Greater Lebanon, wrote the French High Commissioner, General Gouraud, in an internal memo addressed to the Quai d'Orsay:

> All of Beirut's Christians took part in these solemn festivities, and all did so with much enthusiasm. Conversely, save for a handful of notables who attended the Governor's reception, Beirut's Muslims refused to participate and refrained from festooning their homes with Lebanese flags to mark the joyous occasion. The message inciting them to abstain from taking part in these celebrations was launched by the Beirut based Muslim Youth Party, a group notorious for its hostility to the Mandate and to the status of Greater Lebanon in its current configuration. This group had even dispatched a telegram of protest to the Syrian Congress in Geneva, and to the League of Nations protesting the establishment of Greater Lebanon. Indeed, the Muslims of Beirut would rather see the entire coastal region of this country, from Tripoli to Tyre, that is to say a good portion of the former Vilayet of Beirut, amputated from the rest of Greater Lebanon. It goes without saying that we cannot allow this sort of dismemberment to take place. [. . .] We must keep in mind that if we were to give in to the demands of these Muslim agitators [. . .] we would be ill disposed to prevent, say, the Bekaa Valley from following suit in the future and seeking attachment to the State of Damascus. With this scenario in mind, and with the possibility of Mount-Lebanon reverting back to its 1860 frontiers, it would be nearly impossible for this state to survive without French governmental subsidies.[91]

The tone, semantics, and content of Gouraud's dispatch are an interesting reflection of the kind of challenges that the French (and the "Greater Lebanese") were facing in the Levant of the early twentieth century. Gouraud's discomfort with the idea of continuous French subsidy of Lebanon's was perhaps a translation of France's intention to eventually leave the country rather than keep it under French domination. Likewise, referring to the State of Damascus as such confirms the notion that Syria as a distinct entity had not yet come into being, and, indeed, would not become a reality until much later in 1936.

The early twentieth-century dangers lurking around the newly formed state of Greater Lebanon were real, from the perspective of both the French authorities and the Christian component of this emerging republic. And so, the over-reliance on French protection—and indeed the ardent support that Lebanon's Christians lent to the Mandate regime, a general attitude incarnated in the body of Charles Corm's literary work and his other intellectual and social activities—may not have been without reason. Yet Corm had been eager to separate Lebanon from France in the court of world opinion and on the international stage. Indeed, on the day of his arrival in New York City, on April 15, 1939, Corm solemnly and proudly announced to a *New York Times* reporter being "the first Lebanese citizen" to have set foot on American soil.[92] As will be remembered from earlier chapters, Charles Corm had indeed spent an extended period of time in New York City, between 1912 and 1914, so his April 15th "landing" in New York was certainly not his first visit, and he could not have possibly been the "first Lebanese" to have set foot on American soil in 1939. Yet Corm's allegation to the contrary may not have been faulty; indeed, his claims were to have been the "first Lebanese citizen" and not merely the "first Lebanese" to have landed in America. It should be remembered that before World War I Lebanon had been "part of the Ottoman Empire," as noted the *New York Times*; it later "became a French mandate, and last year [1938] it achieved the status of a republic."[93] Still Lebanon would not gain independence from France until 1943, and the last French troops would not withdraw from Lebanon before 1946. But such was the "romance" between Lebanon and France—one that is made abundantly (and publicly) clear in the Lebanese exhibit as will be shown below—that the French occupation of Lebanon would not be perceived as occupation at all; at least not by the Lebanese of Charles Corm's persuasion! And so, it may be argued that on April 15, 1939, Charles Corm might indeed have become "the first Lebanese citizen"—and by all accounts the first Lebanese "diplomat"—to have landed in America; the capstone of generations of earlier immigrants from Mount-Lebanon who might have been Lebanese emotively and spiritually but not legally, and who might have ultimately lain the groundwork to Corm's own "official" landing.[94]

In a report summing up his own work at the Fair from the spring of 1939 until the winter of 1940, Charles Corm wrote that "a nation's international relations are a foundational component of its public life and the most salient sign of its vitality."[95] Betraying the businessman he had stopped (albeit never really ceased) being a mere five years earlier, Corm affirmed that a country's international dealings are indeed its very identity and its brand name as it were. "No country that wished to prosper and live in peace could live in isolation," he wrote.[96] In this sense, he noted,

> a country is not all that different from a businessman, whose capital and creditworthiness derive from the size and the "goodwill" of his clientele; it is for this very reason that a company's corporate name in the French language is referred to as *"raison sociale."*[97]

This "raison sociale," argued Corm, was the "reason" for and the logic behind a company's "social being"; its identity and *raison d'être* as it were, in both the juridical and conventional sense.[98] The same applied to the existence, the presence and personality, and the legitimacy of a nation in his view—and the Lebanese nation in particular. Furthermore, a nation's identity in the international arena, he wrote, requires a host of complex, deliberate, and onerous representative bodies—a diplomatic corps for instance, and an intellectual elite steeped in the nation's local traditions, yet disciplined, cultured, urbane, and well-versed in the ways of the world.[99] That is indeed the role that Corm arrogated himself at the Fair; not so much—and not only—as Commissioner General, but as outright "ambassador" of Lebanon, an emissary on its behalf, and both its voice and the bearer of its message to the world.[100] In a 1938 report to Lebanese Minister of National Education Khalil Kseib, Charles Corm wrote that "World's Fairs are above all else a nation's work of Art, Propaganda, and Prestige," and that *that* was precisely Corm's commission and mission at the Fair.[101]

By taking the initiative to participate independently in the New York World's Fair, noted Corm in his private papers and in reports filed with the Lebanese government in early 1940, Lebanon had for the first time in its modern history partaken of such an event of global significance, all on its own, at its own risk, and in such a deliberate, dignified official capacity.[102] This is all the more important when considering that when Lebanon received President Franklin Roosevelt's official invitation to take part in the New York World's Fair in 1939–1940, the presidential dispatch was sent through the intermediary of the American mission to Beirut, addressed to the American Consul General Theodore Mariner, in "Beirut-Syria," somehow suggesting an inchoate Lebanon as an addendum to a well-defined Syria.[103] It is no wonder that Corm insisted Lebanon's participation be made independently of France's exhibit, and that it showcase a sumptuous pageantry of national artifacts, pride, history, and sovereignty.

A matter of a powerful symbolic significance is worth mentioning in this regard: When President Roosevelt dispatched the official invitations to foreign governments requesting their participation in the New York World's Fair, a number of Middle Eastern countries including Egypt, Syria, Iraq, and Morocco initially expressed strong interest in taking part. Yet, they never followed through and never signed the requisite contracts pledging their participation—with the exception of Iraq, whose exhibit opened behind schedule and barely attracted any attention. With Syria out of the picture, in October 1938 Charles Corm would request that the exhibit space initially slated for that country—some 10,000 square feet of Section GF-4 in the Hall of Nations—be given to Lebanon. And as indicated by a number of telegrams from Beirut, Corm was insistent that Syria's section in particular be given to Lebanon.[104] The fact that Section GF-4 was considerably larger than what had been initially assigned to Lebanon may have played a role in Corm's motives. However, the importance—and indeed the symbolism—of the fact that a lot that had initially been Syria's, and which can now be claimed to Lebanon, must not be discounted! Lebanon's borders during the 1930s were still amorphous and their validity still disputed. So were Lebanon's identity and distinct personality often negated by proponents of irredentist Syrian and Arab nationalism. For Lebanon to take possession of something considered to be Syria's sent a strong message of defiance to those impugning Lebanese sovereignty and nursing irredentist passions; a squaring of the circle as it were, and to irredentist Arab nationalists a doze of their own medicine.

This was Lebanon's moment to shine. Yet, there had been no precedent in the country's recent history that could have prepared it for such a weighty enterprise, wrote Corm in his private papers, and by going to New York, the Lebanese Commissioner General set out on a mission bereft of any prior experience and devoid of any preliminary channels that would have otherwise facilitated his contacts with the American authorities, introduced him to the diplomatic and consular corps present in New York, or familiarized him with representatives of some fifty-seven foreign countries and forty-eight American states to whom it was both his responsibility and duty to promote and represent Lebanon on a daily basis.[105] In this sense, there were no "second chances" afforded Corm; he was allowed only one attempt to make a good first impression. The Commissioner General of the Lebanon Pavilion, he wrote,

> did not have the benefit of the smallest Lebanese vice-consular representative, nor even the tiniest token of a consular officer to assist in the daily tasks of running the Lebanon Pavilion. There was no local residence for the Lebanese delegation [limited as it was to Charles Corm and his wife, Samia], no local staff, no local information center to guide and advise the Commissioner General as he navigated the intricacies of American culture and international affairs. [. . .] Indeed, the Commissioner General of the Lebanese Republic was the only Commissioner General of his kind among his foreign peers; the only emissary cut off from his home country, who couldn't so much as hope for assistance from his home state in Beirut, and who couldn't even rely on a local representative body of the Lebanese government to lend a hand, since no such body [and no such hand] existed.[106]

And so, one of Corm's major challenges as Commissioner General of the Lebanon Pavilion, and what differentiated him and his tasks from the organizers and managers of other exhibits, was the complete lack of institutional, political, moral, and financial support of his home country once he was in New York. No fiscal or budgetary support was forthcoming from Lebanon—besides the initial funds to cover some of the *objets d'art* designed by Corm, and their shipment to New York. Moreover, as Corm noted above, there was no political entity in New York representing Lebanon—no diplomatic mission, consular staff, or the like—that could have lent guidance and assistance. Indeed, at their own expense, Charles Corm and his wife, Samia, resided at the Park Central Hotel for the duration of their stay, not on the grounds of some official "Lebanese mission."[107] It should be mentioned that spending upwards of seven months at one of midtown Manhattan's most glamorous addresses of the times was not an affair for someone with modest means or a limited budget. Certainly the Lebanese government had not the wherewithal back in those days to cover the living expenses of its Commissioner General at the Park Central. Nor would it have been becoming of the emissary of a sovereign nation to reside at a New York address with a lesser reputation or name recognition than that of the Park Central. And so, if the Park Central Hotel of the Roaring Twenties had been the haunt of the likes of Tommy Dorsey, Jackie Gleason, Mae West, or First Lady Eleanor Roosevelt, who kept a permanent private suite there, so would it also, and in the absence of a proper Lebanese Consular Compound, be worthy of Lebanon's first "Ambassador" to the United States and the Commissioner General of the Lebanon Pavilion at the New York World's Fair. Thus, for the duration of Corm's stay in New York, from mid-April to mid-November 1939, the Park Central Hotel would become the official address of the Lebanese government: an upscale elegant and extravagant address, maintained at Charles Corm's own expense; a place befitting the image of Lebanon that he aimed to project to the world, and a home base where he entertained foreign dignitaries, conducted the affairs of state, and managed the construction and operation of the Lebanese Pavilion.[108]

Yet this was no consolation to a sensitive young poet who would still have preferred the dignity of a proper, permanent Lebanese residence, worthy of Lebanon's station as a sovereign nation. In his private journal relative to the Fair, Corm described himself as an "abandoned orphan, drowned in the opulence, responsibilities, and spectacular political, economic, military, and naval displays" of other foreign representatives, their consular personnel, and their national pavilions.[109] For in the case of Lebanon, even the minutest logistical and housekeeping details pertaining to the Fair—from hiring building contractors, to supervising Corm's architectural and interior design for the Lebanon Pavilion, to maintaining and landscaping the Lebanese grounds—were all Corm's responsibility.[110] Navigating the details of American political culture, social etiquette, and business and labor relations were also his duty and his liability. To wit, in his blueprints of the Lebanon Pavilion, Corm had to make allowances for engineering and plumbing and electrical installations conforming to American specifications; nothing was to be taken trivially in the construction of the Lebanon Pavilion; everything had to be accounted for, from snow removal services, to labor relations, workman compensation, and health department inspections and fire codes, to the maintenance of the interior and exterior of Lebanon's building—including weatherproofing the structure itself, its free-standing sculptures, bas-reliefs, paintings, dioramas, and roofs and parapets where necessary.[111] The fairgrounds were, after all, a city in its own right, larger than the city of Cleveland, Ohio, boasting its own port, its own rapid transit line, its own bus system, and its own police and fire departments.[112] And Lebanon, tiny as it had been in that intricate clockwork, had to function accurately and in perfect timing and harmony within that larger whole. In fact, on a daily basis and for as long as the Fair remained open, its transportation systems had to manage some of the greatest mass movements of people in history (with some 250,000 daily visitors); it featured eighty restaurant able to accommodate forty-three thousand customers at a time (this, without accounting for smaller food stands and national restaurants within each of the pavilions); it had a total of forty-five hundred public restrooms; it featured a six-hundred-strong police force, multiple health centers, ambulant clinics, parking areas with over forty-thousand car capacity, and sixty-five miles of landscaped sidewalks and roadways.[113] This was the kind of immensity, precision, and opulence into which Charles Corm had to fit Lebanon. And to this effect, in March 1939, mere weeks before the official opening of the Fair, he would transfer a down payment of thirty thousand dollars to the New York branch of the French American Banking Corporation, to cover the expenses of fitting up the Lebanese section of the World's Fair before his arrival on April 15.[114] When most countries that had initially expressed strong desire to take part in the Fair retracted, mainly due to financial constraints and the onerous burden that participation would have entailed for them, by March 21, 1939, Lebanon was officially erecting its exhibit in the Hall of Nations section of the fairgrounds—behind schedule to be sure, but determined to make a splash.[115] The total cost of the Pavilion, covering only the structure itself, its roof, its rough walls and rough floors, ran at about seven dollars per square foot (or roughly seventy thousand dollars for a space of ten thousand square feet). This figure did not include the costs of the exhibit itself, the interior paintwork, and the finishing of walls and floors, for which Corm himself was responsible, and which he had to supervise and execute upon his arrival so as to fit this whole into the pieces he was putting on display.[116]

But there were other concerns as well, beyond the logistical, the budgetary, and the diplomatic. Corm was being badgered and harassed, night and day, by the intrigues and backbiting of Lebanese émigré groups, who seemed to have resented him for shunning their personal feuds, their political disputes, and their internecine struggles for leadership and influence within the community and at the Fair. In fact, prior to his arrival to New York, Charles Corm had received correspondence from E. F. Roosevelt calling his attention to individuals attempting to gain entry to the Fair before its opening, some of whom were trying to obtain employment at the Lebanon Pavilion through misrepresentation as Pavilion guards, foremen, or even firemen.[117] It is perhaps this kind of nepotism and cronyism—that may have been as common in New York at that time as it is pervasive in Lebanon of today—that Charles Corm was making an effort to avoid, and which might have in the process angered members of the Lebanese expat community still beholden to these time-honored practices of the old country. There is also evidence that a prominent Lebanese New Yorker from Lower Manhattan, George Dagher, had appointed himself Commissioner General of the Lebanon Pavilion in

April 1938, and was acting on behalf of the Lebanese government without authorization, even though Charles Corm had been officially designated to that post at an earlier date, and later confirmed in it by an October 1, 1938, Presidential Decree.[118] Yet Dagher would continue acting in his self-appointed capacities as Commissioner General, and would continue deceiving the Fair authorities—and obviously himself as well—that "a Committee has been appointed in Lebanon [. . . and has] chosen Mr. Dagher as Commissioner. Final arrangements have been drawn up in a decree which was signed by the President of Lebanon [. . . and] Mr. Dagher expects a cable appointment very shortly," which he had promised to relay to the Fair authorities in due time.[119] Needless to say there exists no evidence suggesting that such a committee was ever appointed, nor that it had chosen Mr. Dagher as Commissioner General; certainly no available presidential directives or special decrees relative to the Fair have come to the mention of Mr. Dagher's name, let alone were there any indicating Mr. Dagher's claimed designation as Commissioner General. In sum, Dagher's conduct amounted to an unauthorized impersonation of a government official, and a misrepresentation of the Lebanese authorities, and Charles Corm set out to clean house upon his arrival to New York, restoring professionalism and integrity to the Lebanese "brand," and bringing the Pavilion under his supervision and back to the distinction and respectability that it deserved and that he had envisaged for it.

Evidently, Corm's unwillingness to stand for the aberrant practices of his countrymen abroad must have earned him the resentment of those still coveting his position, and efforts were made as a result to frustrate his successes and hinder his work, even at the cost of damaging the Lebanon Pavilion and the reputation of its authorized administrators.[120] Already on July 17, 1939, mere days following the inauguration of the Lebanon Pavilion, in a commemorative issue dedicated to the event, *al-Hoda*, one of the leading Lebanese newspapers in America and an organ close to George Dagher, kicked off a (subtly negative) campaign minimizing Corm's efforts and praising those of Dagher and Salloum Mokarzel, owner of *al-Hoda*, both of whom had at one point fancied themselves the *éminence grise* behind Lebanon's participation in the New York World's Fair.[121] This push, perhaps initially one of harmless and subtle innuendos and self-promotion triggered most likely by envy and ambition, escalated into an all-out defamation campaign, ultimately contributing to Corm's decision to return to Lebanon before the closing of the Fair for the winter months of 1939–1940.

Additionally, some members of the Lebanese community, arguably under the leadership of Dagher and Mokarzel, appear to have envisaged the Fair a potential marketplace for them to peddle their wares, market their local businesses, and draw financial profit—whereas Corm's intent had been to put on display a dignified "museum" and a "temple of culture," rather than a "shopping emporium" and a concessionaire's stand.[122] To this effect, in September

1938, at a time when George Dagher and Salloum Mokarzel were still commanding—perhaps more likely commandeering—Lebanon's participation at the Fair, an internal memo addressed to the Fair's Director of Exhibits and Concessions raised concerns about the Lebanon project resolving itself "primarily into a concession operation."[123] "Such an operation is not desirable," noted the memo, and the Fair authorities cannot "permit Lebanon to charge admission, however nominal, to the reproduction of the Holy Sepulcher, which is intended to occupy a prominent place on the main floor of the Lebanon exhibit."[124] It should be noted that none of Corm's blueprints for the Lebanon exhibit featured a replica of the Holy Sepulcher, and the earliest prototypes that he had forwarded to the liaison engineers and exhibits director in New York included detailed sketches of what was to be displayed in the Lebanon Pavilion along with a complete floor plan, none of which came to the mention of a Holy Sepulcher model.[125] Indeed, the main attraction of the Lebanon Pavilion, a central panel occupying the larger portion of the ground floor, was a nine-by-fifteen-meters bas-relief map "showing the Lebanon in its geographical and historical relations to surrounding countries," sitting on a plane area three feet below the ground level.[126] Again, no mention of the Holy Sepulcher. All the preceding challenges were compounded by the fact that, as noted earlier, Charles Corm was frustrated by the confusion and "blank stares" that the name "Lebanon" initially provoked among American visitors in the early days of the exhibit.[127]

But all these early vexations and initial apprehensions were, of course, allayed as thousands of visitors began flocking to the Lebanon Pavilion. Indeed, a total of some three million guests were documented to have visited the Lebanon exhibit by the time the Fair had shut down in early 1940, and Lebanon had as a result garnered unprecedented celebrity and acclaim on the world stage incommensurate with its size, political relevance, or "name recognition." Still, Lebanon's (initial) relative anonymity was a major source of frustration and anguish for Corm; "a pain that was often alleviated by the sentiments of sympathy and friendship that the French and American authorities evinced" towards Lebanon, its exhibit, and the person of its Commissioner General.[128] Without the real amity and empathy of France, wrote Corm in his journal,

> and without the genuine interest of members of the French Pavilion Commission, and the French diplomatic corps as a whole, [. . . indeed,] without the help of the majority of our emigrant community, the Lebanon Commissioner would have been completely lost in legions of officials and world leaders to whom he had the responsibility of projecting a certain image of Lebanon, as well as the initiation of formal relations and the maintenance of the first important official representation of his country on the international scene guaranteeing it rank and honor; without all this help, our participation in the New York World's Fair would have been utterly disastrous.[129]

Thankfully, wrote Corm, although very closely skirted, a disaster was averted, and Lebanon and its representatives ended up fulfilling their destiny and playing their time-honored role of gifted and subtle inter-cultural intermediaries.[130] And so, the Lebanon exhibit turned out to be a resounding success, and the Pavilion that Corm so lovingly put together, and so skillfully managed and promoted, became the talk of the town.

INAUGURATION OF THE LEBANON PAVILION

Although the Fair officially opened its doors on April 30, 1939—a mere two weeks after Charles and Samia Corm's arrival in New York—the Lebanon Pavilion remained "under construction" and would not be completed and officially inaugurated until July 13, on the eve of France's Bastille Day.[131] Indeed, the inaugural ceremonies of the Lebanon Pavilion had followed a luncheon that the French Pavilion had hosted earlier in the day, in honor of both Bastille Day and Huguenot-Walloon history. Later on that evening, in the Hall of Nations, in an address expressing his special pride "to welcome Lebanon [to the Fair], with its long history and biblical importance," Mayor La Guardia would solemnly declare the Lebanon Pavilion officially open.[132]

In addition to New York Mayor La Guardia, the Assistant US Commissioner to the Fair, Charles Spofford, and Julius Holmes, representing the Director of Foreign Government Participation, the Lebanon Pavilion's inaugural ceremonies were attended by the Count René Doynel de Saint-Quentin, the French Ambassador to the United States, and Marcel Olivier, a former colonial officer and the Commissioner General of the French Pavilion.[133] In his address, Spofford spoke of the sense of awe and wonderment with which average Americans could be seen entering the Lebanon Pavilion.[134] Meeting people from Lebanon, he said, and being in the presence of effects issuing from a land transcending history was not something Americans were accustomed to, nor was it an experience that they took lightly and without reverence. Spofford reminded his audience that the cedars of Lebanon, the fragrance of which permeated the Pavilion as he spoke, were a symbol of nobility and grandeur truly befitting the nation they represented: "Those magnificent cedars," he noted, "had their place [. . .] in the temple of Solomon and in the ships of the far-ranging Phoenicians." Those cedars, and their native land are

> known to us, therefore, in many ways, and always in connection with what is excellent and desirable.[135] There must be, we think, a certain magic in your country, which draws strong men. Among your mountains, there may still be seen the castles of the Crusaders [. . .] the very rooms in which Conrad of Monteferrat moved and issued orders to the mailed warriors of France and England. Down your valleys galloped the Black Prince and St. Louis, the

soldier king of France. These things fire our imagination. [. . .] Your country is the threshold of the East, which to the Westerner seems timelessly filled with wisdom. The Crusaders who passed through your sea cities, who established castles on the interior mountains, were moved by a force which is perhaps too little known to their descendants in the western world. There may be an economic and sociologic interpretation of the Crusades, but it can never explain the faith and ecstasy which took men from the green forests of England and the ancient chateaux of France and drew them across mountains and rivers and seas toward the realization of a hope which they called sacred. Their armored footprints are on the pages of your history, together with those of the Roman legions and the armies of the World War. Today, we welcome you in the name of all the brave men who have inhabited the lands of your republic. And we thank you for the beauty with which your name is associated. [We] congratulate you on your industries and schools. [. . .] A new nation is rising out of your storied and incomparable past, a nation of men and women who seek peace for themselves and their children. In this Pavilion, Americans will be eager to see the products of your fabulous intelligence, the fruits of your present achievements. Since you are known to us as a brave and independent people, we are doubly glad to welcome you here today as representatives of a sister republic. [. . .] Knowing this, it is an especial pleasure to welcome you to this New York World's Fair in the name of the Government of the United States of America.[136]

This speech, clearly inspired by the displays of the Lebanon Pavilion celebrating Phoenicians and Crusaders as basic components of Lebanon's foundational myth, set the tone for those who took the lectern following Spofford; this spurred Corm to telegram his American hosts the next morning, formally thanking them and telling them his deep personal gratitude, and how "greatly touched" he had been by the "well studied and inspiring [speeches] with which you honored my country at the official dedication of Lebanon's Pavilion."[137] Corm and the Lebanese present at the festivities were naturally sensitive to the historical references alluded to in Spofford's address: Memories of intrepid Phoenicians as skilled mariners and builders of Solomon's Temple, and remembrances of brave Crusaders and Roman Legions, all bathed in Biblical imagery and redolent with the scent of cedarwood and the soft whispers of mountain brooks, were all familiar themes to Corm and his countrymen. This veneration—almost deification—of the Lebanon Pavilion was also evident in the media reports of the time, often written in Biblical style setting Lebanese history in tone, form, and structure straight out of Scriptures. As explained one *New York Times* reporter to a mysterious "little man" he'd happened upon in one of the galleries featuring Lebanese cedarwood, "these trees stood on the hills of Lebanon. Solomon may have walked beneath their shade, and Sheba's Queen."[138] With a twinkle in his pixieish little eyes and a "deep and resonant voice," the "little man" replied with authoritative, almost divine confidence that "Sheba *did* walk beneath them," further muttering words from 1 Kings 5:1–13 about Sidonian Phoenicians and the construction of Solomon's Temple:[139]

> And Hiram king of Tyre sent his servants unto Solomon; for he had heard that they had anointed him king [. . .] for Hiram was ever a lover of David. [. . .] Now therefore command thou that they cut me cedar trees out of Lebanon; [. . .] for thou knowest that there is not among us any that knoweth how to cut timber like unto the Sidonians. [. . .] And Hiram sent to Solomon, saying, I have heard the message which thou hast sent unto me: I will do all thy desire concerning the timber of cedar, and concerning timber of fir. My servants shall bring them down from Lebanon unto the sea; and I will make them into rafts to go by sea unto the place that thou shalt appoint me, and will cause them to be broken up there, and thou shalt receive them; and thou shalt accomplish my desire, in giving food for my household. [. . .] And there was peace between Hiram and Solomon; and they two made a league together. [. . .] And Solomon's builders and Hiram's builders and the Gebalites [. . .] prepared the timber and the stones to build the house.[140]

But when the reporter turned to respond to that mysterious "little man," he had "passed through the shadowy door into the brightness of the sun [and] was gone."[141] And when the reporter queried the Pavilion staff about his mystical encounter, the responses he received amounted to blank stares and question marks: "What little man?" they sneered.[142] It is this sense of awe and wonderment that Spofford spoke about, overtaking visitors across the board. Yet hearing these legends and miracles of Lebanon issue from the mouth of a foreigner expected to be alien to them—indeed from a representative of a major world power, who nevertheless referred to Lebanon as a "sister republic"—was, so far as Charles Corm was concerned, the embodiment of the Lebanon that he wanted to reveal, and a testament to the success of its exhibits and the purity of its Pavilion's message.

It may be argued that Spofford's extoling of the Crusades might have been offensive to the delicate ears of those who did not deem those twelfth-century European campaigns East a valorous enterprise, especially those Muslims from among Charles Corm's countrymen present at the dedication ceremony, and others still perhaps, hostile to Western involvement in the modern Middle East.[143] But this perspective is tantamount to reading history from the present backward, not in the context of its twelfth-century realities. It further disregards a segment of Lebanese history equally as significant and worth remembering as the Muslim Arab and Ottoman eras. In his excellent essay on Charles Corm and Lebanon's participation in the 1939 New York World's Fair, Asher Kaufman warned that the stress on the Crusades in Corm's exhibit, and the positive aspect in which they were portrayed, both in the Pavilion's displays and by the orators that acclaimed them, might have perhaps been an affront to Lebanese Muslims and their generally negative view of the Crusades.[144] Although a justified concern in the context of mid-twentieth-century, post-colonial history and theory, this claim is not entirely accurate given that such attitudes would have been anachronistic in 1939. If anything, Lebanon's Muslim community, in 1939 still a numerical minority, might have had reservations about the very idea of a Lebanon exhibit—not to say reservations about the very creation of Lebanon as a sovereign nation-state, amputated, in their view, from Ottoman dominions considered the rightful property of the *Umma*. They might have even had Arab and Syrian nationalist, rather than Lebanese nationalist, affections, and would rather have opted for Syrian citizenship, or even a place within a larger Arab-Muslim entity for that matter. But their reservations toward the Crusades will have stemmed not from negative feelings vis-à-vis the Crusades per se, but rather from the Crusades' association with Lebanon's Christian communities and the fact that they figured prominently in the Maronites' collective memory and their nationalist mythology. In 1939, the Crusades had not yet been reframed—however inaccurately—as the early stirrings of Western imperialism. They were, and remain to this day, despite the recent and fashionable claims of post-colonial theorists, a mediaeval Christian phenomenon that had hardly been worthy of the attention of Muslims and Muslim chroniclers.[145] As argued the preeminent mediaevalist Thomas F. Madden, the Crusades, which Muslims viewed as "futile [Christian] attempts to halt the inevitable expansion of Islam," were until the twentieth century "virtually unknown in the Muslim world."[146] Indeed, they were strictly speaking, and from a strictly Christian perspective, Christian defensive wars against conquering Muslims;

> part of a medieval world that is very different than our world today. Christians saw crusades to the east as acts of love and charity, waged against Muslim conquerors in defense of Christian people and their lands. For their part, medieval Muslims had no understanding or interest in the crusades.[147]

Just as mediaeval Christians viewed the Crusades as "acts of love and charity," so does a majority of Lebanon's Christians today still look fondly at the Crusades, and still consider them—not unjustifiably—the bedrock of their physical and intellectual survival as a community. Likewise, what is true with regards to mediaeval Muslims and their attitudes—or lack thereof—towards the Crusades *does* apply to their counterparts of the 1930s. Bernard Lewis wrote that from a European and Eastern Christian perspective, the Crusades were just and justified defensive wars, waged by a Christendom under attack by a triumphant Islam, taking to the East in an attempt to retake by force Christian dominions that had been wrested from Christendom by force during the seventh-century Muslim conquest.[148] Not only were the Crusades no more than a nuisance in the larger context of Muslim history claimed Lewis; the terms "Crusade and Crusader [remained] unknown in contemporary Muslim writings, [. . . and] had no equivalents in Arabic or other Islamic languages [before they] were coined in Christian Arabic writings" in more recent times.[149] Lewis goes on to note that whatever traces the Crusades might have left on the Muslim world today, those traces have to do with the worsening of the status of indigenous Christians and Jews in what became the world of Islam, and the concomitant cementing of relations and cultural, intellectual, ecclesiastical, and commercial exchanges between European Christians and their Levantine—namely their Lebanese—coreligionists.[150] Fashionable as it may be today, the idea of modern Muslims—and Lebanese Muslims of the 1930s no less—being offended by zealous, rapacious, primitive mediaeval Crusaders, sweeping through the Middle East, is an "artificial memory" concocted by Western post-colonialist thinkers and repentant twentieth-century colonial powers, then passed down to modern-day Arab nationalists and Islamists on a quest for catharsis and justification for their cultural and military decline.[151] As part of Christian history, the Crusades were an undeniable part of the history of the Levant and Lebanon as well. Their remnants are a gleaming reality dotting the landscape of Lebanon's littoral and countryside, and pervading the memories of Lebanese Christians, who—again, not unjustifiably—may take pride in their historical association with the Crusades without having to suffer the indignation of those who may posthumously deem them an affront or an aberration. Repackaging this history so as to misrepresent the Crusades or blot out their memory, for fear that doing otherwise may offend, is an obsession of the latter part of the twentieth century; one that did not obtain at the time of the New York World's Fair. Suggesting otherwise oversimplifies, anachronizes, and misleads.

Reflecting these realities of the 1930s, Marcel Olivier also mentioned the Crusades in his own inaugural address at the Lebanon Pavilion; again, not to offend, but to state a historical reality that a majority of Lebanese unashamedly related to. He spoke at great length and with grave tenor of the millennial Franco–Lebanese friendship and the special affection that France and Lebanon held for each other, boasting that when King Louis IX of France— or St-Louis the Confessor, whom Spofford had mentioned earlier— embarked on his righteous and emancipating Crusade, the Lebanese were the first line of Easterners to rush to his aid. This prompted St-Louis to speak his firm conviction that "this nation is verily a part of the French nation, for, its friendship for the French is akin to the friendship that the French themselves hold for one another."[152] Conversely, went on to say Oliver, in the throes of their tragic history under Ottoman rule, it was France who rushed to the aid of the Lebanese, making sure their aspirations for freedom and independence were met.[153] More recently, it was another French friend of Lebanon's, General Henri Gouraud, "a fair-eyed soldier, a generous human being, and a skilled strategist, who created the State of Lebanon in 1920."[154] France's glorious destiny, claimed Oliver,

> which was (and shall forever remain) to scatter and sow with selfless abundance the richest of seeds; seeds that aroused in Mankind the concepts of Liberty and Fraternity; seeds that made Mankind aware of its inalienable rights; seeds that awakened in Mankind the magical powers of hope; [thus France recognizes] Lebanon as a hallowed spot on this earth—"the thrills of Lebanon cover the World" wrote [Maurice] Barrès in memorable lines where intellectual grandeur vied with exquisite linguistic charm. In this tradition, subtle Lebanese poets, artists, and scientists, nourished by our own culture, bring forth on this festive day much honor to their country. Likewise, the deeply moving and often perilous History of Lebanon, and the natural beauty of the country itself, with its deep coves and sheltered harbors, with its snow-capped peaks and fragrant mountains, have inspired the immortal works of our own authors who attained the pinnacles of intellect and poetic genius thanks to Lebanon. [And so, France acknowledges this Lebanon as] a spot were civilization, poetry, science, and divine wisdom were born, [. . . and where,] since time immemorial and pasts lost in the mists of the centuries, and to this very day, redolent with celebration, the free exchange of ideas, peoples, services, and cultures issuing from Lebanon, have sealed our two countries in a friendship that shall never be extinguished.[155]

Although clearly reminding the world—and more importantly his Lebanese audience—of France's station and the lofty bequests of its *mission civilisatrice*, and perhaps even pointing out the debts of gratitude that Lebanon owed France, the words of this representative of French "colonial power" did not seem to intimate ascendency or even the power relationships that ordinarily regulated the "unbalance" between colonizer and colonized. To the contrary, France's emissary in this official act of power seemed to pay homage to an unsung protectorate, a subordinate entity as it were, extoling its virtues and praising its own bequests to mankind *and* to France, placing Lebanon, culturally speaking, on par with France itself.

One of imperialism's main battles, wrote Edward Said in *Culture and Imperialism*, pertained to issues of culture and who owned the rights to culture; "nations [. . .] *are* narrations," he claimed, and the "power to narrate, or to block other narratives from forming and emerging, is very important to culture and imperialism, and constitutes one of the main connections between them."[156] Yet this does not seem to have been the kind of power relationships at play between Lebanon and France. Indeed, rather than teaching its own history—as might have been its habit with its other colonial chattel—France celebrated and taught Lebanon's own historical narrative during the Mandate period, and indeed cultivated among the Lebanese— namely among the Maronites—a sense of pride and distinctness similar to France's own. In his Preface to René Ristelhueber's *Traditions françaises au*

Liban, French diplomat and member of the *Académie Française* Gabriel Hanotaux declared Lebanese history to be part of France's own heritage, "consistent with the natural order of France's existence, as God willed it and as man achieved it."[157] Mount-Lebanon never reaches the highest of summits, he wrote,

> yet it remains the loftiest of pinnacles in the universal history of mankind. From the times of Solomon to Renan's own days [in the mid- to late nineteenth century,] the gentlest noblest of human wisdom has dwelt in the shadow of Lebanon's millennial cedars. Those simple peasants of Mount-Lebanon, who have jealously safeguarded their freedom, their religion, and their lineage by making their stand *here*, alongside those stubborn cedars, while others around them bowed down to their conquerors; those farmers—indefatigable friends of France, from father to son, and for the past twelve centuries—stem from a family-tree as old as their magnificent cedars.[158]

No such flattering commentary was ever attributed to Frenchmen—French statesmen and colonial officers to boot—speaking of, say, Algeria, Morocco, or Cameroun, the *other* possessions of France's colonial enterprise. But things, as we saw, were otherwise when it came to Lebanon. To paraphrase Said's indictment of colonialism and colonial history, France certainly maintained its "power to narrate" in the case of Lebanon; yet, not only did it not block Lebanon's own narratives; it put them on par with its own traditions, praised them, nurtured them, and condoned their formation, emergence, and normalization—in contravention of conventional French colonial practice.[159]

In keeping with this tradition, at the dedication of the Lebanon Pavilion, Marcel Olivier would go on to reveal, on that solemn eve of Bastille Day's sesquicentennial anniversary no less, that France would have been honored and proud to have welcomed Lebanon into its own French Pavilion, and to have drawn the attention of America and the world to this nation's glorious history, to its present vitality, and to its future achievements. Alas, he admitted wistfully,

> The Lebanese Government, with her wisdom, anxious to give to the New World a spectacle of the vitality, the cohesion and the free perseverant activity of her people, has decided to create this charming Pavilion, organized and set up with so great a love and taste by my eminent friend, Mr. Charles Corm. With what eagerness, responding to his desire, have I come to this dedication day, to bring along the affirmation of my friendship and my faith in the bright future of his country. [. . .] Tell me then, is there any country better made to be understood and loved than Lebanon? My native country [France] in many places bears on its soil the perfectly minted creative signs of those indefatigable builders who were the Phoenicians, the ancestors of the Lebanese people. [. . .] It is therefore with tremendous personal joy today—as I have done

always, throughout the world, and every time I have come to be in the presence of the children of this ancient race, these purveyors of admirable ethics, diligence, tenacity, and subtle intelligence and probity—it is with tremendous personal joy today that I bring to those Lebanese who are alongside me on these banks of the Hudson River, the pledge of my heartfelt admiration, and my wish that in continued peace and prosperity, the fervent, free, and proud lifeblood of their nation will continue, will endure, and will remain.[160]

It should be noted that Marcel Olivier had been a committed French colonial officer, Governor General of Madagascar, author of multiple works on France's African colonies, and a close associate of Maréchal Hubert Lyautey, a leading officer in France's colonial wars and the first Resident General of the Moroccan Protectorate. Olivier had also assisted Lyautey in setting up and directing the 1931 International Colonial Exposition of the *Bois de Vincennes* near Paris, acting as the event's Commissioner General. As such, Olivier was committed to his country's "prodigious" colonial enterprise and its "Overseas Empire," and Lebanon had figured prominently in this, France's "Homeric Odyssey" as it were, "reaching the remotest confines of this world, tirelessly converting primitive continents into civilized realms."[161] But again, among the primitive and uncivilized that France's colonial enterprise sought to enlighten and refine, Lebanon stood out as a "rose among thorns"; a nation not only wont to polish and civilization, but one bequeathing polish and civilization to others as well—to the French themselves, no less.[162] Indeed, Lebanon had been represented at the Paris *Exposition Universelle* of 1900, putting on display murals and paintings by none other than David Corm, Charles Corm's own father—even though for all intents and purposes no such country had come into existence yet in 1900.[163]

Marcel Olivier's address was followed by brief remarks delivered by the French Ambassador to the United States, who reminded his audience that, "always yearning for independence, Lebanon had always preserved its distinct personality, and always persevered [in the cause of freedom] through centuries of vicissitudes"; he also noted how France's doting and faithful sympathies vis-à-vis the Lebanese people have contributed to Lebanon's endurance and continuity.[164] The French ambassador also mentioned the "spirit of selflessness" that had guided France's altruistic mission in Lebanon, shepherding it through time, but especially in the past twenty years, through the adversities of political independence, and vigilantly protecting Lebanon's security; French succor and guidance as it were, "without which the conservation of Lebanon's sovereignty will have remained hollow words."[165]

One particular aspect of the inaugural ceremony that might have been deemed tantamount to a *lèse majesté* as far as Doynel de Saint-Quentin was concerned, was the fact that it did not feature the *Marseillaise*, the French national anthem. In a dispatch filed from Washington, DC, following the festivities, the Ambassador expressed his displeasure at the omission of France's national anthem.[166] He also reported that Marcel Olivier, who was on very friendly terms with Charles Corm, gently chided the poet for neglecting to feature both the *Marseillaise* and "The Star-Spangled Banner" alongside the Lebanese national anthem on such a solemn occasion: "This is a clear departure from the established norms of inaugural ceremonies attended by dignitaries and representatives of foreign powers," sternly remarked Olivier.[167] A visibly embarrassed and apologetic Charles Corm replied that the *Marseillaise* had indeed been included in the original program, but that he'd been stymied in his efforts to feature it by "some influential elements of the Lebanese émigré community."[168] France's representatives seemed satisfied with that pretext—flimsy as it might have been—especially in light of the agitations that some elements of the Syro-Lebanese émigré community had been fomenting in the United States, on account of the French authorities' ceding the *Sanjak* of Alexandretta to the Republic of Turkey earlier in June of 1939—a province that some Syrians had hoped to include in a future Syrian Arab Republic.

At any rate, Corm's real saving grace out of this "diplomatic bungle" had been his unimpeachable Francophilia, his own personal charm, and the assurances that he later conveyed to the French Ambassador, speaking of "his countrymen's attachment to France," and stressing that "the Lebanese would never allow themselves to be drawn into the anti-French sentiments of the Syrians."[169] What's more, added Corm, even if he hadn't expressly mentioned it in his seemingly impromptu remarks, France's presence in the Lebanese Pavilion had been ruddy and radiant, with a special section of the exhibit dedicated to Franco-Lebanese relations, and many of its *objets d'art*, high-relief maps, and reproductions of various artifacts, having been produced with the guidance and assistance of French artists, artisans, and archaeologists.[170] For good measure, on July 14, 1939, Corm would dispatch a conciliatory telegram to the French Ambassador, thanking him for gracing the Lebanon Pavilion with his presence at the inaugural ceremony, reassuring him of the inveterate Franco-Lebanese friendship, and essentially reiterating in writing what he had already relayed to him in person the evening prior. The telegram, worth reproducing in its entirety here, read as follows:

> To His Excellency, Ambassador de Saint-Quentin:
>
> Your noble presence at the opening ceremonies, your deeply moving speech, and your benevolent personal reminiscences of Lebanon have all happily strengthened our Franco-Lebanese friendship; a friendship that constitutes one of our most glorious titles of honor, of which we the Lebanese are duly and most infinitely proud. Your presence among us has further enhanced the importance of our inaugural ceremony, adding to it the prestige of France's

grandeur. On behalf of His Excellency, Mr. Émile Éddé, President of the Republic of Lebanon, on behalf of our fellow citizens at home, and on behalf of our emigrants in the United States and around the world, whom France has never shied away from devotedly looking after, I wish to thank you for the honor you have kindly bestowed upon us, and ask that you please accept the respectful assurances of my profound gratitude.[171]

Notwithstanding the validity of the excuses offered by Charles Corm—that is to say the obstructions that he might indeed have encountered by some anti-French members of the Lebanese émigré community—it is worth mentioning that this Lebanon Pavilion, at the New York World's Fair, had been this nascent republic's "baby steps" as it were in an international arena; its first solo performance on a major world stage. And so, fastidious, methodical, and deliberate as Corm might have been in his design and construction of the Lebanon Pavilion, and sophisticated as he might have appeared in the ways of the world and the protocols of officialdom, it is not entirely unfeasible that the diplomatic blunder for which he was blamed might have simply been the innocent lapse of a newcomer to the etiquettes of international relations. Still, the always "congenial and quick-witted Corm," as described by Saint-Quentin, had yet again demonstrated his innate competence and finesse, averting a major international incident—involving two major superpowers no less—and sparing his young country the hurts and aches of political growing pains.

Charles Corm would conclude the oratories of the opening ceremony with an equally moving pronouncement as the ones delivered by those who took the stage before him; only his remarks were presented without notes, in French, English, and dialectal Lebanese.[172] During his "long and florid speech," as described in Saint-Quentin's correspondence with the Quai d'Orsay, Corm placed Lebanon at the center of human history, mentioning France—to Saint-Quentin's chagrin—only once, and only in passing in the context of the French Jesuit mission in the Levant and its Beirut Université St-Joseph.[173] During his address, Corm also transmitted a brief message from Lebanese President Émile Éddé, and from Gabriel Puaux, France's High Commissioner in Beirut at the time—whom Corm had referred to as H. E. the Ambassador and High Commissioner of the French Republic, suggesting he were a mere diplomatic representative of France's, not its military governor in Lebanon.[174] In his message, Puaux echoed Olivier, and spoke of his pleasure that Lebanon took the initiative to participate in the New York World's Fair on its own, in order to "bring forth to the Lebanese of the diaspora a stirring image of their mother country." Among many impassioned national effects that the Lebanese of America will find on display at the Fair, noted Puaux, "they will also bear witness to the moving timeless ties that have united our two countries through the ages, and the solid guarantees of happiness and prosperity that this passionate attachment will continue to bring Lebanon."[175]

Although Corm's address did not tarry long on Franco-Lebanese relations, his remarks paid homage to the Lebanese diaspora, their contributions to the Fair itself, and "their noble energies as faithful Lebanese and grateful and productive American citizens."[176] This was in an era where Lebanese immigrants were becoming more vociferous in their attempts to distinguish themselves from other Arabic-speaking immigrant communities that were being galvanized by festering "Arab-Israeli" disputes—or rather the Muslim-Jewish rivalries in the Levant—and a consequent Arab "anti-Americanism" nourished as it were by the United States' expressed sympathies towards the Zionist project in British Mandatory Palestine. Indeed, the main New York–based Arabic-language Lebanese newspaper of the times, *al-Hoda*, was scathing in its attacks on Syria, Egypt, Saudi Arabia, and other Arab-defined countries that had ostensibly refused to participate in the New York World's Fair on account of America's purported "Jewish sympathies." In fact, noted *al-Hoda* in one of its December 17, 1939, articles, the Syrian government had even attempted to badger Lebanon into withdrawing its commitment to participate in the Fair, impelling it to burnish putative Arab credentials and demonstrate a sense of solidarity with the Arabs of Palestine.[177] But Lebanon must remain outside of the disputes of others insisted *al-Hoda*; "The Lebanese," it noted, "are conscious of both the noxious and salutary effects issuing from this conflict, and will always remain amenable to sober and conciliatory language dealing with it."[178] What's more, the newspaper took great pains to differentiate the Lebanese from the Syrians, and both Lebanese and Syrians from the Arabs—miniscule as "Arab" immigrant groups had been in the Americas of the 1930s. "We the Lebanese of the diaspora," wrote *al-Hoda*,

> users of the Arabic language, regardless of our political affiliations, are inseparable from the body of the American nation, and it is our duty to defend this nation against slanderous attacks issuing from the heated disputes between Arabs and Jews over the Palestine Question. [. . .] Furthermore, this newspaper is keen on safeguarding the reputation of its readers, by warding off accusations that seek to paint them in shapes and forms that contravene their true selves and impugn their true identities. [Our readers] are Syrians and Lebanese, and it is imperative that a distinction be made between them, and between themselves and the Arabs, [especially Arabs] who are leveling ridiculous insults at the President of the United States.[179]

In line with this, Corm would spend a good part of his inaugural address speaking to the rationale behind Lebanon's participation in the Fair as a distinct sovereign nation, and its desire to make a contribution toward peace, rapprochement, solidarity, reconciliation, and mutual understanding between nations, in a world teetering on the verge of strife.[180] "On behalf of all my countrymen," said Corm in language reminiscent of his press releases leading up to the inauguration, "in Lebanon and America,"

> I am honored to salute this great democracy of the New World; a great democracy that undertook to put forth this magnificent exhibition and testament to Mankind, despite the difficulties looming in our times; issuing a challenge as it were, a triumphal challenge of goodwill against the coalitions of Evil that are threatening our way of life. At this fine meeting of unity and concord, in the shadow of this grandiose edifice to international friendship, we, as Lebanese, wish to lend our hearts and our unreserved support, our modest little stone as it were, to this noble enterprise of peace. At the Lebanon Exhibit you shall find that this "little stone" of ours has been a "work in progress," honed by 6000 years of history. And so, a modest stone it is! But it is a beautiful stone, a solid stone, a valuable stone, and a precious stone, because it bears the markings—often overlooked markings, but eternal and eternally renewed markings—of the creative, enlightened, and peaceful genius that constitutes the national character of Lebanon. Visitors to this exhibit shall also discover that this "little stone" of ours, is one of the cornerstones of our common humanity and human civilization, carved out of the purest of quarries, chiseled by the love and faith of our people, and honed by the spiritual strengths that still move them and will still remain ablaze within them, so long as God remains alive![181]

In a handwritten draft copy of a speech dated July 11, 1939—that is to say two days before the inauguration of the Lebanon Pavilion on July 13 and the delivery of the actual address—Corm spoke with great passion and conviction of the common bonds of kinship and the kindred values that associated Lebanon to America. Lebanon's small size notwithstanding, he wrote, its similarities with America are striking.[182] "I must therefore maintain a modicum of humility while laying bare our kinships before you," began Corm's address, which, again, although perhaps based on prepared notes, was delivered from memory, in English, French, and dialectal Lebanese:

> Not unlike the United States of America, which has initiated the movement of liberty and democracy in the New World, we, the Lebanese, in ancient times, when we were still known as Phoenicians, have also lived the wonderful experience of being the first in the world to institute democratic and federal states, several centuries before Christ. In the book *Politics*, his treatise on government, Aristotle stated that our [Lebanese] Constitution must have been exemplary to have lasted hundreds of years. Another similarity that comes to mind [between Lebanon and America] is when the United States of America is often described as the "Melting Pot" in the New World; we also, in the Near East, have preserved our tradition of hospitality and have welcomed over a hundred thousand refugees from everywhere and every country after the Great War; and hence, we too may be called the "Melting Pot" of the Levant. Another similarity to which I must draw your attention is that we also have a non-sectarian political system [in Lebanon.] Freedom of worship, press, speech and

association are a sacred heritage to us Lebanese. And while the majority of our population is Christian, there is no restriction whatever placed on any faith, and no preference placed on one creed over another. As a matter of fact, our country can boast the coexistence of almost all the religious traditions under the skies of the Sun, all of them flourishing harmoniously in Lebanon.[183]

Some may raise issues of accuracy with some of Corm's claims in this address. Yet when placed in their historical context, the comparisons he makes between the United States and Lebanon, the positive light in which he depicts the Phoenicians as ancestors of the modern Lebanese, and the liberal pluralist political ethos practiced (as he claims) by the nascent Lebanese Republic do indeed appear to be veridical and accurate depictions of Lebanon of his times—that is to say, Lebanon as the only democracy in the Middle East and, in the telling of modern political scientists, a successful (albeit tempestuous) exemplar of inter-communal coexistence and cooperation; a "federation of minorities" as it were, who, suppressed and persecuted as they may be elsewhere in the Middle East, enjoy unhindered equality and fair representation in Lebanon.[184]

The remainder of Corm's address read like a breviary of the Phoenicians' accomplishments, from the invention of the alphabet, to glassmaking, to chemical dyeing, to shipbuilding and navigation, all the way to the very "invention" of Europe and the initiation of that continent's humanistic values. All of these contributions figured prominently in Corm's inventory; "you certainly know a lot [. . .] about our tiny country," he proudly noted.

> From your classical studies you may still remember that this same Lebanon was famous in ancient times under the name of Phoenicia, and that the Phoenicians were the people who gave the world the first Alphabet, [. . .] from which our modern writing is derived. You certainly know that we still use [this Phoenician Alphabet] when every one of us signs his name in English or in any other European or Oriental language; [this was an Alphabet] designed 4000 years ago under the skies of Lebanon. [. . . Furthermore,] the Phoenicians of Lebanon were the first people to have manufactured and commercialized glass and glasswares. [. . .] The Glass Exhibit at the Fair attests this reality. Those same Phoenicians were the first shipbuilders and navigators, the first people to invent chemical dyeing.[185]

Corm went on to elaborate on the Carthaginian maritime empire, "which lasted over ten centuries," and which "was founded by a girl from Tyre [Lebanon,] a girl named Dido, whose love and the love of Aeneas, the Founder of Rome, was immortalized in Virgil's famous Epic [*The Aeneid*.]"[186] Even the very European continent, said Corm, the progenitor of America as it were, was the namesake and progeny of a Phoenician princess, Europa, the daughter of the King of Tyre, whom the god Zeus had abducted from the shores of Phoenicia and spirited away to a dark continent that would forever bear her name.[187] Corm would continue running down the list of Phoenician bequests, noting: the Carthaginian General Hannibal Barca, a brilliant military strategist who dispirited mighty Rome, who inspired Napoleon, and whose military feats and stratagems are still taught and studied at the world's leading war colleges, West Point included; he too was of Phoenician (and therefore Lebanese) extraction acknowledged Corm; so was St. Augustine, one of the fathers of the Roman Church, a Phoenician who still spoke a variant of the Phoenician language in the fourth century after Christ; Ulpian and Papinian, authors of the famous Roman Law Codex bearing their names, were Phoenician jurists who taught at the world famous Roman Law School of Beirut; "six Roman Emperors and six Roman Popes, were directly related by blood to today's Lebanese."[188]

From classical antiquity, Corm's speech moved into modern times and spoke at some length of the Lebanese bequests to the world of today. He mentioned Lebanon's contributions to the revival of Arabic *belles lettres*, the enrichment of Anglophone and Francophone literatures, and his countrymen's active participation in the cultural, academic, and political life of the Americas of the nineteenth and twentieth centuries.[189] A country's greatness is never measured by the degree of its accomplishments, added Corm, nor by the size of its territory or its population:

> A country, as well as the individual, are only as great as their contribution to the general welfare of Mankind. A country and a man, are only great by the measure of what they can endow and give unto others, and never by the amount of what they can extract or receive from others. All of the wealth of the Rockefellers or Carnegies did not make them into great Men. It is only what they bequeathed [. . .] on to others, to the world around them; it is the universities and the institutions that they brought forth, which made them rank among the most famous and celebrated sons of America.[190]

The greatness of America, noted Corm, is measured by the spirit of liberty, independence, and moral dignity that the American people have generated, and which have inspired the French Revolution and promoted democracy across the globe.[191] Likewise, he went on to say, Lebanon in modern times, bereft of natural resources, transmits to the world something loftier than material wealth, "something better than men; brains," and "something better than brains; love."[192] And what Lebanon expects in return for its bequests is neither glory, nor fame, nor admiration, nor gratitude; what Lebanon seeks in return is friendship, said Corm.[193] He concluded with a word of gratitude to the United States and to the American educational mission in Lebanon, then paid homage to France's millennial friendship and its affections toward his country and his people, giving comfort to the Lebanese and standing at their side through their challenges and the labors of their political rebirth, noting that in the Lebanon Pavilion "we have practically nothing to sell, [. . .] no dollars to gain, but we have our souls unveiled seeking communion with your souls."[194]

It was arguably this noble demeanor of Corm's that prompted New York City Mayor La Guardia to publicize the Fair as an event featuring Lebanon as a centerpiece, where visitors could indulge in "hamburgers and frankfurters sold for a dime each" and feast their senses at "the Pavilion of Lebanon."[195] That is how large the modest Pavilion of tiny Lebanon had loomed under Charles Corm's watch. Yet Lebanon remained unknown in the early days of the Fair, and many high-ranking American officials, foreign dignitaries, and even intellectual elites confounded it with other place-names in the region—Syria for instance.[196] "Even the Honorable Mayor La Guardia himself," wrote Corm,

> was initially astounded to learn that a country named "Lebanon" still existed in this world. He was all the more pleasantly surprised that this "Lebanon" was a republican democracy. His attitude was representative of the quasi totality of the American public, even the educated among them, who up to that point had deemed our country nothing more than a faint memory and a nostalgic reference to Biblical times.[197]

The success of the Lebanon Pavilion, wrote Corm in his private papers, was due in the main to its innocuous, largely historical and cultural character, and to a humanist universalist bent setting it apart from most other exhibits, which focused primarily on commercial, industrial, and technological aspects of the various countries on display.[198] Indeed, the little exhibit from Lebanon was so alluring in its simplicity, profundity, and didactic elements that it drew the attention of the local and national media, giving it publicity and exposure to degrees disproportionate to its size and significance in the state order of the times. Corm noted that in a period of nine months—from May 1939 to January 1940—national and local New York radio outlets dedicated no less than eighteen broadcasts, ranging from twenty to thirty minutes each, treating exclusively and in great detail topics from Lebanese history culled from the Lebanon Pavilion. Such renowned broadcasters of the time, like the iconic radio interview host Martha Deane and Radio City's (RCA) Richard Thomas, were instrumental in making the Lebanon exhibit a prime destination at the Fair, and indeed, the event's precious gem.[199]

THE LEBANON PAVILION:
PLACE OF PILGRIMAGE, TEMPLE OF CULTURE

On the morning of September 1, 1939, nineteen years to the day since General Henri Gouraud solemnly declared the establishment of Greater Lebanon, half way across the world, on the southern edges of Central Park in midtown

Manhattan, three luxury American automobiles, with the New York World's Fair logos emblazoned on their driver and passenger sides, pulled up to the front entrance of the Park Central Hotel. The party of fourteen dignitaries that the limousines were dispatched to transport included the French Ambassador to the United States, the French Consul General to New York City, and Charles Corm, the Commissioner General of the Lebanon Pavilion and the official host of that morning's reception at the Park Central Hotel; a ceremony celebrating the Republic of Lebanon's Independence Day. By 11:00 a.m. the motorcade, led by a New York City Police motorcycle escort, with lights flashing and sirens blaring, began racing down 7th Avenue, past the Theatre District, and on to Queens Boulevard over the East River. Barely a half hour into the ride, the convoy started to slow down as it approached the World's Fair Boulevard Gate in Flushing Meadows. After receiving a nineteen-gun salute (an honor customarily reserved to foreign ambassadors and the Vice President of the United States), the guests of honor oversaw a changing of the guard as their convoy was led further down the boulevard by a World's Fair Police motorcycle escort. By 11:40 a.m. the motorcade came to a halt at Perylon Hall, where the French Ambassador and the Commissioner General of the Republic of Lebanon were met by Grover Whalen, President of the New York World's Fair, who, following the official welcome, escorted them to the signing ceremony of the distinguished guests book. Corm, the French Ambassador, and their guests were then led to the Court of Peace, where the Lebanon Day celebrations were to be inaugurated later that afternoon at the conclusion of the luncheon that the United States had hosted in honor of the Commissioner General of the Lebanese Pavilion.[200]

The protocolary privilege given Lebanon's representative on this solemn day was the kind of recognition that the Republic of Lebanon had striven for since the day it accepted President Roosevelt's invitation to participate in the New York World's Fair. And although the gun salute in this case may have been given in honor of the French Ambassador, not the Lebanese Commissioner General, one can only imagine the sense of pride that Charles Corm and the Lebanese delegates must have felt to be included in such dignified company, and to be received with such pomp and circumstance, worthy of diplomats and official representatives of foreign governments. Likewise signing the distinguished guests book alongside Ambassador de Saint-Quentin, but also on pages graced by such dignitaries as King George VI of the United Kingdom, Princess Elizabeth, the future Queen, and First Lady Eleanor Roosevelt, must have given the Lebanese delegation—and Lebanon's first diplomatic envoy to the United States, Charles Corm—recognition and distinction beyond what they had expected or even dreamt of. Later that day, a visibly elated Lebanese legation would proudly preside over one of the most festive national celebrations in Lebanon's recent history, featuring the Lebanese national anthem played by a ceremonial band alongside "The Star-

Spangled Banner" and the *Marseillaise*. This was perhaps in compensation for the bungled omission of both the French and American national anthems during the Pavilion's inauguration a few weeks earlier on July 13. Soon thereafter, the anthems were followed by a "sword dance" performed by Lebanese girls festooned in national costume, a performance of a Lebanese national choir, and a traditional mountain-*dabké* folk dance. The festivities concluded with a ceremony during which twenty Lebanese girls in traditional dress presented the New York Superintendent of Parks with a thousand Lebanese cedar seeds. The ceremony wound down with a retreat parade to the Court of Peace and a formal reception in the Federal Building featuring a theme of "Peace and Common Accord Among the Nations of the World"; a venue where the American authorities normally entertained foreign dignitaries and visiting heads of state.[201]

No Army! No Navy! No Internal Debt! No External Debt! No Class Struggle! Those were the words that greeted visitors entering the first floor of the Pavilion of the Lebanese Republic. Writing on the week of this nineteenth anniversary of the establishment of Greater Lebanon, Bertha Jaffe of the *Forest Hills Times* declared the exhibit a representation of "6,000 years of peaceful activity in the service of mankind."[202] In order to deliver this Lebanon to the Fair, and to the world at large, Charles Corm had brought through the New York Port Authority tons of materials, artifacts, paintings, sculptures, art reproductions, and various museum pieces: those included some twenty-five cases of native Lebanese marble (weighing three metric tons); forty-two cases of manufactured glass, wood, and plaster of Paris bas-reliefs; eleven cases of manufactured marble, manufactured plaster, and carved cedarwood; one case of original paintings; two cases of art reproductions; thirteen cases of books, paintings, earthenware, and marble statues.[203] Dozens of Lebanese, French, and Belgian artists, historians, essayists, decorators, mosaicists, architects, and craftsmen were enlisted to turn Corm's vision into reality. Those included distinguished French archaeologist Maurice Dunand, Lebanese sculptors Arminée Baronian, César Gemayel, Youssef Hoyek, and Saliba Douaihi, French and Lebanese painters Omar Onsi, Blanche Ammoun, Georges Michelet, Georges Cyr, and Mustapha Farroukh, and essayist Evelyne Bustros among others, all bringing to life the main Phoenician contributions to mankind, which Corm had wanted paraded: the Alphabet, Navigation, Glass-Making, and Purple Dyeing, all four of which were illustrated in massive murals executed by Lebanese artist and student of Corm's art studio César Gemayel, and which were the first displays greeting visitors as they entered the first floor of the Lebanon Pavilion.

Likewise the four "Peace Treaties" that the Phoenicians signed with Romans, Macedonians, Egyptians, and Israelites were represented in imposing paintings executed by then-eighteen-year-old Blanche Ammoun. Corm's intent in these (seldom remembered) scenes from Lebanese history was to emphasize the purity, humanity, and inherent pacifism of Phoenician society thousands of years ago—that is to say, the sincerity, goodwill, honesty, and commitment to peace that were the creed of the Phoenicians according to Corm. The Phoenicians were gentle pacifists, he wrote, not because war disrupted their commercial activities and jeopardized their maritime empire; rather, they were loath to violence because it was the very antithesis of their liberal and conciliatory religious spirit.[204] Concluding a peace treaty, wrote French historian Fustel de Coulanges in his *Cité Antique*, was nothing short of an act of faith. In this sense, the Phoenicians took their oaths and their faith to heart. Deeply religious by nature, they carried their local gods along with them on their travels, fixing them on the bows of their vessels, setting them atop high altars in their new settlements, and housing them in magnificent temples.[205] Taking their gods as witness to their sincerity, the Phoenicians' peace treaties had strikingly solemn, sacrosanct, and religious characteristics to them."[206] This is an important element of "Lebanese Humanism" that Corm was very keen on bringing to the New York World's Fair, as it fit snugly into the vision of the organizers, as well as his own.

And so, in order to do that, and to trot out the best possible image of his country, Charles Corm used every inch of the walls, ceilings, and floors of the building assigned to Lebanon, turning them into veritable art galleries and a stunning museum attraction. He featured the Phoenicians' "first land discoveries," depicting their fleets landing in Cameroun, circumnavigating the Cape of Good Hope, and slithering with skill past the icebergs of the northern fjords, landing in unknown territories—possibly in Ireland, England, and even in the "New World."[207] "Thousands of years before Christ," wrote William Bernbach and Herman Jaffe in the *Book of Nations*, exploiting the solid cedar wood of thick forests that once covered the totality of Lebanon's terrain, the Phoenicians built the most advanced maritime fleets of antiquity, and conquered the waves of treacherous oceans in search of new horizons, rounding Africa, landing in England and Ireland, importing amber from the Baltic, building "hundreds of cities in Western Europe and on the Atlantic Coast of Africa, long before Homer wrote his Epic."[208]

Other murals depicted the Phoenicians' best-known architectural handiwork, including the Temple of Solomon in Jerusalem, the Temple of Eryx in Sicily, the Admirality Palace in Carthage, and the Pillars of Hercules—or Melkart, to use the original Phoenician name. Four scenes from classical mythology, featuring the legends of Venus and Adonis, both born along Lebanon's Mediterranean coast, were portrayed in gold inlaid carvings on dark fragrant cedar wood and staged on the first floor of the exhibit. And then there was the striking bas-relief, three-dimensional, walk-around map of Lebanon, standing sentry, as it were, in the middle of the main lobby, revealing in exquisite detail the country's terrain features, with its mountains, highways, rivers, plains, and shorelines. Around the map, dominating the four corners of the lobby, were four dioramas executed with painstaking accuracy by French painter Georges Michelet, depicting the cities of Tyre and Sidon (the birthplace and launching pad of the Phoenicians' maritime empire), the city of Byblos (home of the Phoenician alphabet and place of pilgrimage to an infant Pythagoras and his Phoenician family), and an awe-inspiring replica of Carthage, the most illustrious of the Phoenician *outre-mer*, a "New Land" as its Phoenician etymology indicates—not unlike "New York"—and an "Empire State" in its own right, which dominated antiquity and challenged mighty Rome the way the "Empire State" of the New World drives and stimulates today's modern world.[209]

The mezzanine level of the exhibit offered a display of Lebanese arts and crafts produced by the *Artisanat Libanais*, a guild of professional craftsmen and artisans founded by Laudie Éddé, wife of Lebanese President Émile Éddé, and today one of Lebanon's most prestigious artisanal societies. Additional items on display in the mezzanine, in a gallery designated "The Presidential Alcove," included needlepoint portraits of Abraham Lincoln, George Washington, and Franklin D. Roosevelt (produced by the *Artisanat Libanais*) and sections dedicated to the "Lebanese in the World" as well as "France and America in Lebanon." Each of these galleries featured paintings and murals depicting Phoenicians and modern Lebanese dealing in one way or another with Europeans (namely Frenchmen) and their modern descendants (Americans) through different stages of history; from the Phoenician Carthaginians' crossing of the Alps with the help of the French Gauls, to the Crusaders under French King St-Louis being welcomed to the East and guided to Jerusalem by a company of Lebanese scouts.

The general message of these illustrations, wrote Asher Kaufman, was to emphasize a timeless Franco-Lebanese friendship stretching from classical antiquity, and before, into modern times, and to affirm the distinct—that is to say the non-Arab—essence of Lebanese history and Lebanese identity.[210] As we saw earlier in the speeches delivered by Corm, Spofford, and the representatives of France's colonial authority, the interconnectedness between Lebanon and France and the interpenetration of the traditions of the West and the East were part of a phenomenon that both the French and Lebanese acknowledged and took ample pride in.

In its special commemorative issue celebrating the Lebanon Pavilion, *al-Hoda* described this exhibit as a solemn, historical moment and a sumptuous triumph for Lebanon on a global scale; The Lebanon Pavilion, the paper boasted, was a veritable "conquest for the children of the cedars."[211] None of the visitors and participants, it further observed, could hide their fervor, their euphoria, and indeed their pride as they processed down the boulevard leading up to the Hall of Nations and caught their first glimpse of the Lebanon flag fluttering proudly aloft among others in the Court of Peace—towering, as it were, majestically over the structure housing the Lebanon exhibit.[212]

The Lebanon Pavilion presented the world not only with a "museum of culture and civilization," proudly claimed *al-Hoda*, it was "a veritable masterpiece in and of itself, and a monument to perfection poured straight out of the heart of the author of *The Hallowed Mountain*, and presented to the children of Lebanon, residents and émigrés alike, so that they may take pride in their country of origin and flaunt its bequests among the nations of the world."[213] All of the beauty, art, history, and glory put on display in this Pavilion, went on to say *al-Hoda*, are indeed representative of Lebanon itself; yet none were as closely representative of the pride of Lebanon, or the gentleness of Lebanon's children, or the tenderness of their morals, or the effervescence and affability of their character as was the person of Charles Corm himself.[214]

The local New York media corroborated this mainspring of *al-Hoda*'s ebullience, patriotic swagger, and pride in Corm himself: "Lebanon Opens Pavilion at Fair Amid Praise" read a *New York Herald-Tribune* headline on July 14, 1939; "Tiny Republic Charms Visitors at Fair," and "Country's Poet Designed Building," chimed in the *New York Times* on July 20; or, wrote another *Times* reporter, "We stood [. . .] in the high-ceiled Lebanon Pavilion, awed by the antiquity of the exhibits [. . .] then as through a mist, [. . .] imagination carried us completely out of the World of Tomorrow"—the overarching theme of the Fair—and into a venerable ancient past represented by modern Lebanon.[215] Even the notoriously unflappable Mayor La Guardia was in awe of the stunning display that Charles Corm had brought to the Fair. In his inaugural remarks at the Lebanon Pavilion, the mayor marveled at the ingenuity, resilience, and endurance of the Lebanese maintaining their memory, their civilization, and their identity intact, and sailing with skill, resolve, and grace the turbulent waters and deep time span of their 6,000 years' existence.[216] "We enter this exhibit with awe," said La Guardia on inaugural night, indeed as if entering a sacred temple:

> What impresses me more than anything else is the fact that [the Lebanese] have kept the faith for 6,000 years; a people who could have gone through many dark centuries of hardship, and yet retain its identity, is ample proof that they are truly deserving of our admiration, and that they are a match to the tenacity of their Cedars and the endurance of their mountains. [In view of] what the Phoenicians have given to civilization and to the construction of our modern world, five thousand years ago and many hundreds of years before the discovery of America, [we are] proud to have you here in our World's Fair. It is gratifying for us who were pioneers in the idea of a world's fair that we were able to bring [you among] nearly sixty countries and peoples together around the Court of Peace.[217]

Referring to the three-dimensional model of the ancient Phoenician port-city of Byblos, the mayor expressed some embarrassment as a New Yorker comparing his own twentieth-century city planning to that of the Lebanese thousands of years earlier:

> When I look at Byblos thousands of years ago, and then look at many of the streets in New York, I am ashamed and I [can't] find an alibi for them.[218]

Although the mayor spoke of his pride in having succeeded to put the entire world on display at the Fair, he was "specially proud to welcome Lebanon, with its long history and biblical importance."[219] Besides the diorama featuring Byblos, of which the mayor spoke, there was the famous three-dimensional walk-around map mentioned earlier, which took center stage at the Pavilion's first floor, greeting visitors as they passed through the entrance hall. The map's topography, executed by students of the Lebanese School of Arts and Crafts, depicted with poignant realism Lebanon's mountains, plains, Mediterranean coastline, and all of its cities, towns, and villages, down to its smallest hamlets. Its landscapes were covered with native plants, rocks, and soil giving the impression that a veritable miniature Lebanon was brought over and placed on display in New York. Charles Corm's wife, Samia Baroody, recalled, not without emotion, the fervor with which Lebanese immigrants visiting the Pavilion would slowly circumambulate this life-like model of their old country, as if on pilgrimage, gazing searchingly, cravingly up and down its roadways, slopes, and coastlines until they've identified their native villages. Then, overcome with emotion, they would come to a halt, cling to the "iron lace" balustrade surrounding the map, and weep softly as if in silent prayer.[220]

Said one visitor to the Pavilion, what I saw at the Lebanon exhibit was a veritable symposium of art and beauty;

> a miniature image of an impavid mountain, with all its cities, its valleys, and its plains spreading before us in a splendid medley of colors and fragrances. [. . .] I saw clear blue skies, hovering overhead, above these scattered ancient artifacts that is Lebanon, brought forth to us, to the West, from the East, like an eloquent sermon, a lesson in beauty about enchanting Lebanon and its selfless gifts of art, inspiration, genius, and creativity bequeathed to the universe. I saw all this and more [. . .] and when I awoke from my ecstasy, I found myself caressing the sacred wood [of Lebanon's cedars] with reverence and nostalgia, as if I'd been in a temple of worship, where the ancient gods of beauty, art, and imagination had suddenly come to life. And as I stood there enraptured, I heard the whole pavilion erupt in applause. "A man of great stature must be visiting the Lebanon exhibit," I said to myself. I was soon to find myself in the presence of a poet, an artist, and a faithful ardent patriot; one of Lebanon's finest; the man who brought us Lebanon in all its brilliance, laying it before us in all its glory among the beautiful exhibits of the greatest nations of this earth. [. . .] And so my heart fluttered and my soul swooned. [. . .] And in awe of

what I beheld, I closed my eyes in prayer, with yearnings in my heart and a tear rolling down my face.[221]

There was more! The Lebanon exhibit, wrote Lebanon native and Princeton Semitist Philip Hitti,

> in its minutest details and its most glorious displays, had dwelt as a dream in Charles Corm's fancy, and a poem in his lyrical yearnings. Yet here it is today a concrete reality; [. . .] a testament to the hardiness of the children of Lebanon and a confirmation of their resolve, the soundness of their bodies, and the purity of their minds; a glimpse into the mysteries of their glory and their determination to keep their faith and weather their hardships and carry on with continued progress and success. [. . .] A nation that gives birth to someone like Charles Corm must not be anguished by what may lie ahead in its future.[222]

This outpouring of emotion and admiration might have been normal issuing from Lebanese immigrants stirred by nostalgia and longing for the land of their birth. However, just as we have seen how such sentiments had been unanimous among the Fair's organizers—perhaps the result of diplomatic platitudes and courtly niceties—they had also been consistent among average Americans visiting the exhibit. "I have come to the World's Fair," wrote one such visitor from St. Paul, Minnesota, "for the cultural and historical and have found mostly the commercial"; but then there was the Lebanon exhibit, he said, where he was overcome with emotion, and where he came upon history, culture, ancient temples, alphabetic writing, the grandeur of the Phoenicians, their benevolent empire, and the examples they set for the rest of mankind in cosmopolitanism, peace, and trade among all peoples.[223] The privilege of having seen "actual samples from the cedars" wrote this visitor, left a "profound and intensely satisfactory impression on me; one which I shall never forget."[224]

And so, not only was Corm able to put on display, for the entire world to behold, an independent sovereign Lebanon at the Fair. The very image of Lebanon that he trotted out was one of a powerhouse of culture and civilization, and a conception of the country, its history, and its identity that corresponded with his own Phoenician sympathies and those of the American-Lebanese community, which was itself heavily invested in the Pavilion and its consequences and the benefits it may present to their status and reputation as American citizens.

During the inauguration of the Lebanon Pavilion, Cypriot-born, Lebanese-American composer Anis Fuleyhan gave impassioned renditions of the Lebanese national anthem (*Kulluna lil Watan*), the *Marseillaise*, and "The Star-Spangled Banner."[225] Fuleyhan was but a small example of the wide range of international and Lebanese artists—from Lebanon proper and from the large émigré community—that Corm marshaled to bring about an exhibit described by all accounts as a "class act," driving even Fiorello La Guardia to use it in his own publicity campaigns.[226] In his private journal entries pertaining to the Fair, Corm relates the remarks of the Consul General of Great Britain in New York, who reportedly told him, "you have built in New York a pavilion that has stunned the world. [. . .] And given the miniscule size of your country, you are indeed the nation that has made the finest contribution to this international exhibit."[227]

Additionally, among the hundreds of anecdotes attesting to the Lebanon Pavilion's success, which Corm included in the official report he filed with the Lebanese government, was one of particular significance. A Lebanese immigrant, related Corm, a typesetter at the New York–based *al-Hoda* newspaper was rushed to a local emergency room to receive treatment for an injury he had sustained at work. Having identified him as a Lebanese, the triage nurse was reported to have exclaimed with enthusiasm: "you come from the beautiful country that I saw in that magnificent Pavilion at the Fair?"[228] The immigrant in question subsequently saw himself surrounded by an over-attentive medical staff eager to tend to his wounds and dote on him. Admitting a perhaps over-exaggerated sequence of events as related to him, Corm could not help noting a novel form of benevolence accorded this Lebanese immigrant, perhaps as a result of Lebanon's newfound celebrity deriving from the Fair.

As mentioned earlier, this was a remarkable accomplishment not only because Corm and the World's Fair were in a sense defying a looming global conflagration, nor because the festivities were being held while most of the world was still suffering the devastating effect of the Great Depression. This was a feat because, arguably, there was no independent sovereign Lebanon to speak of at the time—let alone was there such a country to flaunt at an international exhibit. Yet the Lebanon Pavilion that Corm erected almost singlehandedly loomed large. As boasted one *New York Times* article in August 1939, "Lebanon Presents Story in Pavilion; Tiny Republic, in First Exhibit at International Exposition, Charms Visitors at Fair; Cedars Prompt Queries; Trees 2,000 Years Old Supply Woodwork, Maps—Country's Poet Designed Building."[229] The article went on to note that, "[o]fficially one week old this evening, the pavilion of the Republic of Lebanon has got off to an encouraging start, although most of its 4,000 to 5,000 daily visitors could not have found the country it represents on the map."[230] Yet, again, the impression it left on visitors had a lasting effect. Writing in the *New York Post*, Henry Beckett could not help wedding poetry to Biblical symbolism in his descriptions of an exhibit that was as real as any other at the Fair, but one that, more so than others, appealed to his olfactory as well as his other senses. Beckett's article quoted an entire poem by Ian Duncan Colvin, which kept tugging at him as he walked through the exhibit.[231] With Colvin's intrusions dominating his prose, Beckett wrote:

Come with me from Lebanon, my spouse, with me from Lebanon, / Down with me from Lebanon to sail upon the sea. / The ship is wrought of ivory, the decks of gold, and thereupon / Are sailors singing bridal songs, and waiting to cast free. / Come with me from Lebanon, my spouse, with me from Lebanon, / The Rowers there are ready and will welcome thee with shouts. / The sails are silken sails and scarlet, cut and sewn in Babylon, / The scarlet of the painted lips of women thereabouts. / Come with me from Lebanon, my spouse, with me from Lebanon, / They are hauling up the anchor and but tarrying there for thee; / The boatswain's whistling for a wind, a wind to blow from Lebanon, / A wind from scented Lebanon to blow them out to sea.[232]

The fragrances from Lebanon, olfactory as well as historical, were too overwhelming to be ignored, and the romance and legend associated with them were a resource that Charles Corm capitalized upon, and exploited in the best interest of his country's image in America.

BEGRUDGING THE LEBANON PARTICIPATION

Perhaps from its inception, the idea of an independent Lebanon Pavilion had been an affront and a challenge, and was consequently impugned by those who opposed it. Albeit mildly, it was resented by the French authorities, which according to Kaufman took the opportunity of international world's fairs to display their own colonial achievements and showcase their own empire's possessions, *not* highlight their colonies' individuality and sense of independence.[233] But Lebanon's participation in the Fair, an audacious act of autonomy and a pageantry of national sovereignty, was also begrudged by Arab and Syrian nationalists, both inside and outside Lebanon. Fakhri al-Baroody for instance, a leading Syrian politician and a close friend of Charles Corm, preferred that Syria be represented at the Fair *instead of*, not alongside Lebanon. Indeed, in the context of the New York World's Fair, Arab nationalists spoke of Lebanon as an addendum to an eventual Syrian exhibit, reflecting a prevailing irredentist bent in their worldview, imagining Lebanon a district (Ar. *qutr*) of an illusive Greater Syria.[234] After all, Lebanon's legitimacy as a discrete legal entity, and its very national identity as one separate and distinct from that of its neighbors, were still ideas as contested in the 1930s as they are today. Yet, as mentioned earlier, not only was Syria itself not represented—in fact, Syria lacked the financial and organizational wherewithal to construct a Syrian Pavilion—but some Syrians, imbued in Arab nationalist hubris, mounted a vicious press campaign against the Fair itself, and against its host country, taking great umbrage at America's Zionist sympathies and attempting to intimidate Lebanon into reneging on its commitment to participate in an event ostensibly organized by Zionist sympathizers.[235]

Indeed, and to the great dismay of Fakhri al-Baroody himself, Arab nationalists even coerced a Syria under his leadership into withdrawing its commitment to take part in the exhibit.[236] Like Corm's representation of Lebanon, al-Baroody's aim as a potential participant had been to raise with his own hands "Syria's sacred banner in the skies above New York."[237] But his noble efforts were frustrated, and he was deeply troubled by those who endeavored to impede his hands.[238] In response to those who invoked the pretext of "prevalent Zionist propaganda in America" as justification for Syria's non-participation, al-Baroody wondered if Arab nationalists could identify a better way of countering alleged Zionist propaganda than discharging their own Arab counter-propaganda. "What better publicity for us," he said, "than participating in the New York Exposition, and taking this opportunity to showcase our culture and demolish the Zionists' claims that Arabs are incapable of attaining industrial, agricultural, and artistic progress; that our culture is unsuited for the elements of civilization and modernity?"[239] Still, the same resentful nationalist impulses that depicted Syria's likely participation in the Fair a betrayal of Arab causes, also motivated al-Baroody to protest Lebanon's own participation as a distinct, sovereign state.

A prominent politician, Fakhri al-Baroody (1889–1966) was the charismatic leader of Syria's National Bloc. An Arab nationalist coalition of parties—not to be confounded with Lebanon's own National Bloc, which was firmly Lebanese nationalist and reflected the worldview of its founder, Lebanese President Émile Éddé, and his friend Charles Corm—the Syrian National Bloc called for "Syrian unity"; that is to say, it demanded the unification of the autonomous States of Aleppo, Damascus, Druze Mountain, Alawite Mountain, and the *Sanjak* of Alexandretta into a single Syrian entity. As such, al-Baroody was also an avid proponent of the attachment of the Republic of Lebanon to that yearned-for, larger, future Syrian entity. Curiously enough, a very close friendship developed between Fakhri al-Baroody and Charles Corm, and indeed al-Baroody became somewhat of a fixture at Corm's *Amitiés Libanaises* cultural salons during the 1930s. In a June 1935 issue of *La Syrie*, Lebanese journalist Ibrahim Maklouf described both Corm and al-Baroody as two opposites that completed and complemented one another; one of them represented the conscience of Lebanon and its Mediterranean soul, the other embodied the essence of Syria and its presumptive Arab culture.[240] Charles Corm, wrote Maklouf, "was powerful and dynamic, impetuous and subtle, sensitive and deeply emotional."[241] Fakhri al-Baroody on the other hand, "who had neither the physical stature nor the glowing fire burning in Corm's eyes, still had something resembling Corm's inner strength, his passion, his raging emotions, his eloquence and his skill."[242] Yet this was the unlikeliest of friendships, given Corm's Lebanonist credentials and al-Baroody's firm Arabist beliefs. But as mentioned earlier, Corm was not one to allow the pettiness of ideology and political leanings to stand in the way of friendship, and his affinities to people were as varied as they may have seemed unlikely. To wit, Amin Rihani, one of Lebanon's early twentieth-century exponents of Arabism, was not only a family friend and a fervent admirer of Corm's work—despite his disagreement with its Phoenicianist content—he was also the godfather of Corm's second son, Hiram. Even *he*, his Arab nationalist predilections notwithstanding, could not resist Corm's personal charm and the profound humanism of his brand of Lebanese nationalism. Reading *La Montagne Inspirée*, wrote Rihani in praise of his friend in 1934, one cannot help loving and identifying with Corm and his Phoenician Lebanon—even though Rihani would remain dubious as to whether or not the Phoenicians were truly worthy of Corm's love and adulation.[243] "You are a lover of the human race," wrote Rihani in praise of his friend and philosophical adversary,

> your heart bears within it oceans of affection, and your soul shines like bright sunlights of affection. You abscond both Frenchmen and Arabs, but you regale us with canticles emanating from the depths of your heart and soul, singing with devotion your boundless love for the peoples of your land.[244]

Still Rihani was at a loss to explain Corm's enthusiasm for the vanished Phoenicians while remaining lukewarm vis-à-vis the "living Arabs." Yet he could not help admitting that Lebanon was well deserving of Corm's love, dubbing *The Hallowed Mountain* the "Phoenicians' Song of Songs," writing that:

> Lebanon and Charles Corm are a single inseparable moral and spiritual unit. Corm's unbounded love for Lebanon is incarnate in Lebanon's Cedars and Mountains, and in turn Lebanon's Cedars and Mountains willingly prostrate and melt before him, rendering themselves incense and emanations of light to be offered at his exalted national altar. [...] I read Corm's *Hallowed Mountain* and I feel as if transported from one festival of light to the next, from one orchard to the next, and from one raging volcano to the next; yet I remain firmly planted on Lebanese soil.[245]

Even Khalil Takieddine (1906–1987), another Lebanese Arabist, confided his sheer inability to resist the charisma, energy, and affection that Corm's work—and his person—exuded. Even for one committed to Lebanon's Arab identity as Takieddine had been, the lure and temptation of Phoenicianism were rendered exquisite, irresistible, and profoundly compelling through the magic flowing from Charles Corm's literary work. Khalil Takieddine admits not being a fan of "national literature"; yet Corm's poetry, he revealed, commanded our attention because it broke free from the constraints of time and space and persons, and "it soared high above and beyond Lebanon, to heights far removed from narrow nationalism and into a most spacious universalism."[246] Corm's work is universal and humanist in the true sense of the terms, wrote Takieddine, and it is the outcome of Corm's own spacious, universalist, vigorously and profoundly humanist formation; "a fine, delicious culture that eludes a good many of our company of literati in Lebanon today."[247] And while Amin Rihani's Arabist leanings compelled him to criticize Corm's use of French instead of Arabic, Khalil Takieddine merely wished Corm had written in Arabic, "if only to show those so-called Arabic-language poets of our times—who are in reality scribblers and poseurs and cheap wordsmiths—how true poetry makes the heart flutter, how it makes the eye yearn for the sublime, and how its music lets loose one's feelings and stirs the emotions."[248]

Kaufman rightly noted that those Lebanese opponents of Lebanon's representation at the New York World's Fair feared that Corm would use that platform in order to flaunt Lebanon's Western character—or at least the Lebanese character as seen from Corm's own Phoenicianist perspective[249]— and in the process eclipse the prospects of the Arab unity that they yearned for. Their apprehensions were not unfounded. Indeed they came true. But opposed as some of them might have been to Corm's worldview and to its validation and valorization at the Fair, they could not but respect Corm's person, even when diverging from his endeavors.

Oddly enough, some of those who resented Charles Corm's enterprise might have come from inside his own camp—that is to say they might have been some of his most-dedicated admirers, albeit admirers overcome by envy and a craving for a limelight they lacked. Based on his own narrative in a report filed on April 22, 1940, to Lebanese Secretary of State Abdallah Beyhum, Charles Corm noted that he had been reluctant to take the helm as Commissioner General of the Lebanese Pavilion at the New York World's Fair in 1939, and that he had consented to accept the nomination and take on the mission entrusted him at the insistence of the government of President Émile Éddé.[250] "The government went on rejecting my entreaties that I be spared this responsibility," wrote Corm in that report, until Émile Éddé himself interceded and made him reconsider. Corm ultimately, and reluctantly, left his two sons, a toddler and a newborn, behind, and made that voyage to New York accompanied by his young bride.[251] He further wrote that he had every intention of returning home to his young children as soon as the Lebanon Pavilion had been erected and organized, and the exhibits inaugurated. "My wife accompanied me," he wrote,

> not for the pleasure of embarking on such a long trip, so far away from home; nor did she come along with me for the pleasure of my company over that of our own two children, one of whom a newborn. She came along strictly to keep an eye on me and watch over my ailing health. And I had hoped to return home as soon as the Pavilion had been constructed.[252]

At that time Corm had indeed been suffering excruciating chronic pain from stomach ulcers and gallstone disease, and at one point during the trip to New York, on the leg between Athens and Paris, his wife, Samia, was on the verge of returning with him to Beirut for fear that the gallstone attacks that had gripped him while at sea would put his life in further danger.[253] But the couple would forge ahead, and the Corms would land in New York on April 15, 1939, a full two weeks following their March 29 departure from Beirut. Charles Corm was visibly ailing and physically feeble on the day their ship docked in New York, but he was nevertheless possessed of an inner energy determined to make of his Lebanese Pavilion a sensation for the world to behold.

Charles Corm's written recollections of the events surrounding his work at the Lebanon Pavilion were drafted after his return to Beirut—during the winter closure of the Fair in late October—with some distance and hindsight, and in light of the vicious accusations made against him claiming he had undertaken this project for pure financial gain and in order to be able to sell artifacts and artwork for his own personal profit.[254] The accusations notwithstanding, it should be noted that all of the Lebanon exhibit's concessionaires' items put together, if sold, could not have covered a fraction of the personal expenses that Charles Corm and his wife had incurred and the private family funds that they had themselves expended for the construction and maintenance of the Lebanese exhibit.[255] The cost of advertising the Lebanese exhibit in the local American press alone, according to Corm's calculations, amounted to about $1,000 per month, for a grand total of $9,000 for the nine months during which the exhibit was open.[256]

But Corm claims to have had a premonition of these accusations, even before they ever took place. "I had obstinately resisted becoming the Commissioner General" he wrote,

> not to avoid responsibility, nor to spare myself the personal and financial sacrifices that such a post would have entailed, but rather for fear of triggering exactly the accusations leveled against me today and against the exhibit itself, its content, and its purpose. Such are the kinds of polemics and resentments that holders of public office in Lebanon are bound to bear in our political culture. I am acutely aware of—and indeed I am personally familiar—with these kinds of animosities and calumnies.[257]

Corm went on to minutely document the negative campaign mounted against him personally by the Arabic-language Lebanese press in New York—namely Salloum Mokarzel's *al-Hoda*, and his cousin Joseph's satirical *al-Dabbour*, the latter published in Beirut. Among the accusations that both Mokarzels leveled at Corm, some claimed that he had undertaken the Fair project purely for personal financial gain. Yet, Corm's minute record keeping—a 215-page "Administrative and Financial Report" filed with the

Office of the Lebanese Secretary of State—demonstrates that the exhibit, valued at about a million dollars, cost the Lebanese treasury some sixty thousand dollars, with the rest of the expenses covered from Corm's own personal funds, with a small fraction issuing from secondary contributions made by members of the Lebanese émigré community.[258]

Samia Corm recalls her and Charles being initially received warmly by the Lebanese community of New York. She mentions with particular fondness that the Mokarzels of *al-Hoda* had gone out of their way to honor the great "Hallowed Poet," celebrating him in a deluge of hyperbole on the pages of their newspaper, referring to him as a "national treasure," "the poet prodigy of Lebanon," and suchlike.[259] Indeed, the articles of *al-Hoda*, from around 1934 (when the paper began reproducing excerpts of *La Montagne Inspirée* in Arabic translation) until September 1939, were at times exceedingly adulatory of Corm, and beginning in early 1939 the newspaper started writing with eager anticipation, awaiting his arrival to New York. But soon after the inauguration of the Lebanon Pavilion—and more so after the Lebanon Day festivities of September 1, 1939, during which Corm was given the honors of a bona fide diplomatic representative of Lebanon—the honeymoon effects began waning, and the Mokarzels began waging a very public and very nasty defamatory campaign against the Commissioner General of the Lebanon Pavilion, on the pages of both *al-Hoda* and *al-Dabbour*. This behavior was all the more intriguing given *al-Hoda*'s strong Lebanese nationalist bent and the place of honor that its pages had given Lebanese history and the Phoenicians as ancestors and progenitors of the modern Lebanese. Indeed, in a report filed to the French High Commissioner in Beirut, the French *Mission de Propagande* (or Propaganda Service) in New York described *al-Hoda* as an essentially "Maronite, Francophile mouthpiece," anti-clerical, secular, and sympathetic to the French Mandate and to Greater Lebanon.[260] Yet the report still painted the journal's founder, Naoum Mokarzel, in somewhat unflattering terms, describing him as "independent minded," but also as a megalomaniacal "intransigent, even authoritarian character."[261] The report further spoke of Mokarzel as

> a man whose sometimes outrageous brand of inflammatory [. . .] polemical journalism earned him many friends and even more enemies, all equally immoderate in both their admiration and hatred of him. [. . .] His newspaper is, above all, his own mouthpiece, self-serving, dedicated to the advancement of his own interests. He is founder of the "Committee for Lebanese Renaissance" [. . .] and is a strong advocate for the establishment of a sovereign independent Lebanese homeland, distinct from Syria. [. . . In sum,] *al-Hoda* is a precious organ of the Franco-Lebanese cause; yet it is regrettable to see it at times forgo moderation, which would have made it an even more valuable organ in the service of our cause.[262]

This is perhaps a statement on *al-Hoda*'s character, and arguably a window into what might have gone awry between the Mokarzels and the Corms in New York. According to Samia Corm's recollections (and Charles Corm's own reports and personal journal entries), the Mokarzels and their own circle of Lebanese émigrés had cast themselves in a brighter light than was actually theirs to claim, and had fancied themselves forerunners and progenitors of the idea of Lebanon's participation in the New York World's Fair.[263] They had also hoped to make use of the Lebanon Pavilion as a platform to sell their own, as well as their families' and friends', homemade artifacts and crafts, promote their own local business interests, and boost their personal standing within the Lebanese émigré community. At one point, they pleaded with Charles Corm to let them set up tables and commercial kiosks at the Pavilion's entrance to purvey trinkets and bagatelles in the manner of Oriental bazaars, to the strong objections of Charles Corm, who insisted on keeping the Lebanon Pavilion representative of the "hallowed grounds" that had become its image at the Fair—a symbol that both legally and as a matter of principle Corm had the responsibility of upholding. Furthermore, as Commissioner General and official representative of the Lebanese government, Charles Corm was bound by contractual obligations to the Fair Corporation, and under the laws of the State of New York, to observe the terms of the "Exhibit Agreement," which expressly read that the Fair Corporation remain the sole authority granting "Concessionaire Licensing" at the exhibits.[264]

Nevertheless, Charles Corm did make an effort to indulge the appetites of the Mokarzels, more specifically Joseph Mokarzel's of the *Dabour*, and gave in to his desire to sell—for his own profit—old copies of his Beirut-based newspaper and other personal relics at the New York World's Fair. And no sooner had Charles Corm left Beirut on his way to the Fair in late March 1939, Joseph Mokarzel showed up at the Lebanon Pavilion warehouse on Damascus Road, on the western edges of Corm's *Maison Blanche* compound, demanding that employees preparing the materials destined to the Fair include in their shipments a number of paintings, books, and old newspapers that Mokarzel had wanted sold at the Lebanon Pavilion. A total of three boxes ended up being shipped to New York, to the benefit of Joseph Mokarzel and at his behest, charged to the Lebanon Pavilion budget, and without prior knowledge or approval of Charles Corm.[265] Yet, and for the sake of avoiding a confrontation, once the items were discharged by the New York Port Authority, Corm decided it was "too late—not to say pointless—discussing the items' relevance to the Lebanon exhibit"; he therefore resolved to display them prominently in the "Books Section" showcase of the Pavilion.[266] However, not a single copy of Mokarzel's merchandise ended up being sold, in spite of the cheeky publicity campaigns that Joseph Mokarzel had attempted with Lebanese visitors and émigré groups. Furthermore, Corm himself was eager to move that merchandise, not so much to please Mr.

Mokarzel as to avoid the burden of it crowding the already cramped space of the Lebanon Pavilion, or having to pay for its storage and eventual shipment back to Lebanon at the event's conclusion.[267] So, Corm too set out to peddle Mokarzel's stock, inappropriate as the items might have been in terms of both content and price, and unsuitable as they were to the general theme of the Lebanon Pavilion.[268]

By mid-July 1939, Joseph Mokarzel had arrived in New York, with his visit being billed by *al-Hoda* as the tour of the "Special Envoy" to Lebanese President Émile Éddé.[269] This claim was clearly the kind of family flattery and self-encomium for which the Mokarzels and their publications had become notorious; for, besides the pages of *al-Hoda* and *al-Dabbour*, no available Lebanese or American sources relative to the New York World's Fair had come to the mention of either Salloum or Joseph Mokarzel as official— nor even as unofficial—representatives of the Lebanese government in the New World. Still, and in recognition of the semblance of friendship that Salloum Mokarzel had extended to the Corms upon their arrival in April 1939, Charles Corm hosted a luncheon at the Park Central Hotel in Joseph Mokarzel's honor, and he apprised him of the status of his merchandise and the fact that it had not yet attracted many—not to say any—buyers. Joseph Mokarzel was visibly shaken by the news—and all the more so by the fact that he had also brought along with him thousands of additional booklets and newspaper back issues that he had hoped to unload at the exhibit.[270] He had also brought over a number of miscellanies and other curiosities, from Abyssinian snakeskins to Sudanese ivory and amber-bead rosaries, which he had hoped to also hawk at the Lebanon Pavilion.[271] Joseph Mokarzel also proposed that Corm allow him to sell stamps collections; thirty thousand dollars worth; small envelopes for a dollar each, which Mokarzel himself had prepared for the occasion and brought along with him from Beirut. Corm approved of the idea, only to find out that Mokarzel's collection was a motley of sundry stamps from random countries that could be neither displayed nor sold at the Lebanon Pavilion, *not* because Corm will have refused to feature them, but because contractually speaking the New York World's Fair Corporation would have forbidden such a practice: Stamps from, say, Venezuela, Argentina, Brazil, and elsewhere could only be sold at their respective Pavilions, noted Corm to Mokarzel.[272] Furthermore, as per the "Exhibitor's Concession Agreement" that Charles Corm had signed on behalf of the Lebanese government, and by which he was legally bound, concessionaires were licensed to sell items strictly for exhibit, not commercial, purposes, and the items in question had to be Lebanese native—not foreign—products.[273] As such, the Lebanon Pavilion was specifically authorized

> to sell, within the Project, copper articles, cotton, silk, wool, rayon articles, carved wood, leather goods, straw articles, and postage stamps, it being under-

stood and agreed that all of the merchandise shall be imported from Lebanon [. . . and] specifically limited in character to the Project and the Republic of Lebanon. [. . .] The Concessionaire shall furnish to the Fair Corporation for its written approval [. . .] complete lists of all merchandise to be sold and prices to be charged therefore.[274]

This legal document would have clearly banned the practices that the Mokarzels had intended to get under way, and prohibited the merchandize that they had hoped to sell at the Lebanon Pavilion. Yet they insisted on getting their way. And when Corm spurned their wishes—not out of malice or disregard, but stemming from the standpoint of his legal obligations and the commitments that he had made to the creative and aesthetic framework of the Lebanon exhibit—they began "spewing their venom against the Lebanon Pavilion and its Commissioner General."[275] In one instance, two weeks prior to the Lebanon Day festivities of September 1, 1939, Joseph Mokarzel showed up at Charles Corm's office at the Lebanon Pavilion, and proceeded to scream out insults and level accusations at the Commissioner General, denouncing him for slighting his cousin Salloum Mokarzel, owner of *al-Hoda*, and alleging Corm to have been working with the enemies of *al-Hoda* and the enemies of Lebanon to undermine Salloum's standing in the Lebanese immigrant community; that Corm was a traitor to his country; that "the Mokarzels were a national treasure for Lebanon" that Corm had disdained; that the Lebanese government had consented to putting together a Lebanon Pavilion at the New York World's Fair *only* at the Mokarzels' behest and in deference to their desires; that Charles Corm could have done a better job complying to the Mokarzels and their wishes; that by not doing so, Charles Corm was in clear breach of the Lebanese government's directives; and that he had disobeyed the Lebanese government's decree that Salloum Mokarzel be appointed Assistant to the Commissioner General of the Lebanese Pavilion.[276]

Of course there were no Lebanese directives—official or otherwise—suggesting Salloum Mokarzel be appointed Corm's *aide de camp*; nor was there any evidence in Corm's conduct, from the day he took on the responsibilities of Lebanon's Commissioner General and began laying down the groundwork for the Lebanon Pavilion, suggesting his conduct has been anything but ethical, altruistic, and wholly dedicated to the greater good of his country. Yet Joseph Mokarzel would carry on with his antics that evening at the Fair, lashing out at Corm, leveling false accusations, and making a spectacle out of himself and the Pavilion. Alerted by the ruckus of one strange man flying off the handle, visitors to the Lebanon Pavilion began gathering on the ground floor of the exhibit seeking answers. But Mokarzel remained undaunted, even as Corm kept trying to reason with him attempting to understand how he could have been mislead. But it was all to no avail, and it wasn't until Samia Corm, the Commissioner General's wife, who'd been looking after the *Artisanat Libanais* kiosks on the mezzanine floor, rushed over to her husband's side that Mokarzel began regaining his composure. Samia calmly remonstrated Mokarzel, urging him to take up whatever quarrels he may have had with her husband outside of the Lebanon Pavilion, and refrain from turning a national symbol into a freak show: "how can you have Lebanon's best interest at heart," she asked, "while turning its Pavilion into your personal battleground?"[277] Though still seething with anger, Joseph Mokarzel hung his head in shame and left the premises never to be seen again, and Charles Corm resolved to no longer have any dealings with him from that day on. But the damage was done. The Mokarzels never gained the recognition they thought was owed them by the Lebanese government—therefore subverting the image they had built for themselves in the diaspora—and so, they set out to tarnish Corm's reputation, a man they now viewed as a rival warranting being destroyed, even at the cost of damaging Lebanon's own prestige in the process.

As alluded to earlier, it seems that the Mokarzels were steeped in nepotism and expediency, and their newspapers, although solidly opposed to Arab nationalist narratives and committed to a certain Lebanese particularism, were also used almost as a "family mouthpiece" and an organ for self-promotion and self-adulation. To wit, for the duration of his stay in the New World, Jospeh Mokarzel undertook trips to various Lebanese immigrant communities soliciting subscriptions to the Beirut-based *Dabbour*, which even in Lebanon, where Arabic was widely used, was suffering a dwindling readership. In America on the other hand, where the numbers of first-generation Lebanese immigrants were declining and their descendants, molded in American schools, were ill-equipped to understand Arabic let alone read it, *al-Dabbour*'s prospects at swelling its readership appeared to be even dimmer. Yet the Mokarzels remained hard at work trying (against great odds) to raise their newspapers' standing and increase their circulation. In a December 1938 letter from *al-Hoda* to the New York World's Fair corporate office at the Empire State Building, Salloum Mokarzel appealed to the organizers urging them to advertise the Fair on the pages of his newspaper where the rates stood at "one Dollar per inch single column, [with *al-Hoda*] undertaking the translation" into Arabic at no additional charge.[278] To sweeten the deal, Mokarzel reminded his correspondents that *al-Hoda* was the oldest and most widely read Arabic language newspaper in America, and that its Syrian and Lebanese readers, enterprising business people as they were, would materially benefit the New York World's Fair if the Fair itself knew how to approach them and essentially appeal to their business instinct.[279] "I trust you will favor us with some patronage [. . .] for the appeal [that] such patronage would have in attracting visitors and exhibitors from [. . .] countries of the East where *al-Hoda* enjoys a wide circulation."[280]

As mentioned earlier in this chapter, the energy and commitment that the Mokarzels had devoted to the Fair and to the Lebanese participation in it were no doubt driven by genuine national interest and patriotic duty—although financial gain and personal advancement must not be discounted as added incentives. Yet, based on the content and tone of the letter quoted above, Salloum Mokarzel appeared unaware that the Fair was hardly the money-making enterprise that he might have imagined (or hoped) it to be, for it was in fact "classified by the United States government as a charitable enterprise," with its revenues to be consigned to the future improvement of the fairgrounds and their eventual transformation into a permanent park.[281] Furthermore, the Fair's officers and directors served in their positions without compensation and as part of their duty as civil servants of the United States and the State of New York. So, in a sense, the Mokarzels' later *ad hominem* attacks against Charles Corm seemed to rebut their earlier adulations of the poet as a "national icon," a "hallowed poet," and a "veritable powerhouse" behind Lebanon's representation at the Fair. The fact that they were initially stepping over each other to rally members of the Lebanese émigré community around Corm, organizing receptions for him and his wife, was all the more curious in view of their sudden about face. The fact that a considerable content in the newspaper adulated the Mokarzels themselves—and their role as leaders in the Lebanese émigré community—at times read like pure puffery and (almost Soviet-style) propaganda bordering on hack journalism. The fact that Salloum Mokarzel's attempts to cast himself—at least in the eyes of the Arabophone readers of his newspaper—as one of the "Three Knights of the Fair" were rebuffed and ultimately failed, may explain much of his later antics and the defamatory vindictive that he unleashed against Charles Corm.[282] Furthermore, Corm's refusal to allow Mokarzel a platform at the Pavilion to sell subscriptions to his newspaper and solicit donations from Lebanese visitors (for the building of a "National Mausoleum" in Lebanon for Naoum Mokarzel, the deceased founder of *al-Hoda*) clearly vexed Salloum and Joseph Mokarzel, and morphed them from erstwhile friends to committed foes.[283]

This experience and the vicious defamatory campaign that ensued from it were deeply troubling to Charles Corm, aggravating his already ailing health, and contributing to his decision to return to Lebanon before the inauguration of the second season of the World's Fair in 1940. And although the services he rendered to his country earned him further adulation and added respect upon his return, Charles Corm was a changed man in 1940, and his public life underwent profound changes in the years that followed. To be sure, he continued to earn official decorations and literary and popular accolades: He was awarded the Lebanese Republic's highest honor given to a civilian in 1940, the Medal of the Knight of the National Order of the Cedar for services rendered to the nation. He also became recipient of the Golden Medal of

Merit, awarded him by the State of New Jersey, and another Golden Medal of Honor bestowed by New York City Mayor Fiorello La Guardia "for services rendered to the United States of America." Additionally, three times he was awarded the French Croix de la Légion d'Honneur, France's highest civil decoration, and three times Charles Corm turned down that distinction—doing so perhaps to demonstrate that, although a committed Francophile, his affections for France were far from Pollyannaish, and could never have exceeded his love for his country. But also, and in his own words, Corm refused to accept the Cross of the Legion of Honor "because too many enemies of France and too many traitors to Lebanon had been recipients of this decoration in the past."[284]

But the 1940s was a decade pregnant with significant and dramatic changes, both on the global and local stage. The world was self-immolating in yet another world war; Arab nationalism was on the upswing; and Lebanon was politically and culturally going in a direction that Charles Corm had not anticipated. And so, the "Patron Saint" of *The Hallowed Mountain* and the "Poet Prodigy of Lebanon" would retreat to the turrets of his Beirut tower, writing feverishly in the stillness of night, and sleeping only agitatedly in the bustle of daylight. Arab nationalists would never forgive Charles Corm his audacity, daring to chart Lebanon an independent course and flaunt its distinct identity, both within the country and abroad. And so would rumors and vicious slander continue to swirl around Charles Corm and his eccentric lifestyle, and so would the avatars of an ever assertive and irredentist Arabism proceed to assail and dismantle his Phoenicianist edifice. But the "little man" of the Lebanon Pavilion, the hermit of the *Maison Blanche de Beyrouth*, the "Child of the Mountain" continued to cast a shadow larger than life, and went on igniting and throwing light brighter than light on Lebanon's cultural, social, and political life, long after his life-lights were snuffed out on September 19, 1963.

NOTES

1. See for instance Asher Kaufman's *Reviving Phoenicia; The Search for Identity in Lebanon* (London and New York: I. B. Tauris, 2004), 88.
2. Letter from Julius Holmes to Charles Corm, *The New York World's Fair 1939–1940 Records,* Manuscripts and Archives Division (New York: The New York Public Library, Astor, Lenox, and Tilden Foundations), Box 1470, Folder 10.
3. *The New York World's Fair 1939–1940 Records,* Box 1470, Folder 10.
4. Administering his estate after his death, Charles Corm's children discovered that he had liquidated a sizeable New York Stock Exchange portfolio of triple A shares in order to fund the expenses of the Lebanese Pavilion at the World's Fair. This was in addition to contributing portions of his own personal savings. David Corm notes that had his father left those stocks untouched, he would have been counted among Lebanon's richest men during the 1960s.
5. See *The New York World's Fair 1939–1940 Records,* Box 1497, Folder 6, and Box 2221, Folder 11.

6. See for instance Émile Schaub-Koch's "Le Poète Libanais Charles Corm," a series of three essays published in *La Revue de l'Université Laval* between September and November 1958 (Vol. XIII, No. 1–3.) Schaub-Koch wrote that "while Lebanese *belles lettres* may have a rich history in three different languages, English, French, and Arabic, it would be fair to add Spanish and Italian to the lot. [. . . It is also important to note] that one of the great leaders of this powerful and awe-inspiring movement of modern Lebanese literature is Charles Corm. [. . .] The beauty and majesty of Corm's literary movement is in the fact that one may call it 'Francophone Lebanese Humanism.' For, Charles Corm is specifically Lebanese in his poetry, [. . .] yet he renews the French poetic genius by way of a Lebanese genius."

7. See for instance the special issue of *al-Maarad* dedicated to Corm's *La Montagne Inspirée* and titled "The Mountain's Awakening; Art and Literature in Lebanon" (Beirut: Issue 38, July 4, 1934).

8. Youssef al-Saouda, "al-Jabal al-Mulham, Mihbat al-Wahi" [The Hallowed Mountain, Sanctuary of Revelation], *al-Maarad* (Beirut: Issue 38, July 4, 1934), 9.

9. Assaad Younis, "al-Jabal al-Mulham, Muharrer al-Arwaah" [The Hallowed Mountain, Redeemer of Spirits], *al-Maarad* (Beirut: Issue 38, July 4, 1934), 4.

10. Younis, "al-Jabal al-Mulham," 3–4.

11. Ironically, Takieddine al-Solh, a committed militant Arab nationalist, was expelled from Lebanon by the Syrian regime, which had ostensibly entered Lebanon in 1976 on behalf of Arab nationalism, and in order to "protect Lebanon's Arabness." Solh would die in his Parisian exile in 1988.

12. Asher Kaufman, *Reviving Phoenicia; The Search for Identity in Lebanon* (London and New York: I. B. Tauris, 2004), 143.

13. Kaufman, *Reviving Phoenicia,* 143.

14. Takieddine al-Solh, "al-Jabal al-Haa'er" [The Perplexed Mountain], *al-Maarad* (Beirut: Issue 38, July 4, 1934), 21.

15. The phrase "father of lies" is attributed to Voltaire, who calls Herodotus both "the father of history" and "the father of lies." See for instance Alba Amoia and Bettina Knapp, *Multicultural Writers from Antiquity to 1945; A Biographical Sourcebook* (Westport, CT: Greenwood, 2002), 171, and Kenton Sparks *Ethnicity and Identity in Ancient Israel* (Warsaw, IN: Eisenbrauns, 1998), 58, where the author writes that even in antiquity "Herodotus had acquired the reputation of being unreliable, biased, parsimonious in his praise of heroes, and mendacious."

16. Joel Carmichael, *The Shaping of the Arabs* (New York: The Macmillan Co., 1967), 5.

17. Abu Khaldun Sati' al-Husri, *Abhaath Mukhtaara fi al-Qawmiyya al-'Arabiyya* [Selected Texts in Arab Nationalsim] (Beirut: Markaz Dirasaat al-Wihda al-'Arabiyya, 1985), 80.

18. Solh, "The Perplexed Mountain," 23.

19. Paul Morand, *Méditerranée, Mer des Surprises* (Paris: Éditions du Rocher, 1990), 206.

20. Solh, "The Perplexed Mountain," 30–31.

21. It should be worth mentioning that Charles Corm was the first French translator of Kahlil Gibran's English masterpiece, *The Prophet*. Corm subsequently collaborated with close friend Hektor Klat on the translation of *The Prophet* into Arabic.

22. Charles Corm, *La Montagne Inspirée* (Beirut: Éditions de la Revue Phénicienne, 1987), 53–59. *Antar* (also known as *Antara Bin Shaddad*) was a pre-Islamic Arabian warrior and poet, notorious for his courage in battle and his romantic escapades. His chivalrous values, love life, and legendary courage were immortalized in Classical *Jahiliyya* (pre-Islamic) poetry, and became the themes of popular story telling throughout the Middle East, Lebanon included. *Harun al-Rashid* was a seventh- to eighth-century Abaasid Caliph who also became the stuff of legend and the topic of popular tales. The *Djérid* is an Ottoman, Arab, and Persian mock-fight on horseback, comparable to the mediaeval European martial games like knight jousting. Note also the comprehensive glossary of terms that Corm himself drew up for the 1945 Arabic translation of *La Montagne Inspirée* by Fr. Estephan Farhat. The glossary's Arabic title, *Mouhjame*, consisted of 118 pages of explanatory notes for 181 terms, names of personalities, and historical, geographic, and mythological references. This glossary was not part of the original 1934 French edition, but was subsequently included in later reprints. See for instance the 1987 French edition, pages 109–34, and the 2006 Arabic edition, pages 125–37.

23. Corm, *La Montagne Inspirée,* 53.

24. Corm, *La Montagne Inspirée*, 65. See also Charles Corm's speech during the inauguration of the Lebanon Pavilion at the New York World's Fair on July 13, 1939; *Discours à l'Inauguration du Pavillion Libanais* (Beirut: Charles Corm Archives, July 11, 1939), 4.
25. Selim Abou, *Le Bilinguisme Arab-Français au Liban* (Paris: Presses Universitaires de France, 1962), 157–58.
26. Marius Deeb, *Syria, Iran, and Hezbollah: The Unholy Alliance and Its War on Lebanon* (Stanford, CA: The Hoover Institution Press, 2013), xiv–xv.
27. Jamil Jabr, *Al-Jabal al-Mulham* [The Hallowed Mountain] (Beirut: Éditions de la Revue Phénicienne, 2006), 7.
28. Salah Labaki, "Al-'Aashiq, Shaarl Qorm" [Charles Corm the Beloved], *al-Maarad* (Beirut: Issue 38, July 4, 1934), 16.
29. Saouda, "al-Jabal al-Mulham, Mihbat al-Wahi," 9.
30. Corm, *La Montagne Inspirée*, 102.
31. Abou, *Le Bilinguisme*, 177–79.
32. Abou, *Le Bilinguisme*, 191–95.
33. Charles Corm, *Participation Libanaise à l'Exposition de New York, 1939: Rapport Administratif et Financier sur les Recettes et les Dépenses du Budget de la Participation Libanaise à l'Exposition de New York; du 1er Octobre 1938 à Mars 1940;* a detailed administrative and financial report on the Lebanese participation in the New York World's Fair, submitted by Charles Corm to Abdallah Bey Beyhum, Secretary of State of the Lebanese Republic (Beirut: Charles Corm Archives, April 22, 1940), 10–11.
34. See March 25, 1939, letter from Charles Corm to E. F. Roosevelt, *The New York World's Fair 1939–1940 Records*, Box 1497, Folder 6.
35. See various documents relative to this in *The New York World's Fair 1939–1940 Records*, Box 1497, Folder 6. See for instance "Cost Estimates" telegrammed to Corm by Roosevelt on January 19, 1939, totaling some $25,000. Those estimates included $2,400 for electric bills, $5,000 for painting, $4,000 for utilities, $4,000 for cleaning, and $4,500 for miscellaneous expenses. These figures did not include the actual building of the Lebanon Pavilion, the cost of which Corm himself also covered from his own personal funds. See for instance Corm's January 21, 1939, transfer of $30,000 as down payment to the New York branch of the French American Banking Corporation, covering the early expenses of fitting up the Lebanese section of the World's Fair.
36. William Bernbach and Herman Jaffe's *Book of Nations* (New York and Washington, DC: Burland Printing Company, 1939), 106. See also *al-Hoda*'s Special Commemorative Issue, (New York: Volume 42, Number 122, July 17, 1939).
37. During the 1920s and 1930s Sally Rand acted on stage and in silent movies. She became a dancer after the introduction of sound movies, and popularized the erotic "fan dance" that La Guardia referred to in his quip; a burlesque, traditionally performed by a female dancer, often in the nude.
38. "Mayor at Chicago Scores Fair Critics," *New York Times,* August 11, 1939, 1.
39. *The New York World's Fair 1939–1940 Archives,* The New York Public Library, Manuscripts and Archives Division, Box 1497, Folder 6.
40. *New York Times,* August 11, 1939.
41. *New York Times,* August 11, 1939, 1 and 9. See also Frederick King Poole, "They Went to the Fair," *Saudi Aramco World* (July/August 1973), 5.
42. *New York Times,* August 11, 1939.
43. *New York Times,* August 11, 1939.
44. *New York Times,* August 11, 1939.
45. See for instance "Lebanon Presents Story in Pavilion," *New York Times,* July 20, 1939, 14, where Lebanon's capital city Beirut is spelled "Peirut." See also an October 10, 1939, letter by W. H. Standley about Foreign Government Participation, responding to Charles Corm's request that Section GF-4 of the Hall of Nations be assigned to the Lebanon Pavilion, and where Standley requests a telegram of acceptance be sent to Corm about the "Lebanonese [*sic*] Participation," *The New York World's Fair 1939–1940 Records,* Box 315, Folder 9.

46. Introductory remarks made by Mr. E. F. Roosevelt in connection with the introduction of speakers on Lebanon's opening day, July 13, 1939, *The New York World's Fair 1939–1940 Records,* Box 1497, Folder 6.
47. Transcript of Julius Holmes's speech, July 13, 1939, *The New York World's Fair 1939–1940 Records,* Box 1470, Folder 10.
48. Transcript of Julius Holmes's speech, and text of a telegram sent by Grover Whalen to Lebanese President Émile Eddé, *The New York World's Fair 1939–1940 Records,* Box 1470, Folder 10.
49. See October 26, 1939 letter from E. F. Roosevelt, Director of Foreign Government Participation, to Charles Corm, *The New York World's Fair 1939–1940 Records,* Box 1497, Folder 6.
50. *The New York World's Fair 1939–1940 Record,* Box 1497, Folder 6.
51. See Charles Corm, *Curriculum Vitae* (Beirut: Charles Corm Archives, November 27, 1948), 6. See also *The New York World's Fair 1939–1940 Records,* Box 1497, Folder 6.
52. October 10, 1939, letter to Jamil Baroody, from Gretl Urban, the New York World's Fair's Music Consultant, *The New York World's Fair 1939–1940 Records,* Box 697, Folder 28.
53. Perhaps the best-known iconic representations of those events are the Crystal Palace in London (1851), the White City in Chicago (1893), and the Eiffel Tower in Paris (1900).
54. *The New York World's Fair 1939–1940 Records,* Box 296, Folder 9.
55. *The New York World's Fair 1939–1940 Records,* Box 296, Folder 9.
56. Jessica Weglein et al., *New York World's Fair 1939 and 1940 Incorporated Records 1935–1945* (New York: The New York Public Library, Manuscripts and Archives Division, 2008), vii.
57. See Bernbach and Jaffe, *Book of Nations.*
58. Bernbach and Jaffe, *Book of Nations,* 7.
59. "Senate Also Approves $3,000,000 for Fair," *New York Times,* July 7, 1937, 8. It should be noted that in 1937 three million dollars had the buying power of some fifty million dollars in today's money.
60. *The New York World's Fair 1939–1940 Records,* Box 774, Folder 17.
61. Bernbach and Jaffe, *Book of Nations,* 105. See also Bertha Jaffe, "Lebanon Exhibit at the Fair Marks 6000 Years of Peace," *Forest Hills Times,* September 8, 1939, *The New York World's Fair 1939–1940 Records,* Box 1497, Folder 6.
62. "The President of the United States Opens the World's Greatest World's Fair," *New York Times,* May 1, 1939, 5.
63. "The President of the United States," 5.
64. "The President of the United States," 5.
65. "The President of the United States," 5.
66. "The President of the United States," 5.
67. See Charles Corm, *Curriculum Vitae* (Beirut: Charles Corm Archives, November 27, 1948), 6. See also *The New York World's Fair 1939–1940 Records,* Box 1497, Folder 6. According to his CV, Corm received the Golden Medal of Merit of the State of New Jersey. He was also recipient of the Gold Medal of New York City "for services rendered to the American people." He was also designated an "Honorary Citizen of New York City" by Mayor La Guardia, at the General Assembly of New York City's Municipal Council.
68. La Guardia was fluent in Yiddish (his mother, Iren Coen, was Jewish), German, French, Italian, and Croatian. Although Corm was also fluent in English, his dealings with La Guardia were primarily in French, and their written correspondence was in both French and English. For more on this, see *The New York World's Fair 1939–1940 Archives,* The New York Public Library, Manuscripts and Archives Division.
69. Charles Corm, "Méditations Nationalistes," *La Revue Phénicienne* (Beirut: Éditions de la Revue Phénicienne, Volume 1, Number 3, September 1919), 174.
70. Paul Noujaim, "La Question du Liban; Étude de Politique Économique et de Statisque Descriptive," *La Revue Phénicienne* (Beirut, Éditions de la Revue Phénicienne, Volume 1, Number 2, August 1919), 66.
71. Corm, "Méditations," 174.
72. Corm, "Méditations," 174.

73. Corm, "Méditations," 174–75.
74. Corm, "Méditations," 175.
75. See for instance Charles Corm's *La terre assassinée ou les Ciliciennes* (Beirut: Éditions de la Revue Phénicienne, 2004). Written in 1928, *The Murdered Homeland or the Cilicians* was Corm's memorial to the Armenian Genocide and his indictment of aggressive irredentist nationalism, as much as it was his celebration of the humanism and compassionate nationalism as he saw them practiced in Lebanon. Said his characters in the conclusion of *Les Ciliciennes*, "It is here, in Lebanon, since time immemorial, that every minority, whenever mistreated and abused, elsewhere in the Near East, has found sanctuary, and safe refuge from tyranny. Even Druze and Shi'as, even Muslims themselves, when persecuted by majorities among them, have always found peace, freedom and security, in the shadow of the Lebanon! And so here are we, us the Armenians, ever since the persecutions of 1875, and during the massacres of Red Abdulhamid, in 1895, then in 1915, and later in 1916, '17 and '18, and to this very day, it's always near the hearth of the Lebanese homeland that a brotherly welcome has been granted us! Without hesitation, always with devotion, the Lebanese have given their exquisite friendship. They've given us convents and churches and handsome homes; mountains impregnable, and lands arable; they've given us charming climes, and beautiful blue skies; most importantly perhaps, they have given us, unhindered freedom, to move about and grow! And so, in the embrace of Lebanon, we shall dwell in the Lord!"
76. Corm, "Méditations," 175.
77. It is important to reiterate the relevance of World's Fairs as international fora and staging grounds for political and cultural visibility in the early twentieth century—events similar to our day's Olympic Games. For the Mayor of New York City to have called Hitler a fanatic and a danger to world peace in 1939 would have been analogous to Anatoly Pakhomov, Mayor of Sochi, Russia, and host of the 2014 Winter Olympics, using similar language in reference to the leaders of today's Islamic Republic of Iran or the Kingdom of Saudi Arabia.
78. Bernbach and Jaffe, *Book of Nations*, 105.
79. "Lebanon Presents Story in Pavilion," *New York Times*, July 20, 1939, 14.
80. Corm, *La Montagne Inspirée*, 104.
81. "Lebanon Presents Story," 14.
82. Corm's first stay in New York was between 1911 and 1914, on the eve of the Great War (1914–1918). Nazi Germany had already begun its invasion of Poland on September 1, 1939, date of the inauguration of the "Lebanon Day" at the Fair.
83. Corm, *La Montagne Inspirée*, 106.
84. Bernbach and Jaffe, *Book of Nations*, 68–70.
85. Cédar, "Les Impressions d'un Jeune Phénicien d'Aujourd'hui," *La Revue Phénicienne* (Beirut: Éditions de la Revue Phénicienne, July 1919), 30. Cédar is one of the pennames used by Charles Corm.
86. Cédar, "Les Impressions," 31.
87. Cédar, "Les Impressions," 31.
88. See for instance *Note sur le Grand Liban,* an October 16, 1919, letter from Archbishop of Zahlé, Cyrille Mogabgab, addressed to the French High Commissioner, Henri Gouraud, (Paris: Archives du Ministère des Affaires Étrangères (MAE), Quai d'Orsay, Série E-Levant, Sous-Série Syrie-Liban, Volume 266).
89. See for instance the report of Maronite Patriarch Elias Pierre Hoyek, President of the Lebanese Delegation to the Versailles Peace Conference, presented at the Conference; *Les Revendications du Liban; Mémoire de la Délégation Libanaise à la Conférence de la Paix* (Paris, MAE, Série E-Levant, Sous-Série Syrie-Liban, Volume 266).
90. Charles Corm, "Lettre Ouverte au Général Gouraud," *La Revue Phénicienne* (Beirut: Éditions de la Revue Phénicienne, Volume 1, Number 4, December 1919), 218.
91. Untitled memo by French High Commissioner Henri Gouraud, dated September 5, 1921 (Paris, MAE, Série E-Levant, Sous-Série Syrie-Liban 1918–1940, Volume 127), 19.
92. "Lebanon Envoy to Fair Here," *New York Times*, April 16, 1939, 2. This is before the era of commercial air travel, and the trip from Beirut to New York ordinarily took some two weeks at sea. Corm had set sail by steamship form Beirut on March 29, 1939. See the Charles Corm Archives, *D'Une Campagne de Presse contre le Commissaire du Liban à l'Exposition de*

New York (Beirut: Charles Corm Archives; Corm's Private Papers, ND), 3. See also *al-Hoda* (New York: Volume 47, Number 45, April 15, 1939), 3.

93. Ibid.

94. See March 25, 1939, letter from Charles Corm to E. F. Roosevelt, *The New York World's Fair 1939–1940 Records,* Box 1497, Folder 6.

95. Charles Corm, *Participation Libanaise à l'Exposition de New York, 1939: Rapport Administratif et Financier sur les Recettes et les Dépenses du Budget de la Participation Libanaise à l'Exposition de New York; du 1er Octobre 1938 à Mars 1940* (Beirut: Charles Corm Archives, April 22, 1940), 202.

96. Corm, *Participation Libanaise,* 202.

97. Corm, *Participation Libanaise,* 202.

98. Corm, *Participation Libanaise,* 202.

99. Corm, *Participation Libanaise,* 202.

100. Corm, *Participation Libanaise,* 202.

101. Charles Corm Archives, report submitted to Khalil Kseib, Lebanon's Minister of National Education, Beirut, July 29, 1938.

102. Corm, *Participation Libanaise,* 203.

103. See *The New York World's Fair 1939–1940 Records,* Box 296, Folder 6.

104. See October 10, 1938, memorandum from Corm to the Director of Foreign Government Participation requesting Section GF-4 in the Hall of Nations be assigned to Lebanon, *The New York World's Fair 1939–1940 Records,* Box 315, folder 9.

105. Corm, *Participation Libanaise,* 203.

106. Corm, *Participation Libanaise,* 204.

107. See also *al-Hoda* (New York: Volume 47, Number 45, April 15, 1939), 3. See also Corm's correspondence while in New York, *The New York World's Fair 1939–1940 Records.*

108. See for instance *The New York World's Fair 1939–1940 Records,* Box 1404, Folder 4, for official Charles Corm/Lebanese government letterhead, with the Park Central Hotel address.

109. Corm, *Participation Libanaise,* 204.

110. See for instance a letter from E. F. Roosevelt to Corm, October 23, 1939, *The New York World's Fair 1939–1940 Archives,* The New York Public Library, Manuscripts and Archives Division, Box 1404, Folder 4.

111. Ibid.

112. "Fair Times; Chicago Convention Issue" (New York, December 1936), *The New York World's Fair 1939–1940 Archives,* The New York Public Library, Manuscripts and Archives Division, Box 778, Folder 8.

113. See Facts About the Fair, *The New York World's Fair 1939–1940 Records,* Box 774, Folder 17.

114. See March 18, 1939, letter from Corm to E. F. Roosevelt, *The New York World's Fair 1939–1940 Records,* Box 1497, Folder 6. Based on the 2013 Consumer Price Index, $30,000 in 1939 would have been the equivalent of $500,000 today.

115. *The New York World's Fair 1939–1940 Records,* Box 295, Folder 7, and Box 296, Folder 5.

116. E. F. Roosevelt to Corm, *The New York World's Fair 1939–1940 Records,* Box 1497, Folder 6.

117. E. F. Roosevelt to Corm, *The New York World's Fair 1939–1940 Records,* Box 1497, Folder 6.

118. *The New York World's Fair 1939–1940 Records,* Box 1497, Folder 6.

119. *The New York World's Fair 1939–1940 Records,* Box 1497, Folder 6.

120. Corm, *Participation Libanaise,* 204.

121. *al-Hoda,* "How Was the Idea of Lebanon's Participation in the New York World's Fair Born?" (New York: *al-Hoda,* Volume 42, Number 122, July 17, 1939), 7.

122. Corm, *Participation Libanaise,* 204. See also issues of *al-Hoda* after July 17, 1939, which will become a platform for mounting *ad hominem* attacks against Corm. Salloum Mokarzel, owner of *al-Hoda,* had fancied himself "Lieutenant Commissioner General" of the Lebanon Pavilion; when Corm politely rebuffed the hints that he be assigned that post, Mokar-

zel initiated a smear campaign against the Commissioner General on the pages of his own paper in New York, and his cousin Joseph Mokarzel's satirical journal *al-Dabbour* (The Hornet), published in Beirut. See for instance *al-Hoda* July 17, 1939, where the caption above a picture of Corm, Mokarzel, and an associate of the latter read "The Three Knights of the Fair," clearly attempting to cast Mokarzel, in the eyes of the readers of his newspaper and the Lebanese émigré community as a whole, in a larger light than was actually his. When this sort of imposture failed to sway Corm, Mokarzel resorted to public confrontation, and all the fawning and flattery that *al-Hoda* had initially showered on Corm, up until the inauguration of the Lebanon Pavilion, morphed into defamation and acerbic vindictivness.

123. *The New York World's Fair 1939–1940 Records*, Box 315, Folder 9.

124. *The New York World's Fair 1939–1940 Records*, Box 315, Folder 9. Note that no replica of the Holy Sepulcher was ever proposed—let alone was one planned—for the Lebanon Pavilion; at least not by Charles Corm. This was primarily because such an exhibit would not have fit into the Lebanese cultural and historical themes which Corm was putting on display, and would have been in violation of the Fair's regulations, which demanded that exhibitors put on display items relevant to, and associated with, their countries of origin. There had, however, been a gallery in the Lebanon Pavilion featuring a replica of Solomon's Temple in Jerusalem—the reason being the Phoenicians' involvement in the building of that temple.

125. See for instance the December 14, 1938, "Memorandum NYWF 1939," *The New York World's Fair 1939–1940 Records*, Box 315, Folder 9.

126. "Memorandum NYWF 1939," December 14, 1938, *The New York World's Fair 1939–1940 Records*, Box 315, Folder 9.

127. Corm, *Participation Libanaise*, 204.

128. Corm, *Participation Libanaise*, 204.

129. Corm, *Participation Libanaise*, 204–5.

130. Corm, *Participation Libanaise*, 205.

131. See for instance *al-Hoda*'s Special Commemorative Issue (New York: Volume 42, Number 122, July 17, 1939).

132. Russell B. Porter, "Four Nations Join at Fair to Observe Huguenot-Walloon Day," *New York Times*, July 14, 1939, 10.

133. See "À l'Exposition de New-York" in *Phénicia* (Beirut, Volume 2, Number 13, July–August 1939), 45.

134. "Republic of Lebanon at the New York World's Fair 1939," *The New York World's Fair 1939–1940 Records*, Box 1497, Box 6.

135. "Republic of Lebanon at the New York World's Fair 1939," *The New York World's Fair 1939–1940 Records*, Box 1497, Box 6.

136. "Republic of Lebanon at the New York World's Fair 1939," *The New York World's Fair 1939–1940 Records*, Box 1497, Folder 6.

137. July 14, 1939, telegram by Charles Corm, *The New York World's Fair 1939–1940 Records*, Box 1470, Folder 10.

138. Meyer Berger, "At the World's Fair," *New York Times*, August 18, 1939.

139. Berger, "At the World's Fair."

140. Berger, "At the World's Fair." See also 1 Kings 5:1-13.

141. Berger, "At the World's Fair."

142. Berger, "At the World's Fair."

143. See for instance Asher Kaufman, "Too Much French, but a Swell Exhibit; Representing Lebanon at the New York World's Fair, 1939–1940," *British Journal of Middle Eastern Studies* (London: Volume 35, Number 1, 2008), 74.

144. Kaufman, "Too Much French," 74.

145. Thomas Madden, *The New Concise History of the Crusades* (Lanham, MD: Rowman and Littlefield, 2006), x.

146. Madden, *The New Concise History*, 222.

147. Madden, *The New Concise History*, 222.

148. Bernard Lewis, *Islam and the West* (New York and Oxford: Oxford University Press, 1993), 12.

226   *Chapter 3*

149. Bernard Lewis, *The Muslim Discovery of Europe* (New York and London: W. W. Norton and Company, 2001), 22–24.
150. Lewis, *The Muslim Discovery*, 25.
151. Madden, *The New Concise History*, 222.
152. *Discours de Marcel Olivier 13 Juillet 1939, The New York World's Fair 1939–1940 Records*, Box 2155, Folder 17.
153. *Discours de Marcel Olivier 13 Juillet 1939, The New York World's Fair 1939-1940 Records*, Box 2155, Folder 17.
154. *Discours de Marcel Olivier 13 Juillet 1939, The New York World's Fair 1939–1940 Records*, Box 2155, Folder 17.
155. *Discours de Marcel Olivier 13 Juillet 1939, The New York World's Fair 1939–1940 Records*, Box 2155, Folder 17. See also "À l'Exposition de New-York," *Phénicia* (Beirut, Volume 2, Number 13, July–August 1939), 45, and *al-Hoda'* s Special Commemorative Issue celebrating the inauguration of the Lebanon Pavilion at the New York World's Fair, "Speech of the French Pavilion's Commissioner General, Mr. Olivier" (New York: Volume 42, Number 122, July 17, 1939), 2.
156. Edward Said, *Culture and Imperialism* (London: Chatto & Windus, 1993), 8.
157. René Ristelhueber, *Traditions françaises au Liban* (Paris: Librairie Félix Alcan, 1918), v.
158. Ristelhueber, *Traditions françaises*, v–vi. Emphasis in the original text.
159. Said, *Culture and Imperialism*, 8.
160. *Discours de Marcel Olivier 13 Juillet 1939, The New York World's Fair 1939–1940 Archives*, The New York Public Library Manuscripts and Archives Division, Box 2155, Folder 17. See also "À l'Exposition de New-York," *Phénicia* (Beirut, Volume 2, Number 13, July–August 1939), 45, and *al-Hoda*'s Special Commemorative Issue celebrating the inauguration of the Lebanon Pavilion at the New York World's Fair, "Speech of the French Pavilion's Commissioner General, Mr. Olivier" (New York: Volume 42, Number 122, July 17, 1939), 2.
161. Catherine Hodeir and Michel Pierre, *L'Éxposition Coloniale* (Paris: Éditions Complexe, 1991), 13–14.
162. This is a phrase attributed to Pope Leo X (ca. 1510). Speaking of Lebanon's Maronites, and thanking Divine Providence for having safeguarded them through dire times, described them as a "rose among thorns; an impregnable rock in the sea; unshaken by the waves and fury of the thundering tempest."
163. See *al-Maarad*, op. cit., 28.
164. Archives Diplomatiques Nantes, "L'Ambassadeur de France aux États-Unis À son Excellence Monsieur Georges Bonnet, Ministre des Affaires Étrangères" (Nantes: Archives Diplomatiques, Mandat Syrie-Liban, Inauguration du Pavillon Libanais à l'Éxposition de New York, Carton 1442, July 20, 1939), 129.
165. Archives Diplomatiques Nantes, Carton 1442, "L'Ambassadeur de France aux États-Unis," 130.
166. Archives Diplomatiques Nantes, Carton 1442, "L'Ambassadeur de France aux États-Unis," 132.
167. Archives Diplomatiques Nantes, Carton 1442, "L'Ambassadeur de France aux États-Unis," 132.
168. Archives Diplomatiques Nantes, Carton 1442, "L'Ambassadeur de France aux États-Unis," 132.
169. Archives Diplomatiques Nantes, Carton 1442, "L'Ambassadeur de France aux États-Unis," 132.
170. Archives Diplomatiques Nantes, Carton 1442, "L'Ambassadeur de France aux États-Unis," 132. For a list of French contributors to the Lebanon Pavilion, see for instance Corm's official report to the Lebanese Secretary of State, "Participation Libanaise À L'Éxposition Mondiale de New York, 1939" (Beirut: Charles Corm Archives, April 22, 1940). Some of the names included in that list are Maurice Dunand, Pierre Bompard, and Romain Delahalle.
171. Archives Diplomatiques Nantes, Carton 1442, "L'Ambassadeur de France aux États-Unis," 133.
172. "À l'Exposition de New-York," *Phénicia*, 45. See also *al-Hoda*, July 17, 1939.

173. Archives Diplomatiques Nantes, Carton 1442, "L'Ambassadeur de France aux États-Unis," 130.

174. Charles Corm, *Trois Communiqués À La Presse Libanaise D'Amérique* (Beirut; Charles Corm Archives, Private Papers, undated, uncatalogued). It is important to note the reference to Puaux as "ambassador" here, as France in 1939 was still the colonial administrator of the Republic of Lebanon, and as such had no diplomatic relations with the state warranting diplomatic exchanges at the ambassadorial level. Puaux was a High Commissioner and a "colonial officer" pure and simple; the French governor of a French-defined territory, not a French diplomat representing his government before a sovereign state!

175. Corm, *Trois Communiqués*. See also Charles Corm, *Discours à l'Inauguration du Pavillion Libanais* (Beirut: Charles Corm Archives, July 11, 1939), and *al-Hoda*'s Special Commemorative Issue (New York: Volume 42, Number 122, July 17, 1939).

176. Corm, *Trois Communiqués*.

177. *Al-Hoda*, "Syria and the New York World's Fair" (New York: *al-Hoda*, Volume 41, Number 268, December 17, 1939), 4.

178. *Al-Hoda*, "Syria and the New York World's Fair" (New York: *al-Hoda*, Volume 41, Number 263, December 6, 1939), 5.

179. *Al-Hoda*, "Syria and the New York World's Fair" (New York: *al-Hoda*, Volume 41, Number 263, December 6, 1939), 5.

180. Corm, *Trois Communiqués*.

181. Corm, *Trois Communiqués*.

182. Charles Corm, *Discours à l'Inauguration du Pavillion Libanais* (Beirut: Charles Corm Archives, July 11, 1939), 2.

183. Corm, *Discours à l'Inauguration*, 2. See also *al-Hoda*'s Special Commemorative Issue (New York: Volume 42, Number 122, July 17, 1939), 6.

184. "The government of Carthage," wrote Aristotle in *Politics*, "seems well established, and in many respects superior to others; [. . .] this may show how well [the Carthaginians'] government is framed, that although the people are admitted to a share in the administration, the form of it remains unaltered, without any popular insurrections [. . .] or degenerating into a tyranny."

185. Corm, *Discours à l'Inauguration*, 2–3.

186. Corm, *Discours à l'Inauguration*, 3.

187. Corm, *Discours à l'Inauguration*, 3.

188. Corm, *Discours à l'Inauguration*, 3.

189. Corm, *Discours à l'Inauguration*, 4.

190. Corm, *Discours à l'Inauguration*, 4.

191. Corm, *Discours à l'Inauguration*, 4.

192. Corm, *Discours à l'Inauguration*, 4.

193. Corm, *Discours à l'Inauguration*, 4.

194. Corm, *Discours à l'Inauguration*, 4–5.

195. *New York Times*, August 11, 1939. See also Poole, "They Went to the Fair," 5.

196. Corm, *Participation Libanaise*, 206.

197. Corm, *Participation Libanaise*, 206.

198. Corm, *Participation Libanaise*, 178.

199. Corm, *Participation Libanaise*, 178. Note that Martha Deane was the radio character of Mary Margaret McBride, a pioneering American radio personality sometimes referred to as "the first lady of radio," whose show spanned some forty years, and whose career also spilled into the early days of television—although she never transitioned entirely into television broadcast.

200. Lebanese National Day, September 1, 1939, *The New York World's Fair 1939–1940 Records*, Box 1497, Folder 6.

201. Lebanese National Day, September 1, 1939, *The New York World's Fair 1939–1940 Records*, Box 1497, Folder 6.

202. Bertha Jaffe, "Lebanon Exhibit at the Fair Marks 6,000 Years of Peace," *Forest Hills Times*, September 8, 1939, *The New York World's Fair 1939–1940 Records*, Box 1497, Folder 6.

228				Chapter 3

203. See the inventory of merchandise and materials imported for the New York World's Fair, *The New York World's Fair 1939–1940 Records*, Box 2221, Folder 11.
204. Charles Corm, *6000 ans de génie pacifique au service de l'Humanité* (Beirut: Éditions de la Revue Phénicienne, 1988), 57.
205. Corm, *6000 ans*, 57–8.
206. Corm, *6000 ans*, 58.
207. Jaffe, "Lebanon Exhibit at the Fair Marks 6000 Years of Peace."
208. William Bernbach and Herman Jaffe, *Book of Nations* (New York and Washington, DC: Burland Printing Company, 1939), 104.
209. Corm wrote that by the Greeks' own admission, Pythagoras, this most-venerable master of philosophy and mathematics, and the enduring poet of the *Golden Verses*, was arguably the scion of a Phoenician family. As a child still in diapers, and at the cost of running a great risk to his life, Pythagoras's mother, still loyal to her native soil, set sail with her son from the Greek island of Samos to the Lebanon Afka Temple. There, we are told, a mere fifty kilometers from Beirut, baby Pythagoras was said to have received the lustral consecration—ancient baptismal rites still performed in the Lebanon of the times. Corm also noted that Marcus Porcius Cato Maior (or Cato the Elder), a second-century BC Roman statesman to whom the *Delenda Cartago* aphorism was attributed, sealed the fate of Carthage and paved the way for its devastation. Reflecting the savagery with which Rome set out to erase Carthage from historical memory, some accounts speak of the Romans plowing the city over its inhabitants and sowing it with salt, after having left it in raging flames for seventeen days. Fifty thousand Carthaginians were reported to have perished in 149 BC. See Charles Corm's *6000 ans de génie pacifique au service de l'Humanité* (Beirut: Éditions de la Revue Phénicienne, 1988).
210. Asher Kaufman, "Too Much French, but a Swell Exhibit; Representing Lebanon at the New York World's Fair, 1939–1940," *British Journal of Middle Eastern Studies* (London: Volume 35, Number 1, 2008), 74.
211. *Al-Hoda*, July 17, 1939, 1.
212. *Al-Hoda*, July 17, 1939, 1.
213. *Al-Hoda*, July 17, 1939, 1.
214. *Al-Hoda*, July 17, 1939, 1.
215. Berger, "At the World's Fair."
216. *New York Herald-Tribune*, July 14, 1939, reproduced in *al-Hoda*, July 17, 1939, 7.
217. *New York Herald-Tribune*, July 14, 1939, reproduced in *al-Hoda*, July 17, 1939, 7. See also *al-Hoda*, July 17, 1939, 2.
218. *New York Herald-Tribune*, July 14, 1939, reproduced in *al-Hoda*, July 17, 1939, 7. See also Poole's "They Went to the Fair," 2.
219. *New York Times*, July 14, 1939.
220. Private conversation and correspondence with David Charles Corm (June–July 2012). See also Poole, "They Went to the Fair," 4.
221. *Al-Hoda*, July 17, 1939, 6–7.
222. *Al-Hoda*, July 17, 1939, 6.
223. Letter from Augustus A. Munson, attorney-at-law, Republic of Lebanon at the New York World's Fair 1939, *The New York World's Fair 1939–1940 Record*, Box 1497, Folder 6.
224. Ibid.
225. Corm, *Participation Libanaise*, 179–80. It should be noted that despite Corm's description of events in his report, only the Lebanese national anthem was performed at the Pavilion's inaugural ceremony. In fact, in a memo filed from Washington DC, dated July 20 1939, French Ambassador René Doynel de Saint-Quentin reported to the Quai d'Orsay the Commissioner General of the French Pavilion, Marcel Olivier, having chided Charles Corm for neglecting to arrange for the performance of both the *Marseillaise* and "The Star-Spangled Banner" during the opening ceremonies. "This is a clear departure from the established norms of inaugural ceremonies attended by representatives of foreign dignitaries," noted Olivier. An apologetic and embarrassed Corm replied that that the *Marseillaise* had indeed been scheduled to be performed, but that he was stymied in his efforts to feature it in the program by "some influential elements of the Lebanese émigré community." See Archives Diplomatiques Nantes, "L'Ambassadeur de France aux États-Unis À son Excellence Monsieur Georges Bonnet, Mini-

stre des Affaires Étrangères" (Nantes: Mandat Syrie-Liban, Inauguration du Pavillon Libanais à l'Éxposition de New York, Carton 1442, July 20, 1939), 132–33.
226. Poole, "They Went to the Fair," 5.
227. Corm, *Participation Libanaise*, 211.
228. Corm, *Participation Libanaise*, 210.
229. "Lebanon Presents Story to Pavilion," *New York Times*, July 20, 1939, 14. This is a telling news story featuring an erratum, which Jamil M. Baroody, "assistant to Charles Corm, commissioner-general from the Republic of Lebanon to the World's Fair," corrected in the July 21, 1939, issue of the *Times* (that is to say the next day's issue) clarifying that Michel Chedid, whom the article identified as the Lebanon Pavilion manager, was a clerk, and that "the Republic of Lebanon never was part of the Syrian Mandate." This is an emotionally fraught issue that even scrupulous historians often misinterpret and overlook. To wit, in one of the footnotes of his excellent essay on Lebanon's participation in the New York World's Fair, "Too Much French, but a Swell Exhibit," Asher Kaufman notes that "Jamil Barudi [. . .] Corm's brother-in-law and assistant at the fair published a (*misleading*) [my emphasis] correction in the [*New York Times*] explaining that 'the Republic of Lebanon never was part of the Syrian mandate.'" Yet Baroody's correction might in fact *not* have been all that "misleading," and Kaufman, who scrupulously and expertly mined the French Foreign Ministry Archives in his ground-breaking work on Corm, surely must have noticed that even the cataloguing of French official documents pertaining to the Mandate period had Lebanon and Syria classified separately, and that there was nothing called the "Syrian Mandate" as such in official French documents. Indeed, at the Quai d'Orsay Archives in Paris, Political and Commercial Correspondence holdings are indexed as follows: "Correspondance Politique et Commerciale, Série "E"—Levant 1918–1940, Sous-Série: Syrie, Liban, Cilicie." Therefore, the official headings and subheadings of French archival collections pertaining to (today's) Lebanon and Syria treated them as distinct entities. Furthermore, all internal memos, at least until the formation of the Republic of Syria in 1937, referred to Lebanon, and what later became Syria in 1936–1937, separately and distinctly, albeit there were occasional references to "États Autonomes de Syrie" to include "Grand-Liban," "État de Damas," "État d'Alep," "Djébel Alaouites," and "Djébel Druze"—that is to say "The Autonomous States of Syria" including "Greater Lebanon," "The State of Damascus," "The State of Aleppo," "The State of the Alawite Mountain," and "The State of the Druze Mountain." In sum, Baroody's correction claiming "the Republic of Lebanon" to have "never [been] part of the Syrian mandate" might have been warranted, not necessarily "misleading," given that, indeed, there had been no "Syrian Mandate" per se, and indeed no distinct Syrian entity to speak of, for Lebanon to have been part of. The origin of this misconception may dwell in the fact that it has become second nature among Middle East specialists to speak of such terms as "Greater Syria," and Lebanon being "carved out of Greater Syria," as if this Syria had reflected a political reality preceding the Franco-British takeover of the eastern holdings of the Ottoman Empire. Indeed, that notion of a discrete Syria, and the semantics attached to it, are not only inaccurate and misleading; they are ahistorical. It is important to note in this regard that the Syria of today—as a concept, a name, and a geographic entity—is the outcome of European thought, European geography, European languages, and European conceptions of the Middle East that were not part of the political or geographic discourse of the Middle East of the early twentieth century. In 1907, British traveler Gertrude Bell noted that Syria was "merely a geographical term corresponding to no national sentiment" that can be associated with a discernable Syrian identity or a Syrian territory. Only Europeanized "Levantines," that is to say Arabic-speaking Christians from the Vilayet of Beirut, the Sanjak of Mount-Lebanon, and the Vilayets of Aleppo and Damascus, and elsewhere in what became "Greater Syria" conceptually, who may have been familiar with the languages and concepts of Europe, began describing the lands of their birth collectively as Syria, and themselves as Syrians, in imitation of their European teachers, not as a reflection of an indigenous "Syrian," or even "Arab" precedent. Indeed, conceptually, the terms "Syria" and "Syrian" were used almost exclusively by Levantine Christians to distinguish themselves from Ottoman Turks and Arabs. The Arabs themselves referred to this supposed Syria as *al-Sham*, that is to say "the North," and did so out of a purely geographic, not political, instinct—in the way in which a

European today may refer to "the Alps" or "the Balkans," or the way a North American may refer to "New England."
230. "Lebanon Presents Story to Pavilion," 14.
231. Henry Beckett, "Its Exhibits Portray the Very Beginnings of Civilization," *The New York Post*, August 3, 1939.
232. Ibid.
233. See for instance Kaufman's "Too Much French," 59–77.
234. Kaufman, "Too Much French," 67.
235. *Al-Hoda*, December 12, 1939, 4.
236. *Al-Hoda*, December 12, 1939, 4–5.
237. *Al-Hoda*, December 12, 1939, 5.
238. *Al-Hoda*, December 12, 1939, 5.
239. *Al-Hoda*, December 12, 1939, 5.
240. Ibrahim Maklouf, "En écoutant Charles Corm et Fakry El-Baroudi," *La Syrie* (Beirut, Sunday June 9, 1935), 6.
241. Maklouf, "En écoutant," 6.
242. Maklouf, "En écoutant," 6.
243. Amin Rihani, "Jabal al-Tajalli" [The Mountain of Transfiguration] (Beirut: *al-Maarad*, Special Issue, Number 38, July 4, 1934), 9.
244. Rihani, "Jabal al-Tajalli," 9.
245. Rihani, "Jabal al-Tajalli," 9.
246. Khalil Takieddine, "al-Jabal al-Mulham wa al-Adab al-'Aalami" [The Hallowed Mountain and Universal Literature] (Beirut: *al-Maarad*, Special Issue, Number 38, July 4, 1934), 25.
247. Takieddine, "al-Jabal," 25.
248. Takieddine, "al-Jabal," 25.
249. Kaufman, "Too Much French," 69.
250. Charles Corm Archives, *Rapport Administratif*, Preface, 11.
251. Corm, *Participation Libanaise*, Preface, 11.
252. Corm, *Participation Libanaise*, Preface, 12–13.
253. Corm, *Participation Libanaise*, Preface, 14.
254. See for instance *al-Hoda* and *al-Dabbour* issues beginning in September 1939. The *Dabbour* claimed (wrongly of course) that Corm was charging visitors to the Lebanon Pavilion a $1.00 entry fee, earning him at least three million dollars from this whole affairs and swelling his personal fortune. See for instance the Agreement of Participation in New York World's Fair of 1939 (Box 1279, Folder 21), a document signed by Corm in New York, on May 15, 1939, on behalf of the Lebanese government, expressly spelling out the Fair's rules and regulations, and the Lebanon Pavilion's responsibilities. It is inconceivable to imagine Charles Corm the savvy sophisticated and successful businessman, bound by a legal document, simply putting himself in breach of contract and deciding to charge entry fees to visitors of the Lebanon exhibit when such practices were expressly forbidden—not to mention unheard of—at the Fair. See also the Exhibitor's Concession Agreement, *The New York World's Fair 1939–1940 Records*, Box 1279, Folder 21.
255. Corm, *Participation Libanaise*, Preface, 12.
256. Corm, *Participation Libanaise*, 177.
257. Corm, *Participation Libanaise*, Preface, 13.
258. For instance, musical bands and national insignia and decorations for the "Inaugural Ceremony" and the "Lebanon Day N.Y. World's Fair, September 1, 1939" were provided by Nahum Hatem; the rental costs of a Steinway and Sons grand piano, which was used by Lebanese-American composer Anis Fuleyhan and other members of the Lebanese émigré community for the duration of the exhibit, were covered by Marie El-Khoury, manager of T. Azeez Jewelers in New York City; other Lebanese Americans, among them Corm's attorney, Edward J. Leon, and his brother James, provided other services and various forms of funding for the exhibit. See Charles Corm, *Rapport Administratif et Financier sur les Recettes et les Dépenses du Budget de la Participation Libanaise à l'Exposition de New York; du 1er Octobre 1938 à Mars 1940* (Beirut: Charles Corm's Private Papers, April 22, 1940).

259. See for instance *al-Hoda*, 18, 1939, where in an overkill of hyperbole Charles Corm is referred to (unnecessarily and perhaps even inappropriately) as "the poet, Mr. Charles Effendi Corm," using an Ottoman honorific and a title of Turkish aristocracy that was never before used in reference to the poet, and one to which Corm's own sense of humility would have objected. See also *al-Hoda*, April 15, 1939, where Salloum Mokarzel writes that the audience listening to Charles Corm "was dazzled by his presence and the splendor of his passion for Lebanon, which was apparent as his words got choked in his throat and his eyes welled up with tears every time he mentioned Lebanon."

260. "Les Journaux À New York," Éxtrait d'un Rapport de MM Fares et Debs au Général Gouraud, Mission de Propagande, en date du 21 Février, 1922 (Paris, MAE, Série E-Levant 1918–1940, Sous-Série Syrie-Liban, Volume 129).

261. "Les Journaux À New York" (Paris, MAE, Série E-Levant 1918–1940, Sous-Série Syrie-Liban, Volume 129).

262. "Les Journaux À New York" (Paris, MAE, Série E-Levant 1918–1940, Sous-Série Syrie-Liban, Volume 129).

263. See for instance *al-Hoda*, July 17, 1939.

264. See for instance the Exhibitor's Concession Agreement, *The New York World's Fair 1939–1940 Archives*, The New York Public Library, Manuscripts and Archives Division, Box 1279, Folder 21.

265. See the Charles Corm Archives, *D'Une Campagne de Presse contre le Commissaire du Liban à l'Exposition de New York* (Beirut: Charles Corm Archives; Corms Private Papers, ND), 3. The items that Joseph Mokarzel badgered Corm's employees into shipping to New York included 1,150 copies of a booklet titled "Schmounie" and sixty copies of past issues of the *Dabbour* newspaper.

266. Charles Corm Archives, *D'Une Campagne de Presse contre le Commissaire du Liban à l'Exposition de New York* (Beirut: Charles Corm Archives; Corms Private Papers, ND), 3.

267. Charles Corm Archives, *D'Une Campagne de Presse contre le Commissaire du Liban à l'Exposition de New York* (Beirut: Charles Corm Archives; Corms Private Papers, ND), 3.

268. Charles Corm Archives, *D'Une Campagne de Presse contre le Commissaire du Liban à l'Exposition de New York* (Beirut: Charles Corm Archives; Corms Private Papers, ND), 3. Lebanese immigrant groups were outraged by the asking price for some of those items, especially the $7.50 cost of the *Dabbour* back issues which Mokarzel was demanding, "as if these old newspapers represented vintage issues of the Encyclopedia Britannica in Lebanon."

269. It should be noted that the friendship that banded the Éddés to the Corms is an old and close one indeed. When Charles Corm's father, Daoud Corm, passed away in 1930, the Corms lacked a family burial vault. Daoud's remains were therefore temporarily inhumed in the Éddé family vault, in the Ras al-Nab' Maronite Cemetery across from the *Maison Blanche*, to be exhumed and interred again a few years later in a family crypt that Charles Corm had built right next to the Éddés. "Friends in life shall remain friends in death," was Corm's justification at the time. This story is recounted here to show how unfathomably dubious the Mokarzels' claim would have been without the knowledge of Charles Corm—that is to say the claim that Joseph Mokarzel was dispatched to New York at the behest of President Émile Éddé as his acting "representative" and "Special Envoy."

270. Charles Corm Archives, *D'Une Campagne de Presse contre le Commissaire du Liban à l'Exposition de New York* (Beirut: Charles Corm Archives; Corms Private Papers, ND), 4.

271. Charles Corm Archives, *D'Une Campagne de Presse contre le Commissaire du Liban à l'Exposition de New York* (Beirut: Charles Corm Archives; Corms Private Papers, ND), 4.

272. Charles Corm Archives, *D'Une Campagne de Presse contre le Commissaire du Liban à l'Exposition de New York* (Beirut: Charles Corm Archives; Corms Private Papers, ND), 4–5.

273. Exhibitor's Concession Agreement, *The New York World's Fair 1939–1940 Records*, Box 1279, Folder 21.

274. Exhibitor's Concession Agreement, *The New York World's Fair 1939–1940 Records*, Box 1279, Folder 21.

275. Charles Corm Archives, *D'Une Campagne de Presse contre le Commissaire du Liban à l'Exposition de New York* (Beirut: Charles Corm Archives; Corms Private Papers, ND), 5.

276. Charles Corm Archives, *D'Une Campagne de Presse contre le Commissaire du Liban à l'Exposition de New York* (Beirut: Charles Corm Archives; Corms Private Papers, ND), 5–6. It should be noted that no evidence exist of a Lebanese government decree designating Salloum Mokarzel "Assistant to the Commissioner General of the Lebanese Pavilion."

277. Charles Corm Archives, *D'Une Campagne de Presse contre le Commissaire du Liban à l'Exposition de New York* (Beirut: Charles Corm Archives; Corms Private Papers, ND), 6.

278. December 19, 1938, letter from *al-Hoda* to the New York World's Fair 1939 Corporation, *The New York World's Fair 1939–1940 Records*, Box 1279, Folder 21.

279. December 19, 1938, letter from *al-Hoda* to the New York World's Fair 1939 Corporation, *The New York World's Fair 1939–1940 Records*, Box 1279, Folder 21.

280. December 19, 1938, letter from *al-Hoda* to the New York World's Fair 1939 Corporation, *The New York World's Fair 1939–1940 Records*, Box 1279, Folder 21.

281. May 5, 1937, press release, *The New York World's Fair 1939–1940 Records*, Box 777, Folder 9.

282. See for instance *al-Hoda*, July 17, 1939.

283. See the Charles Corm Archives, *D'Une Campagne de Presse contre le Commissaire du Liban à l'Exposition de New York* (Beirut: Charles Corm Archives; Corms Private Papers, ND), 28. See also all *al-Hoda* issues, beginning in 1933, for various advertisements and pleas for donations relative to the "National Fund intended for the completion of the memorial dedicated to the founder of *al-Hoda*." The advertisement hawks a documentary of the life of Naoum Mokarzel, his New York funeral, and scenes of Lebanon and Beirut. It also urges potential donors to purchase the documentary, organize viewings in Lebanese churches, clubs, and interest groups, and contribute the proceeds to Mokarzel's "National Fund." *Al-Hoda* described the documentary as follows:

> It is an image unlike any other the Lebanese have seen. It is a documentary guaranteed to animate the emotions and arouse the yearnings of its viewers, who, at the mere sight of Naoum Mokarzel and Lebanon, will wish the film will last forever. This is a documentary worthy of being viewed over and over again, as it will quench neither sight nor insight. It is a documentary that will transport the viewer from America to Lebanon. It will review the heroism and the journalistic and national struggles of Naoum Mokarzel, and display the honors with which his struggles were met after his passing, by the Lebanese, at home and in the diaspora. The documentary will also show Naoum Mokarzel, founder of al-Hoda, bursting with life, hard at work in his office; it will then show him a still, lifeless body, carried out of the offices of al-Hoda, for one last time, to the eulogies and cheers of thousands of people crowding the streets of New York, between Washington and Broadway, in the largest funeral processions ever witnessed in Lower Manhattan.

284. See Charles Corm, *Curriculum Vitae* (Beirut: Charles Corm Archives, November 27, 1948), 8. It is ironic that Charles Corm should have shunned such accolades because, as he remarked, they are often bestowed on characters who do not deserve them, alongside many others who may. His prescience might have a singularly relevant plangency in this second decade of the twenty-first century. Although Corm shares the National Order of the Cedar medal with a venerable list of recipients, including Lebanese-Mexican émigré and billionaire philanthropist Carlos Slim, Lebanese-American scientist and director of NASA's Jet Propulsion Laboratory Charles Elachi, Egyptian literati Taha Husayn, and former Archbishop of Paris Jean-Marie Lustiger among others, this same honor has also been awarded to Syrian dictator Bashar al-Assad in 2010, on the eve of the Syrian Civil War, a butchery which may prove to be one of Assad's most salient and lasting legacies.

Chapter Four

Child and Disciple of Humanism

Conclusions

It may have by now become obvious what an exquisite representative of a multifaceted, benevolent culture was Charles Corm. His life and work set against the canvas of the ancient Phoenician coastline and its snowcapped mountains overhead, this Lebanese poet, playwright, historian, painter, and business tycoon was above all a committed representative of a human, humane, and humanist ecumenism.

Thus, identifying, defining, and capturing in the exiguous space of this hasty biography the monumental spiritual and intellectual wealth that was Charles Corm can indeed be a daunting task. No less daunting may be the burden of delineating in this single volume the scope and breadth and variety of Corm's literary output, his cultural and intellectual activities, and his human contacts. In sum, Charles Corm was a living anthropomorphic testimonial and an act of faith dedicated to wide-ranging, universalist, ecumenical values, founded on openness and adaptability to all human horizons, and enamored of all human endeavors and indeed all that is human. Therefore a single monograph incorporating all of Charles Corm's accomplishments can be at best inaugural and introductory, and in that sense incomplete.

Having lived a rich, busy, fulfilling life, leaving behind an exquisite collection of literary and artistic works—two-thirds of which remain as of yet unpublished—Charles Corm never missed an opportunity to promote and uphold humanism: a universalist humanism in general terms and a discernably Lebanese one in particular. And so, Charles Corm's Lebanese version of humanistic values—Lebanonism as it came to be known in the mid-twentieth century—could not be anything if not a system of thought based on the foundations of Corm's ancient Phoenicia, and the high value that Phoenicia and the Phoenician people placed on human interests, human achievements, and human dignity. In this, Charles Corm had been in agreement with former French Prime Minister and Minister of Foreign Affairs Georges Bidault, who, addressing the June 7, 1949, General Assembly of the UNESCO then convening in Beirut, noted that

> having sailed forth from the three-pronged majesty of their skies, their land, and their sea, the Phoenicians set an example and edified a practice that has since become common to all mankind; the habit of moving past and beyond the Mediterranean. [. . .] It is thanks to those Phoenicians that the sea suddenly ceased being a mysterious, terrifying abyss, and instead, was rendered a roadway. [. . .] Indeed, it is thanks to the Phoenicians that human inquiry and discovery and progress had all suddenly become accessible, feasible, common endeavors to all of mankind.[1]

It is this very achievement, one evidently driven by ambition yet deemed a sublime selfless act of love, that would endear the Phoenicians to Charles Corm's heart, and earn them his love and devotedness and his unbridled admiration. To him, the Phoenicians were the epitome of humanism, and their modern Lebanese descendants the rightful heirs to that sublime human value.

Since the very early beginnings of the twentieth century, wrote Charles Corm in the summer of 1949, and especially on the heels of that century's devastating wars, humanism had suddenly become a fashionable fixation, brandished as it were by the era's luminaries, often to "conceal the grins of a bad conscience."[2] And so, after World War II, everyone would conveniently morph into a disciple and votary of humanism, celebrating humanism, advocating for humanism, claiming and acclaiming humanism, and gleefully applauding oneself for upholding that noble virtue.[3] Yet, claimed Corm, very few men can be said to have genuinely and willingly lived, integrated, devoted, and sacrificed themselves for the sake of this vaunted humanism.[4] In fact, scouring the four corners of the world in search of genuine humanism can often yield but a disappointing handful of committed practitioners, he claimed.[5] Yet, wrote Charles Corm,

> on these ancient shores of the Near East, there lay a brave little country, which throughout its storied existence and timeless history, had always been, entirely, in deeds and as a matter of principle, a committed practitioner and a true hero of humanism. This small country is Lebanon![6]

This biography is in a sense the story of that Lebanon; a sentimentalized and idealized story perhaps, but one more authentic and real than reality itself, as grasped and narrated by Charles Corm himself.

CHRISTIAN HUMANISM

But what is this humanism, and how is it that Charles Corm's Lebanon was deemed the "homeland" and "living example" of that doctrine and philosophy of being? Humanism is above all, as Corm defined it, a form of human solidarity, a twining of a thousand disciplines and a thousand attitudes and modes of thought to enrich and strengthen the texture of human life and the very concept of "being human." It is a constant and continuous exchange of men and ideas on a global universal scale. And although its meaning might have fluctuated and changed over time, humanism has nonetheless remained in general terms an instinct and an intellectual current that valorized "human nature" and "humanity," putting an emphasis on "free will," "critical thinking," and "rationalism," as opposed to blind obedience to dogma, doctrinal orthodoxies, and narrow practices and beliefs foregoing moderation, balance, and scientific discourse. And though secularism and skepticism have often been associated with humanist thinking, the movement itself—at least in its Cormian understanding and manifestation—was not inimical to religion. There is always a "love of God and his creation" in Corm's humanism, where one "invariably discerns devotion for God, Humanity, Homeland, and Hearth; the four foundational pillars of that most Excellent of human shrines, which we call Civilization."[7] Indeed, and in full agreement with the humanists of Renaissance Europe, Corm saw no contradiction between humanism and the Christian faith. Like his European predecessors and models, he inveighed against the misdeeds of the Church, but not the Church itself. He also saw Christianity as a synonym of the humanism of his Phoenician forefathers: a primordial impulse for goodness "purified and refined by Christianity," he wrote. Thus, Corm's Christian faith made humanism "more transcendental and spiritual, indeed more human, revealing [this particular religious creed] as the most luminous and radiant wellspring and incarnation of humanism."[8] This doctrine of Corm's was already expressed in *La Montagne Inspirée*: Addressing the Muslim component of Lebanese society, which he chided for being still beholden to an irredentist Arabism and dismissive of Lebanese specificity, Corm wrote,

> Muslim brother, do take note of my candor: / I am true Lebanon, genuine and observant; / I am all the more Lebanese, that my Faith represents / the heart of the pelican. / And if my fervor for Lebanon is bound up to the Church, / It is so because, in my eyes, it embodies universality; / For, I cannot believe in a god that divides this immense humanity. / Jesus teaches me to love both Moses and Mohamed, / All the while holding fast to my Christian beliefs; / For, the Gospels were written, precisely in defiance, / Of all ventures that try, to pit my faith against your own. / And the teachings of Christ, as my humble soul perceives them, / Enjoin me to love without reserve, even my enemy, / For, I

am much closer to you, if I am without guile / A friend to all mankind, and all the human race.[9]

This wedding of humanism to the Christian creed is not a Cormian innovation—although Corm himself might have been an especially faithful apostle of this particular interpretation. As alluded to earlier, humanism can claim roots in the traditional catechism, teachings about humans being created in the image of God; a belief that valorizes human dignity, individual and collective freedom, rationalism, and the right to self-fulfillment and happiness. In that sense, and in Corm's own telling, not only does humanism complement Christian beliefs, often overlapping with them; it indeed emanates from them. It is worth noting in this regard that the pelican in Catholic tradition—and in the context in which it was mentioned in Corm's strophe above—symbolizes "Christ the Savior" who gave his life to redeem mankind. Indeed Catholic ethics, in which Corm himself was very deeply steeped, deem the image of the "parent pelican" feeding its young out of its own entrails a traditional symbol of the Eucharist and Christ the savior; the epitome of "Caritas" and one of the three divine virtues taught in catechism. The fact that Corm seamlessly equated Christian—and indeed his own Catholic—charity with universalist humanism is simply a natural, and indeed an innocuous, outcome of his own socialization in a Christian (Mediterranean) environment.

In an essay published in *Phénicia* (March–April 1939), Jean Desthieux, president of the *Amitiés Méditerranéenes* society of which Corm was a prominent member, wrote that it had precisely been this "Christian humanism" that Islam had embraced and fertilized in Castille, in both peace and in war, reminding us of Pope Pius XI's locution that, spiritually speaking, Christians were Semites, from whose traditions both Judaism and Islam were ultimately shorn.[10] And so, in this vein, addressing the Mediterranean Academy's October 1935 conference on *The Principles of a Mediterranean Humanism*, Charles Corm noted that if humanism, as he thought it ought to be defined, were "a certain benevolence and hospitality of both the heart and mind"; if it were this ability to

> receive and conceive; accept and appreciate; give and forgive—that is to say, never condemn—any and all of that which is in the purview of human nature; if humanism were this supreme blessing of Mankind's, bestowed upon Mankind above and beyond all other riches, allowing Mankind possession and transfer, as well as exchange and bestowal of all spiritual fortunes from wherever and whomever they may derive; if humanism were this ability to treat with dignity, in one's own home, all the pilgrims of the mind, to be so enamored of the truth, so passionate for justice, so acutely sensitive to love, so partial to kindness and compassion, and so unequivocally supportive of the human community at large, to the point that nothing of that which is human

can be deemed alien, then Lebanon can be legitimately claimed to be the supreme incarnation of this humanism, and it can claim the honor of having contributed not only to the founding of Mediterranean civilization, but also to the founding of civilization tout court—better yet, the founding of a civilization that is immeasurably human and humanistic, selflessly bestowing gifts, through both time and space, upon all peoples of the world.[11]

The preceding is in short the condensation of Charles Corm's life as both an intellectual and a patriot; it painted, as this monograph attempted to do throughout, the Lebanese as Charles Corm himself saw them and as he'd hoped they would remain. In Corm's telling, and since the remotest antiquity, at a time when they were still known as Canaanites,

and later as Phoenicians, the Lebanese had created, preserved, defended, affirmed, and advanced an expansive and liberal civilization with universal impulses and predilections so accessible to other peoples, to the point that some of those, even the loftiest and brightest among them, came to assimilate these attributes of Lebanese civilization as if they were their own, identifying them with their own national genius.[12]

This, in Corm's view, was the incarnation of humanism. And in that sense, not only was Lebanon a most exquisite practitioner of humanism; it was an eloquent purveyor of that most human of human virtues, contributing to the "building of a better human community, and a more humane humanity."[13]

PHOENICIAN HUMANISM

The main misfortune of the Phoenicians, the architects of what Corm considered the most invaluable of human inventions, the phonetic alphabet—which remains to this day unsurpassed in its functionality and efficiency and simplicity—is that they have left us almost nothing of their intellectual work or cultural achievements. That is to say, nothing besides the "Justinian Code"— a corpus of Roman law that is still extant in some of our modern legal charters, and whose authorship is owed to two "Phoenician" jurists, from the city of Beirut, the famous Ulpian[14] and Papinian.[15] In a sense, Beirut of the *Pax Romana* may be compared to what modern Americans refer to as a "college town"—the Boston or Cambridge of antiquity. Even during the third century BC, on the eve of the first Punic War, Beirut was already a thriving cosmopolitan center and a crossroads of ideas and universalist tendencies. At the dawn of the Christian era, it had become a remarkable center of science, literature, jurisprudence, and the arts, earning it in due time the Roman title of *Nutris Legum* (Mother of Laws). That sobriquet was acquired on account of the city's famous law school, and its reputation in forming some of the

Roman Empire's most illustrious jurists and magistrates. And although the school was demolished by a particularly severe earthquake in 551 AD, and was never subsequently rebuilt, "Beirut's only law school," wrote Charles Corm,

> still spread its teachings to upwards of twenty-seven countries around the ancient world, even though many of these nations, some of which situated as far afield as Gaul and Iberia, had their own prestigious law schools. Yet, those schools were dwarfed by the immensity of the Beirut college, the most eminent of its day, more so than the institutes of Byzantium, Alexandria, and Rome, supplying the latter with their best scholars, poets, diplomats, and public officials. More importantly, Beirut provided the Roman Empire with its most respected jurists; among them Ulpian and Papinian, to whom we own the revamping of the Justinian Code.[16]

Yet very little of this glory remains, and a trifling of it is even related by the Phoenicians themselves, in their own language and their own alphabet. It may be true, however, that in general terms the Phoenicians were more eager to live and interact with others than they were interested in writing. They were, after all, as attested to by all those who came into contact with them—even their adversaries—the greatest seafarers of the ancient world. Like the Hebrews—the moralists of antiquity—the Phoenicians were trendsetters of sorts: they were purveyors of culture, fashion, and the fundaments of long-distance trade and international relations. And so, if one might say the Hebrews were "the conscience" of the ancient world and perhaps its "puritans," their Phoenician cousins were the "iconoclasts," the "hedonistic jet-setters," and the "bad boys" of antiquity. To put things in modern terms, the Hebrews would have ruled over the "Vatican" of their times, whereas the Phoenicians' capitals of Beirut, Byblos, and Tyre would have conjured up images of what are today London, Paris, New York—or even hedonistic Ibiza, an early Phoenician colony.

Although Phoenicia itself fluctuated widely in terms of borders and dimensions throughout antiquity, it generally embraced all of what is today Lebanon and most of northern Israel and the western portions of today's Syria. Like modern-day Lebanon, largely mountainous and inhospitable to sustained large-scale "commercial" agriculture—unlike, say, the Nile Delta and Mesopotamia—Phoenicia made for an attractive haven for hunted down people seeking sanctuary. The coastal strip of this Phoenician homeland, hemmed in by the snow-capped mountains of Lebanon, "compressed" the early inhabitants of the region nearer to the coast—a natural harbor and doorway to the Mediterranean—rendering those inhabitants more amenable to taking to the sea whenever land and its resources became scant. It should be noted that the high Lebanon mountains also served to intercept weather systems coming from Europe, producing abundant rainfall and heavy snows on the Mediterranean slopes of Mount-Lebanon, thereby allowing for small-scale crops without the need for artificial irrigation. Still, given the geographic position of Phoenicia, maritime trade was almost a natural impulse and a survival necessity. This was aided by the profusion of natural harbors along the coast, and the lush cedar forests of the highlands, which would become one of the major ingredients of the Phoenician ship-building industry, and a valued trading commodity with neighbors in want of the precious timber of Mount-Lebanon. Thus developed the legend of the Phoenicians as merchants and navigators, traveling far afield, circumnavigating Africa, mining for silver in Spain, and even perhaps penetrating as far into northern Europe as Brittany in France and Cornwall on the British Isles. Some even claim the Phoenicians to have sailed as far afield as the New World, two millenniums or more before Columbus.

At any rate, the Phoenicians were intrepid sailors, believed to have been the first civilization to sail the high seas using astral references (the stars, the moon, and the movement of celestial bodies) rather than earlier human sailing methods hugging the coastlines. Most notably perhaps, and as mentioned earlier, the Phoenicians were credited with being the inventors of the alphabet, from which our own is ultimately derived, and a feat that Charles Corm took unbounded pleasure memorializing and showcasing in his own work. In our times, he wrote,

> no one would fathom holding / The invention of writing, to be the greatest miracle of all, / One whereby human genius, raised us up mere mortals / To the status of Creator-gods, / With a simple sleight of hand! / For, the simple act of writing, breathes life into otherwise fading words, / Granting them plain form, and an eternal face; / Indeed the act of writing yields a lucid image / To the sounds of our words, / And assigns a high altar to our fleeting thoughts! / [. . .] For, the simple act of writing, / Is like gushing out of one's own empty twilights, / It is an act of defiance against nothingness [. . .] / For, when God set out to redeem his sinful creation, / The Word became flesh, so as to defy death. / Likewise, when our ancestors, spawned the miracle of writing, / The word was finally given everlasting form![17]

This bequest, from Corm's perspective, was another confirmation of Phoenician selfless humanism. They were renowned for their liberal, urbane cosmopolitan instincts; yet they were not a conquering, colonizing warrior people. Their overseas possessions, strewn around the classical Mediterranean world, were acquisitions gained more through cultural seduction and allure rather than the common methods of their times (and our own)—that is to say, belligerence, war, coercion, and conquest.

The colonial possessions of the Phoenicians—if one could call them that—were similar to today's European Union; a commonwealth joined willingly, not forcefully; one whose members had to conform to onerous and demanding cultural and ethical norms. Some of the most potent and beautiful imageries of the expansive commercial universe once commanded by the Phoenicians were those described in the Jewish Bible, namely by prophets Isaiah and Ezekiel's poetic visions of Tyre and Sidon—some of them even mourning the destruction of Tyre by Alexander the Great ca. 332 BC, seeing in it an ominous foreboding for the destruction of the world. Says Isaiah 23:

> Wail, you ships of Tarshish! For Tyre is destroyed and left without house or harbor. . . . From the land of Cyprus word has come to them. Be silent, you people of the island, and you merchants of Sidon, whom the seafarers have enriched. On the great waters came the grain of Shihor; the harvest of the Nile was the revenue of Tyre, and she became the marketplace of the nations. Be ashamed, Sidon, and you fortress of the sea, for the sea has spoken: ". . . Wail, you people of the island . . . Wail the old, old city, whose feet have taken her to settle in far-off lands Who planned this against Tyre, the bestower of crowns, whose merchants are princes, whose traders are renowned in the earth?"

So, there is no shortage of information on—often praise—of the Phoenicians, mainly left to us by other nations. And as mentioned earlier, the Phoenicians themselves left behind much in terms of etchings and texts of dedications and incantations to the gods. Yet they remained silent in terms of literature—even though no written literature by "others" would have been possible without the Phoenicians' own alphabet. On this alphabet, French archaeologist and philologist Maurice Dunand wrote in his *Byblia Grammata*, that it was the singular, most ingenious, and most perfect of human accomplishments; one that has not been improved upon or transcended in more than four-thousand years of its existence.[18] Certainly, claimed Dunand, the Byblian alphabet had gone through major transformations in its millennial history and has been adapted, amended, and rearranged to fit the needs of the disparate sounds of Man's different languages. Yet, the concept of a phonetic alphabet itself—that is to say the system of symbols representing human sounds, single phonemes, and ultimately abstract concepts, rather than pictograms representing concrete objects—that concept itself has not yet been matched in the pantheon of human accomplishments.[19]

HUMANISM IN DEEDS

In an homage published in a special issue of *Al-Hikma* dedicated to Charles Corm three months after his death in September of 1963, Antoine Abi-Haila wrote that Corm "was a man who woke up before dawn, walked all day long, and noticed only at sundown that everything still needed to be done over."[20] He was a true Lebanese beacon of light, one of the first Lebanese intellectuals of the early twentieth century to have made battle on behalf of Lebanon, its particularism, its proud history, its glorious Phoenician heritage. He was also Lebanon's first industrialist, who succeeded in amassing fortune upon fortune, but who never forgot his humanity and never lost touch with humility. In every endeavor he undertook, he pioneered and excelled; yet he never despaired of searching, and never tired of yearning for an ideal world, an ideal universe, and ideal human existence. To him this search—"searching for a man" to borrow from his 1939 lecture recalling Diogenes—was an act of faith, a devotional endeavor, a prayer, a humanist's quest. His greatness, his genius, was to have bequeathed upon those he left behind the gift of self-denial, humanism, and humility—guiding principles that he lived by and died for.[21]

It was this humility and self-denial—notwithstanding Charles Corm's undeniable gift—that made him a charming human being, an exquisite humanist, and a national icon. Charles Corm influenced—nay, he captivated and entranced—his elders, wrote Hektor Klat. Modern Lebanon's greats—from literati to glitterati, and from Saïd Akl, to Michel Chiha, to May Ziyadé and dozens of others—stood on the shoulders of a giant, Charles Corm, asserted Hektor Klat; a man who influenced and molded those born to times before his own.[22] Klat further described Corm's "genius and generosity" as "débordante," that is to say, "overflowing and boundless, [. . .] and most importantly perhaps, incredibly altruistic."[23] "Oh, what an incredible year 1934 had been," he wrote recalling the publication of *La Montagne Inspirée*:

> It was a sumptuous year for francophone Lebanese belles lettres. And what a Patron-Saint and Poet Laureate we had walking among us, bringing us that year into being! [. . .] Barely three months after the publication of his *La Montagne Inspirée,* and at the rhythm of one volume every three months, Charles Corm published successively Elie Tyane's *Le Château Merveilleux,* Michel Chiha's *La Maison des Champs,* and [my own] *Le Cèdre et les Lys.* And so, our junior had officially—and deservedly—become our leader.[24]

But Charles Corm's humility never allowed him to bask in titles and public accolades. It also tempered his unbounded patriotism, which, at any rate, he had always deemed coterminous with humanist ecumenism. And so, although identified almost exclusively with *La Montagne Inspirée*, Corm also wrote on behalf of *other* patriotisms—e.g., *La Montagne Assassinée ou Les Cilicienne* (1928), dealing with the Armenian Genocide, and *Le Volcan Embrasé ou Le Djebel Druze* (1939), valorizing Druze "specificity." He even wrote in favor of Turkish patriotism and the founding of the modern Turkish Republic, in spite of the harsh criticism that he had reserved for the Ottomans.[25] If anything, this spaciousness of spirit is perhaps evidence of Corm's ability to surpass the narrowness of self-love (whether expressed in innocuous patriotisms or less innocent nationalisms) and his advocacy on behalf of universal humanistic values.

This, Corm's openness to the other and his sensitivity to the plights of the other, the apprehensions of the other, and the hopes of the other, are certainly a reflection of his own view of Lebanon, its multifarious history, its layered identities, and the tormented passions and misfortunes that have afflicted and rent its soul asunder through six millennia of existence. Yet Corm remained an optimist in his vision of the future. "Let us keep the faith," he admonished his audience at the *Cénacle Libanais* in June 1949:

> Let us have faith in ourselves and in our destiny, my fellow patriots! We *must* have faith in ourselves and in our destiny! Whether flourishing or failing, our homeland is our mother; an irreplaceable mother. And those of us who have no affection towards this mother are unworthy of the life that we all owe her. Let us always love our mother! Let us always love our country, as it is the best way for us to love one another. Let us be good patriots; but at the same time, let us always remain friends to all, and good citizens of this universe! And, should we happen to glimpse a few gloomy clouds today, darkening the heavens above our Mountains; and should we, alas, feel more than a storm brewing around the world, let us keep in mind that we have seen many more storms in our day, and we have suffered many more vexations throughout our long history! Yet, let us not forget that in the end they all come to pass! And they all come to pass rather quickly, jostling in their path, above all, the very offenders that had brought them forth in the first place. And let us further keep in mind that forever shall this beautiful Lebanon endure, and forever shall it remain! [26]

This vision of Lebanon and the world around it, conforming to a certain political order and a system of values to which Corm had subordinated his own being and all his literary, political, spiritual, personal, and commercial endeavors, is essentially what this biography attempted to bring to light. And so, through this quest after the thought and ideas of Charles Corm, in all their subtlety, simplicity, and sinuosity, the aim of this biography had been to begin untangling the principal stations in Corm's life, and the role that he played in charting modern Lebanon's intellectual, cultural, and political trajectory. In doing that, this biography attempted to give due attention to the relationship between ideas, politics, and civilization, and their importance to human history as surveyed and evaluated by Charles Corm. In that sense, Charles Corm's thoughts and bequests were placed in the context of contemporaneous currents with which his own ideas were in turn both concordant and discordant. Among those ideas that were given consideration in the course of this biography were the concepts of liberalism, nationalism, Arabism, patriotism, and humanism. Some of those ideas Corm supported and shored up with passion; others he protested and denounced for their alleged dehumanization and enslavement of individual freedoms and human dignity.

At a challenging juncture in the history of the modern Middle East, the history of Lebanon included, when new waves of totalitarianism sweep through the region testing old orders, shaking brittle democracies, imperiling entrenched dictatorships, and replacing old tyrannies with newer, potentially crueler ones, it is perhaps useful to revisit Charles Corm, his life, his ideas, his works, and his calls for social organization framed around equality, tolerance, power sharing, diversity, and humanist value systems. The word of caution that he sounded out in the face of mounting resentful nationalism in the Middle East of the early twentieth century is perhaps worthy of being revisited in these tumultuous early decades of the twenty-first century. Glorious as one's ancestors might have been, he wrote in 1949, "one must be wary of the senseless conceits and the base sense of hubris that generally seep out of narrow nationalism, unleashing the corrosive hysterias of unbridled jingoisms and flag-wavings."[27] We must steer clear of those "so-called nationalisms," he warned, frenzies "whose heightened, blinkered and self-absorbed egotism, hostile towards others—and towards the world at large—often devolve into gruesome savageries of the heart and mind."[28] Indeed, while continuing to piously cling to the most uplifting of past "national memories," urged Corm, only that which honors mankind must be drawn from those memories. All peoples, of all times, he stressed, "even and especially those who might have been our sworn enemies once, must have had [. . .] at one time in their history—and for all times—some honorable benevolent accomplishments."[29] Let us make certain, he concluded, to brandish those accounts of our neighbors' fine humane accomplishments, for our own sake to be sure, and for the sake of those neighbors as well, so as to better confront our modern challenges. Finally, Corm called for tapping into the inexhaustible wellsprings of Lebanon's history, to draw out the true riches that will truly make the Lebanese into the veritable masters of their being and the free agents of their own destiny; "masters of this world and the 'chosen-ones' of the world to come."[30]

NOTES

1. Charles Corm, *6000 Ans de Génie Pacifique au Service de l'Humanité* [6,000 Years of Peaceful Contributions to Mankind] (Beirut: Editions de la Revue Phénicienne, 1988), 52.
2. Corm, *6000 Ans de Génie Pacifique*, 11.
3. Corm, *6000 Ans de Génie Pacifique*, 11.
4. Corm, *6000 Ans de Génie Pacifique*, 11.
5. Corm, *6000 Ans de Génie Pacifique*, 11.
6. Corm, *6000 Ans de Génie Pacifique*, 11.
7. Charles Corm, "Déclaration de M. Ch. Corm," *Les Principes d'un Humanisme Méditerranéen* (Monaco, November 1935), 25.
8. Corm, "Déclaration de M. Ch. Corm," 24.
9. Corm, *La Montagne Inspirée*, 61.
10. Jean Desthieux, "Sur L'Idée Latine et L'Idée Méditerranéenne," *Phénicia* (Beirut: Volume II, Number 11, March–April 1939), 4.
11. Corm, "Déclaration de M. Ch. Corm," 25.
12. Corm, "Déclaration de M. Ch. Corm," 24. See also Corm's *6000 Ans de Génie Pacifique*, 7.

13. Corm, "Déclaration de M. Ch. Corm," 24.
14. Ulpian (170–223 AD) was a Roman jurist, also known as Ulpian of Tyre, and of Phoenician ancestry.
15. Like Ulpian, Papinian (142–212 AD) was also one of the most-respected Roman jurists of his time, and a native of Phoenicia.
16. Corm, *6000 Ans de Génie Pacifique,* 100.
17. Corm, *La Montagne Inspirée,* 47–48.
18. Maurice Dunand, *Byblia Grammata* (Beirut, 1945), 195. See also *Cahiers de l'Est,* Vol. 6 (Beirut, 1946), 151.
19. Dunand, *Byblia Grammata,* 195.
20. Antoine Abi-Haila, "Le Message de l'Absent," *Al-Hikma* (Beirut: The Hikma Institute, Volume 11, Number 9, December 1963), 1.
21. Abi-Haila, "Le Message de l'Absent," 1.
22. Hektor Klat, "Charles Corm, Mon Ami," *Al-Hikma,* 6.
23. Klat, *Al-Hikma,* 6.
24. Klat, *Al-Hikma,* 6.
25. He was arguably an admirer of Atatürk, the father of modern republican Turkey, and had a bust of Atatürk's on display in his library.
26. Charles Corm, *6000 Years of Peaceful Contributions to Mankind* (Beirut, Éditions de la Revue Phénicienne, 2013), 193. Emphasis in the original.
27. Corm, *6000 Ans de Génie Pacifique,* 115.
28. Corm, *6000 Ans de Génie Pacifique,* 115.
29. Corm, *6000 Ans de Génie Pacifique,* 115.
30. Corm, *6000 Ans de Génie Pacifique,* 116.

References

ARCHIVES

Archives Diplomatiques (AD), Nantes, France.
Archives du Ministère des Affaires Étrangères (MAE), Paris, Série "E"—Levant 1918–1940.
    Sous-Série: Syrie, Liban, Cilicie, Correspondence Politique et Commerciale, Paris, France.
Archives Jésuites, Vanves-Malakof, France.
Charles Corm's Archives and Private Papers, Beirut, Lebanon.
The New York Public Library Manuscripts and Archives Division, New York, NY, USA: *The New York World's Fair 1939–1940 Archives.*

PUBLISHED DOCUMENTS

Berchet, Jean-Claude. *Le Voyage en Orient; Anthologie des Voyageurs Français dans le Levant aux XIXe Siècle.* Paris, France: Éditions Robert Laffont, 1985.
Ismail, Adel. *Le Liban, Documents Diplomatiques et Consulaires Relatifs à l'Histoire du Liban.* Beirut, Lebanon: Éditions des Oeuvres Politiques et Historiques, 1979.
Université St-Esprit, Kaslik. *Les Dimensions du Nationalisme Libanais.* Kaslik, Lebanon: Editions de l'Université Saint-Esprit, 1970.

INTERVIEWS AND CORRESPONDENCE

Conversations and correspondence with David Corm, 2010–2014.
Conversations and correspondence with Hiram Corm, 2012–2014.
Correspondence with Carole Corm, 2009.
Conversations with Virginie Corm, 2012.
Conversations with Charles David Corm, 2012.

REFERENCE WORKS, COMPILATIONS, AND BIBLIOGRAPHIES

Les Années *"Cénacle."* Beirut, Lebanon: Dar al-Nahar, 1997.
Book of Nations. New York and Washington, DC: Burland Printing Company, 1939.

The Brill Encyclopedia of Arabic Language and Linguistics. General Editor Kees Versteegh. Brill, 2009. Brill Online. Boston College.

NEWSPAPERS, JOURNALS, AND PERIODICALS

As-Safiir (Beirut)
Beirut Daily Star (Beirut)
British Journal of Middle Eastern Studies (London)
La Bourse Égyptienne (Alexandria)
Les Cahiers de l'Est (Beirut)
Cahiers de l'Oronte (Beirut)
Christian Science Monitor (Boston)
Al-Dabbour (Beirut)
Domestic and Foreign Research (New York)
Forest Hills Times (New York)
Al-Hikma (Beirut)
Al-Hoda (New York)
The Journal of Democracy (Washington, DC)
Al-Maarad (Beirut)
Al-Manarat (Jounié)
Middle Eastern Studies (London)
Le Monde (Paris)
An-Nahar (Beirut)
New York Herald-Tribune (New York)
New York Post (New York)
New York Times (New York)
NOW-Lebanon (Beirut)
L'Orient le Jour (Beirut)
The Palestine Post (Jerusalem)
Le Petit Parisien (Paris)
Phénicia (Beirut)
La Revue du Liban (Beirut)
La Revue du Liban et de l'Orient Méditerranéen (Paris)
Revue du Monde Musulman (Paris)
La Revue Phénicienne (Beirut)
As-Safiir (Beirut)
Saudi Aramco World (Houston)
La Syrie (Paris)
The Voice of Freedom, Baghdad Times (Baghdad)

DISSERTATIONS AND UNPUBLISHED WORKS

Corm, Charles. *Curriculum Vitae.* Beirut, Lebanon: Charles Corm Archives, November 27, 1948.

———. *D'Une Campagne de Presse contre le Commissaire du Liban à l'Exposition de New York.* Beirut, Lebanon: Charles Corm Archives, Private Papers, ND.

———. *Participation Libanaise à l'Exposition de New York, 1939: Rapport Administratif et Financier sur les Recettes et les Dépenses du Budget de la Participation Libanaise à l'Exposition de New York; du 1er Octobre 1938 à Mars 1940.* Beirut, Lebanon: Charles Corm Archives, Private Papers, ND.

Thackston, Wheeler, Jr. *The Vernacular Arabic of the Lebanon.* Cambridge, MA: Dept. for Near Eastern Languages and Civilizations, Harvard University, 2003.

PRIMARY SOURCES: BOOKS AND ARTICLES

Abi-Haila, Antoine, Fr. "Le Message de l'Absent." *Al-Hikma*. Beirut, Lebanon: The Hikma Institute, Volume 11, Number 9, December 1963.
Abou, Sélim. *Le Bilinguisme Arab-Français au Liban*. Paris, France: Presses Universitaires de France, 1962.
Abousouan, Camille. "Présentation." *Les Cahiers de l'Est*. Beirut, July 1945.
Adonis. *Al-Kitaab, al-Khitaab, al-Hijaab* [The Scriptures, the Discourse, the Hijaab]. Beirut, Lebanon: Dar al-Aadaab, 2009.
———. "*Risaala Maftuha ila al-Ra'is Bashar al-Assad; Al-Insaan, Huquuqihi wa Hurriyaatihi, aww al-Haawiya*" [An Open Letter to President Bashar al-Assad: Man, His Rights and Freedoms, or the Abyss]. *As-Safir*. Beirut, Lebanon: June 14, 2011.
———. *Waqt bayan r-ramaad wal ward* [A Lull Between the Ashes and the Roses]. Beirut, Lebanon: Dar al-'Awda, 1972.
Aflaq, Michel. *Fi Sabiili l-Baath* [For the Sake of Arab Resurrection]. Beirut, Lebanon: Dar al-Talii'a, 1963.
Akl, Saïd. "Charles Corm." *Al-Hikma*. Beirut, Lebanon: The Hikma Institute, Volume 11, Number 9, December 1963.
Alamdeddine, Rabih. *The Hakawati*. New York: Alfred Knopf, 2008.
Arcache, Jeanne. "La Bourse Egyptienne." Alexandria, Egypt: February 8, 1935, in *Extraits de la Critique*. Beirut, Lebanon: Éditions de la Revue Phenicienne, 1935.
Bardakjian, Kevork. *Hitler and the Armenian Genocide*. Cambridge, MA: The Zoryan Institute, 1985.
Barrès, Maurice. *Une Enquête aux Pays du Levant*. Paris, France: Librairie Plon, 1924.
Bell, Gertrude Lowthian. *Syria: The Desert and the Sown*. London, UK: William Heinemann, 1919.
Bernbach, William, and Herman Jaffe. *Book of Nations*. New York and Washington, DC: Burland Printing Company, 1939.
Burton, Isabel. *The Inner Life of Syria, Palestine, and the Holy Land*. London, UK: Henry S. King, 1875.
Carmichael, Joel. *The Shaping of the Arabs*. New York: The Macmillan Co., 1967.
Charrier. "Domestic and Foreign Research." New York: November 25, 1934, in *Extraits de la Critique*. Beirut, Lebanon: Éditions de la Revue Phenicienne, 1935.
Chehabi, H. E. *Distant Relations: Iran and Lebanon in the Last 500 Years*. London, UK, and New York: Centre for Lebanese Studies, I. B. Tauris Publishers, 2006.
Chiha, Michel. "Entretiens de Patrice." *La Revue Phénicienne*. Beirut, Lebanon: Éditions de la Revue Phénicienne, August 1919.
———. *Le Liban d'Aujourd'hui (1942)*. Beirut, Lebanon: Éditions du Trident, 1961.
———. *Visage et Présence du Liban*. Beirut, Lebanon: Cénacle Libanais, 1964.
Cleveland, William. *The Making of an Arab Nationalist; Ottomanism and Arabism in the Life and Thought of Sati- al-Husri*. Princeton, NJ: Princeton University Press, 1972.
Corm, Charles. *6000 Ans de Génie Pacifique au Service de l'Humanité*. Beirut, Lebanon: Éditions de la Revue Phénicienne, 1988.
———. *Contes Érotiques; Variations sur le Mode Sentimental, 1912*. Beirut, Lebanon: Éditions de la Revue Phénicienne, 2011.
———. *L'Exemple*. Bhamdoun, Lebanon: Société des Amis des Arbres du Liban; Fête de l'Arbre, May 5, 1935.
———. "Les Impressions d'un Jeune Phénicien d'Aujourd'hui." *La Revue Phénicienne*. Beirut, Lebanon: Éditions de la Revue Phénicienne, July 1919. (Written under the *nom de plume* Cédar.)
———. "*Je Cherche un Homme.*" *La Revue du Liban*. Beirut, Lebanon: October 26, 1963.
———. "Méditations Nationalistes." *La Revue Phénicienne*. Beirut, Lebanon: Éditions de la Revue Phénicienne, September 1919.
———. *Les Miracles de la Madone aux Sept Douleurs*. Beirut, Lebanon: Éditions de la Revue Phénicienne, 2010.
———. *La Montagne Inspirée*. Beirut, Lebanon: Éditions de La Revue Phénicienne, 1987.

———. *Petite Cosmogonie Sentimentale*. Beirut, Lebanon: Éditions de la Revue Phénicienne, 2004.

———. "Les Principes d'un Humanisme Méditerranéen." *Académie Mediterranéenne*. Monte Carlo, Monaco: November 1935.

———. *Programme de l'Association des Amis des Arbres* [Program of the Association of the Friends of the Trees]. Jounié, Lebanon: Missionaries' Press, 1934.

———. "Les Propos d'un Français" [In the Words of a Frenchman]. *La Revue Phénicienne*. Beirut, Lebanon: Éditions de la Revue Phénicienne, August 1919. (Written under the *nom de plume* E. Le Veilleur.)

———. "Rendons le Sol au Paysan" [Let us Give the Land Back to the Peasant]. *La Revue Phénicienne*. Beirut, Lebanon: Éditions de la Revue Phénicienne, Christmas 1919.

———. *La Terre Assassinée ou les Ciliciennes*. Beirut, Lebnaon: Éditions de la Revue Phénicienne, 2004.

———. *Trois Communiqués À La Presse Libanaise D'Amérique*. Beirut, Lebanon: Charles Corm Archives, Private Papers, undated, uncatalogued.

Corm, Samia. "Charles Corm as I Knew Him; An Interview with Samia Corm." *Al-Hikma*. Beirut, Lebanon: The Hikma Institute, Volume 11, Number 9, December 1963.

Deeb, Marius. *Syria, Iran, and Hezbollah: The Unholly Alliance and Its War on Lebanon*. Stanford, CA: The Hoover Institution Press, 2013.

Duboscq, André. *Syrie, Tripolitaine, Albanie*. Paris, France: Librairie F. Alcan, 1914.

Dunand, Maurice. *Byblia Grammata*. Beirut, Lebanon: 1945.

Epstein, Eliahu. "Lebanese Renaissance: La Montagne Inspirée by Charles Corm." *Palestine Post*, Jerusalem, February 24, 1935.

Farah, Samar. "So You'd Like to Learn Arabic. Got a Decade or So?" *Christian Science Monitor*, Boston, MA, January 17, 2002.

Farroukh, Omar. *Al-Qawmiya al-Fusha* [Modern Standard Arabic Nationalism]. Beirut, Lebanon: Dar al-'Ilm lil-Malaayeen, 1961.

Gershoni, Israel, and James Jankowski. *Egypt, Islam, and the Arabs: The Search for Egyptian Nationalism, 1900–1930*. New York: Oxford University Press, 1986.

Ghsoub, Youssef. "Shaarl Qorm: Sawt Lubanaan al-Madwiyy" [Charles Corm: The Resounding Voice of Lebanon]. *Al-Hikma*. Beirut, Lebanon: The Hikma Institute, December 1963.

El-Hajj, Unsi. "Charles Corm." *An-Nahar*. Beirut, Lebanon: September 20, 1963.

Herm, Gerhard. *The Phoenicians; The Purple Empire of the Ancient World*. New York: William Morrow and Company, 1975.

Hitti, Philippe. *Taarikh Lubnan* [The History of Lebanon]. Beirut, Lebanon: Dar al-Thaqafa, 1985.

Hodeir, Catherine, and Michel Pierre. *L'Éxposition Coloniale*. Paris, France: Éditions Complexe, 1991.

Al-Husri, Abu Khaldun Sati'. *Abhaath Mukhtaara fi al-Qawmiyya al-'Arabiyya* [Selected Studies in Arab Nationalism]. Beirut, Lebanon: Markaz Diraasaat al-Wihda al-'Arabiyya, 1985.

Jabr, Jamil. *Al-Jabal al-Mulham* [The Hallowed Mountain]. Beirut, Lebanon: Éditions de la Revue Phénicienne, 2006.

———. "Charles Corm and Lebanon." *Al-Hikma*, Vol. 11, No. 9. Beirut, Lebanon: September 1963.

Jumblat, Kamal. "La Mediterranée, Berceau de Culture Spirituelle." *Les Années Cénacle*. Beirut, Lebanon: Dar al-Nahar, 1997.

Karsh, Ephraim. *Islamic Imperialism: A History*. New Haven, CT, and London, UK: Yale University Press, 2006.

Kaufman, Asher. *Reviving Phoenicia; The Search for Identity in Lebanon*. London & New York: I. B. Tauris, 2004.

———."Tell Us Our History; Charles Corm, Mount-Lebanon, and Lebanese Nationalism." *Middle Eastern Studies*, Vol. 40, No. 3, May 2004.

———. "Too Much French, but a Swell Exhibit; Representing Lebanon at the New York World's Fair, 1939–1940." *British Journal of Middle Eastern Studies*. London, UK: Volume 35, Number 1, 2008.

Khairallah, Khairallah. "La Syrie." *Revue du Monde Musulman*. Paris, France: Vol. 19, 1912.
Khoury, Eli. "Daaesh wa Iftidaah Taarikhina Ghayr al-Sahiiq" [ISIS and the Hazards of Our Not So Abysmal History]. *NOW-Lebanon*. Beirut, Lebanon, August 6, 2014. http://mme.cm/U22U00.
Klat, Hektor. "Charles Corm, Mon Ami." *Al-Hikma*. Beirut, Lebanon: The Hikma Institute, Volume 11, Number 9, December 1963.
Kramer, Martin. *Arab Awakening and Islamic Revival*. New Brunswick, CT, and London, UK: Transaction Publishers, 2008.
Labaki, Salah. "Al-'Aashiq, Shaarl Qorm" [Charles Corm the Beloved]. *al-Maarad*. Beirut, Lebanon: Issue 38, July 4, 1934.
Lamartine, Alphonse de. *Voyage en Orient 1832–1833*. Paris, France: Librairie de Charles Gosselin, 1843.
Lawrence, T. E. *Seven Pillars of Wisdom*. New York and London, UK: Anchor Books, Doubleday, 1991.
Leichtenberger, André. "Une Interview du Général Gouraud." *Le Petit Parisien*. Paris, France: June 7, 1922.
Lévi-Strauss, Claude. *Tristes Tropiques*. Paris, France: Plon, 1995.
Lewis, Bernard. *Islam and the West*. New York and Oxford, UK: Oxford University Press, 1993.
———. *The Multiple Identities of the Middle East*. New York: Schoken Books, 1989.
———. *The Muslim Discovery of Europe*. New York and London: W. W. Norton and Company, 2001.
Lochner, Louis P. *What about Germany?* New York: Dodd, Mead & Co. 1942.
M, E. "La Revue du Liban et de l'Orient Méditerranéen." *Extraits de la Critique*. Paris, France: February 1934, and Beirut, Lebanon: Éditions de la Revue Phenicienne, 1935.
Maalouf, Amin. *Discours de réception et réponse de M. Jean-Christophe Rufin; Réception de M. Amin Maalouf*. Paris, France: Académie Française, June 14, 2012. http://www.academie-francaise.fr/discours-de-reception-et-reponse-de-m-jean-christophe-rufin.
Maalouf, Rushdy. "Yabisat Arza" [A Cedar has Dried Up]. *Al-Hikma*. Beirut, Lebanon: The Hikma Institute, 1963.
Madden, Thomas. *The New Concise History of the Crusades*. Lanham, MD: Rowman and Littlefield, 2006.
Makiya, Kanan. "A Model for Post-Saddam Iraq." *The Journal of Democracy*, Vol. 14, No. 3. Washington, DC: July 2003.
Maklouf, Ibrahim. "En Écoutant Charles Corm et Fakry El-Baroudi." *La Syrie*. Beirut, Lebanon: Sunday June 9, 1935.
Le Monde. "Amin Maalouf Reçu Jeudi à l'Académie Française." Paris, France: June 14, 2012. http://www.lemonde.fr/culture/breve/2012/06/13/amin-maalouf-recu-jeudi-a-l-academie-francaise_1717909_3246.html.
Moosa, Matti. *Extremist Shiites*. Syracuse, NY: Syracuse University Press, 1988.
Morand, Paul. *Méditerranée, Mer des Surprises*. Paris, France: Éditions du Rocher, 1990.
Naccache, Albert. *L'Orient*, Beirut, Lebanon, January 14, 1934.
Noujaim, Paul. "La Question du Liban; Étude de Politique Économique et de Statisque Descriptive." *La Revue Phénicienne*. Beirut, Lebanon, Éditions de la Revue Phénicienne, Volume 1, Number 2, August 1919.
Qabbani, Nizar. *Arfudukum* [I Reject You]. www.titanic-arwad.com/vb/showthread.php?t=16762.
Raymond, Jean. "Le Liban: Terre Traditionnelle de Liberté; Textes Commentés, Tirés des Récits des Voyageurs Occidentaux du 16ème au 18ème Siecles." *Cahiers de l'Oronte*, No. 7. Beirut, Lebanon: 1967.
Renan, Ernest. *Mission de Phénicie*. Third Facsimile Edition. Beirut, Lebanon: Editions Terre du Liban, 1998.
Reynaud, Charles. "Catholiques et Français, Toujours!" In *Le Voyage en Orient; Anthologie des Voyageurs Français dans le Levant au XIXème Siècle*. Paris, France: Robert Laffont, 1985.
Ristelhueber, René. *Traditions françaises au Liban*. Paris, France: Librairie Félix Alcan, 1918.

References

Said, Edward. *Culture and Imperialism*. London, UK: Chatto & Windus, 1993.

Saghieh, Hazem. "Daaesh wa Iftidaah Tawaarikhina al-Saahiqa" [ISIS and the Hazards of Our Abysmal Histories]. *NOW-Lebanon*. Beirut, Lebanon, August 5, 2014. http://mme.cm/PM2U00).

———. *Wadaa' al-'Uruuba* [The Swansong of Arabism]. Beirut, Lebanon, and London, UK: Dar al-Saqi, 1999.

Salameh, Franck. *Language, Memory, and Identity in the Middle East: The Case for Lebanon*. Lanham, MD: Lexington Books, 2010.

Salibi, Kamal. "Fakhreddin al-Thani w al-Fikra al-Lubnaniyya" [Fakhreddin II and the Lebanese Idea]. *Les Dimensions du Nationalisme Libanais*. Kaslik, Lebanon: Editions de l'Université Saint-Esprit, 1970.

Al-Saouda, Youssef. "Al-Jabal al-Mulham, Mihbat al-Wahi" [The Hallowed Mountain, Sanctuary of Revelation]. *al-Maarad*. Beirut, Lebanon: Issue 38, July 4, 1934.

Schaub-Koch, Émile. "Le Poète Libanais Charles Corm." *La Revue de l'Université Laval*. Québec, Canada, 1958.

Seymour, Charles. *The Intimate Papers of Colonel House*. Vol. 3. Boston, MA: Houghton Mifflin, 1928.

Al-Solh, Takieddine. "Al-Jabal al-Haa'er" [The Perplexed Mountain]. *al-Maarad*. Beirut, Lebanon: Issue 38, July 4, 1934.

Tabet, Jacques. *La Syrie Historique, Ethnographique, Religieuse, Géographique, Économique, Politique et Sociale*. Paris, France: Alphonse Lemerre, 1920.

Tayyah, Charbel. "L'idée de Dieu et la 'Spiritualité' dans L'Œuvre de Charles Corm." *Al-Manarat; Revue de Sciences Religieuses*. Jounié, Lebanon: Congrégation des Missionnaires Libanais, Vol. 31, No. 1, 1990.

Tyane, Élie. *Lumière sur la Montagne*. Beirut, Lebanon: Éditions de la Revue Phénicienne, 1935.

Valéry, Paul. *Eupalinos ou l'Architecte, Précédé de l'Âme et la Danse*. Paris, France: Editions de la Nouvelle Revue Française, 1921.

Vicomte de Vogüe. "Voyage au Pays du Passé." In *Le Voyage en Orient; Anthologie des Voyageurs Français dans le Levant au XIXème Siècle*. Paris, France: Robert Laffont, 1985.

The Voice of Freedom, *Baghdad Times. The Antalya Conference Urges Assad to Resign*. Baghdad, Iraq: June 6, 2011. http://www.baghdadtimes.net/Arabic/?sid=75390.

Yamak, Labib Zuwiya. *The Syrian Social Nationalist Party*. Cambridge, MA: The Center for Middle Eastern Studies, Harvard University, 1966.

Younis, Assaad. "Al-Jabal al-Mulham, Muharrer al-Arwaah" [The Hallowed Mountain, Redeemer of Spirits]. *al-Maarad*. Beirut: Issue 38, July 4, 1934.

Wood, Ghislaine. *Essential Art Deco*. London, UK: Bulfinch, 2001.

Zamir, Meir. *The Formation of Modern Lebanon*. Ithaca, NY, and London, UK: Cornell University Press, 1985.

Index

Abou-Mady, Eliya, 160
Abou, Sélim, 161
Abou-Shabké, Elias, 160
Académie Française, 16, 51–53, 103, 191
Adonis (Phoenician god), 66, 161, 202
Adonis (river), 128, 131
Adonis (poet Ali Ahmad Saïd), 46
Aflaq, Michel, 33, 40
Ahirom (King of Tyre), 66. *See also* Hiram
Ajami, Fouad, 161
Akl, Saïd, 15, 49, 63n57, 83, 92, 99–100
Alameddine, Rabih, 53–54
Alawites, 33, 38, 42–44, 55, 59, 113, 209, 229n229
Albert I of Monaco, 102
Aleppo, 7; vilayet of, 34, 42, 59, 90, 91, 113, 148n161–148n162, 209, 229n229
Alexander the Great, 142n54, 240
Alexandria, 47, 147n160, 238
alphabet, 146n150, 151n179, 206; Phoenician, 52, 53, 197, 201, 203, 237, 238, 240
Amchit, 78–79
Amitiés Libanaises. *See* Charles Corm. *See also* Charles Corm
Amitiés Méditerranéenes, 236. *See also* Charles Corm
Ammoun, Blanche, 201
Antalya Declaration, 37–38, 44
Antoura (monastery), 68

Arab identity, 28–47; and Charles Corm, 159–163, 172, 210, 219, 235; in Lebanon, 20–21, 27, 47–50, 58–60, 67–71, 83, 86, 88–90, 104–105, 110, 140n25, 146n149, 157–159, 176, 179, 195, 210
Arab nation. *See* Arabism; Arab identity
Arab nationalism. *See* Arabism; Arab identity
Arab spring, 29, 32, 37, 45, 66
Arabia, 34, 88–89, 157–160
Arabic language, 29–30, 39–40, 146n149, 158–163, 198, 211–213
Arabism, 21, 30, 32, 33, 39–40, 43, 45–46, 88–89, 91, 110, 157–158, 161–74, 210, 235
Aramaeans, 31, 39, 44, 67
Armenians, 31, 35–37, 54–55, 66, 73, 162, 163; genocide, 19, 105–107, 148n162, 223n75, 241
art deco, 3–14
Artisanat Libanais, 203, 217
Ashrafiyyé (Beirut), 1, 14, 93, 124–125, 135, 148n163
al-Assad, Bashar, 43, 46, 232n284
al-Assad, Hafez, 43
al-Assad, Suleiman, 42–43
Astarte (Phoenician goddess), 111, 145n147
Augustine, saint, 156, 198
Aurelius, Marcus, 146n148, 149n171

Awan, Tawfiq, 30

Baal (Phoenician god), 111
Baath Party, 33, 40, 43–44
Bahaïs, 7–8
Barcelona (1929 International Exhibition), 18, 168–170
Baronian, Arminée, 201
Baroody, Jamil, 229n229
al-Baroody, Fakhri, 208–209
Baroody, Samia. *See* Samia Corm
Barrère, Camille, 57
Barrès, Maurice, 78, 79, 151n178, 190
Bashir II (Emir Bashir Shehab), 76–77, 80
Baudelaire, Charles, 84, 141n51
Bauhaus, 168–169
Beckett, Henry, 207–208
Beirut, 8, 9, 13; vilayet of, 27, 32, 55, 66, 73, 80, 89–90, 147n160–148n161, 172, 177
Bell, Gertrude, 33
Benoît, Pierre, 15, 103
Ben-Zvi, Rachel, 15, 103
Berger, Meyer, 153
Beyhum, Abdallah, 211
Bialik, Haim Nahman, 15, 103
Bidault, Georges, 234
Bikfayya, 143n103
Bourg Hammoud, 19
Boustany, Fouad Ephrem, 15, 83
Breuer, Marcel, 17
Briand, Aristide, 55, 60, 70
Broadway, 23n2, 101, 232n283
Burton, Isabel, 33
Burton, Sir Richard Francis, 33
Bustros, Evelyne, 201
Byblos, 47, 53, 72, 75, 111, 145n147, 146n150–146n151, 205

Cadmus (Phoenician Prince), 52, 53
Café des glaces (*'Ahwet le-'zééz*), 149n173–150n174
de Caix, Robert, 41, 59, 104
Canaan-Canaanites, 9, 25n30, 45, 48, 51, 83, 136
Carthage, 47, 202–203, 227n184, 228n209
Le Cénacle libanais, 242
Cercle de la jeunesse catholique de Beyrouth, 95

Chagall, Marc, 16, 103
Chanel, Coco, 25n34, 158–159
Chehim earthquake, 8, 24n23–25n24
Chicago World's Fair, 154, 168
al-Chidiac, Sham'un (Semaan), 76–77
Chiha, Michel, 15, 45, 48–50, 70, 81, 87–88, 241
Cicero, 156
La Colline Inspirée, 151n178
Colvin, Duncan, 207–208
Corm, Charles,: Amitiées Libanaises and, 15–17, 83, 103–104, 155, 159, 209; Amitiées Méditerranéenes and, 236; as architect, 11–14; Association des Amis des Arbres, 96–98; as businessman, 7–10, 19, 23n13–24n14, 100, 102; education of, 76, 81–96; as environmentalist, 96–99, 143n103, 145n144, 166; family background of, 76–77; Humanism and, 17, 20, 22, 48, 51, 60, 75–76, 87, 96, 98–99, 103–105, 107, 137, 151n179, 161–162, 170–171, 210, 223n75, 234, 235–237, 239–242; *La Montagne Inspirée*, 22, 49–50, 84, 86, 91, 108–112, 114–124, 146n149, 149n171, 151n178, 156–158, 159–160, 161, 162–163, 173–174, 174, 204, 210, 213–219, 235–236, 241; on New York radio, 199; in Palestine, 7, 15–16, 97, 102; Young Phoenicians and, 9, 12, 21–22, 27–28, 47–53, 55, 57, 65, 70, 74, 88, 98–99, 112, 121, 137, 140n25, 144n142–145n143, 147n153, 150n176, 153, 156–162, 169–170, 186, 191, 196, 197, 201–204, 206, 210, 213, 225n124, 234, 237, 238–240
Corm, Daoud, 16, 76–81, 83, 125, 231n269
Corm, David, 1, 4, 6–7, 11, 16, 18, 81
Corm, Hiram, 1–2, 4, 6–7, 16, 18, 84, 96–97, 210
Corm, Madeleine, 2, 5
Corm, Samia, 6, 92, 174, 180, 185, 205, 212, 213, 214, 216–217
Corm, Virginie, 2, 3, 4, 23n5, 25n33
de Coulanges, Fustel, 202
Crusades, 68, 71, 163, 185–189
Cyr, Georges, 201

dabké (dance), 160, 201

Damascus, 7, 71, 80, 88–91, 102; Vilayet of, 18, 32, 33–34, 42, 59, 72, 73, 88–91, 113, 148n161–148n162, 177, 209, 229n229
Damascus Road, 18, 214
Deane, Martha, 199
Desthieux, Jean, 236
Diogenes, 85–86, 142n54, 241
Djérid (dance), 160, 220n22
Dog River (*Nahr el-Kalb*), 146n148, 149n171
Dorsey, Tommy, 180–181
Douaihi, Saliba, 201
Duboscq, André, 71
Dunand, Maurice, 146n150, 201, 240

Eddé, Emile, 163, 194, 203, 209, 211, 215, 231n269
Éddé, Laudie, 203
Eiffel, Gustave, 25n43–26n44; tower, 25n43–26n44, 168, 222n53
Elizabeth II, 200
Environmental Protection Agency (EPA), 96, 98
Epstein, Eliahu, 16, 103, 111–112
Eupalinos, 11–13
Europa, 51–53, 197
Exposition Universelle de Paris (1900), 80
Ezekiel, 66, 240

Fakhreddin II, 71–72, 146n150, 149n173–150n174
Farhat, Germanos, 49–50
Farhi, Joseph, 103
Farroukh, Mustapha, 80, 201
Farrukh, Omar, 39
Fitzgerald, F. Scott, 14, 15, 103
Flushing Meadows-Corona Park, 168–171, 200
Ford, Henry, 23n2, 101–102
France: attitudes towards Lebanon and the Maronites, 56–57, 67–68, 71, 73–74, 147n158, 161, 174–179, 189–194; League of Nations Mandate, 56–57, 59–60, 94–95
Fuleyhan, Anis, 206, 230n258

Gaulmier, Jean, 83
Gemayel, César, 80, 201

George VI, 200
Ghazir, 76–79, 81, 121
Ghosta, 76
Ghsoub, Youssef, 2, 81–83, 160
Gibran, Kahlil, 49–50, 80, 160, 220n21
Gleason, Jackie, 180–181
Gouraud, Henri, 41, 56–57, 59, 63n77, 110, 113, 114, 146n148, 175–177, 189–190
Greater Lebanon, 42, 55–57, 59, 72, 74, 76, 80, 108, 110, 113–114, 144n138, 144n142–145n143, 199, 201, 212–177, 213, 229n229
Greenpeace, 98
La Guardia, Fiorello, 164–165, 166–167, 171, 173, 185, 199, 204, 219

Haifa, 7–8, 23n13–24n14, 148n161
Hannibal, 197–198
Hanotaux, Gabriel, 90
Herodotus, 51, 145n147, 157, 220n15
al-Hikma, 240
Hiram (king of Tyre), 16, 111, 187. *See also* Ahirom
Hiram-Aviv, 22, 103
Hitler, Adolph, 107, 170, 173, 223n77
Hitti, Philippe, 70, 76, 206
al-Hoda: and Arabism, 195, 213; and the New York World's Fair (1939), 203–204
Holmes, Julius, 157, 166, 185
Homer, 126, 147n152, 192, 202
House, Colonel Edward Mandell, 28–29
Hoyek, Patriarch Elias Peter, 57–59, 79–80, 223n89
Hoyek, Youssef, 201
Humanism. *See* Charles Corm
al-Husri, Sati', 39–40, 110, 158

Ibrahim Pasha, 73
Isaiah, 240
Israel, 25n35, 35, 67, 85, 103, 105, 145n147, 148n161, 167, 195, 238

Jacobson, Victor (Avigdor), 16, 103
Jaffe, Bertha, 201
Jahiliyya, 220n22
Jerusalem, 7, 24n14, 90, 203; Solomon's temple in, 16, 159, 202, 225n124

Jesuits, 76–81, 100, 101, 125, 194
Jewish Agency, 103
Jumblat, Kamal, 47
Justinian, 156, 237, 238

Kaufman, Asher, 100, 157, 187, 203, 208, 211, 229n229
Kedourie, Elie, 38–39
Khoury, Eli, 21, 61n2
el-Khoury, Bechara, 85–87, 104–105
el-Khoury, Marie, 230n258
Klat, Hektor, 81, 83, 100, 160, 241

Labaki, Salah, 162
Lamartine, Alphonse de, 25n31, 53, 109
Lammens, Henri, 77–78
Lawrence, T.E., 29, 33–34, 42, 71
Lazarists, 68
Lebanese National Museum, 1, 15, 18, 102
Légion d'Honneur, 219
Lewis, Bernard, 30, 188–189
Lincoln, Abraham, 203
Louis IX (king of France), 185, 189, 203
Louÿs, Pierre, 136
Lyautey, Maréchal Hubert, 192

Maalouf, Amine, 16–17, 51–54
Maalouf, Rushdy, 16, 51
Maan dynasty, 71, 74, 76
Madden, Thomas, 187–188
Maison Blanche, 14–15, 18, 24n23, 25n43; Charles Corm's home, 17, 83, 96, 104, 214; Ford Motors Headquarters, 7, 11, 19
Makiya, Kanan, 31–32, 38
Maklouf, Ibrahim, 209
Maronites, 33, 35–36, 41, 56, 65–69, 71–74, 104–105, 145n144, 163, 188; and Lebanon, 56–58, 67–69, 71–74, 108, 145n144, 148n163, 190–191, 213
Martyrs' Square, 149n173–150n174
Matisse, Henri, 101
Mediterranean Sea and culture, 8, 36, 47, 52, 54, 65–66, 68, 70, 74, 75–76, 78, 89, 94, 102, 145n143, 146n148, 147n153, 148n163, 149n171, 159, 162–165, 234, 236–239
Melkart, 202
Michelet, Georges, 201

Mokarzel, Joseph, 212–215, 216–217, 224n122
Mokarzel, Salloum, 183, 212–218, 231n259, 232n276
La Montagne Inspirée. See Charles Corm
Morand, Paul, 15, 25n34, 158–159
Mount-Lebanon, 25n31, 27, 35–36, 49–50, 53, 56, 66–74, 89–90, 92–95, 144n142, 147n153, 151n178, 163, 172, 177, 191; famine in, 74, 92–93, 107, 129–130, 144n142–145n143, 148n161, 149n167
Mutasarrifiyya. *See* Mount-Lebanon

Naccache, Albert, 112
an-Nahar : tribute to Corm, 82, 84
al-Nahda (Arabic literary renaissance), 49, 160
Napoleon III, 146n148, 149n171
National Pact, 104–105, 160
Nazareth Quarter (Beirut), 1, 14
New York Herald Tribune , 204
New York Post , 207
New York Times , 153–154, 164, 174, 177–178, 186, 204, 207
New York World's Fair (1939), 153–156, 164, 167, 169–171, 182; Charles Corm addresses and correspondence relating to, 193–194, 195–199; Charles Corm Commissioner General at, 163–164, 166–167, 179–185, 196–197, 211–214, 228n225, 229n229; Lebanon Pavilion at, 154–156, 164–165, 166, 173–175, 185–187, 189, 191–192, 193–194, 196–197, 198–201, 203–208
Nike of Samothrace, 110, 118, 145n147
Noujaim, Paul (Jouplain), 90, 172

Olivier, Marcel, 185, 189, 191–194, 228n225
Onsi, Omar, 201
Orloff, Chana, 16, 103
Ottoman Empire, 27–32, 35–37, 41–42, 55–59; Lebanon under the, 66–74, 89–94, 107, 147n158, 147n160–148n162, 149n173–150n174

Palestine, 38, 55–56, 71–72, 105, 111, 148n161, 167, 176, 195
Pan-Arab Nationalism. *See* Arabism

Papinian, 156, 198, 237–238
Paris Peace Conference, 58, 223n89
Park Central Hotel, 180–181, 199–200, 215
Phaedra, 12–13
Phoenicians. *See* Charles Corm
Pillars of Hercules, 202
Pius IX (Pope), 80
Pius XI (Pope), 236
Pius XII (Pope), 85
place des canons, 149n173–150n174
Pliny, 146n150
Plisnier, Charles, 15, 103
Puaux, Gabriel, 194, 227n174
Pythagoras, 203, 228n209

Qabbani, Nizar, 45–46

al-Rashid, Harun (caliph), 160, 220n22
Ravitaillement Civil de Beyrouth (Post-War Beirut Relief Committee), 19, 95–96, 102
Règlement organique, 36, 73, 147n158
Reich, Lilly, 17–18
Renan, Ernest, 53, 77–79, 90
Renan, Henriette, 53, 77–79
La Revue Phénicienne, 48, 88, 96, 100, 112, 155, 176
Rihani, Amin, 15, 16, 157, 160, 210–211
Ristelhueber, René, 90
Roman Codex of Justinian. *See* Justinian
Roosevelt, E. F., 166, 182
Roosevelt, Eleanor, 180–181, 200
Roosevelt, Franklin D., 170–171, 179, 200, 203

Saadé, Antun, 44–45
Sabet, Habib, 8–9
Saghieh, Hazem, 20–21, 32, 61n2
Said, Edward, 190
de Saint-Quentin, Count René Doynel, 185, 192–194, 228n225
Salibi, Kamal, 71–72
Sanjak. *See* Mount-Lebanon
al-Saouda, Joseph (Youssef), 81, 160, 162
Shehab dynasty, 76
Shulamite (Song of Songs), 100, 210
Sicily, 13, 202

Sidon, 47, 53, 72, 75, 111, 149n173, 159, 187, 203, 240
Sloucshz, Nahum, 15–16, 25n37, 103, 143n112
Socrates, 12
al-Solh, Riyad, 81, 104
al-Solh, Takieddine, 157, 158–161, 163, 220n11
Solomon (King), 16, 66, 68, 90, 103, 153, 159, 186–187, 191, 225n124
Spofford, Charles, 185–189, 203
Strabo, 146n150
Sunnis, 33, 44, 59, 66–67, 104, 147n160, 148n163, 150n174, 157
Sykes-Picot, 31, 34, 36
Syria, 30, 31–39, 42–46, 58–59, 67, 69–72, 113, 147n160–148n161, 179, 208–209. *See also* Aleppo; Damascus; Greater Syria, 208, 229n229–230n230; Shaam, 35; Syrian Social Nationalist Party, 44–45; Syrians, 88–90, 105

Tabet, Jacques, 35, 69, 176
Takieddine, Khalil, 210–211
Taylor, Elizabeth, 3
Thales of Miletus, 156
Theophanes, 146n150
Thomas, Richard, 199
Thoreau, Henry David, 96
Turkey, 28, 42, 128, 148n161, 193
Tyane, Élie, 109, 166
Tyre, 47, 51–53, 66, 74, 75, 103, 111, 159, 177, 187, 197, 203, 238, 240

Ulpian, 48, 156, 198, 237–238
UNESCO, 85, 146n151, 234
Union Libanaise, 70
Université Saint-Joseph, 1, 15, 25n33, 77, 85, 125, 194

Valéry, Paul, 11–15, 103
van der Rohe, Ludwig Mies, 17–18, 169
Vatican, 80, 238
Vaudoyer, Jean-Louis, 21–22
Venus of Milo, 110, 118, 145n147
Versailles. *See* Paris Peace Conference
Versailles World's Fair (1889), 80
Virgil, 197

Volney, Constantin François de
    Chasseboeuf Comte de, 53, 68–69

Washington, George, 203; inauguration of,
    169, 171
West, Mae, 180–181
Whalen, Grover, 154, 166, 199–200
Wilson, Woodrow, 28

al-Yazigi, Ibrahim, 49
al-Yazigi, Nassif, 49
Yishuv, 15, 97, 103
Young Phoenicians. *See* Charles Corm
Younis, Assaad, 156–157

Zamir, Meir, 67
Zionist movement, 103, 112, 195, 209
Ziyadé, May, 160, 241

About the Author

Franck Salameh is associate professor of Near Eastern Studies at Boston College, Department of Slavic and Eastern Languages and Literatures, and founding editor in chief of *The Levantine Review* journal. His academic work has focused on the history of ideas, political thought, cultural history, and linguistic nationalism in the Levantine region of the Near East. His scholarly articles and essays have been published in a number of academic journals and media outlets, including *Middle Eastern Studies*, the *Middle East Review of International Affairs*, the *Middle East Book Review*, the *Middle East Quarterly*, and the *National Interest*, among others. His first book, *Language, Memory, and Identity in the Middle East: The Case for Lebanon*, was also published by Lexington Books.